CH00794248

Slave Law and the Politics of Resistance
in the Early Atlantic World

Slave Law and the

Politics of Resistance

in the Early Atlantic World

EDWARD B. RUGEMER

Harvard University Press

Cambridge, Massachusetts

London, England   2018

Library of Congress Cataloging-in-Publication Data
Names: Rugemer, Edward Bartlett, 1971- author.
Title: Slave law and the politics of resistance in the early Atlantic world /
    Edward B. Rugemer.
Description: Cambridge, Massachusetts : Harvard University Press, 2018. |
    Includes bibliographical references and index.
Identifiers: LCCN 2018013048 | ISBN 9780674982994 (cloth)
Subjects: LCSH: Slavery—Law and legislation—Great Britain—Colonies. |
    Slavery—Law and legislation—United States. | Slave insurrections—Jamaica. |
    Slave insurrections—South Carolina. | Slavery—Barbados.
Classification: LCC K3267 .R84 2018 | DDC 342.08/7—dc23
    LC record available at https://lccn.loc.gov/2018013048

For Kate and our boys,
Henry, Philip, and James

North Atlantic Ocean

North America

Boston
Newport
Providence
New York
Philadelphia
Charles Town
Savannah
New Orleans
St. Augustin

Caribbean Sea

South America

Recife

Salvador

Rio de Janeiro

The Early Atlantic World

BAHAMAS

CUBA

Cap-Français • HISPANIOLA

JAMAICA ST. DOMINGUE
Kingston

ST. THOMAS

Caribbean Sea

GUADALOUPE

MARTINIQUE

CURAÇAO

BARBADOS

TRINIDAD

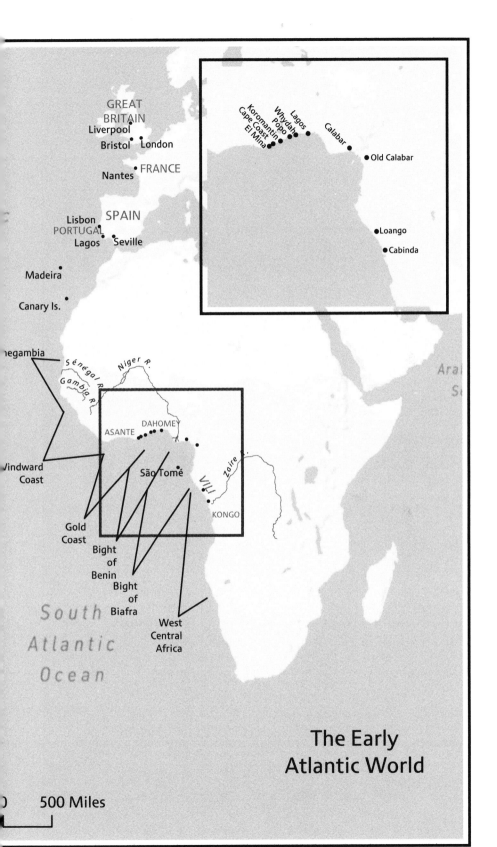

GREAT
BRITAIN
Liverpool
Bristol   London

Nantes   FRANCE

Lisbon   SPAIN
PORTUGAL
Lagos   Seville

Madeira

Canary Is.

negambia   Sénégal R.   Niger R.

Gambia R.

Windward
Coast

ASANTE   DAHOMEY

São Tomé   Zaire R.

VILI

KONGO

Gold
Coast

Bight
of
Benin

Bight
of
Biafra

South

Atlantic

Ocean

West
Central
Africa

Koromantin   Whydah   Lagos
Cape Coast   Popo   Calabar
El Mina

Old Calabar

Aral

S

Loango

Cabinda

The Early
Atlantic World

500 Miles

Contents

List of Maps

Slave Law and the Politics of Resistance
in the Early Atlantic World

The West Indian slave laws of the 18th century mirror the society that created them. They reflect the political traditions of the European colonisers and the political necessities of a way of life based upon plantation slavery.

—Elsa V. Goveia

The question of abolishing slavery was ultimately a question of power.

—David Brion Davis

At the Heart of Slavery

THE STRUGGLES OVER racial slavery make for an epic tragedy central to the formation of our world. An ancient human practice that persists in various forms today, slavery is at its heart the violent exercise of power to degrade the dignity of a person toward the status of an animal, the master's aspiration to impose absolute subjection. Enslavement often generates resistance among its victims, who struggle for power over the self in order to restore the human dignity that people need.[1]

Resistance violated the terms of enslavement in the early Atlantic World, and masters usually turned again to violence to reestablish their power. In Western culture, such power had its ethical sanction in the law, which justified the often brutal relation between the master and the slave. Slaveholders were white men and women, as well as some free people of color. There were slaveholders who did not possess the physical size, or violent inclination, to impose their will on another human being. But in a slave society, the law empowered all slaveholders, regardless of disposition, to maintain the threat of violence over their slaves, albeit through the hands of other men, including officers of the state. The human need for dignity, however, meant that slave law could never resolve the core conflict, the existential struggle between the master and the slave. This conflict at the heart of slavery festered throughout the Americas for almost four hundred years.

1

The slave systems of the Atlantic World developed a novel form of animate capital—enslaved Africans and their descendants—which generated significant revenue and proved fundamental to the expansion and productivity of the Atlantic empires. Slavery was essential, profitable to those invested in it, and fundamentally at war with the humanity of the people enslaved. Slave societies revolved around this war. Enslaved people struggled daily for some bit of dignity in their lives while their masters compelled the overwhelming portion of their labors. A few writers described this system as abhorrent in the seventeenth century, and more followed in the eighteenth, but moral censure did little to curb slavery's expansion. Over time, however, a small but growing number of free men and women, in Europe and the Americas, came to believe that slavery was morally wrong. Social movements emerged around this idea, first in Great Britain and later in the United States, but this would not happen until the late eighteenth century. Racial slavery's incompatibility with human dignity proved unsustainable, but only after an epic struggle of eight generations.[2]

Slave Law and the Politics of Resistance in the Early Atlantic World explores two centuries of the dialectic between slave resistance and the laws of slavery. In the British Empire, slaveholders often controlled the legislative assemblies, especially in the Caribbean and in the South. One way they dealt with the problem of slave resistance was to pass laws. These laws reveal the nature and extent of slave resistance, as well as the sophisticated apparatus of social control that masters created to control enslaved people. Patrols, jails, brutal punishments, runaway slave advertisements, slave catchers paid by the state—such were the everyday coercions that masters wielded. The pervasive extent of these practices across time and space attests to the significance of slave resistance. Each of these powers flowed from the laws of the slave society, which in turn were responses to the resistance of enslaved people.[3]

This book brings together Jamaica and South Carolina within the same historical narrative, allowing us to see each slave society in the light of the other. Both were formed by the rise of the North Atlantic slave system, and both were influential within their respective political communities, the British Caribbean on the one hand, and British

North America and later the United States on the other. Jamaica and South Carolina were stable and lucrative slave societies that lasted a very long time, yet slavery ended in Jamaica in 1834, thirty years before it ended in South Carolina, and it ended through an act of the British Parliament, not as the result of a brutal civil war. By placing the origins of these slave societies at the beginning of a history that ends with abolition in one of them, we are able to consider the deep roots of the abolition of slavery.[4]

It is useful to distinguish between "day-to-day" resistance and the more aggressive forms of resistance waged by enslaved people against their condition. Everyday resistance included actions such as feigned illness, pretended incomprehension, tool breaking, and stealing, while active resistance involved running away, fighting back against the master or overseer, or, at its most extreme, organized rebellion.[5] Studies of everyday resistance have richly illuminated the lived experience of enslaved people, but this book focuses on active resistance, especially the organized violence of rebellions. While rebellions were rare, they had great political significance in the formation of slave societies over the *longue durée*. Rebellions were critical events of profound social crisis that not only laid bare the exercise of power but also generated precious documentation of the actions and ideas of enslaved rebels.[6]

Comparative history and the concept of the *longue durée* allow for a novel approach to understanding the political dynamics of slave resistance and their relation to the law. The French historian Marc Bloch argued that two societies close together in space and time, and similar in structure, invite comparison as an exploration of historical change. Different outcomes might point to different causes, while similar outcomes can suggest underlying patterns. Any two societies might be compared, but only when the chosen societies have a combination of similarities and differences will comparative analysis yield the richest insights. Likewise, the *longue durée* approach to history pioneered by Fernand Braudel situates historical events within a very long chronology. The creative tension between "the instantaneous and the time that flows slowly" allows for both the lively drama of events and the understanding that comes with attention to the deep contours of historical time.[7]

This book traverses about two hundred years in the history of American slave societies. Beginning in the seventeenth century, English colonists in Barbados developed the "large integrated plantation" based on enslaved African labor, a system that spread into both Jamaica and South Carolina by the end of the century.[8] All three of these colonies became mature slave societies, as did many other British colonies. But Jamaica and South Carolina played outsize roles in the rise and fall of racial slavery in the Anglo-Atlantic World. The violent maturation of these slave societies during the eighteenth century, the tumult of the Age of Revolution, and the manner of abolitionist influence shaped in distinctive ways the coming of abolition in each slave society. Slavery ended in Jamaica in 1834, more than a generation before it ended in South Carolina.

The physical settings of Jamaica and South Carolina share an awesome natural beauty that masks horrid scenes of oppression still buried in the sediment and histories of these lands. An island with numerous natural harbors of clear blue water but no navigable rivers, Jamaica's dramatic topography sweeps from the Blue Mountains in the east, which soar seven thousand feet above the sea, to the strange, steep, bush-covered hillocks of the Cockpit Country in the west. The earliest European settlements were concentrated on the broad, fertile coastal plain that came down to the sea on the southern coast. This plain features broad savannahs and once held thick forests of mahogany and lignum vitae. But throughout the island, the steep ranges are cut by rich valleys of brilliant green that were planted with canes during the eighteenth century. What became South Carolina was a long stretch of the southeastern woodlands of North America, a coastal region cut by a series of navigable rivers centered on the confluence of the Cooper and the Ashley Rivers, two hundred miles south of Chesapeake Bay. Early English settlement clung to the Lowcountry, a swampy land crossed by innumerable creeks and estuaries that flowed through cypress swamps festooned with Spanish moss, savannahs thick with tall grasses, stands of longleaf pines, majestic live oaks, and soaring palmettos. Fertile barrier islands line the coast, and as one traveled inland north and west, the land rose gently toward a low range of rolling sand hills that divide the middle country of level, fertile lands from the mountainous back country, where the old mountains of the Blue Ridge spread north and south. Fierce hurricanes devastated each colony from time to time, though with greater frequency in Jamaica. The climates are subtly different, with summers in both places that are hot, humid, and long, and winters that are mild. In South Carolina, there are freezes that annually suppress bacterial pestilences. Well within the tropics, Jamaica's climate proved entirely too hospitable to the germs that devastate human populations.[9]

These lands were not empty when the English arrived, and differences among their Indian inhabitants had a lasting impact. Both colonies were situated on the periphery of Spain's American empire, which meant that the Indians who peopled these lands had already been transformed by the European arrival in the Americas. The Taino of the Greater Antilles had been numerous before the arrival of the Spanish. When Christopher Columbus first visited Jamaica in 1494, a dozen of the island's caciques approached his ship in huge canoes hewn from single trees and paddled by large entourages of men. The caciques were richly adorned with feather headdresses and cotton clothing of local manufacture. These men governed large towns of between twenty and fifty houses, and scholars believe the island to have been densely populated with a precontact population of perhaps five hundred thousand people. The Taino practiced agriculture by heaping soil into tall, round *conucos* that they would plant with cassava, corn, squash, and beans. The island had no gold, but when the Spanish discovered gold in neighboring Cuba and Hispaniola, they enslaved the Taino of those islands, and when the slaves died in large numbers and ultimately rebelled, the Spanish began to raid neighboring islands for slaves, not only for their labor but also to sell their bodies in Europe. By 1519 most of the Taino of Jamaica had been enslaved, killed, or lost to mass suicide; in 1611, when Abbot Bernardo de Balbuena reported on the state of the colony, he counted only seventy-four Indians. When the English conquered the Spanish colony in 1655, they reported no native presence.[10]

Unlike the Taino of the Caribbean, the peoples of the southeastern woodlands of North America posed a vigorous military and political challenge to the English who sought to settle there. Estimates of the precontact population of the southeast vary greatly, but they are within the same range as those for Jamaica, suggesting a less dense population over a larger area. Diseases introduced by the Spanish *entradas* of the sixteenth century, as well as the establishment of Saint Augustine and its mission system, had weakened these peoples. By the time the English began to arrive in the 1670s, Indian populations were greatly reduced, but they were far more robust when compared with the populations of the Greater Antilles. The Indians of the southeast had begun to coalesce into loose confederacies— Cusabo, Tuscarora, Catawba, Cherokee, Guale, Yamasee, Creek, Timucua, and Apalachee. These peoples lived in towns that sometimes coordinated for defense but otherwise retained their autonomy. The borders of what would become South Carolina would have made no sense to them, but the lands of Carolina were important and well known. Footpaths that carried goods, people, information, and war crisscrossed the southeastern woodlands, and the English had to learn their routes and uses. All of these native peoples practiced agriculture, hunted widely, and had traded with Europeans for about a century before the English arrival. By the best estimates, these groups numbered about seventy thousand people when the English began to arrive.[11]

The political histories of slavery in Jamaica and South Carolina, unlike those of other American slave societies, share remarkably parallel narrative arcs that end in dramatic divergence. Each was a "colony of a colony," settled in part by emigrants from Barbados. The Jamaican colonists established a political economy on the Barbadian model by 1670, and the Carolinians did much the same by 1700. Jamaica produced sugar while South Carolina produced rice, and Carolinian planters enslaved numerous Indians while Jamaicans enslaved mostly Africans. The Assembly of Jamaica borrowed its first slave laws directly from Barbados, but as the colony grew and Africans rebelled, the assembly made key innovations in the law. Jamaica solidified a racial regime to control enslaved Africans through violence, and it refined the law of slave property. Slaves were neither chattel nor real estate but rather a combination of both. They could be bought and sold like cattle, and through natural reproduction they accrued value over time. Slaves were people, of course, but they were also significant capital investments. When the South Carolina General Assembly established its own slave code in 1691, legislators borrowed the Jamaican law word for word.[12]

Both colonies became slave societies with African majorities during the eighteenth century, and by the 1770s their planter classes had become the wealthiest colonial elites in their respective regions of the British Empire, the Caribbean and North America. Each planter class developed its own distinctive mode of governing slaves, made evident in the laws they passed. The legal innovations adopted by each colony responded in part to the threat of slave rebellions and in part to wars with internal enemies, the Maroons of Jamaica and the Indians of the southeastern woodlands, especially the Yamasee. Many of Jamaica's enslaved Africans hailed from the Gold Coast region of West Africa, where the Akan states had developed highly sophisticated military cultures. Led by skilled rebel leaders such as Nanny, Apongo, and Samuel Sharpe, Jamaica's slaves rebelled more than those in any other Atlantic slave society. And as a result, Jamaica's masters developed an ever more militarized mode of governance that rested on extreme brutality, a permanent garrison of imperial troops, local militias, and, after 1740, an alliance with the Maroons, with whom they had fought to a draw.[13]

The first generations of Carolinians lived in a very small colony on the periphery of both the British and Spanish Empires, where they were surrounded by Indian polities that were more numerous and powerful than the English colony. The Carolinians secured their foothold on the continent through trade with the Indians, especially the trade in Indian captives taken in war by the English and their Indian allies. Along with skins and furs, the Charles Town merchants shipped these Indian captives to other English colonies, where they were sold as slaves. Early Carolinians like Thomas Nairne gradually built an agricultural export economy based on provisions, lumber, and ultimately rice, but during the colony's first decades, slaving was their most lucrative activity. The Carolinian traders indulged in indiscriminate brutality against the Indians, and in 1715 a war that broke out between the colony and the Yamasee spread through all the Indian towns that traded with the Carolinians. The war devastated the colony, and in its aftermath, the assembly gradually ameliorated the legal regime that governed slaves, removing sanctions from the more horrendous punishments and incorporating statutes that defined masters' responsibilities toward their slaves. To be sure, Carolinian masters retained great and violent powers that justified the beheading and disemboweling of the Stono rebels as the necessary violence of slaveholding. But in contrast to the militarized slave society that emerged in Jamaica, the Carolina Assembly of masters made a concerted effort to domesticate the slavery at the core of their colony so that it could endure.[14]

The fundamentally different regimes of social control developed by the Assemblies of South Carolina and Jamaica had a profound impact on the role each colony played during the American Revolution. The imperial crisis created opportunities for black people like Thomas Jeremiah of Charles Town or Sam, Daphnis, and Quamina of Lucea Bay, Jamaica, to make a move for their freedom. And while the radical Whig ideology of the North American patriots was influential in Jamaica, the colony's dependence on imperial troops rendered it loyal to Great Britain. In contrast, the threat of rebellion in South Carolina motivated its planters, led by Henry Laurens, to move quickly and forcefully toward independence. Most importantly, the tendency to use "slavery" as a political metaphor to describe tyranny became interwoven with antislavery critiques of racial slavery. Consequently, slave resistance during the Revolution gave antislavery ideas a new political force. The struggles over slavery during the American Revolution initiated the transformation of slavery's politics from a visceral struggle between the masters and the slaves into an epic contest between masters, slave rebels, and abolitionists that would shake the seats of power—Parliament and the United States Congress—until 1863.[15]

The different paths taken by South Carolina and Jamaica during the American Revolution might suggest a break in their similar development, but the abolitionist movement that emerged first in Britain in the wake of the imperial crisis generated quite similar responses from each planter class. This first wave of abolitionists challenged the permanency of slavery on either side of the Atlantic, and the most aggressive proslavery spokesmen were Stephen Fuller and Edward Long of Jamaica and the South Carolinian delegation to the Constitutional Convention in Philadelphia: John Rutledge, Pierce Butler, Charles Pinckney, and Charles Cotesworth Pinckney. These men succeeded in the political defense of slavery, but within a few years, a slave revolt in French Saint-Domingue grew into the Haitian Revolution, a seismic event in the worlds of Atlantic slavery, when an enslaved people rose up in violence, destroyed the master class, and emerged as an independent nation. Enslaved people in both Jamaica and South Carolina conspired to rebel in the wake of Haiti, but would-be rebels faced empowered slaveholders who suppressed discontent and survived relatively unscathed. In addition to introducing the threat of violent upheaval, the Haitian Revolution also destroyed the biggest producer of sugar and coffee in the Atlantic World, inaugurating a period of economic expansion known as the second slavery.[16]

At this very moment of slavery's renewed expansion, the divergence between Jamaica and South Carolina began to materialize. South Carolina's slaveholders enjoyed a comparative political advantage over their Jamaican counterparts that stemmed from American independence and the federal constitution. They were part of a group of well-represented slaveholders from an important region of the new nation—the South. American slaveholders served in the legislatures of the states and the federal government; twelve of the first sixteen presidents of the United States were slaveholders. In contrast, the Jamaicans hailed from a region that had declined in importance within Britain's empire and thus were poorly represented in Parliament. The abolitionist movement coalesced and thrived in Great Britain when abolitionism in the United States did not yet resemble a movement. American abolitionists formed societies, wrote pamphlets, and sent petitions to Congress, but in comparison, American abolitionists could only whisper while their British counterparts had begun to roar.[17]

The ultimate divergence between the histories of South Carolina and Jamaica followed a series of rebellions and conspiracies of the enslaved—the aftershocks of Haiti—that brought fear and tumult to

Barbados (1816); Charleston, South Carolina (1822); Demerara (1822); Jamaica (1823–1824); Southampton, Virginia (1831); and Jamaica again (1831–1832). Creolization within the enslaved population transformed the nature of these rebellions, and abolitionism shaped their course and reception. In Great Britain, the combination of rebellion and abolitionist agitation led to legislative action, the British Parliament's Act for the Abolition of Slavery throughout the British Colonies, passed on August 28, 1833. In sharp contrast, while the Virginia legislature debated the gradual abolition of slavery in 1832 after the Nat Turner revolt (a bill that did not pass), the combination of abolitionism and insurrection generated a forceful proslavery reaction distinctive to South Carolina. Led by John C. Calhoun, the Nullifiers of South Carolina advanced a constitutional theory that asserted a state's right to nullify specific acts of the federal government, a theory consciously designed as a protection for slavery. Nullification failed, but the proslavery argument that followed became the intellectual bedrock for the power of slavery in American political life for another generation. The planters of Jamaica lost their mastery to rebellious slaves and abolitionists, while the same historical actors enabled South Carolinians to secure their mastery on the grounds of a racist and sophisticated proslavery argument that echoes in some circles today.[18]

The planters built their slave societies on a deep contradiction. In both South Carolina and Jamaica, the planters aspired to the Barbadian pattern of economic growth that made a few white men rich and left Africans and their descendants racialized and enslaved. As a political class embodied in legislative assemblies, the planters crafted laws to establish the social stability that made economic growth based on racial slavery possible. And because of the violation of human dignity inherent to slavery and the endemic resistance that resulted, the governance of slaves became an urgent problem that faced every generation of slaveholders.

CHAPTER 1

England's First Slave Society, Barbados

THE ENGLISH ADOPTED the practice of using enslaved Africans as agricultural laborers in the late 1620s without much thought because their imperial competitors in the Atlantic—the Portuguese and the Spanish—had been doing so profitably for more than a century. As the English founded their first slave society in Barbados during the mid-seventeenth century, two hundred thousand enslaved Africans survived the Atlantic crossing in Dutch or Portuguese slave ships and were sold in Brazil or the Spanish mainland. A small percentage were sold in the rough young colonies of the English, but in the early decades of England's empire, indentured servants from Europe provided most of the labor. The first Barbadian planters found success in growing cotton and tobacco, and servants were cheaper and more widely available, so they predominated. The planters built a plantation economy based on the labor of indentured servants and, soon, of enslaved Africans who were compelled to do the same work in similar conditions of inhumane brutality.[1]

The English began to develop their own slave trade with West African merchants in the 1630s, and in the 1640s the Barbadian planters learned the art of making sugar, which the Iberians had known for a hundred years. Sugar brought in more profits than either cotton or tobacco, and its production required more capital, as well as more labor. Sugar brought success to fewer and richer colonists, and the intensity of its production worsened the exploitation inherent in the plantation economy. Servants and slaves resisted the erosion of human dignity at the heart of this exploitation, generating a political struggle that would last for two hundred years.[2]

Despite the importance of liberty in European intellectual discourse, few people of power had ever challenged the morality of slaveholding. In 1518 Bartolomé de Las Casas, outraged by the brutal enslavement and slaughter of the Indians of the Greater Antilles, proposed to the Crown that the practice of enslaving Indians be replaced with the purchase of enslaved Africans. While Las Casas later regretted his proposal, the suggestion accurately represented the growth of African slavery within the expansive merchant capitalism that linked northern Europe to the Mediterranean and West Africa by the end of the fifteenth century. The expansion of Mediterranean sugar production, as well as the European sugar market, had fostered these connections, for when the Ottomans captured Constantinople in 1453, barring Christian merchants from the slave markets of the Black Sea, Mediterranean sugar planters turned increasingly to the slave markets of North Africa and the Iberian Peninsula.[3]

There had always been a few black Africans in these slave markets, those who had survived the trans-Saharan journey, but as the Portuguese began to explore the West African coast, they opened a trade with African merchants in gold and slaves. In 1444 some 235 Africans arrived in Lagos, a port in southern Portugal, and in the following decades Genoese and Castilian merchants were also dealing in African slaves. By the 1490s slaves from sub-Saharan Africa were known to Europeans as *sclavi negri*, literally "black slaves," and in Sicily they were predominant on some of the sugar plantations. Over the next half century, the Portuguese extended their domain and brought the sugar plantation to the Canaries, Madeira, and especially São Tomé. They purchased African slaves to do most of the labor in all of these islands. In Brazil, discovered by Europeans in 1500, the Portuguese enslaved Indians at first to plant a sugar industry there, but during the 1580s they began to import Africans, and by 1620 most slaves in Brazil were African.[4]

In the 1480s English merchants demonstrated interest in what was then known simply as the "Guinea trade" when King Edward IV sought the blessing of Pope Sixtus IV for an African trading venture planned by John Tintam and William Fabian. It was a fitful start to a sixty-year period of haphazard attempts to establish a regular trade with West Africa. William Hawkins the elder—father of the infamous slaving pirate—made three successful ventures to Guinea and Brazil in the 1530s. He traded for ivory in Africa and "behaved himself so wisely" on the Brazilian coast that an unnamed Indian king willingly traveled back to England and appeared before the court of Henry VIII. The English established a regular trade with West Africa by the 1550s, though without any permanent presence, and when William's son John left for West Africa in 1562, he behaved quite badly. John Hawkins had already traded in the Canaries and the Spanish West Indies, where he learned that "Negros were very good marchandise in Hispaniola, and that store of Negros might easily bee had upon the coast of Guinea." Hawkins led three more slaving ventures to West Africa over the next few years, and in depositions taken after the Spanish disrupted Hawkins's fourth voyage, the English merchants William Clark, John Tommes, and William Fowler demonstrated extensive knowledge of the slave markets of Hispaniola and Vera Cruz.[5]

The compendiums of Richard Hakluyt kept alive the knowledge of Hawkins's voyages, and trade with West Africa continued to attract the interest of English merchants, albeit a relative few. The English merchants who engaged in overseas trade in this era established companies that sought royal charters that granted a monopoly for a particular trade—in exchange, of course, for a stream of revenue to the Crown. So the Muscovy Company focused on northern Europe, while the Spanish Company, the Turkey Company, and the Levant Company invested in different portions of England's trade with the Mediterranean. The English merchant companies established a diaspora of trading factories in northern Europe, Spain, and the Levant, and by the 1590s there were English merchants based in Madeira. In the early seventeenth century a more sustained trade with West Africa developed as an offshoot of the Mediterranean trades; ivory, dyewoods, and pepper were the principal commodities.[6]

By 1618, England's Guinea trade had become significant enough to motivate the merchants involved to seek a royal monopoly. "The Company of Adventurers of London Trading to Gynney and Bynney" included merchants such as Humphrey Slaney, Nicholas Crispe, and William Cloberry. Slaney, the most experienced merchant in the group with interests in the Levant, Spain, and the Barbary Coast, developed a significant trade in redwood during the 1620s with Crispe, Cloberry, and John Wood. They traded in more than dye, however, for in 1629, a French privateer seized the *Benediction*, a company ship that was loaded with slaves. When the company faced bankruptcy, Crispe engineered its reorganization, and it gained a new charter in 1631. Crispe hoped to branch out from the redwood trade of Sierra Leone into the gold trade to the east, the stretch of coast between Cape Three Points and the river Volta known as the Gold Coast, where the Portuguese and then the Dutch had opened a trade in gold and slaves with Akan merchants. But if this proved too difficult, Crispe was confident that the sugar trade with São Tome would be lucrative.[7]

At some point in the 1620s, the English Guinea merchants realized that a moderately successful trading voyage in redwood and ivory could become profitable by taking on sugar in São Tomé, and by doing so, they would have learned about what the historian Philip Curtin called the "plantation complex." This engine of merchant capitalism that would shape the Atlantic World brought together European merchants with access to capital and markets, tropical land with a climate suitable to sugar production, and a regular source of enslaved laborers, who in São Tomé came from West Central Africa. This political economy began to develop in the Mediterranean in the fourteenth century and reached its mature form in São Tomé by 1500. By the time the English began to plant colonies beyond the European pale, the sugar plantation founded on African slavery had been critical to economic development and imperial expansion for several hundred years. The English merchants who went to São Tomé to buy sugar understood this.[8]

Under the leadership of Crispe, the reorganized African Company made key innovations in the trade with Akan merchants with the assistance of Arent de Groot, a Dutchman who had traded for the Dutch West India Company. De Groot introduced the English to the Dutch trading system of keeping resident merchants, or factors, at permanent trading stations whose security depended on agreement with the local African ruler. In 1632 De Groot negotiated a treaty on behalf of the English with Ambro, the Fante ruler, for the exclusive right to trade from Kormantine, Egya, and Anomabu, ports that lay within his authority. De Groot planted the flag of His Royal Majesty of Great Britain at Kormantine and established the first trading factory held by the English on the Gold Coast.[9]

For the next twelve years, Crispe and his associates worked assiduously to grow the trade with the Akan merchants of the Gold Coast. English factors learned the ways of the African trade and made connections with local merchants while English ship captains learned the tricks of the route to Guinea. Success came slowly, but late in 1636 a ship returned with gold that brought investors profits of about £30,000. The English began to build a fort at Kormantine in 1638 and by 1640 posed a serious challenge to the Dutch. Crispe became increasingly wealthy, and in 1640 he was knighted and became a chief customs farmer for Charles I. But as the turmoil of the English Civil War intensified, Crispe suffered for his connections to the King. In 1641 the Committee of Grievances accused Crispe of being a monopolist (which he was) and forced him to give up his patents to the trade in redwood and gold. Crispe fled London and joined the King at the onset of war, and in 1644 Parliament sequestered Crispe's shares in the company, which reverted to John Wood. By 1649 one of Wood's partners in the company was Maurice Thompson, a former interloper in the Guinea trade who had been invested in every English colonial enterprise in the Americas since the 1620s. So it was that at the very moment English planters in Barbados began to plant sugarcane, the English trade to the Gold Coast had developed into a profitable and growing enterprise. By the late 1640s the branches of commerce that connected African slave merchants to England's tropical colonies through European merchants with access to capital and markets had passed into the hands of men deeply invested in all of these things.[10]

The English began to plant colonies in the Americas in the early seventeenth century, 1607 in the Chesapeake and then New England and the Lesser Antilles in the 1620s. In 1627 Barbados became the second island settled, after Saint Christopher, when the London merchant William Courteen and his associates gained permission from the proprietor of the colony, James Hay, the Lord of Carlisle, and put up capital to fund the first settlers. During that very first year, Captain Henry Powell, the island's first governor, brought an unknown number of enslaved Africans to the island, whom he had captured from a Spanish or a Portuguese vessel. While Spain and England were at peace, Spain considered the entire Caribbean as part of its domain according to the Treaty of Tordesillas of 1494, which drew a line down the center of the Atlantic. The area to the west was Spanish, including the Caribbean islands (some of which the Spanish had already claimed through conquest), as well as the continental Americas. Portugal claimed everything to the east, including Brazil, Africa, and all of Asia. England under Elizabeth, the Stuarts, Oliver Cromwell, and the Stuarts again after 1660 consistently challenged the Iberian claims, as did the Dutch and the French. Just as in the era of Hawkins, the English encountered African slaves whenever they encountered the Spanish.[11]

Maurice Thompson had been involved in English colonial expansion almost from the very beginning. Born around the turn of the seventeenth century, Thompson, young and ambitious and from a large family without fortune, made his way to Virginia by 1617, the very year that Virginians made their first shipment of tobacco to London and just two years before a Dutch merchant brought the first Africans to the colony.[12] He established himself as a ship captain in the provisioning and servant trades, but in 1626 he returned to London as a merchant with interests in all of the American colonies, importing tobacco, furs, and fish while exporting provisions, equipment, and indentured servants. One of Thompson's first ventures as a London merchant was a partnership with the cash-poor tobacco planter Thomas Combes of Saint Kitts. In 1628 Thompson sent sixty African slaves to work on Combes's plantation.[13]

Virginian success with tobacco fostered the "first American boom," and the earliest Barbadians followed suit, hoping to tap into the new market for this stimulating weed. Henry Winthrop wrote from Barbados in 1627 that he and his servants had planted tobacco, which in three years he hoped would be "very profitable." He sought assistance in bringing over more servants, two or three "everye yere," who would be bound to serve him for three to five years and could expect no more than ten pounds a year. He described Barbados as "the pleasantest iland in all the West Indyes," with a small settlement of only sixty "christyanes," all of them English, and between forty and fifty slaves, "negeres and Indyenes." Winthrop's father, John, replied some months later that he could only procure boys who were willing to indenture themselves in Barbados and that the tobacco Henry sent was "foul, and full of stalks." No one would buy it, not even his relatives.[14]

Not all Barbadians were so careless with their tobacco, however, for in 1638 Thompson imported twenty-five thousand pounds of the stuff, and tobacco remained an important form of currency on the island until 1648.[15] But in 1640 the aspiring planter James Dering considered tobacco to be a "dead commodity" that could not compete with the Virginian product in a market now glutted with the crops from Nevis, Saint Kitts, and Montserrat as well.[16] Barbadians expanded into cotton and indigo and, based on the production of these commodities, developed the plantation model of agricultural production—sizable estates dependent on unfree labor—that they would soon adapt to sugar.[17] Indentured servants did most of the labor during this period, but as the testimony of Henry Winthrop shows, African slaves were part of the workforce from the very beginning. Barbadians may have been the first among the English to codify the slave status of Africans, for in 1636 the Barbados Council resolved that "Negroes and Indians, that came here to be sold, should serve for Life, unless a Contract was before made to the contrary." At this early stage in socioeconomic development, then, Barbadians made distinctions between those who "served for Life" and those who worked under a contract. These English did not yet define

slavery in racial terms, for the council allowed the possibility that
an African or Indian might arrive under a contract, just as indentured laborers from Europe did. Then again, nothing suggests that
the council applied the same distinction to European indentured laborers; they would never "serve for life."[18]

Indentured servants were, however, far more important to the
early development of Barbados than were African slaves. From a
small settlement of 100 people that was about 40 percent African in
1627, there were 6,000 people ten years later and only 200 were Africans, a mere 3 percent.[19] The English had only begun to establish
a presence on the Gold Coast during the 1630s, yet by 1643 there
were 6,400 Africans on the island, about one-fourth of a population
of at least 25,000. Landholding was relatively widespread in 1643,
with 8,300 proprietors among the European population of 18,600.[20]
Two-thirds of those proprietors were probably former servants who
raised cotton, tobacco, and food provisions without the assistance
of servants or slaves. Often working in partnerships, these men had
used the money they received at the end of their indentures to purchase small amounts of marginal land. They cleared it, sold the
lumber to their wealthier neighbors, and then planted food and commodities, mostly cotton and tobacco. A third of the proprietors owned
the service of two or three servants, and there were a handful of
planters who owned the labor of more than ten servants. Tobacco and
cotton were most popular because they required very little capital to
begin, just seeds, land, and hoes. Tobacco and cotton also demanded
far less and lighter labor than sugar did.[21]

The development of plantation agriculture in tobacco, cotton, and
indigo created a robust society that grew more rapidly than any other
English colony in the Americas. The increase of the enslaved African
population was less than the growth in the servant population, but
it was still significant. Most of Africans on the island in 1643 had
arrived fairly recently, and most of them had been brought by English merchants. Barbadian planters had acquired some capital, and
as Thompson's early investment in slaves for Saint Kitts attests,
English merchants knew very well that African slaves made for a
sound investment. In 1638 Thompson invested in an interloping

voyage to the Gold Coast, probably for slaves, but Crispe remained influential and protective of his monopoly and customs officials prohibited Thompson's ships from sailing. Wood, working with Crispe, began to expand the Guinea trade into slaves for the Americas during the 1640s, and by 1650 about 4,500 enslaved Africans had arrived in Barbados.[22]

The expansion of African slavery in Barbados took place at precisely the same time the English began to ramp up their activity in the transatlantic slave trade. These developments were interdependent, stemming from calculated ventures of perhaps a dozen men with investments in the expanding Atlantic economy. The expansion of African slavery began in the early 1640s because of economic growth based on the production of tobacco, cotton, and indigo, and in 1643 James Drax, who had arrived on the island with £300 in the late 1620s, performed the first successful experiment with sugar production. Richard Ligon, who lived on the island for three years in the late 1640s, noted the presence of "Portugal Negroes" on Drax's plantation. These men and women had probably come from Brazil, and they probably had some knowledge of sugar production.[23] Thompson invested in sugar production in Barbados, and other London merchants such as William Pennoyer, Martin Noell, Thomas Povey, John Vincent, and Anthony Ashley Cooper (later Lord Shaftesbury) invested in Barbados plantations. By 1645 40 percent of the island was covered with fields of cane.[24]

Sugar brought greater profits than tobacco, cotton, or indigo, but it also required more labor, as well as more capital to begin production. Sugar had to be at least partially processed before it could be shipped, so in addition to land, the planter had to invest in a "sugar works"—a sugar mill, a structure to house it, and several more buildings: a boiling house, a curing house, numerous cauldrons and clay pots for processing, horses and oxen to power the mill, and far more laborers than other crops required. The sugar harvest, which could last six months, involved hacking down canes that could be as thick as a man's arm and processing them before they spoiled. Laborers in Barbados put the canes through horse-powered mills that were known to take off the arm of the unlucky person who snagged a finger in between the rollers. The cane juice flowed through pipes into the cauldrons of the boiling house, where the boiler, a skilled and experienced worker, would stir the juice and adjust the fires so that the cauldrons would boil at just the right roll. They would skim it for impurities several times, and at a particular moment that only a skilled boiler knew, he would temper the juice with a mixture of ash and water, which initiated crystallization. The boiler then decided when it was time to strike, or kill, the fire. Once this mass of sugar and molasses cooled, the boiler poured the syrup from the hot iron cauldrons into conical clay pots. Slaves carried these to the curing house, where the molasses slowly drained, leaving the crystalline essence of sweetness behind. A combination of sheer greed and the fragility of the cane juice drove most planters to keep their mills running night and day, with brush fires burning at night to provide light for exhausted servants and slaves. The work was brutal, so most sugar planters hired overseers to manage the pace of their laborers with liberal applications of the whip.[25]

The combination of more arduous labor and greater profits seems to have deepened the exploitation of Barbadian laborers, enslaved or indentured, and intensified social conflict. An anonymous writer of a 1650 account noted that servants customarily received only ten pounds after four years of service, significantly less than what Winthrop described in 1627.[26] Ligon believed that servants were treated worse than the slaves. He described their poor diet of potatoes, the inadequate lodgings, and the cruelty of overseers who would "beat a Servant with a cane about the head" until the blood flowed freely. Father Antoine Biet's account of the island in 1654 described how Barbadians settled "their differences by fist fighting. They give each other black eyes, scratch each other, tear each other's hair." Such everyday violence reflected the tensions of an oppressive society in which the laborers were treated more brutally than their Old World counterparts.[27]

But Biet's account does not concur with Ligon's judgment that the servants were treated worse. Biet noted the same poor diet and lodgings, as well as the brutality of the overseers with both classes of laborers. Yet he described the treatment of black slaves with far more gruesome language. Masters beat servants and slaves with similar violence, but black slaves could be "brand[ed] all over their bodies which makes them shriek with despair." One cruel overseer sliced off one of his slave's ears, roasted it, and forced the poor man to eat it.[28] In 1654 John Berkenhead wrote that Barbadians killed their slaves with impunity and ranked them with "dogs." Henry Whistler described a multiethnic servant population of "English, French, Duch, Scotes, irish," and Spanish Jews, along with the "miserabell Negors borne to perpetuall slauery thay and thayer seed."[29] Whistler's remarks are particularly suggestive; they reflect a far wider net for indentured servants than the predominantly English population Winthrop had described, and they indicate the Barbadian adoption of hereditary slavery. The Barbados Council in 1636 had not described slavery as hereditary, and the transition by the 1650s simply followed the practice of the Iberians, whose slave law descended from ancient Rome. This transformation took place simultaneously with the rise in the African population, which grew mostly from importation and some natural reproduction, though the latter could not have been great. Sugar and the enslavement of Africans became entrenched in the political economy of Barbados during the same historical moment.[30]

Despite such miserable developments, the labor demands of the expanding sugar industry increased significantly during the 1640s, and the population more than doubled with rising numbers of indentured and enslaved immigrants. By 1650 the European population had grown to about thirty thousand, and most of these newly arrived thousands came as bound servants. The plantations also had drawn about 6,500 more Africans since 1643, and they now were about one-third of the island's population.[31]

The dramatic expansion of Barbados attracted a third group of migrants who had the resources to generate opportunity from the transatlantic crossing. As Barbados had grown, England had become increasingly riven by the English Civil War, which would bring regicide and the rise of Cromwell by the end of the decade. Men of the lesser gentry either fled or simply departed England for Barbados. This latter group included the Walrond brothers, Humphrey and Edward, who arrived in 1645; Thomas Modyford, a trained barrister and later the governor of Barbados and Jamaica, who arrived in 1647 with Ligon; and John Colleton, who would become a proprietor of South Carolina and came to the island in 1650. These men and others like them had capital and access to credit, which they immediately invested in slaves and sugar plantations. Humphrey Walrond, for example, acquired a prime seaside plantation of 250 acres worked by ten servants and 29 slaves, while Modyford, with Thomas Hilliard, bought into a plantation of 500 acres, twenty-eight servants, and 102 slaves. The political economy of slavery had taken root in Barbados; these men would foster it, expand it, and make their fortunes.[32]

The wealthy migrants who arrived in Barbados during the 1640s were fierce political partisans who threatened to disrupt the relative political unity that had characterized the emerging Barbadian elite. Ligon wrote that when he arrived, the tradition held that "whosoever named the word Roundhead or Cavalier" must host a feast for everyone present at the onset of political disagreement.[33] This distaste for political acrimony among the elite reflects a concern with political challenges from servants and slaves. Servants had organized a conspiracy to rebel as early as 1634, and when Beauchamp Plantagenet visited the island in 1648, he reported seeing "rich men having sugar mills" and "many hundreds Rebell Negro slaves in the woods."[34] Early laws passed by the assembly show that indentured servants ran away from the plantations in significant numbers, and they sometimes struck back against violent overseers and stole from their estates.[35] Land prices rose consistently with the growth of the export economy, and a trickle of former servants without prospects on the island began to leave for other parts of the Atlantic World. As they left, the proprietors became smaller in number, and servants and slaves became even larger in proportion.[36]

On January 30, 1649, the Parliament in London ordered the execution of Charles I as a traitor to the Commonwealth of England. In Barbados, a group of at least eighteen servants began to form a conspiracy to cut the throats of their masters and "make themselves not only freemen, but Masters of the Island." Ligon believed the conspiracy grew from their "suffereings" and the inability of some "to endure such slavery." The planters discovered the conspiracy when a servant of Justice Hothersall informed him of the plot. Hothersall spread the word, and the planters identified the principal leaders and halted the plot before it began. Ligon was told that the conspiracy reached throughout the entire island and that most servants were involved. Eighteen people were executed, and their "haughty" demeanors in the midst of discovery terrified the planters.[37]

The servants may well have taken advantage of the execution of Charles to make their move for freedom, and in this fraught moment of barely foiled conspiracy, the civil war that had overtaken England erupted in Barbados. Resident royalists rejected the authority of Parliament, seized control over the colony, and forced more than a hundred of their opponents into exile. The exiles included some of the big planters, such as Drax, Thomas Middleton, James Futter, and Thomas Noell (the brother of Martin Noell), who returned to London and began to pursue their interests with Parliament. In November 1650, Parliament's Council of State, which governed the colonies, made Sir George Ayscue, Daniel Searle, and Michael Pack commissioners charged with raising a force to reduce Barbados to the submission of Parliament. Ayscue was to lead the force, and Searle was to become governor once the royal colonists were defeated. Ayscue's fleet arrived in October; by the end of the year, the royalists on the island had been defeated. Many were pardoned, but the most ardent royalists were exiled, leaving in power those planters who were most concerned with stability and prosperity. Searle became governor, and Barbadian freeholders elected a new assembly.[38]

The new assembly voided the laws passed by the royalist assembly, reenacted some of them, and passed additional laws "thought necessary for the good government of the Island." John Jennings, clerk of the assembly, began to assemble a compilation of these new and reenacted laws once they were confirmed by the governor. In 1654, Jennings published a slim volume of Barbadian law, the first such publication, which illuminates the dialectical contest between masters, servants, and slaves. These early slave and servant laws reflected the aspirations of Barbadian planter-legislators as they codified the practices of New World mastery. Beyond the physical brutality used on the plantations, the passage of laws governing servants and slaves represents the first political actions of English planters in the epic struggle that embedded slavery in the political economy of England's empire.[39]

The laws do not reflect the social reality of Barbados; rather, they provide a refracting lens that allows us a glimpse of the actions of indentured and enslaved individuals responding to the oppressions of plantation labor. And with more clarity, the laws reveal the prescriptive actions that legislators saw as necessary to establish the order they sought. The laws of slavery distill the political struggle that emerged and changed over time as slave societies developed.[40]

Indentured servants still predominated in the Barbadian labor force during the 1640s and 1650s, and as a result there were some laws that treated servants and slaves as if they held equivalent status. No master, one law stated, should "entertain," or take into service, "any man, or woman, White or Black . . . if he did not know him to be a Free-man." Violators genuinely ignorant of a servant's status would be fined one hundred pounds of sugar; violators who willfully broke the law would be fined five hundred pounds of sugar. Freedom rather than race was the critical attribute, for the statute clearly implied that a black person could legally be taken into service by a master. Another law treated both servants and slaves as property that could be seized by a creditor for payment of debt, placing both groups of people within the same category as cattle, stock, and horses. Another law banned both servants and slaves from trading, with a fine imposed on the merchant rather than the servant or slave. These laws defined the economic role played by servants and slaves: both were animate capital more akin to farm animals than people; they created wealth for others and, despite their humanity, were prohibited from engaging in trade, a fundamentally human activity.[41]

These laws governed servants and slaves with the same language, but they did not treat personal behavior, and in this respect, the laws had much more to say about servants than slaves. The laws prescribed punishments for a whole range of servant behaviors deemed inappropriate by the planter-legislators of the assembly. Servants must not hit their masters or overseers; they must not steal, especially cattle; they must not violate the Sabbath; they must not marry; and servant men must not impregnate servant women. The punishments for all of these infractions involved additional service to their master, or to the master of the woman in the case of a pregnancy. Violating the Sabbath could result in thirteen lashes on the bare back, and stealing cattle could result in several days in the pillory and the loss of both ears. Servants were not protected in any way from the abuse of masters; only disputes about the amount of time served could be brought before two justices of the peace, positions that were held by planters, not recently freed men. The laws relating to slaves touched on none of these issues, reflecting the planters' collective sense that the behavior of servants warranted more attention.[42]

The law's distinction between servants and slaves can also be seen in the Act to Restrain the Wandring of Servants and Negros. The law sought to suppress runaways, but with different punishments for servants and slaves. Servants were to serve an additional month for every two hours away from the plantation; slaves would be "moderately whipped" and escorted under guard back to their master's plantation. Moreover, the law spoke to servants directly, threatening them with extended servitude. But the law approached slaves indirectly, punishing Africans who absconded by commanding others to detain and whip them. For the trouble of capturing, whipping, and escorting an African runaway, the captor would receive ten pounds of sugar for each mile traveled. There were no such provisions for the capture of servants. Like free persons, servants were subject to the laws and the enforcement of legal officers. Africans, however, stood outside the law, and their violations of the social order became subject to the enforcement of any free person.[43]

There were also special laws protecting slaveholders that did not extend to the masters of servants, which suggests that while servants remained a mainstay of labor, the interest in African slaves was ascendant. For example, one law governing runaway slaves but not runaway servants stipulated that no person could hold a runaway slave for more than forty-eight hours. The person who did so risked a fine of one thousand pounds of sugar, to be split between the rightful master and the informer. The servant who acted as an informer in such a case could gain his or her freedom for providing such "honest information," a significant incentive for Barbadian servants to enforce the rights of slaveholders. The creation of privileges for servants not available to slaves would become a favorite tactic of the assembly as the slave society developed.[44]

The expanding plantation economy created even greater demand for labor, and fortunately for the planters, the English state proved entirely willing to provide them with servants. As Cromwell completed the conquest of Ireland, the English state sent thousands of Irish to Barbados as political prisoners. Others deemed "undesirable" were kidnapped from the streets for shipment to the Caribbean. "Barbadozz'd," meaning "to be forcibly transported to the colonies," became a verb during this period.[45] This happened to Marcellus Rivers, who testified in a petition to Parliament that he had been arrested during the Salisbury Rising (though he claimed to have no part in it), held for a year in prison, and then shipped to Barbados in 1656. When he arrived he was sold for 1,550 pounds of sugar, and he was bought and sold several more times during his indenture. Rivers stated that he and others were "whipt at [the planters'] whipping pofts, as Rogues, for their mafters pleafure"; they slept in "ftyes worse than hogs in England," ate nothing but potatoes, and drank nothing but water.[46]

It is hardly surprising that servants resisted such conditions and that the Irish, with political experiences distinct from those of the English or the Scottish poor, were at the forefront of organized resistance. In 1655 in Saint Philip Parish, "several Irish servants and negroes [were] out in rebellion" plundering the estates, and in 1656 Governor Searle received another report from the same parish of a "riotous and unruly lot" of Irish servants wreaking havoc. The next year Searle made a public declaration that cited the many Irish who were "now forth in rebellion" and instituted a series of regulations, including a pass system and a ban on Irish servants' possession of weapons. Such laws, made in response to aggressive resistance from below, are significant, for over the next century, as the plantation model spread, planter-legislators of later generations applied them to Africans as they forged the systems to control slave societies that would last for two hundred years.[47]

The restoration of Charles II in 1660 created the historical moment when the English state formally embedded racial slavery in the process of imperial expansion. Cromwell died in 1658, and in May 1660 Charles II returned to England from his long exile in the Netherlands. His restoration had been orchestrated in part by George Monck, a cousin of the planter Thomas Modyford. Monck served on the Privy Council, which took a series of steps that consolidated racial slavery at the very heart of the imperial project. In July, the Privy Council established the Lords of Trade, a committee with responsibility for the governance of the American colonies. In November, the Privy Council established the Council of Trade and the Council of Foreign Plantations; both advised the Lords of Trade. Then, in December, Charles issued a charter for the Company of Royal Adventurers Trading to Africa (precursor to the Royal African Company), empowering it with a monopoly on the West African trade.[48]

At least six of the men involved in these committees had personal knowledge of Barbados and the increasing importance of African slavery in the development of that colony. The Privy Council included Anthony Ashley Cooper (later Lord Shaftesbury), who had invested in a sugar plantation in Barbados. The merchants Martin Noell and Thomas Povey, both with investments in Barbados, sat on the Councils of Trade and of Foreign Plantations, as well as the board of the Royal African Company. Joining them in all three bodies were Crispe, who had played so crucial a role in founding the English Guinea trade, and John Colleton, the Barbadian sugar planter. Drax, the single largest slaveholder in Barbados and the planter who had introduced sugar to the island, served on the Council of Trade and the Council of Foreign Plantations. So it was that the men who had profited most from the English embrace of sugar and slaves in Barbados were appointed to positions of great influence in the governance of England's empire at the dawn of the Restoration.[49]

The new committees and the Royal African Company created the administrative structure to consolidate slavery, but it fell to the Assembly of Barbados, England's first slave society, to codify the manner of internal governance. In the fall of 1661, the newly elected Barbados Assembly formulated two distinct comprehensive labor codes: an Act for the Good Governing of Servants, and Ordaining the Rights between Masters and Servants, and an Act for the Better

Ordering and Governing of Negroes. Governor Humphrey Walrond signed these laws within three days of each other in September 1661, suggesting that the assembly worked out this legislation as one comprehensive project for the governance of the island's
laboring class. The distinctions between the treatment of servants
and slaves evident in previous legislation appear in the very titles of
these new acts. Both servants and slaves required special laws, but
only servants deserved the codification of their "Rights." And while
servants were named by the contracts they had signed, slaves were
named as a peculiar people, Negroes.[50]

The preambles of both acts emphasized group histories of criminality, but uniquely, the law asserted that the criminality of Negroes
stemmed from an inherent barbarism. Unruly servants had engaged
in the "bold extravagancy" of running away from their masters, and
the assembly sought to establish a "continual strict course" for their
governance. Likewise, slaves had been guilty of "many . . . misde-
meanour, crimes, and offences," but Africans were further described
as a "brutish" people who required harsher "punishionary Laws for
the benefit and good" of the colony.[51]

Presumably, the alleged barbarism of Africans precluded them
from the possession of rights as the English understood them, and
unlike contemporaneous Iberian slave law based on the medieval
Siete Partidas, the 1661 Slave Act of Barbados did not attribute any
positive rights to slaves whatsoever.[52] Yet the rights noted in the title
of the Servant Act were much expanded since 1652, when the only
right clearly stated was that two justices of the peace were to hear
disputes between servants and masters over time served. The new
comprehensive legislation prohibited the indenture of "children of
the English nation" under the age of fourteen (though the status of
Irish and Scots remained unclear). Disputes between servants and
masters over time served would now be heard under the common law
in court, rather than by two justices of the peace, and the 1661 Servant Act allowed for disputes on wages to be considered as well. The
law obliged masters to care for servants who became ill and prohibited masters from simply turning them out, as had been the prac-

tice. If married servants arrived from Europe together, masters could not separate them; rather, the law ordered that the couple be "sold together." To be sure, indentured servants still could not marry without their masters' consent, women could not become pregnant, servants could not trade, and masters could not entertain them, but considering all, the Servant Act of 1661 expanded the rights allowed to servants.[53]

Based on the allowance of servants to bring disputes over time served to a court of common law, we might presume that servants had access to the courts in other suits as well. Not so with African slaves. The assembly created a distinct procedure for judging and punishing crimes such as theft, murder, and robbery when committed by enslaved people. "Negroes[,] . . . being brutish Slaves," did not deserve to be tried for such offenses by a jury of twelve of their peers as English law prescribed. Rather, the assembly established what would come to be known as the slave court. Slaves accused of crimes would be judged by an impromptu court of two justices of the peace and three freeholders, who were endowed with the power not only to pass judgment on the accused but also to decide on and execute a punishment in accordance with the law. The Barbados Slave Act did not prescribe specific punishments for most crimes (subsequent Assemblies would do so). Presumably, this decision was left to the men convened as a court in each particular instance.[54]

Among both servants and slaves, to run away from the authority of the master was the most common action performed in resistance to oppression. The 1652 runaway laws made a two-pronged distinction between servants and slaves that separated these groups by their relationship to the law and by the dissimilar punishments ordered for the same offense. The 1661 acts retained the distinctive relationships to the law; they also embellished the differences in punishment.

The provisions of the 1661 Slave Act governing runaways made slaveholders and their agents responsible for restricting the movement of slaves. The law required masters or overseers to write tickets for any slave sent off the plantation. Masters or overseers who failed to provide tickets were to be fined five hundred pounds of sugar; half of this went to the informer and the other half to the public treasury. The slaveholder or overseer who failed to capture and whip a runaway slave faced a fine of five hundred pounds of sugar. While designed to limit enslaved people's freedom of movement, the mechanism of the law targeted the response of Europeans to African assertions of a right to movement. Moreover, through the use of informers—a group that could have included indentured laborers—the law created an incentive structure within the society to monitor their neighbors' management of slaves.[55]

In contrast, the masters of servants had no such responsibilities; rather, the Servant Act of 1661 made the servant responsible for procuring a ticket if he or she wished to go abroad. And the punishments and enforcement mechanisms for servants and slaves caught off the plantation diverged widely from previous law. The assembly significantly reduced the punishment for runaway servants from an additional month to an additional *day* of servitude for every two hours' absence. In the same moment, the assembly increased the punishment of runaway slaves from a "moderate" to a "severe" whipping. And while the enforcement of runaway servants was still left to the justice of the peace, the assembly created an elaborate enforcement structure for the capture, punishment, and imprisonment of Africans who ran away. The financial incentive for capturing a runaway African rose from ten pounds of sugar per mile escorted to a flat fee of one hundred pounds of sugar. Slave catchers were to bring runaways to the owner, if known, or to the provost marshal of the island, who was charged with their maintenance and imprisonment until redeemed by the owner. The legal status of servants made them subject to the law like any free person; slaves' indirect relationship to the law, however, made them subject to the power of free society at large. The mastery of slaves required the participation of the entire free community, and the law encouraged the brutal treatment of Africans by any free person. The laws governing the mastery of servants did no such thing.[56]

With simultaneous action, the comprehensive acts of 1661 raised the status of indentured laborers and reduced the condition of African slaves.[57] This process can be further seen in the treatment of insurrections, and in the governance of the far more common physical altercations between a master and a laborer. The servant conspiracy of 1649 terrified the planters, and rebelliousness had not dissipated during the 1650s. Yet the Servant Act of 1661 has no specific clause relating to servant rebellions or bands of runaways. The Slave Act does. Over the *longue durée*, bands of Maroons and insurrections posed major threats to slave societies across the Americas. Maroon communities never developed in Barbados to the extent they did in Jamaica, Brazil, or Suriname, but in the seventeenth century, there were still "Woods and other fastness of the Isle" where bands of runaways hid and did "mischief" on neighboring plantations. The Slave Act empowered militia captains to raise companies for the specific purposes of capturing these bands. Captains were empowered to raise a posse of "not more than twenty" members and pursue and apprehend the members of these bands "dead or alive." Members of the company would receive five hundred pounds of sugar for each runaway captured or killed, paid by the owner if captured or by the public if killed. In the case of insurrection or even a conspiracy among the slaves, the law ordered the governor to declare martial law, which would allow for the execution of any of the "Actors, Contrivers, raisers, fomenters, and Concealers" of rebellion. So that slaveholders would be encouraged to disclose the rebellious plans of their slaves, the law promised compensation from the public treasury for any slave executed by the state.[58]

According to previous law, the indentured servant who struck his or her master could be subjected to two additional years of servitude; in 1661, the assembly reduced this punishment to one year. If similar legislation existed regarding African slaves, it has not survived, but in the Slave Act of 1661 any "Negro" who struck a "Christian" could be severely punished. The first offense incurred a severe whipping; on the second the offender would have his or her "nose slit" and face branded. The third offense demanded unspecified but "greater Corporal punishment," probably death. Significantly, the language of this law replaced the term "master" with "Christian," significantly broadening the group protected under the statute to include indentured servants as well as slaveholders, another legal distinction between these groups of laborers. And the slave law introduced a level of physical disfigurement that had not been evident in previous laws.[59] The sixteenth-century vagrancy codes that Barbadian legislators probably consulted prescribed both whipping and branding, but for no crime did these laws require the mutilation of the nose. Slitting of the nose would have left the face of the victim permanently deformed in an unsightly fashion that illustrates the "animalization" of the enslaved at the heart of slavery.[60]

Past assemblies had threatened whites with physical disfigurement as well. Previous laws punished those who absconded with cattle with two weeks in the pillory and the loss of their ears. Another statute punishing obnoxious behavior on the Sabbath prescribed thirteen lashes on the naked back of any indentured laborer so convicted. The assembly renewed neither of these statutes in the years after 1661.[61]

Finally, men in the Assembly of 1661 acknowledged that some masters had taken the punishment of servants and slaves to the point of death. The surviving laws we have did not address this question, but the comprehensive acts of 1661 did so in harshly different terms. The Servant Act prohibited masters from burying any Christian servant who died on his or her plantation until a justice of the peace and two freeholders had viewed the body, presumably to detect foul play. Punishment for violation of this statute was twenty thousand pounds of sugar. In stark contrast, if a master killed an African slave during punishment, he or she had committed no crime. In the case of a killing that resulted from "cruel intention," the assembly prescribed a fine of only three thousand pounds of sugar.[62]

By distinguishing "Christians" from "Negros" in the physical punishment of the body, the Barbados Assembly laid the empirical foundation for racial ideology. The Slave Act's preamble provided words to introduce that ideology into English law. "Negroes," the assembly stated, were a "heathenish, brutish and uncertain dangerous pride of people." The code employed "Negro" throughout rather than "slave," which asserted equivalence between slave status and the complexion of sub-Saharan Africans. "Negro," meaning "African," derived, of course, from Portuguese and Spanish usage and was rooted in the word for black. The language of the law therefore linked blackness to religious otherness, but it also attributed black people with "brutishness," an English word associated with beasts, and "uncertainty," which, when applied to people, meant "fickle and capricious." Moreover, the law considered Africans not as individuals but as a "pride of people," the word used to describe a band of lions. The law defined "Negroes" not only by their blackness but also through the allegation of offensive cultural characteristics, and it established their animalization as dangerous, exotic lions who needed to be caged. While later generations would articulate ever more sophisticated and insidious articulations of race, we can see the kernel of it here in 1661 with the assertion of cultural and biological difference. In slave law, race served as an intellectual technology to justify the brutally distinct treatment of a people defined as inferior.[63]

The usage of "Christian" rather than "white" to denote people of European descent is also significant. While Barbadians did use the term "white" on occasion, neither comprehensive act of 1661 did so, preferring the term "Christian servant." The ideology of race developed slowly, even while the technology of race began to operate. The use of physical violence by one person on another lay at the core of enslavement, and the perceived duty to protect "Christians" from the violent actions of blacks created a privilege within the laboring class reserved for "Christians." European indentured servants suffered great brutality in seventeenth-century Barbados, but the comprehensive acts of 1661 sought to protect them from the violent actions of blacks, a phenomenon that evolved into what we might describe today as white privilege. The comprehensive acts of 1661 sought to divide the laboring class into two groups, "Christian" and "Negro," that were separate and unequal. And because of their views about Africans, men in the assembly could not imagine a Negro as legitimately Christian. Race as an ideological construction had not yet fully emerged, but race as an exercise of power was clearly at work.

In December 1667, Barbados governor William Willoughby wrote to the Privy Council of his concern for the "great want of servants in this island." As sugar had become ever more dominant, the price of land had increased and the opportunities available to servants at the end of their terms had diminished. The migration of former indentured servants had turned into an exodus, peopling England's Atlantic empire. At the same time, the transatlantic slave trade from

Africa to Barbados had more than tripled. By 1670 people of European descent would form less than 40 percent of the island's population. Servants were needed not only for their labor, Willoughby wrote, but also for "the safety of this place, [which] will always be in question; for though there be no enemy abroad, the keeping of slaves in subjection must still be provided for." Willoughby's concern for the domestic tranquility of the island speaks to the perpetual struggle between the masters and the slaves that lay as the foundation of Atlantic slave societies.[64]

The laws of the Barbados Assembly governing servants and slaves not only reflect the essence of this political struggle; they also made a critical contribution to the formation of the political economy of slavery at the heart of the imperial project. The Barbados Assembly established a sophisticated system of laws, fines, courts, and rewards to encourage free people of European descent to employ a vicious brutality to control the behavior of enslaved Africans. They divided their society into Christians and Africans, making it abundantly clear that Africans were closer to beasts and should be treated as such, and that Christians were a privileged people. These were insidious acts that would shape the development of slavery, racism, and empire among English-speaking peoples for the next two centuries.

CHAPTER 2

Animate Capital

In an arc of expansion that shot west across the Caribbean and up the North American coast toward the Chesapeake, the political economy of slavery that the English forged in Barbados spread into the Lesser Antilles, Jamaica, and then South Carolina. The same elite men who had profited from the slave colony in Barbados, and who advised the consolidation of imperial governance under Charles II, played a critical role in the expansion of racial slavery into Jamaica and South Carolina. Likewise, many of the settlers for the new colonies embarked from Barbados, which had a profound impact on the formation of the slave societies that would develop in these places.

The development of slave law in the English Atlantic of the seventeenth century was an imperial endeavor in which the colonial assemblies learned from one another, with occasional guidance from the Crown. Unlike the Spanish Empire, which hewed to a tradition of slave law that stretched back to the medieval *Siete Partidas*, or the French Empire, in which the Crown played a central role in the formulation of slave law, the colonial assemblies of the English Atlantic crafted the laws that governed slaves.[1] In 1664, the Jamaica House of Assembly adopted the Barbados Slave Act of 1661 almost word for word. When pressed by the Lords of Trade to revise its slave laws, the Jamaica Assembly developed a new comprehensive slave code in 1684 that strengthened the coercive force of the colonial

state and refined the status of property in slaves. In 1691, the South
Carolina House of Assembly followed the same pattern with the
adoption of Jamaica's Slave Act of 1684, again almost word for word.
Jamaica was an established and profitable slave society, and its law
was at the cutting edge in the development of racial slavery. The law
imposed racial distinction and it empowered whites with the free use
of violence to control black slaves. Simultaneously, it carefully described the proper uses of slave property in wills and dowries and in
the payment of debts. The law worked to classify and dehumanize.
It sought to reduce African people to animate capital.

As people, slaves suffered the unceasing efforts of their masters
to strip them of dignity, to control their bodies, and to curb their
intellects—in short, to reduce their humanity to a mere animal state.
As property, slaves were not real estate, but they were not simply
chattel either. Slaves were long-term, capital investments that retained useful liquidity. They generated profit with their labor and
required minimal reinvestment, and their value in the market brought
credit to their owners. The enslaved could be given as dowries and
left to heirs; and as people who loved and had children, their numbers could increase, a disturbing form of compound interest. Among
English colonists, the Jamaicans were the first to codify slave property with the sophistication that capital investments require, and it
is highly significant that when the assemblymen of South Carolina
decided to adopt a slave code, they chose the Jamaican law. When
these colonial assemblies returned to their slave codes in 1696, the
question of property was settled. The planters focused on physical
restraint, the reduction of African humanity that violence could
never break down.

Jamaica became English because of a series of astonishing military
blunders that cost the lives of a thousand men. In 1655, Oliver
Cromwell had sent his "Western Design" to seize Hispaniola from
the Spanish, but when his forces were devastated, Admiral William
Penn and General Robert Venables led their surviving troops on a
short sail west to Jamaica, which the Spanish had never developed
and barely garrisoned. The English marched on Saint Jago de la Vega

(present-day Spanish Town) in May 1655 and demanded the surrender of the island.[2]

The Spanish fought intermittently for about a year, but the fiercest
resistance to the English came from the "Spanish Negroes" who
were, for all intents and purposes, freed by the English invasion. In
April 1656 Captain William Godfrey reported that while most of
the Spanish had abandoned the island, his men still faced resistance
from "the negroes and mulattoes who slew about 40 of our soldiers
about a month since." When the English ventured into the countryside to catch wild pigs and cattle, these first Maroons "butchered
them with lances." A few years later, an English expedition discovered "a town" built by the Spanish blacks with "200 acres of provisions" already planted. They had probably discovered one of the
earliest Maroon communities to coalesce in the Blue Mountains
after the English conquest.[3]

Sir Francis Drake had aligned with Maroons almost a century earlier in Panama, and in April 1660 Cornelius Burough reported a similar English alliance with Maroons in Jamaica. Burough's unit joined
with one group of Maroons in an attack on "two settlements of other
negroes." This alliance led the English to the last encampment of
Spaniards, who only then were driven from the island. Burough later
described the Africans who allied with the English as "our blood-
hounds" and reported that together they "were daily making depre-
dations" on the other Maroon bands. Before the English had even
secured their authority, the island Maroons were a potent military
force fully able to maintain their strength and autonomy.[4]

Unlike the Maroons, the English occupiers were entirely unwilling
to work in the fields to provide themselves with sustenance. Moreover, as most were new to the Caribbean, they saw terrible losses
from mosquito-borne disease. Despite their victory over the Spanish,
the English population suffered a dramatic decline in these first years
of settlement. Their population dropped to as low as 2,200 men in
1660 (from the expedition of about 8,500 who had attacked Hispaniola), and only through immigration from England and Barbados did
their numbers begin to increase. In the first census taken under English governance of the island in 1662, there were 3,653 whites and
554 blacks.[5]

In January 1664, the Lords of Trade appointed Thomas Modyford governor of Jamaica. He had advised policy makers for the
Western Design and had secured appointment as the agent of the
Royal African Company in Barbados in 1663. Modyford went to
Jamaica via Barbados, where he convinced some two thousand land-
hungry Barbadians to accompany him. Modyford's reign as governor
has been characterized as tyrannical. The first English settlers of
the island must have resented his popularity with the new migrants,
and in the new assembly elected in October 1664 there were only
four members from the first assembly. The new assembly was
marked by severe factionalism, even the murder of one of its members, and it met for only five months during the six years of Modyford's
governance. Yet it was this assembly that laid the legal foundation
for slave society in Jamaica. It passed barely altered versions of both
the Slave Act and the Servant Act passed by the Barbados Assembly
in 1661, as well as a declaration of war on the "outlying Spanish
Negroes."[6]

Consider the distinct moments of slave law codification in Barbados and Jamaica. In Barbados in 1661, the colony was more than
thirty years old, the plantation economy had fully developed, sugar
had become the main staple crop, and African slaves made up about
half of the total population. In Jamaica in 1664, the colony was not
quite a decade old, the colonists had developed few plantations,
and the black people were only about 15 percent of the island's population. Jamaica's moment of codification reflected economic aspirations
rather than socioeconomic reality. Modyford certainly understood
the evolution of slavery in Barbados, as well as the comprehensive
labor codes the Barbadians had established. The Jamaica Assembly's adoption of the same code reveals the expectation of a similar
pattern of development. If these Englishmen wanted the wealth
generated by a staple economy in the Barbadian mode, they would
face a growing population of enslaved Africans and the daily violent
resistance that slavery entailed. Sugar production had to be brutally
enforced, and the Barbadian law provided the blueprint.

The English established a plantation economy in Jamaica within
a generation, and as in Barbados, the initial crop was not sugar. The
Spanish had developed extensive cacao walks, and the English took

advantage of them. Cacao trees need to mature for several years before they bear fruit, and these Spanish walks were already established. In February 1660, Captain William Dalyson sent 12,400 pounds of cacao to England and 4,000 more in April.[7] Modyford himself invested in cacao production, and by 1670 the island exported 188,000 pounds of cacao nuts.[8] Modyford also facilitated the African slave trade to the island through his connections to the Royal African Company. Dutch merchants had brought enslaved Africans to the new English colony as early as 1659, and in 1663 Peter Merit, an English slaver for the Company of Royal Adventurers, brought about 280 enslaved Africans. From 1664 until 1670 when Modyford left the island, almost 5,000 Africans arrived in Jamaica, most of them from the Bight of Biafara. Sugar production also began during these years. One report on the colony noted seventy plantations capable of producing fifty tons of sugar a year, with forty more plantations under construction. A census taken in 1673 estimated that the black population was 7,768, half of the island's total. It had taken Barbados about thirty years to reach that point; in Jamaica it had taken thirteen.[9]

Island residents became concerned about the rise of the African population well before it reached that point. In January 1669, John Style recommended that every planter who had "six negroes should keep one Christian servant and one hired freeman" in order to "secure the island from danger."[10] There were good reasons to be concerned. In May 1670 the Council of Jamaica reported that the Maroons, now called the "Varmahaly Negroes," had committed "murders robberies and other outrages" with impunity. Style reported that the Maroons could destroy the old settlements "at any time." The council ordered that no persons travel more than two miles beyond their settlement without being armed and that no one trade with the Maroons. The council also ordered financial rewards for the killing of any of the Maroon leadership and offered freedom to any servant or slave who did so. Anyone who did kill the Maroon leadership would also receive the wives and children of these "traitors" as their property. Runaways posed a further challenge to the maintenance of order. Style could not say just how many were "out," but slave catchers were being paid twenty shillings for each runaway and forty shillings if the runaway came from the sparsely populated "North Side."[11]

Persistent slave resistance pushed changes in the law. Hideouts for runaways on the North Side posed such a problem that in September 1672 the council increased the reward for slave catchers to forty shillings regardless of location. The council also acted against a rare leniency in the law. At some unrecorded point after the act of 1664, the ticketing clause had been altered to allow enslaved people a four-mile radius around their plantation where they could venture unmolested without a ticket. This may be evidence for the development of the provision ground system, by which slaves produced their own food on lands allotted to them, lands that were sometimes quite distant from the plantation. The council considered this "extraordinary latitude" dangerous, as the "safety and Interest of all the Planters in this Island does consist in restraining by all ways imaginable the communication of the Negroes one with another." Henceforth, ordered the council, all masters were to keep their slaves on the plantation and allow none to go abroad without a ticket. And any freeman who encountered a slave off his or her plantation without a ticket should exact a whipping right then and there, regardless of the distance from the plantation. Consistent enforcement seems unlikely, but the ordinance speaks to the compounded danger the council feared from the growing black population.[12]

In June 1673, a group of Africans in Saint Elizabeth killed their master, William Groudan, and stood their ground in the woods against the whites who came after them. These were not Maroons, and given their location in Saint Elizabeth, which was distant from the core of settlement in the southeast of the island, they were probably newly arrived Africans. Two were killed and one captured, and we cannot be sure how many escaped. According to the slave code, whites who pursued and captured rebellious slaves were to be rewarded five pounds for each slave brought in "dead or alive." The council considered the law to be "of mighty import to this island," but as Saint Elizabeth Parish was quite poor and Groudan had left nothing of value, the council ordered his heir, one John Yeeles, to pay fifteen pounds to the men who had gone after Groudan's mur-

derers. Slave law stretched throughout the society, from a poor slaveholder to the council and out to a distant relative who may not have
even been in Jamaica.[13]

Jamaica's planters faced tenacious African resistance, but in September 1675, they learned of the most deadly slave conspiracy that
Barbados had experienced yet. It originated among a group the English knew as "Coromantins." The rebels planned to begin the uprising with the sounding of "trumpets to be made of Elephants Teeth
[ivory]," followed by a firing of the cane fields and a general massacre
of the planters. In the event of the rebellion's success, the conspirators would crown their leader, Cuffee, "an Ancient Gold Coast
Negro" on "a Chair of State exquisitely wrought and Carved . . . with
Bowes and Arrows." The planters discovered the conspiracy when
Anna, enslaved to Judge Gyles Hall, heard of the conspiracy and informed Hall, who spread the word among the planters. Governor
Jonathan Atkins declared martial law immediately and called out the
militia. Over the next few days, more than a hundred slaves were arrested and interrogated for more information about the conspiracy;
seventeen were ultimately executed. Some of the young men were
burned alive, and as the fires were lit, the planter George Hannow
harangued one young man to "confess the depth of their design."
The young man called for water and was prepared to speak, but he
was chastised by a man called Tony who was chained beside him:
"Thou fool, are there not enough of our Country-men killed already?
Art thou minded to kill them all?" Effectively rebuked, the young
man held his peace.[14]

Such dramatic dialogue, if overwrought, illustrates the impact of
African political history on Barbados in this moment.[15] There is little
reason to believe that the rebels saw themselves as "Coromantins," but
the evidence does suggests that the rebels were Akan, recently enslaved in war and sold to English slavers from a Gold Coast port. The
name Cuffee is an Akan day name meaning "a male born on Friday."
Akan day names persisted among the enslaved for many generations throughout Britain's American colonies. Some examples include

Cudjoe (male born on Monday), Amba (female born on Saturday), Quaw (male born on Thursday), Abba (female born on Thursday), Quamina (male born on Saturday), and Quashee (male born on Sunday). These distinctly African names stand in sharp contrast to the far more common English names, such as Joe or Sarah, that most slaves bore. The names speak to a powerful cultural influence.[16]

The English identification of Akan people as "Coromantins" probably derived from the fact that the first English trading post on the Gold Coast had been at Kormantine. Governor Atkins wrote that "Coromantins" were a "warlike and robust people" and that their numbers were "greater [than] . . . from any one country" represented on the island. While the records are not clear on the African coastal origin of most captives brought to Barbados during the five years before the conspiracy, we do know that one thousand captives arrived in Barbados from Gold Coast ports in 1674 alone, more than a third of the Africans brought to Barbados during that year.[17]

The conception that Akan peoples were "warlike" did not stem from a unique cultural bent but rather from their distinctive political history. This forest region had rich deposits of gold, and beginning in the fourteenth century, states emerged that derived wealth and power from the trans-Saharan gold trade. The Akan initially panned for gold in forest streams, but in the fifteenth century miners developed more-productive techniques based on slave labor. By the end of the sixteenth century, wealthy men known as *aberempon* brought in slaves to clear the forests near the sources of gold to establish agriculture in proximity to the mines. In this region of West Africa, a political economy founded on slave labor, forest agriculture, and the gold trade facilitated both population growth and state formation, as the *aberempon* competed for access to gold and slaves. During the sixteenth and early seventeenth centuries, the Portuguese and Dutch began to import slaves to the Gold Coast (which they purchased in the Bight of Biafara and West Central Africa) in order to trade with coastal Akan merchants for gold. By the 1670s when England's transatlantic slave trade had taken off, there were a handful of highly organized states among the Akan—Akwamu and Denkyira in particular—that controlled the commerce in both gold and slaves along the Gold Coast. Highly ornamented stools were the symbol of kingship in all of these polities.[18]

The economic stakes were high, and the Akan states often went to war. These wars generated a series of innovations in tactics and weaponry in the mid-seventeenth century that considerably broadened popular participation in war. Where armies of the early seventeenth century had consisted of trained military elites, by the 1660s some states (the first was either Akwamu or Denkyira) had embraced the *levée en masse* in order to raise armies of commoners for wartime. Wars inevitably resulted in captives who were either ransomed or enslaved, depending on an individual's social status. Such military developments were of significant consequence in the Americas, for it meant that beginning in the 1670s many of the enslaved Africans shipped from the Gold Coast would have had at least some military experience. It seems likely that Cuffee of Barbados was a man of status enslaved with some of his soldiers during a war among the Akan states. Once in Barbados, these rebels were able to reforge social bonds with other Akan that enabled them to organize an insurrection. While they were unsuccessful in 1675, later generations of enslaved Akan would continue to test the chains of slavery, particularly in Jamaica, for another century.[19]

In 1675, the Council of Jamaica immediately ordered that none of the "criminal or convicted" Africans exiled from Barbados be allowed to come to Jamaica and fined anyone who did so fifty pounds.[20] But English slavers were unconcerned with the travails of West Indian planters, and they continued to frequent Gold Coast slave markets. In 1673 more than two hundred "Coromantins" on Lobby's estate in Saint Ann's, Jamaica, revolted, killing a dozen whites and establishing themselves in the nearby mountains. In December 1675 Governor Henry Morgan (the former pirate) issued a proclamation that described the "sole cause" of the recent insurrections as "the remissness of all persons in not putting the laws for the right ordering and government of the negroes in due execution." He ordered that the Slave Act be printed and posted by every custos on the island and asked the leading men to consider what new provisions in the law might curtail future disturbances to the "peace and planting of this island." Nevertheless, another group of Africans

escaped from a plantation in Saint Mary's. The council invoked the
powers of the Slave Act and ordered a company of twenty men to
be raised and "kept in pay" for two months in order to rout these
rebels. Specific rewards were offered for the capture or killing of
the principal leaders of the revolt: twenty pounds for Peter and
Scanderberg, fifteen pounds for the "the negro called Doctor," and
five pounds per head for the rest of the band. These acts of mass resistance laid the foundation for the development of further Maroon
bands in the Cockpit Country.[21]

As enslaved Africans coordinated efforts to resist slavery with violence, several actors in the making of England's empire began to
challenge the planters' efforts to establish an unfettered mastery.
Some Quakers had settled in Barbados, and in 1671 the revered
itinerant George Fox visited the island. While Fox did not condemn slavery explicitly, he did criticize the brutal treatment of African slaves and encouraged Friends on the island to welcome
blacks to their meetings. The Barbados Assembly did not approve
and passed a law to ban the practice, to which the Quakers protested
with a petition to the Lords of Trade. Most English ostracized the
Quakers as bizarre religious extremists, and the Lords of Trade refused even to consider complaints brought by "this sort of people."
The Quakers' tendency to disregard mainstream opinion about
slavery would lead to abolitionism in the eighteenth century, but in
the 1670s the Quakers could be silenced with relative ease.[22]

   A similar challenge came from the Bishop of London, however,
who could not be ignored, and who in 1680 ordered that church
leaders in Barbados take measures to Christianize Africans. Absentee
Barbadians in London attended a meeting with the Lords of Trade
to nip this idea in the bud, citing the recent insurrection as a caution against plans for conversion. Africans' "savage brutishness" rendered them "wholly incapable" of religious conversion. They would
"hang themselves or run away" rather than submit to religious instruction, and with some contradiction, the planters warned that
"converted negroes grow more perverse and intractable than others."
Because of the great "disproportion of blacks to whites," the secu-

rity of the island depended in part on "the diversity of the negroes languages," which (contrary to the evidence) prohibited the development of island-wide plots. This measure of security would be "destroyed by conversion, in that it would be necessary to teach them all English."[23] The planters' analysis of the threat of Christian conversion suggests that someone, probably the Quakers, had already worked toward African conversions. The planters responded, employing political influence and legislative power to protect their interests. Left unstated was the fact that the conversion of blacks to Christianity nullified the categorical difference between "Christian" and "Negro" that had been so important for the Barbados Assembly's comprehensive acts of 1661.

During these same years, the Lords of Trade admonished the Jamaica House of Assembly for laws that the Lords considered unacceptable. In 1676 the Lords informed the Jamaica Assembly that they could not accept the word "servitude" in the colony's Act for the Good Governing of Christian Servants. "Servitude" struck them as "being a mark of bondage and slavery," inappropriate to use in a description of persons who were "only apprentices for years."[24] The assembly does not seem to have responded to the Lords until 1681, when they passed a new Act for Regulating Servants. It was easy enough for the assembly to strike the word "servitude" from the law governing servants, but the Jamaica Assembly took innovation still further, employing the new Servant Act to introduce a deficiency clause to address the island's demographic imbalance. The law required every slaveholder to keep one "White Man Servant, Overseer, or hired Man" for every five slaves he or she possessed. While a similar deficiency clause had been part of the Barbados Slave Act of 1661, the Jamaica Slave Act of 1664 had not adopted it, presumably because the demographic situation did not warrant it. The 1681 Servant Act also continued the legal effort to ameliorate the treatment of servants through a ban on the whipping of naked white servants and the prescription of fines for masters who failed to provide their servants with the legally allotted provisions of food and clothing.[25]

As in Barbados twenty years before, the consolidation of slavery involved the governance of both servants and slaves, lifting the status of servants while depressing that of slaves.[26] Even more important, and reflecting a new stage in the development of racial slavery, was the assembly's use of a relatively new word, "white." Previous statutes had consistently used the term "Christian" to refer to European indentured servants, but Jamaica's 1681 Servant Act dropped the term "Christian" and used the term "white" instead. The Barbados Assembly had made clear distinctions between "Christian servants" and "Negro Slaves" in its comprehensive acts of 1661, but the efforts of the Quakers in Barbados and the Bishop of London had begun to undermine this distinction. After all, if "Negros" could also be "Christians," the distinction between Africans and Europeans might begin to lose its potency.[27]

The use of "white" as a racial descriptor is evident in various writings from England's colonial Atlantic, emerging gradually and without consistency.[28] The early Barbados law that prohibited masters from entertaining (or hiring) anyone, "White or Black," if the master did not know the person to be free used racial language, suggesting Barbadian origin. Yet by no means had the language of whiteness become pervasive. In 1669, for example, an anonymous account of the "Carybee Islands" counted "40,000 Blacks" in Barbados and "6,000 Christians in the standing militia." But in describing Montserrat, the writer noted "1400 whites and 300 blacks," most of the whites being Irish. The Jamaica Assembly in 1673 passed one law referring to "negroes" and another to "Christian servants," but in correspondence from the previous year, Sir Thomas Lynch advised Lord Cornbury to stock his newly patented land with "24 white servants" and "100 Negroes." In 1676 the Lords of Trade sent a letter to the governor of South Carolina asking "what number of whites Blacks or Mulattos have been born . . . for these 7 yeares past." Yet in a 1679 account of arrivals to Jamaica, only the terms "Christians" and slaves "from Guinea" were used. The trend of usage suggests that "white" had its origins in Barbados in the late 1640s when the African population began to rise. The term then traveled slowly into the writing of the discursive community of the English empire, where for at least thirty years it was used interchangeably with "Christian." In Jamaica in 1681, perhaps for the first time, the assembly used "white" as a racial descriptor that designated a particular relation of power.[29]

But demands from England for colonial reform continued. In February 1683, the Lords of Trade wrote to Governor Lynch of Jamaica that they were displeased with the provision in the Slave Act that imposed a mere fine on those who "willfully and wantonly kill a negro." The Lords reported that the "King will not confirm this clause, which seems to encourage the willful shedding of blood," and ordered the governor to convey the report to the Assembly, which should develop a gentler provision. In September the new governor, Henry Morgan, addressed the assembly with the King's request.[30] This body of men included some of the most experienced planters of the island. Most had been members of the assembly for more than one term, and several had represented more than one parish in their years of service. One member, Samuel Jenks, had even participated in the first assembly of 1664.[31]

As with the Servant Act, changing the law to meet the King's specific demand was easy enough. The assembly simply added two clauses that changed the punishments for those who "willfully" killed a slave. Hereafter, servants who murdered a slave would receive thirty-nine lashes on the bare back and serve an additional four years of service to the owner of the killed slave. Nonservants would serve three months' imprisonment without bail and be fined fifty pounds, paid to the owner of the killed slave. The King's ministers must have considered these new provisions adequate, for the Crown approved the new law in April 1684.[32]

But the Jamaica Assembly's new Act for the Better Ordering of Slaves did much more than address this single critique. The assembly governed a society in which Europeans were outnumbered three to one by enslaved Africans who worked on profitable sugar plantations and continued to rebel.[33] English slavers brought more than 1,800 captive Africans to the island every year to grow the colony's economy, but in doing so, they exacerbated the politics of resistance that slavery created. In 1678, enslaved people on a plantation in Saint Thomas in the Vale, led by at least one Akan, named Quashee Eddo, rebelled and killed at least twenty whites. While some of the rebels died in the effort, many escaped permanently into the mountains to join the Maroons. Colonial prosperity depended on the labor of Africans, who challenged their enslavement whenever they could. Presented by the Lords of Trade with the opportunity, the Jamaica House of Assembly sought to place racial slavery on a more solid legal foundation.[34]

Jamaica's Slave Act of 1684 made significant innovations in the law of slavery that would have lasting implications. First, in place of the distinction between "Christian" and "Negro" that had under-girded the labor laws of Barbados, the new Jamaican law clarified the power differential between people now classified as white and black. In the ticketing clause, for example, which descended from the Barbados Slave Act of 1661, the assembly allowed that if a "white man" accompanied a slave beyond the plantation, a ticket was un-necessary. From 1661 to 1864 only one word changed in this clause: "Christian" became "white."[35] Moreover, the Jamaica Assembly stated clearly that if a slave were to become a Christian, conversion would in no way alter his or her status as a slave. Jamaica was not the first English colony to make such a law, which stayed consistent with medieval and Iberian practice, but the assembly nevertheless restated the rule. If Quakers or the Bishop of London wanted to at-tempt the conversion of Africans to Christianity, the Jamaica As-sembly would not stand in the way—yet—but they would not allow conversion to erode slavery. They simply changed the law.[36]

Jamaica's new slave law further reshaped three principal arenas: the control of runaways, the regulation of whites' enforcement of slave law, and the nature of property rights regarding slaves. The most extensive innovations targeted runaways. Whereas the act of 1664 had established a flat reward of one pound for the return of runaways, the act of 1684 implemented a mileage charge for trans-porting runaways that accounted for Jamaica's extensive geography and potentially doubled the bounty. Slave catchers would receive twelve pence per mile for the first five miles and eight pence per mile thereafter, with a maximum reward of two pounds. If a slave returned a runaway, he or she was now eligible for the entire re-ward, and any person denying payment to a slave would be fined triple the amount owed. Another provision made it legal to destroy any plantation left vacant for two months, "lest it become a Recep-tacle for Fugitives." Runaways had made use of coastal shipping traffic in Kingston Harbor, evident in a new provision that compelled the master of any boat to post a bond of fifty pounds not to carry slaves without a ticket. The new Slave Act also made it more difficult for whites to avoid participation in the enforcement of the Slave Act by imposing a twenty-pound fine on any freeholder who refused to participate in a slave court. The law also ordered that all fines outlined in the Slave Act could be collected by debt action in the courts, despite the poverty of the negligent white.[37]

And with lasting implications, the assembly's new Slave Act codified slaves as "chattel" property. While enslaved Africans had been bought and sold as chattel for several centuries at this point, the legal nature of slave property remained unclear. The preamble to the Barbados Slave Act of 1661 likened slaves to "other goods and Chattels" but offered no further definition of the nature of slave property.[38] Seven years later, the Barbados Assembly defined African slaves as "real estates," asserting that slaves should be understood as freehold rather than chattel property and thus protected by a far stronger body of law. In passing such legislation, the assembly responded to a series of suits that arose from the deaths of intestate planters. The estates of these men had been stripped of their slaves through the suits of creditors. Heirs and widows had been left "bare Land without Negroes to manure the same." The wealth of the entire island, so important to "His Majesty's coffers," was threatened by these suits.[39]

English law had long protected land as freehold property, real estate that could not be seized by creditors. This legal tradition reflected the political and cultural dominance of England's landed aristocracy, which drew its wealth from rents on their land. In Barbados, however, where an equally dominant aristocracy had emerged (albeit on a far smaller scale), the principal form of wealth came from the sale of commodities produced by indentured and enslaved laborers. Land and slaves had become interdependent forms of capital investment that were profitable only when combined. By codifying slave property as real estate, the Barbadian law aspired to protect the wealth of the big sugar planters, much as English property law protected England's nobility. It meant that heirs and widows could not lose their slaves to the creditors of a deceased slaveholder. Two provisos made clear that slaves could still be bought and sold as chattel by the living, and a statute passed in 1672 declared that slaves could still be sued for in suits and used as chattel in the payment of debts. But the act declaring slaves real estate was not reversed; Barbados law protected a planter's investment in slaves as if they were a landed estate, to be preserved for his descendants. Slaves were therefore a novel form of property, in some ways protected like real estate but in other ways understood as chattel.[40]

The Jamaica Assembly of 1684 modified this understanding of slave property by emphasizing the "chattel" status of slave property and rendering the freehold understanding of slave property the exception rather than the rule. The new Slave Act declared that "as to the payment of Debts, [slaves] shall be deemed and taken as all other Goods and Chattels." If a slaveholder died in debt (as most did), slaves that had been made part of dowries or belonged to heirs must be sold to satisfy creditors. The remaining slaves of the estate would "be accounted as Free-hold . . . and descend accordingly." The Jamaica Assembly's innovation enhanced the liquidity of slave property, which bolstered the credit of the island, so essential to the transatlantic slave trade. The Barbados Assembly had attempted to create a gentry of sugar planters by grafting slave law onto the Old World legal tradition of freehold that privileged landed wealth. Not so with Jamaica. Jamaican legislators looked to the future. Transatlantic commerce depended upon credit. The assembly's new slave law sought to secure the favor of merchants, who could extend credit to Jamaica's slaveholders, would could then buy enslaved Africans, to clear more land, to grow more sugar.[41]

Classifying slaves as chattel property also aligned with the pernicious idea that Africans and their descendants were more like animals than human beings. In English property law, domestic animals were considered chattel, and thus slaves took on the legal characteristics of cattle. The Slave Act's determination that slave status passed from mother to child mirrored not only the precedent of ancient Rome but also the character of property in domestic animals. The principle stemmed from the facts of pregnancy. Pregnancy rendered the profit-generating labor of an animal far less efficient, but resulted in a creature that accrued to the wealth of the proprietor. It was only just, William Blackstone later argued, that while the owner of a cow would be "the loser by her pregnancy, he ought to be the gainer by her brood." The Jamaican law thus rendered property in enslaved Africans the equivalent of that in horses or cattle. Indeed, in most of the surviving plantation inventories of the seventeenth and eighteenth centuries, that is exactly how enslaved Africans appear, in a separate column labeled "Negroes," right next to the column for livestock.[42]

But England's laws of property also recognized that not all animals could be domesticated. Such animals maintained "their natural liberty" unless a man could make them "tame by art, industry, and education; or by so confining them within his own immediate power that they cannot escape." Property in such beings was "not absolute"; rather, such property "may be destroyed" if the animal resumed its "antient wildness." And so it was that the Jamaica Slave Act of 1684 assigned chattel status to black people while simultaneously establishing the laws of violent social control that sought to subdue their humanity.[43]

The planning, exploration, and early settlement of English Carolina resulted from the same political process of imperial expansion. Like Barbados, Carolina began as a proprietary colony. But while Barbados was simply given to Lord Carlisle by a generous monarch as a source of prestige and revenue when England had little empire to speak of, the proprietors of South Carolina were eight powerful men who were well informed about the recent history of Barbados, the expansion into Jamaica, and the centrality of racial slavery to both imperial endeavors.

The idea to pursue the grant of Carolina probably originated with the Barbadian planter John Colleton. Colleton did not have the stature in the court of Charles II to secure the grant for himself, but as we have seen, when the Privy Council reorganized imperial governance in 1661, Colleton secured appointments on the Council of Trade, the Council of Foreign Plantations, and the Royal African Company. Through these appointments, he made connections to five men who were close to the Crown and who would join him in a successful bid for the grant of Carolina. Lord Baron John Berkeley and Sir George Carteret were close to Charles during his years in exile, and each man served on all three of these committees with Colleton. Three of the proprietors—Anthony Ashley Cooper (later Lord Shaftesbury); Edward Hyde, the Earl of Clarendon; and George Monck, the Duke of Albermarle—were members of the original Privy Council that appointed Colleton; and Cooper had himself invested in a Barbados plantation. The seventh proprietor, William Craven, the first Earl of Craven, had also been with Charles in exile, and the eighth, William Berkeley, had been the governor of Virginia since 1641 and was a cousin to Baron Berkeley. William Berkeley had intimate knowledge of the North American terrain, the nature of the Indian trade, and the development of African slavery. By the summer of 1662, these eight men had secured the proprietary grant to a vast tract of North America that the English imagined as Carolina.[44]

By the end of 1663, about two hundred "gentlemen and persons of good quality" had come together as the "Corporation of Barbados Adventurers." They petitioned the proprietors through their agents in London for a grant of land within the new colony. Their agents were Thomas Modyford and Peter Colleton, John Colleton's son. The Adventurers emphasized their capacity as "experienced planters" with "Negros and other servants fitt for such labor" as would be required in the founding of a new settlement. The corporation funded the expedition of William Hilton, who explored the area, encountered the coastal Indians, learned of their trade with the Spanish, and penned a promotional account of his travels. The proprietors pledged to grant land to all colonists who settled in Carolina through headrights for every free migrant, as well as for every servant or slave the migrant brought. During the first year of settlement, each free man or woman would receive 150 acres and an additional 150 acres for each "every able man Sarv^{t}."

Free migrants who brought "weaker" servants or slaves, male or female, would receive 75 acres of land for each. Indentured servants would receive 75 acres of land at the end of their term of service. Free migrants who came in succeeding years would receive less acreage for themselves and their laborers, and servants would receive proportionately less as well. Free male migrants were also to be armed to the teeth, supplied with a gun, ten pounds of powder, and twenty pounds of bullets, as well as six months of provisions. With these concessions, the proprietors hoped to draw migrants to Carolina, migrants who were ready to fight upon arrival.[45]

The Adventurers did not actually settle Carolina, and two other groups of Barbadians and one group of New Englanders also failed in their efforts to settle. The proprietors supported none of these ventures with serious money, and all succumbed to disease and a lack of provisions.[46] Only in 1669 did the proprietors actively support the Carolina venture. Now led by Cooper, the proprietors made preparations for an expedition that would leave from London and pick up more migrants in Barbados on the way to Carolina. In cooperation with his personal secretary, John Locke, Cooper also began to draft the "Fundamental Constitutions," an idiosyncratic document with grand ambitions. Cooper and Locke envisioned a landed nobility of palatines, landgraves, and caciques. They imagined Carolina with a class of "Leetmen" who would be bound to the land like medieval serfs. More concretely, the Fundamental Constitutions established almost complete freedom of religion in Carolina, so long as one believed in God. Cooper and Locke also sought to establish a respectful relationship with "Neighbor Indians," endowing the proprietors with the responsibility for all diplomatic relationships and banning colonists from receiving land from the Indians through either purchase or gift. And most importantly for the Barbadians, the Fundamental Constitutions guaranteed that "Every Freeman of Carolina shall have absolute Authority over his Negro Slaves." Slaves were explicitly allowed to join any church they chose, but the Fundamental Constitutions made it clear that conversion of any kind would not change the lawful "civil dominion" that a master had over the slave.[47]

In August 1669, an expedition of three ships departed from England with more than one hundred settlers on their way to Barbados. They brought along a copy of the Fundamental Constitutions and in Barbados picked up more colonists. Nicholas Carteret, who arrived on the *Carolina* in March 1670, encountered Indians armed with bows and arrows, probably Cusabos, who traded food and deerskins to the English for knives and beads. These coastal Indians were terrified of the neighboring Westos and actively sought English friendship. Maurice Mathews, who arrived on the *Three Brothers* in May, landed on Saint Katherina Island quite close to the Spanish and had a very different encounter. The Indians who met him were initially friendly, but after a few days the Spanish arrived with drums and soldiers and Indian allies. The Spanish drove the English off with volley after volley of "Musket Shott and a cloud of arrows." The *Three Brothers* headed north and brought some Indians along with them, who directed them to Edisto Island, where some of their fellow colonists had begun to establish a settlement. These initial encounters alerted the English that they were attempting to colonize land in a dangerous political arena. They would need to learn these politics if they were to prosper.[48]

The Westos had been in the Carolina region only a few years, and they were not allied with the Spanish; rather, they had trading connections with the English in Virginia. The Westos may have been a northern group of Indians, perhaps known as the Richahecrians, who were driven south by the Iroquois during the 1640s. The Richahecrians settled near the falls of the James River, and in 1656 they defeated a combined force of English colonists and Pamunkeys who sought to dislodge the newcomers. The Virginia colony sued for peace with the new group, which established trading alliances with the Virginia merchants William Byrd I, Richard Stegge, and Theodorick Bland, whose trading operations stretched west and south. The Richahecrians may have become particularly associated with Bland's plantation Westover—thus "Westos," the name the Cusabos used to describe them to the English in Carolina.[49]

The Westos had become slavers by the time they moved to Carolina. They secured guns from the Virginia traders, raided Indian communities without access to guns, and sold their captives in Virginia. Many North American peoples enslaved their enemies in war. Defeated men would be ransomed or killed; women and children would be enslaved and incorporated into the victorious society. The act of enslavement, or the bestowal of a slave, was an established means of gaining or maintaining honor. A young man who sought recognition as a warrior, for example, had to either kill or enslave an enemy to be so esteemed. Likewise, when a warrior died in battle, his family sought his replacement by a slave taken from the enemy who slayed him. If a person was killed unintentionally, what in the Western legal tradition might be called manslaughter, the family of the deceased could demand the first slave captured by the family of the offender. In short, acts of enslavement and the exchange of people among families and larger kin groups had a set of meanings among Indian peoples that operated to appease and compensate the death of valued persons.[50]

But as the Indians of the southeast became entangled in European affairs, and began to value the novel trading goods that Europeans brought, slaving gradually became a far more destructive practice, a historical process similar to the devastating transformations being concurrently wrought in West and West Central Africa by the trans-atlantic slave trade. European merchants supplied rare goods and guns that Indians valued, and Europeans were perfectly willing to trade these goods for slaves who could be easily sold in the slave mar-kets of North America and the Caribbean. Slaving complemented the trade in pelts and deerskins, but it had a far more pernicious im-pact on Native societies. The spread of slavery into South Carolina would thus combine the slaving and marketing of Indians with the importation of enslaved Africans, a more complicated pattern of his-torical development than what had emerged in Jamaica.[51]

The first English colonists depended on trade with the coastal In-dians for food, and they took some of these groups under English protection. Colonists also explored the interior regions. In the late summer of 1670 Henry Woodward traveled north and west from Charles Town and met with many Indian groups. Woodward be-lieved he had discovered the ancient kingdom of Cofitachiqui de-scribed in the *Narrative* of Hernando de Soto's expedition of 1540. Woodward established "a league with ye Emperor & all those petty Cassekas betwixt us & them" and returned with a load of deerskins, the beginning of trade. These groups also feared the Westos, who attacked them with guns and carried off "their Corne and Children."[52]

Woodward would play a central role in Indian relations with the colony for the next twenty years. He had traveled to Carolina with the expedition of Robert Sandford in 1666, a failed effort by the proprietors to promote settlement. Adventurous and keen to serve the proprietors, Woodward had volunteered to stay alone to learn the languages and customs of the Indians. The Spanish captured him during this first sojourn and he had languished in a Saint Augustine prison for two years until liberated when the pirate Robert Searle raided the Spanish in 1668. Woodward signed on with Searle as ship's surgeon and sailed with him until later that year when they shipwrecked at Nevis. The Carolina expedition came through Nevis in 1669 and Woodward immediately signed on, eager to use the language skills he had developed through such hardship. As a first settler, Woodward received 150 acres of the new colony, if only the English could control it.[53]

The proprietors compensated Woodward's efforts quite generously. Upon learning of his expedition to Cofitachiqui, Lord Shaftesbury convinced the proprietors to advance to Woodward one hundred pounds' worth of "servants or goods" on the credit of the proprietors. Shaftesbury sent Woodward an additional twenty-pound credit "as a particular gratuity from my selfe." He valued Woodward's linguistic ability and hoped that Woodward could maintain a "friendship and commerce" with the Indians that would be beneficial to all. By 1674 Woodward had overdrawn his grant's worth of goods by seven pounds and established a flourishing trade in skins and slaves.[54]

Trade with the Indians had become the most lucrative branch of the nascent colonial economy, and while the Westos may have initiated slaving in Carolina, the English exacerbated the practice. Their aggressive wanderings and growing settlement encroached on Indian lands, resulting in violent conflict. As early as 1671, the Grand Council sent an expedition out against the Kusso and empowered the militiamen "to secure and maintaine the Indians they have taken" until they could be transported for sale. Evidence has not survived as to whether captives were actually taken and sold, but the English had clearly taken captives. What did they do with them? Indeed, Shaftesbury would establish his own plantation, Saint Giles, on the depopulated lands of the old Kusso town.[55]

In the spring of 1674, Shaftesbury instructed Woodward to seek out a peace with either the Westos or the Cussitaw (a Creek town), whichever Woodward deemed more powerful, and to establish a regular trade, of which Woodward would receive one-fifth. The colony's population was still quite small, and to the proprietors' frustration, Carolinian planters had not yet discovered "Comodyties produced there, which at the markets they must be carried to, shall really reimburse us." The proprietors had claimed a monopoly on trade with the Indians in their Fundamental Constitutions, and they were eager to secure this trade. Moreover, the Westos posed a threat to the colony that Shaftesbury wished to control. In the fall of 1673 some Westos had murdered an Englishman and made "publick declarations" that they would invade the colony. The Grand Council ordered a party to be raised to march against them in alliance with the Esaughs, and a brief war ensued.[56]

Woodward may have sent word to the Westos that he wanted to meet, or perhaps the Westos sought an alliance with the English, but either way, in October Woodward learned from Shaftesbury's agent and kinsman at Saint Giles, Andrew Percivall, that "strange Indians" had arrived. Woodward suspected they were Westos, and he set out to meet them. He did not know the Westo language, but he had his patron's instructions and the prospect for expanding his trade must have been enticing. A small party of ten Westos had camped out near Saint Giles, and while they refused Percivall's offer to stay the night, Woodward nevertheless set out with them for their town. It rained mercilessly as Woodward and his guides hiked the long journey inland. They ate parched corn and roasted turkey and deer, and they slept in "barke covered Hutts" the Indians erected at the end of each day. Woodward covetously observed the "large pastorable Savanas" and the extensive "vallies of excellent land." After a full week of travel, the company met two Indians armed with fowling pieces who had been sent by the Westo cacique to await Woodward's arrival.[57]

His guides brought him to the main Westo town, Hickauhaugau, and in ritual greeting, Woodward fired his pistol, which was answered by "a volley of fifty or sixty small arms." One hundred Indians approached Woodward "drest up in their anticke fighting garbe," and their chief gave a long address declaring their strength but suggesting friendship. Woodward recognized the exchange for what it was: a display of power. The Westos approached the English from a dominant position in the region; friendship and trade would be on their terms. Woodward spent ten days among the Westos and learned of their extensive trade "from ye northward," where they traveled on a regular basis to exchange "drest deare skins, furs, and young Indian slaves" for arms, ammunition, cloth, and other goods. He learned of their "continual wars" with the "Cowatoe" and the "Chorakae." Two days before his departure, two Savana Indians with Spanish trade goods arrived with news that "ye Cussetaws, Checsaws & Chiokees" would soon combine in war against the Westos. The Westos and Savanas spoke different languages and communicated through signs, but their relations were apparently good and the Westos reacted swiftly. Impressed by their preparations, Woodward described a town surrounded by palisades, one hundred canoes at the ready, and a regular watch set throughout the night. In late November Woodward began his return trek to Carolina. The Westos sent ten men to accompany him and gave him an Indian boy as well, a slave. Woodward sent them back from Saint Giles "very well satisfyed," and he wrote to Shaftesbury that he fully expected the Westo to return in March with "deare skins, furrs, and younge slaves."[58]

Woodward's visit to the Westos inaugurated a terrible expansion of slaving among the Indian peoples of Carolina. Now relieved of the long treks to Virginia to secure the arms and ammunition necessary for their raids, the Westos slaved relentlessly, sending a steady stream of captives down to Charles Town. The trade alliance with the Westos would be the first of several diplomatic configurations meant to keep the growing colony secure. The proprietors still hoped that Carolina would become a productive agricultural colony on the Caribbean model. They continued to search "for plants & seeds proper for your country and for persons that are skilled in planting and produceing vines, Mulberry trees, Rice, oyles & wines and such other comodities that enrich." But the slave trade generated an immediate revenue that took little time or investment to begin. In a manner similar to the harvesting of timber and animal skins but far more insidious, slaving transformed the human bounty of North America into a profitable return.[59]

In the fall of 1677, the proprietors reaffirmed their monopoly on the trade with the Westos, which they sought to control through

Shaftesbury's Saint Giles plantation. Woodward served as their agent. The proprietors sought to secure the colonists and to protect the coastal Indians who had settled near the Carolina colony. But conflict between the English and the Westos persisted, and the colonists still depended on the coastal Indians, whom they did not wish to see enslaved. But trade is not friendship, and slaving for the English market transformed every Indian body into a good to be exchanged. Perhaps further conflict was inevitable once the inland tribes nearest the Westos were defeated and fled or were enslaved. In the summer of 1677 the Grand Council warily considered the security of the colony in light of recent Westo threats. Westos were suspected in the killing of two colonists, and the council expected "satisfaction." The council had also learned that the Westos were "intent to inquire and find out the way, manner, and strength of the settlement." The council banned the Westos from entering the colony or addressing the governor until satisfaction for English blood had been given.[60]

By the spring of 1680 satisfaction had not been given, and the Westos had begun to slave among the coastal Indians. They had "killed, taken, and destroyed severall of [the] Neighbor Indians," reported the Grand Council. Woodward had helped them. He had "purchased" enslaved Indians from the Westos and now held them as "slaves contrarie to the positive orders and directions of the Lords Proprietors." The council banned all trade with the Westo, especially the sale of arms or ammunition, and it commanded all smiths in the colony to refuse to repair the gun of any Westo Indian. The council ordered one Captain Fuller to secure the colony's gunpowder, conveniently stored at Saint Giles for Woodward's trade. The council ordered that the enslaved Indians be freed and it banned Woodward from further participation in the Indian trade.[61]

The Grand Council represented the views and interests of the dominant faction in Carolinian politics, the Goose Creek men. Among the first settlers of the colony, the Goose Creek men were ambitious Anglican Barbadians, so named for their cluster of plantations along the Goose Creek tributary of the Ashley River. They quickly emerged as a political force within the colony through their dominance of the Grand Council, and they consistently opposed proprietary policy, particularly regarding the Indian trade. The Goose Creek men shared the aspiration to transform Carolina into an agricultural colony on the Caribbean model, and as in early Barbados, they planted cotton. But they traded with the Indians as well, and they resented their exclusion from the slave trade with the Westos.[62]

The Goose Creek men used Westo aggression against the settlement Indians as a pretext to break the proprietors' monopoly. They made an alliance with the Savanas, armed them, and sponsored a war against the Westos. War generated further Indian captives, and soon the Westos themselves had been decimated to no more than fifty people. Within a couple of years, the Carolinians joined the Savanas in a slaving war against the Waniahs. The proprietors were outraged. They claimed humanitarian concerns but these are difficult to accept. The Westo war began a sordid chapter in Carolinian history in which the colony's most ambitious men used the value of European goods to attract the allegiance of one Indian group and encourage them to war on another. The Savanas replaced the Westos in this slaving alliance, and the Yamasee would soon replace the Savanas. These alliances forced the march of a miserable train of Indian captives down to Charles Town, where colonial merchants shipped them out to the slave markets of the Atlantic. In the long view, the result of this process was the gradual elimination of Indian power in the region and a severe depopulation of the land. King Charles II had given this land to the proprietors, who in turn granted it to settlers. But without the violent theft of the land from its Indian inhabitants through slaving, the Carolina colony might not have entered history.[63]

Slaving brought immediate revenues to the proprietors and leading men of the young colony, but that had not been the original plan. The proprietors had consciously fostered black slavery in Carolina with the Fundamental Constitutions, and with the apparent success of the settlement in 1670, the proprietors altered the headright system to award free migrants with 150 acres for "every able man servant . . . negroes as well as Christians." In subsequent years they reduced the amount of land granted, but the opportunity to own land stimulated a consistent migration to Carolina. About half of these migrants departed from Barbados, and many brought black slaves or white servants along with them, which enabled them to make large claims of Indian land.[64]

The warrants for land written out for the new settlers by colonial officials provide a glimpse of the growing trickle of black slaves arriving in South Carolina during the first forty years of settlement. We have a surprising amount of information about these people. Many were listed by name and gender, and on occasion a family appears. It is likely that most arrived from Barbados, and based on their names, many either had been born there or had been there long enough to assume an English name. John and Elizabeth, for example, were brought, along with their son John Jr., by Governor William Sayle with the first fleet in September 1670. In February of the following year John Culpeper brought two blacks, Judith and Crow; Mrs. Joane Carner brought her daughter Margaret and her black slave Tony in August 1672. Of the 182 black migrants that these warrants document during the first twenty years of settlement, the names were recorded for 65 people, about 35 percent. African names like Mingoe or Aphee were rare until the 1680s; they represented only about 14 percent of the named individuals. Carolina's first black settlers understood the ways of an English slave society. Some may have been born in Africa and brought to the Caribbean, but if so, they had probably been there for several years and knew the white men and women who brought them to North America.[65]

Most of the grantees who brought black slaves to claim Indian land were of modest means. Six were women and thirty-four were men. Most claims were for fewer than seven slaves, and the average claim was for less than five. The warrants suggest that many white migrants to Carolina intended to create a slave population balanced by gender, one that would naturally grow. Even when grantees did not name the blacks they claimed, they usually identified them as men, women, or children. Thirteen grantees brought balanced numbers of enslaved men and women, and there were at least three, maybe four, black couples with children. We have noted John, Elizabeth, and John Jr., and in May 1679, Stephen and Phillis Fox brought a white maidservant and twelve black slaves: four women, four men, two boys, and two girls; in November 1685 Robert Hull brought Stout, Betty, and Ambros, a little boy. In later decades, when plantation agriculture had fully developed in South Carolina, the transatlantic slave trade would bring more men than women, skewing the gender balance of many black settlements. But while migrants in the seventeenth-century could choose, and many hoped that their investment in black slaves would accrue. Slaveholders clearly understood the investment value of enslaved women. Because women bear children, once en-slaved they became a particular form of capital that generated interest—namely, children. Through the capitalization of this most natural pattern in human life, the enslavement of families could lay a durable foundation for slaveholders' wealth.[66]

But there were just as many slaveholders who did not think so far into the future. The black population arriving in South Carolina was not balanced. Among ninety-four people, there were fifty-seven men and thirty-one women, and at least six were children, three boys and three girls. Nine grantees brought only one or two men each. Twelve grantees listed only "negroes" without further detail, and one sus-pects these were men brought for hard labor. Among these was the Indian slaver Henry Woodward, who used the proceeds from his trade to import "seven negroes" in November 1682 to secure a grant of four hundred acres. The claims laid on black bodies gave these whites the legal rights to more than fifteen thousand acres of Indian land. And because of Indian slaving, depopulation, and the slow con-quest led by the "dealers of Indians," those lands would ultimately be available for planting, if not for them, then for their descendants.[67]

In January 1688 and then October 1689, the royalist governor of the Leeward Islands, Nathaniel Johnson, sent two groups of black slaves, eleven men and one woman followed by nine men and one woman, all of them named, to work on his lands on the Cooper River. These shipments made Johnson the single largest transporter of black slaves to Carolina, and his Caribbean career illustrates the continued salience of the Caribbean political economy to the founders of South Carolina. Johnson received 1,100 acres for these slaves, and the clear gender imbalance of this group suggests that Johnson had one principal interest: hard labor on a working plantation.[68]

Born of a wealthy family in Kibblesworth, Durham County, England, in 1644, Johnson went to Barbados as a young man and served the colony as deputy treasurer in the 1660s. He returned to England in the 1670s, was knighted in 1680, and, like his father before him, served as mayor of Newcastle upon Tyne (1681–1682). Johnson invested heavily in South Carolina during these years. He sent seventeen white servants to Carolina in 1683, for which he received 760 acres of Indian land, as well as a town lot in Charles Town. With this land and labor he established the plantation on the Cooper River that he later named Silk Hope. But Johnson would not yet settle in Carolina. In September 1686 King James II gave Johnson the commission to be governor of the Leeward Islands, and by the summer of 1687 he had arrived in Antigua.[69]

Johnson established a large sugar plantation in Antigua, and it seems likely that the slaves he sent to Carolina came from his own plantation. But the revolution brewing in England soon threatened his Caribbean career. Johnson's royalism went deep, and he refused to serve the new king, William III. He had governed the Leewards with a firm hand in pursuit of James II's pro-French, pro-Catholic policies, and the Leewards planters resented and feared him. Moreover, his investments in Antigua had been quite disappointing. "I have lost another near relative and fourteen more slaves, and have been very ill myself," he wrote to the Lords of Trade in April 1689. "I have been a great sufferer by coming to these parts," he wrote without irony, "where my expenses and losses far outbalance my gains." His political career seemingly ended by the revolution in England, Johnson named Christopher Codrington as his replacement and departed for Carolina in July 1689.[70]

Upon his arrival in Carolina, Johnson immediately attracted the attention of the Goose Creek men, who sought him as an ally in their perpetual struggle with the proprietors. John Stewart, an Indian trader who also managed the Colleton family's Wadboo plantation, wrote to his patron's agent, William Dunlop, about a feast held upon Johnson's arrival by Maurice Mathews, a notorious Indian slaver, along with several others from Goose Creek. In addition to their Indian trade, the Goose Creek men were planters in search of lucrative staples. They expected to load two ships of cotton with the harvest of 1690, and experiments with silk production, indigo, and rice were well under way. Stewart wrote that Johnson had his servants and slaves plant twenty-four thousand mulberry trees for silk production, work that surely began before his arrival. Stewart himself experimented with rice production and wrote that Carolinian rice was "better esteemed of in Jamaica than that from Europe." Carolinian rice sold for a "ryall a pound" in Jamaica and "17/a hundred weight" in Charles Town when "new husk't." Such details suggest that by 1690 rice production and marketing were well under way.[71]

The Goose Creek men needed a powerful ally, and Johnson fit the bill. Since 1686, they had been in conflict with Governor James Colleton, brother of the proprietor and a former member of the Barbados Assembly who hewed to proprietary policy. The most outrageous episode to alienate Colleton from the Goose Creek men was the unanswered Spanish attack on Port Royal in 1686. That summer, in response to the attacks of English pirates and a Yamasee slaving raid on the Spanish Timucua mission of Santa Catarina de Afuyca, Governor Juan Marqués Cabrera of Saint Augustine outfitted three vessels with a force of a hundred Spanish soldiers and fifty-three Indians and blacks. The Spanish force destroyed Port Royal and moved on to Edisto Island, where they ransacked the plantation of then-governor Joseph Morton and carried off thirteen slaves. Two of the blacks returned to the English, but the other eleven went with the Spanish. The serendipitous arrival of a hurricane protected Charles Town, but the damage had been done. The Goose Creek men wanted to strike back, but as Spain and England were formally at peace, the proprietors refused. Nevertheless, the Carolinians raised a force of four hundred men, some of whom were on board their ships when the newly appointed governor Colleton arrived in Charles Town. Colleton carried very clear orders from the proprietors that the expedition must not depart, and in this particular moment, his power proved adequate to enforce the proprietors' will.[72]

The Spanish attack, particularly the seizure of Morton's slaves, had profound implications. Did the Spanish take these slaves as the plunder of war? Or did they intend to free them? The first documented mass escape of enslaved Carolinians, which took place within a year of the Spanish attack, suggests that black Carolinians knew or hoped for the latter. Eight men and two women, one of whom carried an infant at the breast, somehow secured a boat and made their way to Saint Augustine. The Spanish allowed them entry to the colony and put them to work in various occupations, for which they were paid.[73]

Two additional groups of runaways also gained admittance to the Spanish colony, which suggests that the Goose Creek men had been correct in their assessment of the Spanish threat. That these would-be West Indian planters, who were just beginning to find success on their plantations, had been willing to defy the proprietors in an episode fraught with interimperial conflict illustrates the threat that the Spanish posed to the consolidation of racial slavery in Carolina. Colleton had subordinated local concerns to imperial policy, and the Goose Creek men were outraged.[74]

Colleton would not risk war, but in June 1688, he sent a delegation led by Dunlop to Saint Augustine to establish a better relationship with the new Spanish governor, Diego Lequiroga y Cassado, and to secure the return of Carolina's slaves. Morton had since died, but Dunlop carried with him a memo from the executors of the estate, which included the names of the slaves to be secured: Peter, Scipio, Doctor, Cushi, Arro, Emo, Caesar, Sambo, Frank (a woman), Bess, and Mammy. Dunlop presented his demands, but the tangible results of his diplomacy were few. The only English slaves the Spanish acknowledged were the first group of fugitives who had escaped in 1687. There is no evidence that Lequiroga y Cassado even considered returning Morton's slaves, and instead of returning the fugitives they did acknowledge, Lequiroga y Cassado claimed that these men and women had converted to Roman Catholicism and thus could not be restored to slavery. The Spanish governor agreed to purchase these men and women from Dunlop, for 2,000 pieces of eight, payable within the year, but those who had been enslaved remained free. Dunlop thus returned empty-handed, with promises of payment to a handful of Carolinian planters whose slaves had successfully gained their freedom. In a telling letter to Lequiroga y Cassado written in

1690, Colleton complained that Carolina's slaves continued to run "dayly to your towns." The problem of fugitive slaves had not been solved.[75]

In 1690, the proprietor Seth Sothel arrived in the colony, apparently without notice. Sothel had purchased the proprietorship of Lord Clarendon in 1677 and had set out to govern the Albemarle settlement (which became North Carolina). But he was captured by North African pirates and held for ransom in Algiers and forced to perform hard labor. Ultimately ransomed, by the time he arrived in South Carolina in 1690, Sothel was more of a self-interested renegade than a representative of the proprietors. He claimed that under the authority of the Fundamental Constitutions, his proprietorship placed him above Colleton in rank, a de facto governor. Colleton and his supporters rejected the claim, but Johnson and the Goose Creek men supported Sothel and staged an armed confrontation, which Colleton averted by resigning his position. Sothel called for a new assembly, which passed a raft of legislation, including the first comprehensive slave code. Sothel and the Goose Creek men also moved against their political opponents, imprisoning some and banishing Colleton from the colony. This went too far. The proprietors recalled Sothel, restored Colleton, and disregarded all of the laws passed under his administration.[76]

South Carolina's Act for the Better Ordering of Slaves never became law, but its passage in 1691 remains a valuable reflection of the aspirations of Carolina's slaveholders. The Indian slave trade fostered by Carolina's leading men complemented the settlers' less violent endeavors and paved the way for Carolina's development into a staple-producing economy on the West Indian model. For these first twenty years of settlement, the English in Carolina had depended on two branches of trade: one to the West Indies, whereby Indian slaves, beef, pork, corn, and lumber went to the Caribbean, sometimes in exchange for black slaves; and a trade in Indian commodities and forest products with England, whereby pelts and deerskins procured from the Indians, as well as pitch and tar produced by slaves, were shipped to England. Before the liberalization of the transatlantic slave trade in 1698, the Royal African Company could not meet the demands of West Indian planters for enslaved Africans. With their connections to Barbados and the rest of the English West Indies, where enslaved laborers for the growing sugar economies were in high demand, early Carolinians had a market for slaves that was intimately linked to their own economic development. Carolinians held slaves as well, but they did not need as many as their Caribbean counterparts, and sugar planters did not really care whether the slaves were Indians or Africans; they simply needed labor.

The English in Carolina had set out to be slaveholders, not slavers. They were not morally opposed to slaving and would continue to slave for another generation, but as soon as it became evident that the large-scale production of rice had a tangible future, they embraced the legal foundation their West Indian cousins had already established. The South Carolina Assembly of 1691 adopted the Jamaica Slave Act of 1684 almost in its entirety. They added "Indian" to the category of "slave" and dropped a few of the provisions in the Jamaican law that did not apply to their nascent slave society. The rest of the act—word for word—borrowed the Jamaica legislation with no new provisions. Jamaica and South Carolina were part of the same expanding sphere of English imperialism, which in the Greater Caribbean had coalesced around a political economy of racial slavery. As in Jamaica in 1664, the passage of South Carolina's first comprehensive slave code indicated economic aspirations and the expectation, based on experience, that black slaves would have to be governed with a rod of iron.[77]

Two months after the South Carolina Assembly adopted Jamaica's comprehensive slave code, Johnson secured a warrant for 1,200 more acres of Indian land based on his importation of ninety-five "servants and negroes" at "sundry times." Johnson had already made the biggest claims of Indian land based on slaves; now he tripled those claims. The warrant tells us nothing about the gender or race of these new forced settlers, but they were by far the largest group that a planter imported during these first two decades of settlement in South Carolina.[78]

In 1696 the Houses of Assembly in both South Carolina and Jamaica passed revised slave codes that illustrate significant distinctions between these slave societies at the close of the seventeenth century. In South Carolina, the new governor, John Archdale, had fostered a working relationship among the colony's political factions. A Quaker and proprietor who bought Lord Baron John Berkeley's share of the colony in 1678, Archdale laid the political foundation for South Carolina's plantation revolution into large-scale rice production. Jamaica had already begun to produce significant quantities of sugar. Its assembly in 1696 included some of the most experienced planters on the island, men such as Andrew Langley, Thomas Sutton, and Thomas Trapham, all of whom had served in the assembly for almost twenty years. The governor of Jamaica, Sir William Beeston, enjoyed the longest term of the colony's seventeenth-century governors. He owned large sugar plantations on the island, and he had been Speaker of the Assembly in the 1670s and later an agent for the assembly lobbying at Whitehall. As governor, Beeston steered the colony through a devastating earthquake in 1692 and a destructive French invasion in 1694, and he would govern the island until 1702. In short, both colonies were enjoying strong, stable leadership when they passed new comprehensive slave codes in 1696.[79]

Jamaica's society had changed dramatically since 1684, while South Carolina had changed very little since 1691. The black population of South Carolina had risen slightly, Indian slaving continued with both Savana and Yamasee allies, and while rice production had certainly been established, it was not yet the core of the colonial economy and a direct slave trade between Africa and South Carolina had not yet been established. In contrast, Jamaican sugar had begun to generate significant revenues, which stimulated an expansion of the slave trade to Jamaica to an average of about two thousand enslaved Africans every year. The black population of Jamaica had probably doubled by 1696, while the white population had actually declined.[80]

With respect to the law of slave property, each colony's new Slave Act strengthened the chattel status of slave property, but with distinctions that revealed their different stages of development. South Carolina's assembly simply declared that slave status would be determined by the fact of having been "Bought and Sold for Slaves." The simplicity of Carolina's definition ignored the "real estate" distinction altogether; slaves were movable property—nothing more, nothing less. Jamaica's new law did much more than this, indicating a far more developed market for the exchange of slaves. The Jamaica Assembly established a record-keeping system for slave sales that protected property in slaves with the legal power of a deed. Forthwith, every slave sale was to be recorded by the vestry clerk in "a distinct book" to be kept in each parish on the island. The law required each entry to include the vender and the vendee, the date, the price, and "the Name and Mark of the Slave or Slaves." Clerks would receive payment for each entry and faced a ten-pound fine if they failed to enter a slave sale. And in the case of future disputes, the entries of this book would hold the authority of deeds and would be considered "sufficient record and evidence" of property in any court on the island. Through the establishment of these "distinct books," which unfortunately have not survived, the assembly secured slave property with a legal protection hitherto reserved for land.[81]

While the assemblies only needed to tinker with the legislation on slave property to clarify it, in their work on the legislation concerning the consolidation of power, they sought violent retrenchment. Here again, the laws reflected different stages of development. Jamaica's Act for the Better Order and Government of Slaves highlighted the challenge of combating organized resistance waged by the large numbers of newly enslaved Africans brought by the slavers. "Whereas it is found by Experience," the law proclaimed, "that the often Insurrections and Rebellions of the Slaves . . . have proved the Ruin and Destruction of several Families," the assembly developed a brutal code of law intended to subdue a resistant humanity. This preamble reflected recent history, for there had been several major slave rebellions during the living memory of most assemblymen.[82]

In 1685, 185 Africans led by Cuffy organized a major rebellion in Saint John's Parish. The Akan name Cuffy suggests parallels with the conspiracy in Barbados, but scholars have counted only 2,400 Africans from the Gold Coast who arrived in Jamaica during the decade before this rebellion, about 10 percent of the 23,000 who survived the middle passage. Cuffy's prominence in the rebellion suggests that Akan military prowess gave them prominence beyond their numbers. Cuffy's men went from plantation to plantation seizing arms and ammunition. When ultimately confronted by a large body of militia, they fought hard, many died, and the rest dispersed into the mountains. They regrouped a few months later and attacked the whites again, only to retreat again into the mountains, where they formed another community of Maroons.[83]

In 1690 more than four hundred Africans on Sutton's Clarendon plantation—his entire slave force—revolted, murdered the resident whites, and seized fifty muskets, four field cannon, and a "great quantity" of gunpowder. The merchant-historian James Knight would later report that the Maroon leader Cudjoe's father had been a leader of these rebels. Their actions illustrate clear military skills, but they could not convince the slaves of a neighboring plantation to join them, and when they met the white militia in battle, the rebels were routed. Many were killed and some surrendered, but a band of about forty escaped into the mountainous Cockpit Country. In a report on the insurrection, Governor William O'Brien, second earl of Inchiquin, wrote that there had been only six or seven white men on the plantation, "the usual proportion in the island," which made for an astonishing ratio of one to fifty-seven. In 1692 the Jamaica Council raised parties of slave catchers to attempt the capture of bands of rebels that made constant attacks on the colonial settlements. The slavers had brought so many enslaved Africans to the island that the planters could no longer control them. The effort to domesticate Africans, to render them useful capital, had come under serious attack.[84]

Jamaica's 1696 Slave Act aspired to blunt the capacity of enslaved Africans to wage war. "Great Numbers" of slaves had gathered on "Sundays and Holy-Days," when rebels had plotted the "bloody and Inhuman transactions" that threatened to undermine the colony. On too many nights, African drumming pulsated throughout the countryside, and planters feared the sound. The law enjoined masters to prohibit these endeavors—the drumming, the rendezvous, the feast, and the revels. The new act also targeted the resistance of individual slaves. Slave courts were newly empowered to deal with the offenses of both free blacks and slaves, and they could now consider the testimony of slaves in any case that came before them. Slave courts could order the summary execution of any slave who struck a white man—

indeed, any slave who even "imagine[d] the death of any white person" could be executed.[85] The act also targeted the nascent Maroon communities by defining the Maroon as a particular criminal, the "rebellious slave" who had been away from the plantation for twelve months. Whites who killed or captured a "rebellious slave" could collect five pounds; a slave could receive forty shillings and a serge coat for the same act. And once caught, the "rebellious slave" should receive a severe lashing and be transported out of the colony.[86]

In contrast, the new South Carolinian slave code did not even mention drums. The assembly's new Act for the Better Ordering of Slaves opened with a defining preamble that seemed to predict a new era of slavery. It explained the provisions that followed by warning of "too much Liberty" among the slaves, which would prove especially dangerous "as the number of Slaves Shall increase." The South Carolinian code also declared slave status hereditary, which the Barbados and Jamaica acts had not yet done. This measure followed ancient and Iberian precedent, but it would have been particularly important to those who had consciously fostered the growth of a slave population through the importation of enslaved women. South Carolina's legislators were guarded, eager to consolidate their property, and concerned about the dangers they knew to be imminent in the black-majority society they seemed to predict.[87]

Beyond this preamble, the South Carolina Assembly added only a few innovations to the law they had borrowed from Jamaica just five years earlier. The South Carolinian law enjoined masters to keep their slaves away from "strong drink"; it also included a deficiency clause that ordered anyone who owned a "plantation or cowpen" to keep at least one white man in residence. But the assembly's most remarkable innovation was to order the castration of enslaved men who ran away. Slaves over the age of sixteen who absconded for more than two weeks were to be branded with an *R* for the first offense. But for the second offense, the enslaved man was to be gelded, while the woman would lose an ear. The statute further stated that if a slaveholder refused to punish a chronic runaway in accordance with the law, he or she could lose ownership of the slave through a suit in court brought by an informer, who might win possession of the slave. Such an informer would be obliged to carry out the punishment, of course, or face a fifty-pound fine if he or she failed to do so. And if the victim of such punishment were to die from it, the law allowed the master a twenty-pound compensation to encourage the gruesome act.[88]

Carolinians not only codified gelding, they did it. Within a year of the new law's passage, the assembly ordered the gelding of three runaways who attempted to escape to Saint Augustine and awarded the bricklayer Gabrill Glaze sixty-five pounds' reimbursement for Cyrus, one of the victimized men. Why did the South Carolina Assembly prescribe such terrifying punishments, and where did they get such an awful idea? Gelding as a punishment had no precedent in English law, and neither Jamaica nor Barbados legislated gelding in the comprehensive slave laws of 1684, 1688, or 1696. In June 1683, when Colonel Ivey of Jamaica discovered a conspiracy among his slaves, he captured the conspirators and subjected them to all sorts of tortures, including castration. In the aftermath of a slave rebellion in 1693, the Barbados Council paid one Alice Mills for the castration of forty-three rebels. These were fraught moments of terrifying bloodshed when masters resorted to brutal terror to reassert their dominance. But on neither island did such moments lead to a legislative process that made castration formal policy.[89]

Spanish policy and the proximity of Saint Augustine motivated Carolinians to codify terroristic mutilation as a systemic tactic in the governance of slaves. Despite the work of the Dunlop delegation, groups of fugitive slaves escaped from South Carolina in 1689 and 1690. Spanish officials continued to harbor these brave souls; they also sought clarification of Spain's policy toward these fugitives. On November 7, 1693, Charles II issued the *cédula* (edict) that established royal policy with respect to runaways from English Carolina. The king granted "liberty to all . . . the men as well as the women . . . so that by their example and by my liberality others will do the same."[90] Charles clearly sought to undermine the upstart English colony by encouraging their slaves to escape, and some had done so. The House of Assembly responded by terrifying their slaves with bodily mutilations that were generally reserved for animals.

The South Carolinian provision to brand, castrate, and disfigure black slaves who persistently resisted the authority of the master should be understood as intrinsic to the animalization of black people at the heart of racial slavery. It was rooted in the common practice of gelding bull calves. Work shapes the way people live.[91] In seventeenth-century South Carolina, the management of open-range cattle herds played a critical role in the colonial economy. In 1680, Maurice Mathews wrote that there were already "several thousands" of cattle in Carolina and only newcomers did not possess them. Two years later Samuel Wilson wrote that some individuals owned seven or eight hundred head of cattle. With Carolina's extremely mild winters, early cattlemen simply let their herds fend for themselves. The Dutch engineer John DeBrahm described herding practices in the mid-eighteenth century: "The cowpenkeepers determine the number of their stocks by the number of calvs, which they mark [brand] every spring and fall: if one marks 300 calves per annum, he rekons his stock to consist of 400 heifers, 500 cows, and 300 steers, in all 1500 heads." DeBrahm's account suggests a biannual practice of hunting down all of the cows in a herd in order to brand the calves and geld most of the young bulls.[92] Black slaves participated in this bloody work, as many slaveholders entrusted their herds to a few male slaves.[93] The practice of gelding, then, would have been extremely common and well understood by both whites and blacks in early Carolina. By threatening enslaved black men with gelding, the South Carolina Assembly literally treated them as beasts with a procedure that would have been immediately recognizable and terrifying.

By the close of the seventeenth century, the colonial Assemblies of Barbados, Jamaica, and South Carolina had consolidated a law for racial slavery that would undergird its expansion. For Englishmen in the seventeenth century this was quite new, but in the longer flow of human history their actions were as old as slavery itself. The Hammurabi Code did not recognize the killing of a slave as murder, and male slaves were castrated in ancient Rome, medieval Egypt, and sixteenth-century Peru. Slave law ordered the payment of slave catchers in ancient Rome and sixteenth-century Mexico, just as it did in the English colonies. Assertions of the biological difference of slaves were not new either. Aristotle wrote of the "natural slave" and likened them to "tame animals," while medieval Jewish and Muslim writers had views of sub-Saharan Africans that were similar to the image of the barbarous African that festered in the white mind.[94]

The significance of these early colonial slave codes lies not in their novelty but rather in the political work they did in making slavery English. The incorporation of a brutal slavery into the political economy of empire might have begun as an "unthinking decision" and the work of economic forces, but the Restoration marked an important turning point when the profits of slavery attracted the interest of the most powerful men of England. The emergence of powerful colonial assemblies, which represented the planters as a political class, fostered the consolidation and control of enslaved Africans as a novel form of capital investment that would fuel Great Britain's imperial economy. Through a decades-long struggle fraught with blood, terror, and sweat, the plantation order established in Jamaica and South Carolina would create, by the middle of the next century, Great Britain's wealthiest colonies in the Caribbean and North America.[95]

CHAPTER 3

The Domestication of Slavery
in South Carolina

T HE PLANTERS OF South Carolina and Jamaica fostered distinctive systems of social control to make racial slavery pay. In South Carolina, the power of Indian polities and the expansive geography of North America made the formation of its slave society distinct from Barbados and Jamaica. The earliest Carolinian colonists engaged with the Indians out of necessity, but once trade with the Indians began—especially the slaving trade—the colonists profited handsomely and pursued alliances with the most powerful tribes. The Indian slave trade peaked during the first decade of the eighteenth century, but it ended in the Yamasee War of 1715 with a cataclysm of violence that almost destroyed the colony.

South Carolina's commercial development fostered the accumulation of capital that enabled the plantation economy to grow. The English slaving merchants who brought Africans to the Chesapeake and the Caribbean began to send ships to Charles Town in about 1700, and by 1715 hundreds of enslaved Africans were arriving in South Carolina every year. As a result, rice production expanded significantly before Indian slaving ended, and after the war, the Carolinian planters wanted nothing more than to return to the business of importing captive Africans and making them clear forest and plant rice.

But the war posed an existential crisis to the colony, and it shaped the governance of slaves as the planters rebuilt. The war had resulted from the indiscriminate enslavement of Indian peoples by the Carolinian traders who slaved. It taught the planters that the avaricious brutality of men on this dangerous frontier could lead to explosive violence, with disastrous consequences for the entire colonial project. And because many Carolinian planters had arrived through the Caribbean, they knew that such explosive violence could come from African slaves as well as Indians. The Yamasee War transformed the dialectic between resistance and repression that had shaped Anglo-Atlantic slave law since the 1640s. Beginning in 1722, the laws of slavery in South Carolina, which had hitherto fostered a vicious brutality, became, in the hands of wary planter-legislators, a set of tools to domesticate the system of racial slavery at the heart of their colony.

By the early eighteenth century South Carolina had become an expansive slave society pushing outward from Charles Town into the Indian lands of the southeastern woodlands. In 1708, the Lords of Trade requested a report on the colony from Governor Nathaniel Johnson, who had prospered from his move to Carolina and regained the favor of the Crown. Johnson described a bustling settlement deeply embedded in the Atlantic economy. The Charles Town merchants sent ships to Great Britain, the Caribbean, Africa, and the North American colonies, a reflection of the colony's diversified economy. Rice came first among the colony's products, but the settlers and their slaves also harvested hardwood lumber and made pitch and tar from the pine forests, valuable products for shipbuilders. Carolinians grew crops of corn and peas as well, and maintained herds of cattle and pigs. Most of the naval stores went to London; rice went to all of Carolina's markets, but most of the lumber, food provisions, and household manufactures like butter and candles went to the sugar planters on the islands.[1]

Carolina also sold slaves. Enslaved Indians, wrote Governor Johnson, were the first commodities of importance in the trade with the North American ports. Records that might give us numbers have not survived, but the slaving raids had expanded. A significant trade in peltry had also developed, fostered by the backcountry traders who had followed in the footsteps of Henry Woodward and now made annual trips to the hundreds of Indian towns that surrounded the colony. The Charles Town merchants sent at least fifty thousand deerskins annually to London, along with smaller numbers of furs: beaver, otter, wildcat, raccoon, buffalo, and bear. As in the West African commerce of the same era, Indians demanded cloth, guns, manufactures, and alcohol for the skins and slaves they sold. The Charles Town merchants thus imported significant amounts of British manufactures and West Indian rum, building up a considerable capital in the process.[2]

The people who built this economy were perhaps the most intercultural population in the empire. Whites came mostly from England or its Caribbean possessions, but there were also French Huguenots and exiles from the German principalities. In contrast to Jamaica, where the white population stagnated and even declined in these years, in South Carolina whites had increased by about 70 percent since 1690, and children were the largest group. The black population had also grown and now surpassed the whites, though only slightly; blacks outnumbered whites by 4,100 to 4,080. Growth came through a slave trade with the Caribbean and Atlantic Africa, but there was probably some natural increase as well. Black slaves represented more than half of the colony's core population, a far greater proportion than in Virginia, where they made up less than 30 percent of the colony, but much less than Jamaica, where 85 percent of the island's people were African slaves and their children. Enslaved children made up about 30 percent of the black population in South Carolina; officials in Jamaica did not record such numbers. The children of enslaved mothers may have represented a return on investment for their masters, but for the black families that had begun to set their roots in the little plantation villages, children represented hope.[3]

South Carolina's large number of Indian slaves also distinguished this slave society from that of Jamaica. About 1,400 Indians worked as slaves in the colony in 1708—500 men, 600 women, and 300 children—which made the enslaved majority of the colony about 60 percent. Victims of slaving raids into Florida, these Indians labored alongside blacks well into the 1720s. Most of their kin had either escaped the slavers or been transported and sold in the colonial slave markets in North America and the Caribbean. But with the growth of rice production, the demand for slaves grew in Carolina too, and significant numbers of enslaved Indians now remained in the colony.[4]

In almost forty years of settlement, whites in South Carolina had prospered, but the insurrections that had already struck Barbados and Jamaica demonstrated the threats of an enslaved majority. The assembly sought to avoid the Caribbean pattern through legislation. In 1698 the assembly passed the Act for the Encouragement of the Importation of White Servants, which directly subsidized the growth of the colony's white population. The preamble to the law clearly explained the assembly's rationale for this expenditure: "Whereas the great number of negroes" endangered "the safety" of the colony, the law established a subsidy for the importation of white servants: thirteen pounds for a grown man and twelve pounds for a teen. The law also reinforced the deficiency clause established in the Slave Act of 1696 by ordering every plantation with six or more slaves to take at least one new white servant for each six slaves. Constables were to enforce the statute by recording lists of such slaveholders and how many slaves they held so that new white servants could be allocated in accordance with demographic need.[5]

Carolinians enlisted significant numbers of black slaves to serve in the colonial militia. Blacks may have served as soldiers in the colony as early as 1682, but the Act for Raising and Enlisting Slaves, passed in November 1704 after the outbreak of Queen Anne's War, codified the practice. The law required each company commander in the militia to compile lists of "trusty slaves" from among those held in his jurisdiction, and in "time of Alarms" each slave so designated must be armed with either a gun or a lance and be embodied in a party under a white officer. If the slave died in battle, the master would be compensated, and under a revision of the law passed in 1708, if a trusted slave killed or captured one of the enemy, or if the violence of battle left him maimed, he would be freed and the master compensated. Under this legislation almost one thousand blacks had been enlisted into the Carolina militia.[6]

Carolinian colonists trusted some of their black slaves to assist in colonial defense during times of war, but the very same assembly instituted a regular patrol to manage the threat of organized resistance. Warning of the "insurrections and mischiefs" expected from the "great number of slaves" in the colony, the Act to Settle a Patroll established a system of military mobilization whereby militia captains appointed by the governor were to enlist ten men from their district to ride patrol. These men were to have a horse, a set of pistols, a gun, twelve cartridges, and a sword constantly at the ready. During any alarm, or whenever the captain "shall think fit," these patrols were to ride from plantation to plantation, and onto any plantation, arresting any enslaved person who appeared to be on the lam without a ticket. The act enabled the increased enforcement of the comprehensive slave code of 1696 and indicated that the possession and control of slaves demanded rigorous surveillance.[7]

South Carolina remained a small and fragile outpost on a dangerous international frontier. The Spanish and the French threatened from the southwest, and white colonists were outnumbered not only by their slaves but also by numerous Indian peoples whose allegiance could not be certain. Curiously, the Lords of Trade did not ask Johnson about South Carolina's Indian neighbors, but he knew better and took care "to superadd an account of the Indians our allies." Johnson described ten distinct peoples living in about eighty towns, a total population of 8,480 fighting men and an unstated number of women and children. Almost 60,000 Indians lived in the region that Johnson described, and while the governor confidently asserted that alliances made for an English sphere of influence over this huge region, it was strikingly clear that the Carolina colony was literally surrounded by Indian polities that were far more populous than the English and skilled in warfare.[8]

Indian slaving in the southeast had become a destructive cycle that devastated Native peoples and brought much wealth to the South Carolina colony. The Westos and the Savanas had demonstrated that access to English guns enabled Indian warriors to dominate their weaker neighbors. And as the Charles Town market grew, the Yamasee and the Creeks discovered much the same. The Yamasee were Carolina's principal ally. Early victims of the Westos, the Yamasee had moved from Spanish Guale closer to Charles Town to forge an easier trade with the English and acquire the guns and powder they needed to protect themselves. They sold slaves to the English as early as 1685, and by 1707 their alliance with South Carolina had become so close that the assembly passed legislation to protect Yamasee lands from the encroachment of white settlers.[9]

The traditional values that had validated Indian slaving before the arrival of the English had been severely compromised by the trading goods the English brought, especially rum. Indians had not produced alcohol before the arrival of Europeans, and sugar's profitable by-product soon became the addictive poison that continues to devastate Indian communities. The trade in pelts and deerskins was important, but slaves brought the highest prices. In 1705, the Virginia trader John Evans, who had traveled in the Carolina backcountry, recorded in a rare surviving account book that he had purchased Merrak, a ten-year-old Indian girl, for twenty pounds. Based on other entries in the same book, we can see that Merrak brought the same value as a hundred buckskins, or one horseload in the backcountry trade. The Indian slaver and agent Thomas Nairne wrote that one Indian slave could bring a warrior "a gun, ammunition, horse, hatchet, and a suite of Cloathes," far more than could be earned during an entire winter of hunting deer and preparing the skins for trade.[10]

Indians' own interests in slaving meshed with the interimperial rivalries that convulsed the southeastern woodlands. In 1699, the French explorer Pierre Le Moyne d'Iberville rediscovered the mouth of the Mississippi River and established settlements at Biloxi Bay and, later on, Mobile Bay. Carolinians had been trading with the Creeks north of these settlements for about twenty years, and there were traders from Carolina resident in the Creek towns. The Carolinian leadership were quite alarmed to learn of the French presence, for the French already had considerable success with their fur trade in Iroquoia. This trade revolved around Montreal and extended south along the northern tributaries of the Mississippi River. French imperialists hoped to consolidate and expand their North American trade along the entire course of the Mississippi River, from the Great

Lakes region, where they had planted themselves in the 1650s, to the river's mouth in the Gulf of Mexico. If they could embed themselves in the southern trading system and displace the English as the source for European goods, France might emerge as the dominant European power in North America. Iberville believed French and Spanish interests might be compatible in the southeast, and he pursued his plans in correspondence with his Spanish counterparts.[11]

The English had been enslaving Spain's Indian allies in Guale for a generation by this point, and the addition of French involvement exacerbated conflict. The French reached out to the Creek towns as soon as they had established the settlements in Biloxi and Mobile Bay, but the English resident traders were not keen to share this trade. In 1701 a Creek slaving raid with English support sacked the towns of the Spanish-allied Apalachee, and a similar raid the following year destroyed the Spanish Timucuan mission at Santa Fé de Toloco. We have no idea how many were enslaved in this attack, but the raids inspired an attempt at retribution by a force of eight hundred men, Spanish and Apalachee. The Carolinians quickly raised a force of Creeks and defeated the expedition, and more Apalachee were slaughtered and enslaved.[12]

The onset of the War of the Spanish Succession in Europe further intensified the devastation. Unofficial news of the war arrived in the fall of 1702, and it fired martial passions. The South Carolina Assembly voted funds for an expedition of five hundred Carolinians and three hundred Indians to be led by James Moore against Saint Augustine. The English and their allies destroyed the Spanish town but could not breach the fort, and thus they left in embarrassment at the arrival of Spanish reinforcements from Havana. The English vented their disappointment in slaving, again raiding the Apalachee with their allies and destroying three Spanish mission towns. In the winter of 1704, now acting on his own to mend his reputation, Moore assembled an army of fifty Carolinians and marched against the Apalachee with an army of a thousand Indian soldiers, Creeks and Yamasee. Moore assembled a second expedition in the spring, which enslaved thousands more and convinced the remaining Apalachee to either flee or submit to the English. In the coffles driven by Moore's army back to Charles Town walked 325 men bound in leather harnesses and more than four thousand women and children. In January 1708, the Spanish governor of Saint Augustine lamented that the English had enslaved between ten thousand and twelve thousand Indians from the Spanish missions during the war, and countless more in the years before. In July of that same year, Nairne wrote with pride to the Earl of Sunderland, secretary of state for the southern colonies, that the Yamasee had driven the Florida Indians to the Key Islands. They had "brought in and sold many Hundreds of them and Dayly now Continue that Trade." Nairne was equally proud of the Creek and Chickasaw bands who slaved against Indians who had allied with the French. Slaving continued to foster the slow conquest of the southeastern Indians, clearing the land for the expansion of black slavery outward from the colony's plantation core.[13]

Thomas Nairne arrived in South Carolina at some point in the 1690s, and his career exemplifies the experience of ambitious whites. He first appears in the historical record in 1698 when a warrant for land written out for the old Indian trader John Stewart noted Nairne's plantation on Saint Helena Island as a boundary. A Scot, Stewart lived in the settlement at Port Royal during the Spanish attack of 1686 but had nevertheless decided to remain. He began to trade with the Indians under the authority of Governor James Colleton in 1690, lived with the Creeks in Coweta for two years, and has been credited with opening Carolina's trade with the Chickasaw. Stewart's career moved from serving as agent and planter for English patrons to a deep involvement in the Indian trade for himself. With the capital amassed in the Indian trade, Stewart bought land and sought to establish himself as a planter. He participated in a few more slaving raids in the 1700s, but he retired to intellectual pursuits, as well as to agricultural experimentation. We can surmise that Stewart introduced Nairne to the tactics of the Indian trade, and that both men chose to live in the lands south of Charles Town because of their proximity to the Yamasee.[14]

Nairne pursued a rather different career. Like Stewart, he used the proceeds of his Indian trade to establish himself as a planter, but

Nairne remained deeply committed to the Indian trade as imperial policy. Nairne's involvement in the Indian trade dates to the early eighteenth century, and by the end of his life he knew most of the Indian peoples of the southeastern woodlands as far west as the Choctaw. Nairne participated in the failed 1702 attack on Saint Augustine and the slaving raids against the Apalachee in 1704, and he accompanied Yamasee and Creek allies on slaving raids to the tip of Florida. He left a terrifying portrait of this slaving. The night before a raid, the slavers would arrange themselves in a "halfe moon" around a village and march slowly together like the closing of a noose. The party's leader would signal the attack, and every man would give "the War Whoop and then catch as catch can." Nairne considered the reduction of the Florida Indians a matter of pride. These Indians were "Spanish." Slaving had severely weakened them and paved the way for English expansion.[15]

As the most lucrative economic endeavor in the colony, the Indian trade became the subject of intense partisan conflict. Tories and Whigs in South Carolina had conflicting views on numerous issues, including religion, governance, and the nature of empire. On the Indian trade, they largely agreed on the importance of cultivating allies to extend the power of the colony. But while Whigs like Nairne saw commerce and slaving with Indian allies as the wisest imperial policy for English expansion, Tories like Governor Johnson saw slaving and commerce as valuable sources of revenue, not as aspects of diplomacy.[16]

In the summer of 1707, South Carolina Whigs pushed forward the Act for Regulating the Indian Trade, which sought to curb the abusive practices of traders by establishing official oversight. The prohibitions of the statute describe practices that had developed over several generations of intercultural trade. The law's preamble described the traders as "loose, vicious" men who "oppress the people among whom they live." The assembly feared that without change, the traders' practices would "tend to the destruction of this Province." The law banned the selling of rum to the Indians. It imposed a severe fine, or the threat of a flogging, on any trader who enslaved a free Indian. And the new law made all future presents from the Indians to the colony the property of the public. The exchange of these presents, which from the Indians' perspective were the diplomatic requirement for trade, had become a large part of the governor's compensation. The new law established a licensing system to be overseen by a paid agent of the assembly, Nairne himself, who would take on the responsibility of addressing grievances between the Indians and traders and receive an annual salary of £250. The act empowered Nairne to hear evidence and to judge these cases, and it required him to live constantly among the Indians, traveling from one principal town to the next, wherever English traders resided.[17]

By June of the next year, Nairne's efforts as agent landed him in prison on charges of treason. According to his own petition to the Lords Proprietor, Nairne offended Governor Johnson by enforcing the law to the detriment of the governor's income, claiming for the public a present of a thousand skins that Johnson believed was his. Nairne also sought to free a group of Cherokees enslaved by traders who worked for Thomas Broughton, Johnson's son-in-law. Johnson imprisoned Nairne on charges of treason based on the testimony of two individuals that Nairne thought deeply suspect. One of these men, Hakes, was a "a perfect Lunatick," and Nairne had once arrested the other, an Indian trader named John Dixon who was also in Broughton's employ, for being caught in the act of buggering a dog. Janet Tibbs, a widow who once boarded Dixon, testified that he had even bragged about the act. We have Nairne's testimony alone regarding the character of these men, but regardless, they claimed to have heard Nairne declare Queen Anne an illegitimate pretender to the throne, and Johnson had thrown him in jail. Sixty-two of Nairne's supporters petitioned Johnson and the Lords Proprietor for Nairne's release, and he was even reelected to the assembly while in prison. But most assemblymen still feared Johnson. Nairne's friends posted bail, and he fled to England to defend his reputation.[18]

While languishing in prison, Nairne published his *Letter from South Carolina*, which promoted the colony and said not a word about the author's plight. In the guise of a "Swiss Gentleman" writing to a friend in Bern about the prosperous colony he had discovered, Nairne portrayed South Carolina as a budding plantation society. He offered detailed discussions of Carolina's agriculture, the production of pitch and tar, the herds of cattle, and the colony's extensive transatlantic commerce. But despite his deep involvement with the Indian trade, Nairne barely mentioned this important commerce. He understood the sophistication and power of the Indian peoples better than most, but he described them as "a primitive race of mankind" who lived off fruits and nuts. Nairne never described the Indian trade, nor did he name the Indian polities he knew so well. He acknowledged that Indians made up the majority of Carolina's population but also wrote that they were "subject" to the English.[19]

Nairne portrayed the Indians, along with many black slaves, as intrinsic to the defense strategy that had enabled the colony to prosper. Nairne wrote that Indians fought under the command of "*English* Officers" who could quickly raise them in the case of invasion. Whites in the colony, most of whom were planters, were particularly dexterous with firearms because of their constant hunting for game in the woods, and Nairne believed the well-trained militia of Carolina far superior to regular troops. Nairne also noted the inclusion in Carolina's militia of a "considerable number of active, able, Negro slaves," who were given their freedom if they killed one of the enemy. This military force had been quite effective in the recent war, when English forces, with their Indian allies, had utterly defeated the Spanish. The war had destroyed all Indians hostile to the English, and it had brought all others, within seven hundred miles of the colony, into alliance with the English. South Carolina was not a West Indian island besieged by its black majority; rather, South Carolina had integrated its Indians and slaves into an organic system of labor and defense.[20]

Nairne carefully explained the system of colonial governance: its governor and councils, its two legislatures, the passage of laws, its courts, even a presentation of the annual budget. Carolina differed from "those Countries where Slavery is fixed," by which he meant the enslavement of free men to arbitrary rulers. The laws bounded power so effectively in South Carolina that even the highest authorities obeyed. "Liberty is so well and legally established," wrote Nairne, that a "sense of freedom" reigned throughout the province.[21]

Nairne's own experience with Governor Johnson hardly demonstrated this rosy sketch of governance. Nevertheless, he portrayed a free society for white men worthy of their investment. The man who sought to establish himself with "comfort and decency" needed capital of £150 to establish an estate in South Carolina. Two black slaves at £40 a piece would be the principal investment, as well as tools, a canoe, animals, and provisions for a year; aside from the survey fee, the land was essentially free. With a capital outlay of £1500, wealthier migrants could establish an estate that generated £300 a year. Thirty black slaves, fifteen men and fifteen women, represented 80 percent of the suggested investment and proportionately more animals and tools. To be sure, Carolina had "many who settle without any slaves at all," but in the colony Nairne described, prosperity came through slaveholding.[22]

Nairne wrote with the exuberance of a promoter, but he was not far from the mark. The commercial development of Charles Town fostered the accumulation of capital in colonial merchant houses that fueled the expansion of the plantation economy. In 1701, for example, Edward Hyrne of Norfolk, England, "found credit" in Charles Town to purchase a plantation of 2,550 acres, with 200 acres cleared for £1,000. It had 150 head of cattle, four horses, an enslaved Indian boy, some hogs, and a brick house. His creditors, who must have been local, demanded no money up front and accepted payment in Carolina currency. Hyrne owed £500 after his first year of possession, and another £500 after the second year. He also bought a skilled black slave, a cooper to barrel his meat, with only £10 down and the remainder of £50 not due for twelve months. According to his own estimations, Hyrne could pay off all his debts and make "great sumes of money" off his plantation if only he could purchase "a good stock of slaves." While Hyrne returned to England, three of his sons, Edward, Burrell, and Henry Jr., became successful planters and members of the Carolinian elite who served the colonial government in various capacities until the American Revolution.[23]

The Hyrne family gained its footing and rose in stature by riding the expansion of the plantation economy. Exports of provisions, naval stores, and pelts continued, but the level of rice production rose dramatically. The Charles Town merchants exported three hundred tons in 1702, and within seven years rice production had more than doubled; by 1713 production had doubled again. Driving such exponential growth was the development of a transatlantic slave trade directly with Africa. The Lords of Trade broke the monopoly of the Royal African Company in 1698, which opened the trade to independent slavers willing to service the smaller colonial markets such as Charles Town. The following year Royal African Company officials observed a Carolinian ship in the Gambia River, and Captain William Rhett of the *Providence* brought what may have been the first shipment of Africans directly to Charles Town.[24]

There were probably more slavers after Rhett in subsequent years, but the first fully documented slaving voyage arrived in Charles Town in 1710. The men who opened South Carolina's transatlantic slave trade were experienced merchants who had cut their teeth on the slave trade to the Caribbean. In 1709 the London merchants Daniel Jamineau and James Berdoe bought a sloop, the *Loyall Johnson*, hired Captain Zebulon Carter, and began to acquire the trading goods that Carter would need to purchase slaves for the Charles Town market. Carter had been to Africa at least once before when he captained the *Ruby* in 1700. He had loaded 132 enslaved Africans into the *Ruby*'s hold—where in Africa the records do not say—and brought them to Jamaica; 14 died in the middle passage. The *Loyall Johnson* was a bigger ship, for Carter bought 202 enslaved Africans for the voyage to Carolina; 22 died. According to Nairne's figures, the *Loyall Johnson* would have generated revenue of about £4,800 sterling.[25]

Such revenue might not have actually turned a profit, for neither Jamineau nor Berdoe ever again sponsored a voyage to Carolina. These men had been investing in transatlantic slaving since 1698 when the trade first opened, and they had joined together in at least a dozen voyages before the *Loyall Johnson*. Jamineau was by far the more active investor. He had supplied the Royal African Company with beads and cowries for company voyages, and he had put capital behind fifty slaving voyages before the *Loyall Johnson*. He focused on the Caribbean markets in Jamaica, Barbados, and Antigua until about 1705, when he began to invest almost solely in slaving voyages to the Chesapeake markets in Maryland and Virginia. The voyage of the *Loyall Johnson*, then, represents the joint venture of men who were well versed in the opportunities and risks involved in the transatlantic slave trade.[26]

The Charles Town slave market nevertheless attracted further investment. Slavers working out of Bristol sponsored the *Union Sloop* in 1711, which brought Africans from the Gold Coast, and the *Morning Star* in 1713, whose African destination is unknown. Another London slaver arrived from the Gambia in 1714, and in August 1715, the *Sylvia Galley*, captained by John Vennard Jr., also arrived from the Gambia, with 150 enslaved Africans. Vennard's voyage holds particular interest because of its owner, George Barons. Of a merchant family from Exeter, Barons based his operation in Rotterdam in the early 1700s while his brother Samuel established himself in London. Their nephew Richard Splatt migrated to Charles Town around the same time, and in 1720 an official at Whitehall identified Splatt as "ye most considerable merc[hant] in Carolina," and "his unkle" Samuel as the "most considerable trader to Carolina."[27]

The *Sylvia Galley* appears to have been their first investment in the transatlantic slave trade. The ship departed Dartmouth, England, in September 1714 and went first to Rotterdam, where it loaded a cargo of wrought pewter. The ship arrived at the Gambia River in late October and probably traded its pewter with other European slavers for the necessary assortment of trading goods. By August 1715 the ship had returned to Dartmouth with a cargo of rice, ivory, and beaver skins, all of which were reexported to George Barons in Rotterdam. Carolinian goods and the Charles Town market had become fully integrated into the Atlantic world of commerce, a process that drew almost eight hundred Africans into Charles Town and slavery, in just six years.[28]

These captives arrived in a brutal place. The physical violence of enslavement evident in the slaving raids against the Indians had its counterpart in day-to-day life on the plantations. As the English colonist Mary Stafford observed, a settler who could "get a few slaves and beat them well" could make a decent living in South Carolina. The Anglican missionary Dr. Francis Le Jau, who sought to convert both Indians and Africans, wrote with frustration that whites in South Carolina were "generally like those of the West Indies." He had very little cooperation from slaveholders in his missionary efforts—indeed, he found that some whites did not even acknowledge the distinction between "Slaves and free Indians, and Beasts." One master had burned a slave woman to death because he believed she had set fire to his house. Another had invented a cruel coffin-like machine to punish runaways. It slowly crushed the body with a lid clamped to the torso while the victim's feet were tightly chained outside the box. The man typically kept his victims in this contraption for twenty-four hours.[29]

But cruelties against enslaved people were not limited to the actions of a handful of exceptionally abusive men. Rather, the system of violent control found legitimacy in a revision of South Carolina's comprehensive slave code, passed in June 1712.[30] Revision of the law stemmed from the apparent inadequacy of previous slave law, despite its brutality, to manage the resistance of the growing number of African and Indian slaves brought into the colony. The exploits of one particular rebel named Sebastien seem to have precipitated the assembly's action. In June 1711 the assembly offered a reward of fifty pounds for Sebastien's capture, dead or alive. Identified as "the Spanish, or Hidling's Negroe" at one point, and as "the Spanish Indian" at another, Sebastien's ambiguous identification speaks to the racialization of both Africans and Indians enslaved by the English. He had been at large from his plantation for forty days; he had committed arson and murder; and his exploits left the colonists with a sense of dread that stemmed from the "insolence of the Negroes."[31]

South Carolina's revised Act for the Better Ordering and Governing of Negroes and Slaves marked the ongoing effort by the assembly to define with greater precision the appropriate behaviors of masters toward their recalcitrant slaves. Legislators borrowed many of the new law's provisions from the Barbados Act for the Governing of Negroes, passed in 1688, but several clauses dealt quite specifically with forms of resistance particular to South Carolina. Despite the ambiguity of his appearance, Sebastien was clearly Spanish, and a new array of laws attempted to limit what must have been a steady flow of runaways to Spanish Saint Augustine. Some whites in the colony were known to assist slaves who sought freedom in the Spanish territory. The Slave Act of 1712 declared the tempting of slaves with freedom to be a felony, subject to execution. If a white were caught speaking to a slave on the subject of escape, he or she would be fined twenty-five pounds; if caught aiding in the act of escape, said white could be executed. The Barbados law also contained this provision, but it penalized such a crime with a fine, not the threat of execution.[32]

Carolinian legislators broke new ground in the torture of runaways. The new law doubled the reward for slave catchers and made even harsher the series of punishments meted out to slaves who continued to escape. The 1696 law had codified three degrees of punishment for runaways who stayed away for twenty days, but in 1712 the assembly created two additional degrees of torture. The law made the first punishment a severe and public flogging rather than branding, which became the second punishment. If an enslaved woman ran away a third and fourth time, she would again be flogged, branded again, and have both of her ears sliced off. If a man, he would be flogged, branded, lose one ear, and suffer castration. Legislators even imagined that recaptured fugitives—men or women—might run away a fifth time, despite such debilitating tortures. In such a case the law prescribed the slicing of the Achilles tendon of the slave who refused to remain on the plantation regardless of the consequences. Such atrocious legal prescriptions do not come from a vacuum; Carolina's slaves were running away.[33]

The new law prescribed similar punishments for slaves who stole property worth as little as twelve pence, a law borrowed from Barbados. The sight of cropped ears, slit noses, branded cheeks, and scarred backs must not have been uncommon. Slaveholders were held responsible to pay for the execution of all these punishments, and in the case of a slave's death, the master would be financially compensated by the public, the amount to be determined by the judgment of his or her slaveholding peers, who were often generous. An additional act that amended the slave code just two years later noted that the public treasury had been "very much exhausted by the extraordinary sums" that slaveholders had granted to their peers in compensation for the execution of criminal slaves. The amendment limited further compensation to fifty pounds and made transportation the punishment for slaves convicted of all capital crimes with the exception of murder.[34]

The new slave law also drew attention to the emergence of practices that seem to have become customary. Some masters had begun to allow their slaves to work on their own account. They could labor on the docks or in a planter's field, or they could use particular skills like carpentry or cooperage. No power controlled these slaves other than the agreed-on payment schedule established between the master and the slave. Legislators worried that such practices led slaves to seek out "opportunities to steal," not only to pay their masters but also to support their companions "in drunkenness and other evil courses." Masters had also begun to allow their slaves to plant corn, peas, and rice "for themselves," and to keep poultry and livestock on their own account. The practice of allowing slaves their "own time," as well as land to plant for themselves, became the norm in many Atlantic slave societies. In South Carolina, the creation of such slave-controlled provision grounds became the counterpart to the task system of work on the rice plantations, which emerged early in the eighteenth century. Connected to these developments was the emergence of the "black" market in Charles Town on Sundays—the slaves' customary day of rest—when slaves were allowed to sell the surplus from their grounds. The law of 1712 observed this development with great trepidation, noting that "great numbers of slaves" went to Charles Town on Sundays "to drink, quarrel, fight, curse and swear, and profane the Sabbath." These slaves carried clubs and "other mischievous weapons," which the assembly rightly feared could be used for "wicked designs."[35]

In order to ease their own financial burdens, individual masters had begun to allow their slaves greater autonomy to take care of themselves. But the assembly had come to see the liberty of movement that resulted from these practices as dangerous. The new law sought to curb these developments with fines for masters who allowed their slaves these freedoms, and it empowered the constables of Charles Town to establish a special patrol to stop the dangerous congregation of slaves on Sundays. Customary relations had evolved between masters and slaves that subtly acknowledged the slaves' humanity and their need for some time and means to take care of themselves and their families. But when embodied in the House of Assembly, slaveholders as a political class created the means to suppress enslaved people's aspirations. The laws reveal both a customary loosening in the management of slaves and a hardening of the legal apparatus for slave control in the context of intensified rice production.

During the same years the Lowcountry slave society developed and grew, the Indian traders of the colony intensified their involvement in wars of slaving with and against their Indian neighbors. Slaving expeditions departed Charles Town to the west in alliance with the Creeks, and to the north in alliance with the Yamasee. The traders marched back from these wars with coffles of Indian slaves sometimes numbering in the thousands. The Charles Town slave market thrived. Rice planters bought some of these captives, but most found themselves in the holds of merchant ships headed to Britain's colonies to the north or out into the Caribbean.[36]

Le Jau, who had lived in the colony for about five years, wrote to his superiors regarding the various and horrid forms that slavery took in Carolina. In February 1712 he wrote that the "Barberous usage of the poor Slaves" had brought God's wrath on the colony in the form of a deadly sickness that had taken the lives of two hundred whites and twice as many slaves. He wrote specifically of the bodily mutilations promulgated by the Slave Act of 1712, which he had opposed "with all [his] might." Le Jau argued that these measures violated the laws of God, Exodus 21 in particular, which ordained that a slave ought to be set free if he loses an eye or a tooth. The assembly had ordered the opposite.[37]

Le Jau's reflections brought him from these outrages to the enslavement of Indians. A trader had just arrived in Charles Town with a coffle of one hundred Indian slaves, victims of an expedition against the Tuscarora to the north. Le Jau despaired of these "Melancholy Affaires." He hoped these people might find Christian charity, but what he had seen foreshadowed terror. When Le Jau looked out into the pews on Sundays, he saw thirty blacks to one Indian. And the free Indians who lived near the English settlements "goe their own way and bring their Children" with them; they had no interest in "Conversation among us." Le Jau thought he saw "something cloudy in their looks, an argument," he feared, "of discontent."[38]

The slave society had grown, and Le Jau thought its evil had deepened. He believed the planters had become "more Cruel . . . of late Dayes than before." They would "hamstring, maim, and unlimb" the slaves for "small faults." He wrote of an enslaved man in his district who had dropped a parcel of rice and suffered terrible beatings as punishment. The man's suffering became so dire that he procured a knife from a child and took his own life. Le Jau had learned of the slave conspiracy in New York, which he supposed the savage law of 1712 was designed to deflect, but in January 1714 he reported on a conspiracy planned for the Christmas holiday among the slaves in Goose Creek. More than a dozen were implicated; one rebel had been executed and two others "severely chastised." Le Jau hoped the frightful episode might inspire "Serious Reflections" among the colonists, "upon the Judgments wch our Sins . . . bring down upon our heads from time to time."[39]

Misery on the plantations mirrored suffering in Indian country. The Act for Regulating the Indian Trade had been crafted to end abuse and wrongful enslavement, but Indian complaints reveal its utter failure. On September 21, 1710, a delegation of Apalachee appeared with horror stories of enslavement and brutality carried out by the traders. Six Indians—Ventusa and his wife, Massoney, Diego, Wansella (an Ellecombe Indian), and Coloose—protested their wrongful enslavement by Carolinian traders. The trader John Musgrove had threatened the people of Assapallago that he would beat them if they did not hoe his corn. Another trader named Jess Crossley had become so jealous of an Indian woman and her suitor that he had beaten the man "in a barbarous manner." And the trader Phillip Gilliard, who had enslaved Ventusa and his wife, had raped another Indian woman and "cruelly whipped her."[40]

The following July a delegation of Yamasee appeared before the board to complain that the traders continued to sell rum. Addiction had spread, and many Indians had amassed considerable debts. Yamasee leaders considered these "rum debts" illegitimate and demanded that they be forgiven. The commissioners agreed, but they acknowledged their inability to enforce the law. The traders could not be stopped from bringing rum. The chiefs must convince their people not to buy it, and Indians should avoid falling into debt. The chiefs declared that they would soon go to war, and go hunting, in order to pay their debts to the traders, but they had one last complaint. Six white men—Thomas Jones, John Whitehead, Joseph Bryan, Robert Steale, John Palmer, and Barnaby Bull—had established plantations on land that stood within "the Limits" of the Yamasee domain established by law in 1708. The Yamasee protested these encroachments, but in June of the next year, when they returned to the board, they remained unsatisfied.[41]

The traders acted like masters among slaves, especially the new agent charged with enforcing the law, John Wright. A political opponent of Nairne and a litigious moneylender, Wright sought the post of agent for its financial benefits. According to David Crawley, a Virginian who had traded in the same Indian towns, Wright traveled with an entourage of servants "to wait on" him, as well as porters to carry his luggage and his packs of skins. Crawley believed this was "purely out of ostentation," an example of the arrogance among the traders that lent itself to theft and violence. When living among the Indians during the season of trade, the Carolinian traders would kill the Indians' hogs and fowl; gather and eat their corn and peas; or go "into their watermillion grounds" without asking any leave of the owner. And when the owner of the taken goods demanded pay, the traders gave "not half the value." If the Indian "grumbled, or seem discontented," he or she would be beaten "very cruelly." Likewise, the young Indian men who worked as porters for the traders, carrying huge packs of skins along forest trails, were beaten if they complained and just as often were cheated of their pay. Worst of all, the traders raped Indian women. They would approach the women and demand their bodies, and when the women refused to consent, the traders had "proceeded so far as to force them."[42]

On the morning of Good Friday, April 15, 1715, the day Christians remember the killing of Christ by the Romans, Yamasee men who had debated their connection to the Carolinians all night decided on war, which they initiated with the public and brutal assassination of the Englishmen sent to speak with them, Nairne and Wright. The old rivals were taken from their beds that morning, probably tortured, and burned to death.[43]

Nairne and Wright had been sent to meet with the Yamasee only three days earlier, after a meeting of the Board of Commissioners heard from two traders who had returned from backcountry journeys with alarming news. Samuel Warner, who came from the Palachocola towns, had learned that the Creeks were quite vexed with the English traders; that Creek protests had been ignored; and that they would "down with them" upon the next provocation. William Bray, who had a Yamasee wife, learned from his wife's kinsman that the Creeks would soon "cut off" the traders and then "fall on the Settlement." Bray had been chasing runaway slaves on their way to Saint Augustine, but he quickly returned to Charles Town to relay the worrisome news. The Board of Commissioners sent Nairne and Wright directly to Pocataligo, the main Yamasee town, so that all the Yamasee factions might be heard and, hopefully, the danger of war might be averted.[44]

Nairne delivered the commissioners' message of reconciliation, but Wright had been defensive and threatening. According to a Yamasee account, Wright threatened "to hang four of their head men and take all the rest of them for Slaves." Wright's threat of retribution did not convince all the Yamasee, but enough were outraged to begin the bloodshed. And the Yamasee did not act alone. Over the next week, at least ninety of the one hundred Carolinian traders resident in the Indian towns were assassinated by their hosts. One trader in Pocataligo, Seymour Burroughs, survived the initial attack, despite being shot, and made his way to the Port Royal settlement to warn the colonists there. His was a desperate escape, and fortunately for the colonists, a merchant ship in the harbor provided safe haven for the hundreds who fled the Yamasee army that soon arrived. A war had begun that would nearly destroy the colony.[45]

The plantations of Carolina were spread thin over the lands around Charles Town, and some were quite near to the Yamasee towns. As news of the assassinations spread, colonists began to flee into Charles Town, which quickly filled with terrified people. The governor and the militia captains began to raise parties of men to fight, and the assembly met in early May to declare martial law and allocate funds to raise troops. The assembly granted the governor and militia captains the power to seize the materiel of war. Horses, slaves, arms, ammunition, ships, and "all other necessaries" could be pressed into the service of defense; all inhabitants could be pressed into service as well. The text of the act to "raise Forces to carry on the War against Indian Enemies" has not survived, but Le Jau described "good partyes of Men, White, Indians, and Negroes" in battle against the Yamasee under Colonel John Barnwell and Colonel Mackey.[46]

The first published account of the war appeared in the *Boston News* on June 13, 1715. It recounted the assassinations, the early military engagements, and the loss of forty white men. In July a delegation of planters and merchants invested in the colony appeared before the Lords of Trade to testify to Carolina's plight. The colony did not have more than 1,500 men who could bear arms, and they were already surrounded by the enemy. Large skirmishes were few, but colonists who ventured beyond Charles Town were at great risk of attack from small parties of Indians. The colonists needed armed men to assist in their defense, and they could not afford to either pay them or feed them. The Indians had so destroyed the country that the planters could not sow rice that year. The delegation hoped that Carolina could "immediately" come under His Majesty's protection, and that the Lords Proprietor would surrender the government to the Crown.[47]

The proprietors were unwilling to contribute much. A cargo of rice from the previous crop had lately arrived in London, and the proprietors offered the proceeds of its sale to defray the costs of assistance, but they "absolutely refuse either to mortgage their charter or surrender their Government to His Majesty," unless His Majesty was willing to pay. Assistance had begun to arrive from Virginia and North Carolina, including men, materiel, and provisions, but a letter written in Charles Town while the Lords Proprietor argued revealed a situation that had become far more dire. The Apalachee and the Creeks had traveled down the warpaths, burning crops and plantations as they went. The assembly had sent an expedition to the Cherokee to enlist their aid, but it had not borne fruit and the future remained uncertain.[48]

The multiracial military force established by the colony fought well, for by October 1715 at least two observers declared that major fighting had ceased. The Yamasee had moved, in both geography and politics, toward the Spanish in Saint Augustine, who not only welcomed them but also sponsored the occasional forays of small Yamasee parties into the English colony to make the planters feel their pain. John Tate wrote that Carolinian scouts were "daily shott down without ever seeing an enemy," and Le Jau knew "30 good men" already killed in raids that had "carryd their children away." The reverend believed he was "16 or 20 miles away" from the Yamasee camps, and he described a life of perpetual fear.[49]

The explosive rounds of massive violence may have ended, but the raids continued. A "Memorial" from the colony's agents penned in December 1716 charged the Yamasee with "continually murthering & enslaving the inhabitants" of South Carolina and plundering their slaves and cattle. The agents charged the Spanish with "openly" purchasing these stolen goods from the returning Yamasee parties and "plentifully" providing the Yamasee with "arms, ammunition, and provisions." Two months later, a "humble address"—a massive document signed by the Speaker of the Assembly, twenty-three members of the House, and 565 inhabitants—begged the Crown to take the colony under its "gracious protection." The colonists were desperate. "Numerous families" had been ruined and were leaving the province. The signatories, a diverse group that included elite planters like the Moores, the Izards, and the Bees, as well as Le Jau and the weaver Joseph Scott, "earnestly and fervently" asked to be governed directly by the Crown. They sought only to be saved "from Ruin."[50]

At least four hundred white colonists were killed during the Yamasee War, and the Lord Proprietors' failure to provide sustenance in this moment of severe need contributed powerfully to the Revolution of 1719 that ended the reign of their careless authority. The movement to break from the proprietors sprung from multiple causes, but the devastation wrought by the war was crucial. In December 1719, when rumors spread that the Spanish would again attack Charles Town, leading colonists demanded that Governor Robert Johnson

(Nathaniel's son) step down. Johnson refused, and the colony came very close to civil conflict. But the Spanish did not attack, bloodshed was avoided, and the proprietors entered negotiations with the Crown to buy their shares of the colony. In 1729, South Carolina joined the British Empire as a colony governed directly by the Crown.[51]

The war had devastated the land, and the colonists desperately sought to rebuild. The plantations south of Charles Town, which held the largest stocks of cattle and hogs, had been utterly destroyed and most of their inhabitants had fled. The rice crops of 1716 and 1717 were half of what they had been before the war. And while the Indian trade would return to South Carolina, it would be dramatically restructured. The Charles Town deerskin trade began to expand again in the 1720s, and deerskins would be an important export throughout the colonial period. But slaving ended, at least in the lands that became the Old South. A small number of Indian slaves continued to work on South Carolinian plantations, but their numbers diminished as the lucrative slaving raids of past generations were over. Only the Cherokee would revive a friendship with the colony, and they had rarely slaved.[52]

Rebuilding the colonial economy meant further investments in the transatlantic slave trade, for the colonists badly needed labor. On September 13, 1716, the *Ludlow Galley* sailed out of London's harbor with a hold filled with trading goods for the West African coast, destined, its owner hoped, for Charles Town. Samuel Barons, who knew the Carolina market better than anyone, was the sole investor in this voyage, and the captain, Arthur Lone, had slaved at least twice before, bringing Africans to Barbados in 1713 and 1715. The *Ludlow Galley* embarked from London about a year after the major fighting in South Carolina had ended. Barons knew that he would find in Charles Town a ready market for African slaves, but he instructed Lone to drop anchor off the bar that stretched across Charles Town's harbor and send for news of the state of the market before he proceeded. Richard Splatt could be depended on to give accurate information. Lone must have received good news, for he sold 218 people to the merchants of Charles Town. The loss of life on board the ship is sobering: 54 died on the middle passage.[53]

These fifty-four people were only the first to die in the effort to restore Carolina's plantation economy. Five slavers arrived from West Africa in 1717; six arrived during the next year; and by the end of 1725 twenty-eight British slavers with designs on Carolina had purchased almost 4,700 Africans along the slaving coasts of West Africa. We know the African slaving regions for nine of these voyages; at least four did their slaving along the Gambia River, a region known to Carolinians for the rice-growing peoples that lived there. Ten of these ships came from London, seven from Bristol, one from New York, and one from Charles Town itself. The Royal African Company outfitted just two of these voyages; the rest drew from the private capital of just twenty men. The Jefferis brothers of Bristol—William, Richard, and Joseph—had sent their first slaver to Charles Town in 1713; they sent twelve more during the years of rebuilding. The Lougher brothers, Richard and Walter, also of Bristol, invested in six voyages to South Carolina (about 15 percent of their total slaving endeavors). But of the 4,700 enslaved Africans bought with the money of these men, only 3,800 survived the middle passage to Charles Town.[54]

The Africans who disembarked in Charles Town during these years entered a colony bustling with activity. Governor Johnson reported in 1719 that five hundred white migrants had recently settled in South Carolina, and by 1724 there were fourteen thousand white people in the colony. Pitch and tar operations were relatively easy to restart, and imperial bounties for these products fostered development and brought much-needed cash into the colony. The rice planters were able to plant widely in 1718, which nearly doubled rice exports in 1719 and brought production levels past their prewar height. By 1730 rice production would triple. The volume of the transatlantic slave trade expanded simultaneously. In 1726 the London slaver Samuel Wragg, who had been trading in the colony for twenty years, testified before the Board of Trade that the merchants of Charles Town imported about one thousand Africans yearly, a number supported by modern research. By the mid-1730s the Charles Town merchants imported more than three thousand Africans every year, and by 1739 the colony contained almost forty thousand Africans, whose enslavement was enforced by half as many whites.[55]

These Africans disembarked from the slavers to be sold to ambitious colonists who had developed a brutal system of governing slaves. Most enslaved arrivals were men, though there were certainly women and children among them. Forced to rebuild the plantations, to clear more forest, and to plant and reap the fields of corn and rice, these people entered a rapidly growing black society that bore a grueling enslavement. But in the little African villages that popped up on each plantation, they met black people and a few Indians who had been enslaved in the colony for some time, and these people understood the tactics of survival.

The means of surviving enslavement ranged from efforts to build up a little property to ease the forced poverty of slavery, to more desperate efforts to escape Carolina altogether by fleeing to Saint Augustine. These strategies were linked, for one needed material resources and available routes to survive the long trek to Saint Augustine. The brutal law of 1712 had attempted to curb slave autonomy and the southward flow of runaways, but the Yamasee alliance with the Carolina colony had probably been more important. Carolina's Indian allies were in the business of selling slaves, and whether those enslaved were Indians captured in war or runaway Africans would not have made a difference. With the exception of the exploits of the Spanish Sebastien and the law he inspired, there are no documented accounts of successful escapes to Saint Augustine between 1688 and 1715. The war changed everything.[56]

Carolinians claimed that during the fighting in 1715, at least ninety-eight "negroe and Indian slaves [were] taken" and "carried" to Saint Augustine. It is unlikely that the Yamasee captured these people and brought them to the Spanish to sell as slaves. Rather, these Carolinian slaves willfully joined Yamasee warriors who would lead them south because they believed the Spanish would free them. Old-timers around the slave quarter campfires or at the Sunday markets in Charles Town knew the long-standing policy of the Spanish in Florida, and it is not hard to imagine tales told of the valiant efforts to escape there. The Yamasee War transformed the political landscape of resistance by generating a loose allegiance between the enslaved blacks who hated the plantations and the Yamasee warriors who hated the Carolinians.[57]

In March 1718, Carolina assemblymen James Cochran and Jonathan Drake wrote to the proprietors that the Spanish continued to foster Indian animosity against the colony, and that they had accepted many more runaway slaves into their colony. When pressed to return them by the Carolinian government, Spanish authorities claimed that the slaves had "turned Christians" and they could not "deliver them without the King's Order." About a year later, a Yamasee raid killed a white colonist named Tanner and his white servant, and twelve black slaves accompanied the raiders back to Saint Augustine. Then, in the spring of 1720, a group of at least fourteen enslaved men on the Ponds estate developed a "wicked and barbarous plott" to raise a rebellion, kill all the whites, and march on Charles Town. When their plans failed, the rebels sought out an Indian guide to lead them to Saint Augustine. But the man they approached was a Creek whose town was then at war with the Yamasee, and he refused to help them. Creeks and Yamasee spoke the same language and the black rebels may have mistook one for the other, but they had good reason to expect Indian aid. The rebels were later found by a patrol in a "half-starved" condition. The patrolmen brought them down to Charles Town, where some were "burnt, some hang'd, and some banish'd."[58]

Much like the assembly's response to Sebastien in 1712, the First Royal Assembly of 1722 responded to the threat of organized slave resistance with another revision of its comprehensive slave code. These men represented the first generation of colonists to come of age in South Carolina. Almost half had been born in the colony, and most of the others had arrived by 1700. Half of them served as militia officers, and all of them were either planters or heavily invested in land; less than a third were involved in the Indian trade. On average, these men had served in public office for ten years. The Slave Act of 1722 represented the collective wisdom of men long accustomed to and deeply invested in the management of slaves.[59]

Instead of inventing ever more draconian tortures to terrify their slaves into submission, the planter-legislators of 1722 embraced a subtler approach to governance that sought a better balance between the carrot and the stick. The brutal mutilations of serial runaways that the assembly had intensified from 1696 to 1712 were now omitted entirely. Of course, runaways were still flogged, the patrols rode, tickets were required, and there were rewards for slave catchers. The law still prescribed execution for slaves who joined an insurrection, had numerous fisticuffs with whites, or sought to escape to Saint Augustine. But the new slave laws no longer required the beastly slicing of black people who continued to run away.[60]

And for the first time, the law codified the responsibilities of masters toward their slaves. Numerous slaves "under pretense of hunger," the assembly asks us to believe, had begun to steal food, and under previous law such offenses brought execution. The law of 1722 replaced death with branding and flogging for the first two thefts, followed by execution for the third. But the assembly also ordered justices of the peace to investigate any plantation suspected of failing to provide adequate food for the slaves. The fine for planters who did not feed their slaves was small, but while Barbados and Jamaica had passed such legislation in the seventeenth century, the South Carolina Assembly had not done so until now.[61]

The most novel proscription of the new law regarded horses. Some slaves had amassed the wherewithal to carry on the "keeping and breeding of horses," and they had used these animals to "convey intelligences from one part of the country to another," fostering the insurrections that plagued the colony. The law's language suggests that more insurrections had occurred than that of the spring of 1720. The law ordered every justice of the peace in the colony to inquire about the keeping of horses by slaves, and to seize and sell said horses, the proceeds to go to the churchwardens for the benefit of the white poor.[62]

But the law aimed deeper than communication and travel; it sought to curtail the property of slaves. In addition to horses, justices were also empowered to seize any hogs, cattle, or boats held by slaves and likewise sell them. The most industrious slaves had not only eked out surpluses from their provision grounds to bring to the Charles Town market, they had also built up small herds that could grow, as well as horses and boats to travel and bring goods to market. Presentments of the grand jury of the province from a decade later illustrate the prowess of enslaved marketers within the internal economy of Charles Town. They cornered the markets for corn, peas, and poultry by waiting "Night and Day" on the wharves for the small trading boats with provisions from the countryside. They would "buy up" all the essentials of life and sell them to town residents at an "exorbitant Price." A presentment from 1737 complained that slave hucksters would go in "boats and canoes up the country trading with Negroes in a clandestine manner." When the Assembly of 1735 revised the slave code again, its only revisions focused on the slaves' economy, with new regulations on the clothing slaves could wear and a prohibition of "houses of entertainment or trade" operated by slaves. Individual masters had allowed an expansion of mobility and endeavor, and some black Carolinians had been able to carve out a corner of the economy to better their economic condition. But when embodied as a political class, the planter-legislators of the House of Assembly passed laws to curtail these freedoms.[63]

Last, the new law of 1722 limited the rights of black people who had somehow secured their freedom. The 1696 slave law had recognized the rights of slaveholders to manumit a slave for extraordinary service, but it happened seldom. South Carolina's Act for Enlisting Trusty Slaves (1708) granted freedom to slave soldiers who killed an enemy during war, and perhaps this fostered the emergence of a free black population. The law of 1712 compelled free blacks to prove their status before the governor and council of the colony, and the law of 1722 shifted this responsibility to the justices of the court in Charles Town. But the assembly went further in 1722, ordering any master who freed a slave to make provision that said free person leave the colony within twelve months. Failure to do so would result in reenslavement, now codified as the natural status of black people.[64]

The planters had begun to adjust their mode of governance, but almost simultaneously, the Spanish intensified their efforts to undermine the English colony. In February 1723, Governor Francis Nicholson protested to Governor Antonio de Benavides of Saint Augustine that the Yamasee war chief Cherekeeleechee had led a raid

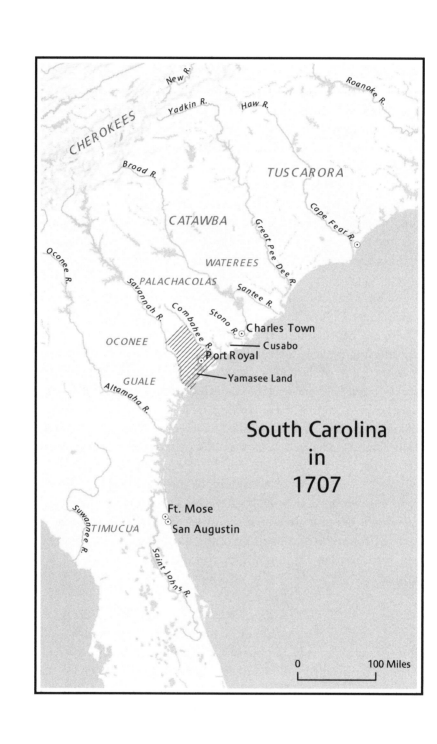

CHEROKEES

New R.

Yadkin R.

Haw R.

Roanoke R.

TUSCARORA

Broad R.

Cape Fear R. ⊙

CATAWBA

Great Pee Dee R.

Oconee R.

WATEREES

PALACHACOLAS

Santee R.

Savannah R.

Combahee R.

Stono R. ⊙

Charles Town

OCONEE

Cusabo

Port Royal ⊙

Yamasee Land

GUALE

Altamaha R.

South Carolina
in
1707

Suwannee R.

Ft. Mose

TIMUCUA

⊙ San Augustin

Saint Johns R.

0   100 Miles

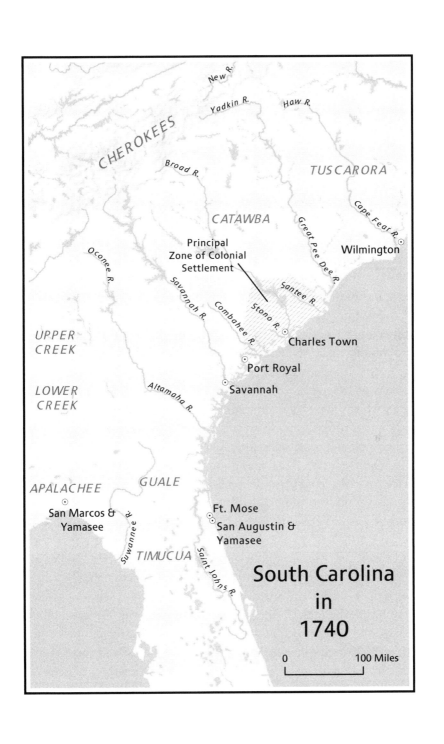

New R.

Yadkin R.

Haw R.

CHEROKEES

TUSCARORA

Broad R.

Cape Fear R.

CATAWBA

Wilmington

Oconee R.

Principal
Zone of Colonial
Settlement

Great Pee Dee R.

Santee R.

Savannah R.

Stono R.

UPPER
CREEK

Combahee R.

Charles Town

Port Royal

LOWER
CREEK

Altamaha R.

Savannah

APALACHEE

GUALE

San Marcos &
Yamasee

Suwannee R.

Ft. Mose

San Augustin &
Yamasee

TIMUCUA

Saint Johns R.

South Carolina
in
1740

0   100 Miles

into Carolina, killed several whites, and brought a black slave to Saint Augustine that Benavides himself had accepted as a gift. Nicholson wrote that many other Carolinian runaways were known to be in Saint Augustine, and he demanded they be returned. They were not returned; indeed, during the following year ten more Africans survived the escape from Carolina with the assistance of English-speaking Yamasee. Two more groups of runaways arrived in Saint Augustine in March 1725, and in May John Bull petitioned the South Carolina House of Assembly that several of his slaves had escaped to Saint Augustine.[65]

In September 1726, a small party of seven Yamasee raided John Edwards's plantation on the Combahee River, murdered him, and returned to Saint Augustine with four black slaves and all of his valuables. In July of the next year, a group of Carolina Indian traders traveling up the Savannah River were attacked by a much larger party of thirty-four Indians, twenty-seven of whom were Yamasee. Several colonists were killed, but three men—John and William Gray and another man named Beans—were captured and imprisoned in the castle in Saint Augustine. While imprisoned, they learned that Governor Benavides offered bounties of thirty pieces of eight for every white scalp and a hundred pieces of eight for every black slave. Carolinian officials supposed that these black slaves were then sold in Havana, and some undoubtedly were.[66]

In October 1727, Benavides fit out a schooner with Spaniards and black fugitives from Carolina for another raid. They sailed north up the coast and into the Edisto River, where they sacked the plantation of David Ferguson and carried away seven more slaves. The South Carolina House of Assembly responded in August 1728 with an expedition of seventy-nine white men and about ninety Indian allies, led by Colonel John Palmer. The Yamasee had established their town right outside the Spanish castle, but through a series of "secret marches in the night," Palmer's men ambushed the Yamasee, killed thirty, and took fifteen prisoners. Because of the formal peace between Britain and Spain, Palmer's men did not attack the Spanish fort, but in October 1733, in Madrid, the Crown issued two *cédulas* that prohibited compensation to Carolina colonists whose slaves escaped to Spanish territory, reiterated the offer of freedom to Carolinian slaves, and commended a company of black fugitives who had fought alongside the Yamasee in defense of their town. News of these events spread through the growing black villages of the Carolina Lowcountry, burnishing Saint Augustine's reputation as a place of refuge in this new world of slavery.[67]

On April 21, 1738, Governor William Bull heard the testimony of one James Howell, a merchant who had been carrying on a trade between Charles Town and Saint Augustine for the past five years. On his most recent voyage, Spanish authorities had detained Howell after he had sold his wares. He remained in Saint Augustine for three months and witnessed several developments that illustrated Spanish designs. A flotilla of thirty-seven vessels arrived while he was there, and he learned from a Spanish captain that they were intended for an attack on Georgia. The garrison in Saint Augustine was also much larger than usual, 1,500 men rather than the 500 he usually saw there, and 200 Florida Indians had arrived from Cape Florida. Last, he had heard a proclamation by the Governor Manuel de Montiano "that all Negroes who did, or should hereafter, run away from the English, should be made free." Howell reported that the proclamation had an immediate effect. Then in the colony were some Carolina runaways who had been sold to Spanish masters; the blacks were immediately "made free and the Purchasers lost their Money."[68]

News of Spanish doings prompted action both in the House of Assembly and in the African quarters of the plantations. The assembly began to debate a new law on the "further security and better Defense" of the colony, and in September 1738 it decided that it could no longer countenance the arming of slaves in the case of an invasion. South Carolina had always turned to the slaves for protection, but times had changed. Outside Port Royal, nineteen slaves from the plantation of Caleb Davis and at least fifty others from neighboring plantations, including women and children, undertook the southward trek to Saint Augustine. Davis followed and found them there, but Governor Montiano refused to give them up. Another contingent of slaves escaped from Granville County in February. One report from the new colony of Georgia noted that so many runaways passed through Savannah on their way south that there were hardly any hogs left; they had all been stolen and presumably eaten.[69]

In his opening address to a new session of the assembly in 1739, Governor Bull warned the assembly, "the desertion of our slaves is a matter of so much importance" that the legislature must take "effectual means" to stop it. The governor sent a delegation of his councilors to Saint Augustine to demand the slaves' return, but Montiano referred to the *cédula* of 1733 and claimed he had no power to do so. However, Montiano had also begun to establish the free black settlement at Fort Mose a few miles north of Saint Augustine, the perfect buffer against English attack and a further invitation to Carolina runaways, erstwhile Spanish allies.[70]

Thus threatened, the legislature began work on yet another law that might better control their slaves. Members established a committee to determine immediate measures to be taken against runaways and opened a debate on how to strengthen the colony's defenses. One motion to compel men to bring "firearms" to church on Sundays failed, though members agreed that all should wear a set of pistols, even in the pew. The committee suggested that the colony establish "a scout boat" with a company of ten men "to guard the water passages" south to prevent further escapes. And to catch slaves who had already gone, the committee recommended substantial rewards for slave catchers calibrated by the gender and age of their prey. Only white men or free Indians could earn these rewards: forty pounds for a man who had escaped beyond the Savannah River, twenty-five pounds for a woman, and ten pounds for a child. If the slave catcher killed a runaway, man or woman, he could slice off the scalp, so long as he included both ears, and turn in the trophy to the Public Treasury for twenty pounds.[71]

The first victim of Carolinian vigilance swung from the gallows before the new law even passed. Slave catchers picked up two black men, Caesar and Alleboy, and brought them before a slave court. The court determined that they were headed for Saint Augustine and that Caesar had led the other man astray. In accordance with the law, the justices and freeholders sentenced Caesar to hang and imposed a flogging on Alleboy. On Saturday morning, April 4, 1739, they had Caesar brought to "Hang-man's Point," directly across the Ashley River from Charles Town, and hung him from the neck until dead. The place was well chosen, according to the *South Carolina Gazette*, to flaunt broken black corpses to the "Negroes passing and repassing by water." The writer claimed that before the hangman did his work, Caesar had given a "sensible speech to those of his own Colour," imploring them to be honest and just and to be warned by his "unhappy example."[72]

The Charles Town merchants had been importing Africans in larger numbers than ever before, and from new places. In the years after the Yamasee War, the slavers had focused on the rice-growing regions along the Gambia River, but for the past decade the overwhelming majority of voyages had come from West Central Africa, specifically, the northern Angola ports of Cabinda and Loango. Between 1730 and 1739, thirty-nine of the eighty-seven ventures to bring Africans to Carolina had departed from West Central Africa; only twelve had come from the Gambia.[73]

More than twenty thousand enslaved Africans survived the passage to Carolina during these years, and a careful look at the runaway slave advertisements printed in the *South Carolina Gazette* tells a little about this community of enslaved Africans, and who among them resisted by running away. In the period before the Stono Rebellion, 188 advertisements described in varying detail the escapes of 273 people. Most were young men like Justice, who fled from Stephen Dwyer's plantation in February 1735. But there were sixty women who escaped as well, and four of them, like Virtue, who was both Indian and Black, ran with children in tow. More than half the fugitives escaped in groups of between two and five people; five groups used a canoe. There were forty-five of these small groups, and thirty-seven of them consisted entirely of young men, like Esham, Exeter, and Boson, who fled along with Justice in their new jackets and breeches made of white cloth. Flora fled with a white man named Richard Ratton and a little girl named Katey who might have been theirs. Most fled in the heat of June when the incessant hoeing of the rice fields began, but almost as many fled in January after the Christmas holiday. Not a day went by without someone considering the dangerous escape from Carolina slavery.[74]

The advertisements suggest that white Carolinians had begun to learn more about the people they enslaved and had begun to classify them into types. Slaveholders used "New Negroe" to describe a newly arrived African, and they described twenty runaways as "this country born." But advertisers described forty-seven runaways with a variety of ethnonyms used to categorize what they perceived as distinct cultural groups among the Africans they enslaved. They used the terms "Pawpaw," "Gold Coast," "Bossue," and "Bambra" one time each; they identified twenty-seven "Angola negroes," eleven "Gambia negroes," and six "Ebo negroes." As with the "Coromantins" identified by Governor Jonathan Atkins in Barbados, what these names actually meant to enslaved people is an important historical question.[75]

Of these names, only "Ebo" (Ibo or Igbo) and perhaps "Bambra" (or Bambara) refer to particular peoples who have a history in Africa. The Ibo lived in the hinterlands of the Bight of Biafara, but in Africa they did not identify as Ibo until the nineteenth century. Bambara might be an ethnic group of the Senegambian region, but the term might also mean "slave soldier" and thus apply to a profession rather than a culture. "Pawpaw" likely refers to Popo, a port in the Bight of Benin, but by the nineteenth century European missionaries in Sierra Leone identified Pawpaw as a language group. Without question, the Gold Coast and Angola were coastal regions, not peoples. The Senegal and the Gambia are separate rivers. The seventeenth- and eighteenth-century meaning of these names is uncertain, yet within the violent confines of American slavery, these names came to represent ethnic identities with African roots that coalesced among enslaved people in the Americas. Consider the man named Peter, with "country-marks cut in the shape of a diamond on each of his temples," who escaped alongside Hector and Dublin. All three were considered men "of Angola." It is hard to say how these men saw themselves before their enslavement, but their coordination to escape slavery, and the recorded observation that they were all "of Angola," suggests a process of cultural coalescence among Africans in Carolina. These identities were not of the Old World but rather of the New. Of the thirty-seven groups of young men who fled their masters, four groups were all Angolans, and four were all Gambians.

The terms used to describe these young men might be close to the way they saw themselves.[76]

These young men were not the majority of runaways, and sometimes blacks born in Carolina ran off with Africans. In June 1738, the Carolina-born Cyrus ran off with Bambra Cain, Ben and Symon of Angola, and Will, who was not further identified. The descendants of Africans born in Carolina came of age in American surroundings and had a deeper knowledge of the colony that enslaved them. Newly arrived Africans faced more significant obstacles. They were compelled to adapt to a new geography, new languages, a new labor regime, and a new political milieu that governed and severely limited the possibilities of a hopeful future.[77]

Some of those who survived the slaving ships brought with them martial skills that intensified resistance. Many of the Africans brought to Carolina from the northern Angola ports were enslaved during the tumultuous civil wars that followed the destruction of the kingdom of Kongo. The ports of Cabinda and Loango were supplied by the decentralized trade networks of Vili merchants who had established connections with British merchants early in the century. The Vili acquired slaves from a broad catchment region of West Central Africa, people who were enslaved by raiders, as punishment for alleged crimes, or through war. There can be little doubt that some of the men brought into Carolina during the 1730s had been soldiers in African armies, accustomed to guns and military discipline. And on September 9, 1739, a group of these men described as "Angola Negroes" deployed their skills and raised a rebellion against the whites, the most widespread insurrection South Carolinians would ever see.[78]

September 9 was a Sunday. By common practice, slaves worked for themselves on Sundays, and the rebels likely spent the day plotting their attack. They lived on the west side of the Stono River, a settled rice district not twenty miles from Charles Town and close enough to the Pons Pons Road for the rebels to know that it ran south toward Saint Augustine. That night, under the leadership of a man named Jemmy, they raided the warehouse of a colonist named Hutchenson who sold guns and ammunition, among other wares. They met resistance from Robert Bathurst and a white man named Gibbs, whom they killed, and according to one report they left their severed heads on the steps of the ransacked store. Now armed, they plundered Godrey's house and killed the whole family, then went to the Pons Pons Road past Wallace's tavern, which they did not molest because Wallace had the reputation for being a good man. They broke into Lemy's house, killed him and his family, and then marched to Thomas Rose's place. Two men and a woman enslaved by Rose hid their master and told the rebels he wasn't there.[79]

As the old soldiers marched south along the Pons Pons Road, they attracted followers, presented banners, and beat the drums of war. At around eleven in the morning on September 10, Lieutenant Governor William Bull and a small party of "gentlemen" were riding north up the same road, returning to Charles Town from Granville County. The rebels pursued the men, but their horses were fast and they escaped to raise the country. The white people of Stono, and no doubt some of the enslaved as well, gathered at Dandridge's Bridge, seeking security in numbers. As the militia began to gather, the rebels marched on. They brought the torch to five more houses and killed any white person who came across their path. Their numbers grew to about a hundred, and perhaps confident of victory, they stopped in a field, drank rum, and sang and danced to beating drums.[80]

About one hundred militia had mustered, and they pursued the rebels down the road. They encountered them in premature celebration at four o'clock in the afternoon. Battle ensued. About half of the rebels, probably those who had joined last, fled back to their plantations and hoped not to be missed. But the others fought on, and at least one determined company of ten fought their way out and continued down the road. The militiamen killed fourteen rebels with their first volley, and those they captured they summarily shot. Some were hanged and others disemboweled right there on the field. There were no slave courts as the law prescribed. As the planters rode back to Charles Town, tracking down the remnants of the band, they fixed the severed heads of African bodies on the mileposts, signaling to all that the road to Spanish liberty was marked by the threat of brutal death.[81]

Colonial authorities immediately increased the rewards for slave catchers to fifty pounds for every rebel caught alive and twenty-five pounds for each one killed. In November, the assembly voted to raise funds for an expedition to demolish the castle at Saint Augustine, as well as to pay "a patrol completely armed" of ten men and two officers to ride constantly in the vicinity of Stono for the next three months. There were still a few rebels at large, but as the assembly investigated the origins and course of the rebellion, they realized that some of the enslaved had "shewed so much Integrity and Fidelity" to their masters that they must be rewarded. The enslaved man July, owned by Thomas Elliot, had fought the rebels and even killed one, saving the lives of his master and family. The assembly gave July his freedom, as well as a shirt, a hat, stockings, a pair of shoes, and a suit of clothes made of fine blue strouds faced with red and trimmed with brass buttons. Not surprisingly, Elliot was a Quaker. He must have been a humane master, for Ralph, Prince, Joe, Larush, and Pompey, all enslaved by Elliot, also fought against the rebels, though they did not kill. These men received the same assortment of clothing and twenty pounds cash. Thirty enslaved people in all, twenty-nine men and one woman, as well as nineteen Indians, received awards from the assembly for resisting the rebels. All received clothing and various amounts of cash in a formal ceremony in the Council Chamber on December 12, 1739, just in time for Christmas. No one but July received freedom.[82]

Carrots and sticks. Bloody heads on mileposts to mark power, new clothes, shoes, and cash for loyal slaves were all tools in the governance of this slave society. While the assembly deliberated on the gifts for loyal slaves, it also ordered a strong patrol to ride during Christmas, a "Time of general Liberty." Legislators would not deny the slaves this holiday privilege, but in light of recent events, the assembly ensured that Christmas would be supervised by heavily armed white men on horseback.[83]

The planters knew that it had been Africans, not Creoles, who had risen in rebellion. And so before they finalized the new comprehensive slave code, the assembly passed the Act for the Better Strengthening of This Province, which put an effective end to the transatlantic slave trade. "Whereas, the great importation of negroes

from the coast of Africa," proclaimed the assembly, "who are generally of a barbarous and savage disposition, may . . . prove of very
dangerous consequences to the peace and safety of this Province,"
the new law established a prohibitive tax on their importation.
They could not tax the British merchants who slaved on the coast
of Africa because these men had the ear of Parliament and the
Crown. But the assembly could tax the planters, many were
planters themselves, and starting in fifteen months, the law stated,
anyone who purchased a slave from a transatlantic slaver would
pay a duty of one hundred pounds per head to His Majesty's coffers in South Carolina, to be used to bolster colonial defense. The
Charles Town merchant Robert Pringle learned of the new law
before it had even passed. He wrote to Samuel Saunders of London,
already the captain on eight slaving voyages, that the new tax
would be "equal to a prohibition." Pringle advised Saunders that
there were still fifteen months before the new tax would be effective and that "a Pretty Many Negroes" might be profitably imported before the ban. Pringle wrote much the same to his brother
Andrew, a merchant based in London, and to Michael Lovell, a
merchant in Antigua.[84]

The law would prove extremely effective. Five more slavers arrived
in 1740, but then there were none until 1744, when the law expired.
Even then, no slavers arrived in Charles Town from 1745 through
1749, and not until the late 1750s did the trade return to the average
importation of the 1730s. Carolinian planters had purchased 23,000
enslaved Africans during the 1730s—6,000 more than their counterparts in Virginia. But after Stono, during a period when British slavers transported 143,000 Africans across the Atlantic and when
Virginians bought 10,000, Barbadians bought 19,000, and Jamaicans bought 68,000 enslaved Africans, South Carolinians bought
only 2,300. The assembly determined that the slave population of
Carolina had become dangerously Africanized by reckless importation. Planter-legislators used the law in an effort to domesticate their
slave population by ensuring that its increase would come only
through the birth of children. And with a new law to govern the
enslaved, the assembly attempted nothing less than a social experiment that might generate "absolute slaves."[85]

For that is how the slave law now defined them—"absolute slaves"—the "people called negroes, Indians, mulattoes and mustizos" long recognized as property. Legislators understood that those they enslaved were human beings, even if they were not white. Slaves needed to be "kept in due subjection and obedience," but the assembly also recognized that the brutality of masters had spiraled out of control. Previous laws had encouraged such brutality, and the suppression of the rebellion in Stono had given awful vent to the violent passions that slaveholding provoked. The assembly hoped the new law would restrain masters "from exercising too great rigour and cruelty" over their slaves, so that "public peace and order" might be maintained. Embedded in this preamble to the new Act for the Better Ordering and Governing of Negroes was the subtle admission that insurrection had resulted in part from atrocious brutality. The assembly sought a domestication of their society. They wanted the black children hitherto born into slavery to be firmly controlled, and to work, but they also wanted to cultivate a greater measure of humanity in the white men empowered to control them.[86]

In pursuit of these aims, the new Act for the Better Ordering and Governing of Negroes combined measures that solidified the authority of masters while increasing their responsibilities toward the people they owned. The law made clear that slave status "shall follow the condition of the mother" and that slaves were "chattels personal." It ended the requirement that manumitted slaves leave the colony and empowered any one justice, rather than a jury of twelve, to grant recognition of free status. But the law now suggested that free people of color needed to have a white "guardian." For if a free person claimed to own a person who might be seen as a Negro, of a range of phenotypical hues, or an Indian, only a white guardian could defend in court the person of color so claimed as property. The law explained that in the case of an attempt at wrongful enslavement, the guardian could "bring an action of trespass in the nature of ravishment of ward." In the eyes of the law, then, free people of color were most similar to orphaned children under the benevolent protection of responsible white men.[87]

The new law further limited the autonomy of slaves by banning their assembly, banning the travel of enslaved men in groups larger than seven, and continuing the prohibitions on slaves' economic endeavors—dressing too well, keeping horses or shops, or trading on their own account. The law maintained the old ticket system, but it added a prohibition on teaching slaves how to write. Legislators were not concerned whether slaves could read—yet—but slaves had written out fraudulent tickets that allowed them to wander from the plantations without the master's knowledge, and this had to stop.[88]

This new slave law tried to smooth out the harshest edges of Carolina's slavery. It required masters to provide enough food and clothing for their slaves, and the new law codified the custom of giving slaves a day off on Sundays. It also banned torturous punishments. Masters could no longer "cut out the tongue, put out the eye, castrate, cruelly scald or burn" or dismember their slaves, a terrifying list that must have had precedent. Likewise, whereas the law of 1735 allowed a white man pursuing a runaway to "beat, maim, or assault" said runaway who resisted capture, the law of 1740 only allowed for moderate correction. To be sure, enslaved people could still be executed for the third offense of striking a white man, and some of the common retaliatory measures that enslaved people employed against their masters—arson, theft, and poisoning—could also result in execution. But in comparison with the slave laws crafted by assemblies past, the law of 1740 was more humane.[89]

There was one caveat. Everything that had been done in the suppression of the Stono insurrection, "all and every act, matter and thing, had, done, committed and executed, in and about the suppressing and putting all the . . . negroes to death, is and are hereby declared lawful." The opacity of such language, the wide range of action it justified after the fact, reminded all who read it that while the assembly wanted their slave society to be kinder and gentler, when faced with black insurrection, the white men of Carolina could and would do terrible violence to maintain their power.[90]

About ten years later, the Georgia settler Johann Martin Bolzius answered a long questionnaire about this slave society of the southeastern woodlands. A pious Lutheran from Salzburg (present-day Austria), Bolzius had settled in 1733 in Ebenezer, Georgia, where he pastored a community of like-minded German farmers. These men and women had migrated to Georgia in part because of its explicit ban on slavery, which ended the next year. The Salzburgers lived intentionally apart from other colonists in their own village of self-sufficient farms, but commerce with Charles Town was indispensable to Europeans living on this frontier and, perhaps inevitably, Bolzius knew well the slavery he despised.

Bolzius wrote privately for a "distinguished gentleman" of Augsburg (present-day Germany) who seems to have taken a great interest in the nature of American slaveholding. Bolzius wrote with sympathy for the enslaved, who felt their burden as "an unbearable yoke." It would be such "to all people," he wrote, who faced the "eternal slavery" of Carolina. And Bolzius knew the system. He knew the range of current prices of slaves, from the "New Negroes" purchased off the slavers to those born in the country and taught a trade. He knew that runaways still escaped to Saint Augustine, where "they receive their freedom," but no, he replied, the Indians no longer helped them. Slaves who rebelled would "give no mercy" to the whites, and it was "not rare" to hear of the outraged slave who had murdered the master. The rebellious slave captured, however, might be "slowly roasted at the fire." Slave resistance had not been suppressed, nor had the outrageous violence of the masters.[91]

The pastor's account offers a reflection of the slave society that had developed over eighty years. Beginning in 1696, the South Carolina Assembly had revised the colony's slave code five different times in the effort to shape how white men governed their slaves. Bolzius described the operation of Carolina's laws with a familiar Latin proverb, *quasi campana sine pistillo*, which means "like a bell without its clanger." The law signaled a repressive arrangement of white control, but like a bell that does not ring, its particular notes often went unheard. Bolzius wrote specifically of the law requiring the owners of ten Negroes to employ at least one white man, which had not been observed, resulting in "thirty times" more blacks than whites in the colony. Bolzius also described the widespread acceptance of the internal economy that the assembly had long attempted to thwart. Despite the law, Carolinian planters allowed their slaves "as much land as they can handle," on which they grew a wide variety of crops, sold their surplus, and bought whatever necessaries they needed. To be sure, the plantations were "constantly patrolled" in accordance with the law, and men went fully armed to church, lest they be caught unawares by an attempt at insurrection. The spirit of Carolina's laws cannot be found in the tracings of obedience to their dicta; rather, it is best found in the behaviors of the masters and the hopes of the people who survived within its bindings.[92]

"They love their families dearly," Bolzius wrote of the Africans, and "none runs away from the other." In Jamaica, children born into slavery often did not survive; the black population there did not grow naturally until 1838.[93] In South Carolina many did survive, and the slaveholding culture Bolzius described, along with the pattern of amelioration evident in the changing laws, helps to explain this difference. By custom, Bolzius noted, one could not "buy a child under 8 years by itself," but only with the child's mother, and children were "spared from work so that they may grow big and strong." The best way to start a plantation, he suggested, was "to buy 2 or 3 families," as one could be assured they would stay together and work.[94]

The postwar revisions of South Carolina's comprehensive slave code softened the law's harshest punishments and asked more humanity of the masters, but it still maintained powerful tools of repression. This long process of legal refashioning was an effort to domesticate the slave system, and the best evidence of its success can be found in the children among the enslaved—an embodiment of a people's hope. This is not to claim that slavery in colonial South Carolina was humane—hardly: the runaway slave ads continued to reflect brutal floggings, and summary executions by slave courts continued. But through a deft manipulation of human skill and the love of kin, the planter-legislators of South Carolina had domesticated a system of racial slavery that perpetuated itself, made them rich, and became the material foundation for the proslavery argument that would emerge among a later generation. Twenty years after Bolzius wrote, Governor William Bull Jr., whose uncle had barely escaped the Stono rebels, noted with pride that the colony had not experienced a slave insurrection since 1739, the result, he argued, of the "particular system of laws" that blended force with humanity. Bull had lived during Carolina's "golden age," when rice and slaves built the fortunes of North America's richest planter class. Stable prosperity grew from a system of social control that nevertheless allowed four generations of Africans and their descendants to carve out a semblance of human dignity from the granite despair of their enslavement.[95]

CHAPTER 4

The Militarization of Slavery in Jamaica

JAMAICA'S CLIMATE AND rich soils made sugar production an immediate success, but its mountainous interior welcomed rebellious Africans, the first-time Maroons. The sugar plantations drew significant capital from Great Britain, and British slaving merchants shipped thousands of enslaved Africans to the island every year. Unlike the colonists of South Carolina, Jamaica's planters did not face powerful indigenous polities with whom they had to contend. Yet through the brutality of their plantations and their dependence on the transatlantic slave trade, the Jamaican planters unwittingly fostered the rise of the Maroons, autonomous communities of Africans who escaped from slavery and adapted to the mountains where they fought for their autonomy, which they secured through formal treaties with the colony at the close of war in 1739.

The Maroons played a similar role in the formation of Jamaica's slave society as Indian polities had in the making of South Carolina. Having barely survived the Yamasee War of 1715, the South Carolina House of Assembly frequently revised their comprehensive slave code in an effort to domesticate the governance of slavery. In their forty-year war with the Maroons, however, the Jamaica House of Assembly passed laws to raise temporary military forces and to intensify internal surveillance. Simultaneously, the planters lobbied

120

Whitehall to secure regular troops for the island, a dependable military garrison to protect colonial investments. This first, long war with the Maroons fostered a militarization of the governance of Jamaica's slave society that persisted. It generated a three-tiered military structure that managed the politics of slave resistance through a responsive militia, imperial troops, and, after 1739, the deployment of Maroon allies. When Coromantee Africans waged a major revolt in 1760, Jamaica's system of governance faced its most severe challenge, which it overcame with brutality and clear success. The planters of South Carolina and Jamaica became the richest slave-holding classes in their respective regions of the British Empire. Yet each planter class over saw a slave system structurally distinct from the other, and each slave system developed through deadly struggles with peoples who would not be enslaved.[1]

The wars among the Akan states of the Gold Coast hinterland in West Africa played a critical role in the politics of Jamaican slavery during the eighteenth century. British slavers purchased more enslaved Africans in the Gold Coast ports than in any other region of Africa, and Jamaica became the destination for more of these ships than any other American site. About 45 percent of the captives who arrived in Jamaica during these years departed Africa from the Gold Coast, making the Akan wars the personal experience of thousands of people enslaved in Jamaica. Significant numbers departed from the Bight of Benin and West Central Africa as well, but the influence of the Akan would be paramount.[2]

The expansion of the transatlantic slave trade between the Gold Coast and Jamaica happened simultaneously with the rise of Asante, which replaced Akwamu and Denkyira as the dominant state among the Akan peoples. Asante traditions hold that the empire was founded by Osei Tutu in the late seventeenth century as a rival to Denkyira. Tutu was the nephew of Obiri Yeboa, king of the small state of Kwamaan, a tributary of Denkyira. Yeboa was childless, which meant the throne would pass to his sister's son Osei Tutu. One oral tradition of the Asante holds that when Tutu was a young man, Yeboa sent him to the court of Denkyira to be trained in the arts of governance.

While there, the handsome Tutu fell in love with Akobena Denusa, a sister of the king of Denkyira, and when she became pregnant, Tutu had to flee. He took refuge in Akwamu, Denkyira's principal rival, and there he befriended Ansa Sasraku, king of Akwamu. When Tutu's uncle died and it became time for him to take the stool of Kwamaan, Sasraku gave Tutu a body of troops to support his ascent to power.[3]

Once enstooled, Tutu called together the kings of Mampon, Kokofu, Kumawu, Dwaben, Bekwai, and Nsuta and convinced them to form a confederacy that Tutu would lead. Both Akwamu and Denkyira had been empowered by the development of commoner armies and the rise of the Atlantic slave trade. Asante's emergence at the center of this rivalry foreboded the terror of enslavement for those in the region without power or protection. The states Tutu brought together were all subject to Denkyira, and with the support of Akwamu, the new kingdom of Asante went to war against Denkyira and defeated its former overlord by 1701. Now the predominant state of the western Gold Coast hinterland, Asante wielded great power, but it also garnered great resentments from the peoples it held subject. For the next twenty years, then, the states subject to Asante would occasionally rebel, inviting retribution that resulted in more war and large numbers of people enslaved by victorious armies throughout the region.[4]

The rise of Asante accompanied further efforts at political consolidation both toward the coast and eastward into the Bight of Benin. The military revolution that transformed warfare among the Akan states spread southward toward the coast and east into the Bight of Benin, emboldening would-be kings and further disseminating military knowledge among the young men of this populous region. In 1708 the small coastal state of Borbor Fante attacked its neighbors Asebu and Fetu, and by 1724 Borbor Fante dominated a coalition of coastal states that included Eguafo and Agona, and it resisted the domination of Asante until 1807. In the Bight of Benin, Allada, Offra, Whydah, Little Popo, and Grand Popo struggled for power among themselves until Dahomey conquered Allada in 1724 and Whydah in 1727, making all these lesser states tributary to Dahomey. These wars fed a dramatic expansion of the English slave trade from the

Gold Coast and the Bight of Benin that replicated the politics of resistance we have seen before, when Akan-named rebels organized
insurrections that fractured the power of Barbadian slaveholders,
or when the "Angolas" of South Carolina challenged their own
enslavement.[5]

African political history marked each transported captive, and
white colonials recognized distinctions among the people they enslaved. Writing in 1746, the former Kingston merchant James Knight
wrote that the Africans of Jamaica came from "more than twenty different countries, or nations," of which he named the Whidahs, Angolas, and Coromantees. As with the runaway slaves in the newspaper
advertisements in South Carolina, it is hard to know whether captive Africans had begun to identify with those among them who had
spent time in the slaving port of Whydah, or passed through the Angola coast. But whites saw cultural differences among Africans, who
very well might have felt them. Knight had more to say about the
Coromantees, who were "of different Provinces or Clans, and not
under the same Prince." He identified three separate groups among
the Coromantees: Fanteens, Shantees, and Achims, names that cor-
respond with kingdoms involved with the Akan wars.[6]

Knight's perceptions speak to the processes of cultural coalescence
within the African population of Jamaica that would have important
political ramifications for the island's history. The English had identified "Coromantins" in seventeenth-century Barbados, but it seems
unlikely that any enslaved Africans saw themselves as such at this
early date. But ethnographic evidence from twentieth-century Jamaica, as well as developments in Asante history during the 1720s,
suggest that by the 1730s "Coromantee" had become a palpable
identity among the Africans of Jamaica that would have important
political consequences.

Anthropologists who have studied among the Maroons have described the oral traditions of a "Kromanti" past that remain strong.
In the 1920s when the American anthropologist Martha Beckwith
visited the Moore Town Maroons of the Blue Mountains, they still
spoke and sung a language they called "Koromanti." The Jesuit Joseph Williams found the same thing in the 1930s, and the Jamaican
linguist Mervyn Alleyne found "Kromanti" sung in the Scott's Hall

Maroon community in the 1960s. Anthropologist Jean Besson has
found that in Accompong, a Maroon town in the Cockpit Country,
there are still burial grounds said to represent the "Congo" and
"Coromantee" origins of the ancestral, or "First Time," Maroons.
According to the anthropologist Kenneth Bilby, the spiritual practice still alive in the Maroon communities of the Blue Mountains is
known as "Kromanti," a clear reference to the "tribe" or "nation" of
origin—the Coromantees—from whom today's Maroons understand
themselves to descend. Many black Jamaicans in the eighteenth and
early nineteenth centuries saw themselves as Coromantee, but an understanding of this connection to the past has survived most clearly
among the Maroons.[7]

The name of this nation that has persisted so long may have roots
in the death of Osei Tutu, who died in battle against Akyem in 1717
or 1718. Tutu's heir to the throne had not been clear, and civil war
broke out within Asante in the aftermath of Tutu's death. Opoku
Ware ultimately succeeded Osei Tutu in about 1720, and according
to Ghanaian historian John Kofi Fynn, Opoku Ware's greatest accomplishment lay in the establishment of the Ntam Kese, the Great
Oath of Asante. Oaths were common among the Akan and typically
referred, though obscurely, to a great tragedy in the past. To recall
the past in this way was to invoke the guidance of the ancestors,
which was not lightly done. The Ntam Kese referred to the death of
Osei Tutu and became the most serious oath in Asante. He had been
killed on a Saturday at Koromantin, and so the most serious iteration of the oath, because it was so specific, was "Meka Kormante me
Memeneda," or "I swear by Koromantin and Saturday." The word
"Kormantin" thus took on great power for many Akan, a signifier of
the kinship that Atlantic slavery sought to deny them. As the name
of an African people, then, "Coromantee" began as a name applied
by the English, but over time and for Africans' own reasons, it became appropriated by the enslaved as a powerful new identity.[8]

Archival evidence of the origin of Jamaica's Maroon communities remains sparse, but James Knight's account of this history is probably
the best contemporary account. Knight spoke with the "old-Standers"

of the colony, a phrase he used to describe the oldest white inhabitants, who still remembered the early battles. Knight probably commissioned one of them to write the "Anonymous History of the Rebellious Negroes," which he used as a source in his own history, though not exclusively, and Knight knew Captain Cudjoe of the Leeward Maroons, who played a critical role in this history.

The Africans of Spanish Jamaica freed during the English conquest withdrew into the mountains and had no connection to the English colony. They probably combined forces with indigenous people never conquered by the Spanish and formed two separate communities, one in the rocky Cockpit Country in the west-central part of the island, and the other in the Blue Mountains. Those in the Blue Mountains would become known as the Windward Maroons, and in these early years their desire for autonomy was so strong that they did not allow fugitive Africans from the plantations to join them. As the colony grew and the planters marched larger numbers of Africans to new plantations, some "began to fly to the mountains in small bodies." Moreover, the surviving rebels from the seventeenth-century insurrections established their own towns in the Cockpit Country. All of these rebel groups included both women and men, which allowed these communities to reproduce and grow in numbers and capability. The new Maroon towns remained separate "under distinct commanders," and separate from the Maroons descended from the Spanish Africans. There were at least five different Maroon communities by 1700, four in the Cockpit Country in the western half of the island and one in the Blue Mountains.[9]

The new Maroons differed from the older Maroons in that they never entirely withdrew from the colony but rather lived in proximity to the plantations and smaller farms. They raided colonial settlements for provisions and manufactured goods, and they kept in touch "with their countrymen" who remained enslaved. The Old Stander wrote that the Maroons were "of different countrys and of different manners and customs in Guinea," as were the slaves in the plantation quarters, which suggests that in the early eighteenth century kinship, language, and trade connected the new Maroons to those Africans enslaved on the plantations. Sometimes people escaped the plantations and joined the Maroons in the mountains, increasing their numbers, strength, and boldness.[10]

The Maroon communities shared a hatred for the whites and for being enslaved, but this did not unite them. The communities knew of one another because their hunters crossed paths in their pursuit of wild hogs and conflicts resulted. It is also possible that reverberations of the Akan wars fostered conflict among these Maroons, who may have organized themselves along West African patterns of identification. In 1718 a significant body of Africans enslaved by one Downs of Saint Elizabeth Parish escaped to form a new Maroon group in Dean's Valley, Westmoreland. This band grew considerably in the following years, led by a "Madagascar" described by the Old Stander as a "resolute cunning fellow." These Maroons came into serious conflict with the other Leeward Maroons, whom Knight described as "mostly Coromantines under the command of a Negro belonging to Mr. Sutton." After a series of "bloody battles" that took the lives of many on each side, including the Madagascar captain, the Leeward Maroons united under the leadership of Cudjoe.[11]

Cudjoe was a born Maroon, raised in the cockpits, and his father was probably the man Knight referred to as the Madagascar's principal foe. Cudjoe's father was said to have led the insurrection on Thomas Sutton's Clarendon plantation in 1690, and if he was a young man of perhaps twenty-five at the time, he would have been in his early fifties during the Maroon battles of the 1710s. That he named his son Cudjoe, the Akan day name for a male born on Monday, suggests the Akan roots of the Coromantee of Jamaica. Akan political traditions were organized around kingship, and Cudjoe seems to have emerged as a king by 1720, though contemporaries did not use this term. The Old Stander described Cudjoe as a "very Sensible Prudent man" who held absolute power. He had several commanders subordinate to him who trained men in the arts of war and led hunting parties and raids on the plantations when necessary. Cudjoe's policy, however, was to remain aloof from the plantations so as to avoid antagonizing the whites. Cudjoe seems to have preferred peace, for his towns were well supplied by the numerous provision grounds planted and maintained by Maroon women throughout the Cockpit Country. To avoid conflict among his towns, Cudjoe prohibited the use of African languages, compelling all his Maroons to speak English only, a measure intended to overcome the ethnic divisions that had driven the battles of the 1710s. This could not have been adhered to strictly, but as a result of Cudjoe's leadership, by 1730 when the colony began to take active measures to suppress the Maroons, the Leewards were strong and united.[12]

The Jamaica House of Assembly responded to the rise of Maroon power with a series of desperate laws that sought to subdue the "rebellious negroes" who challenged the colony's supremacy. The Slave Act of 1696 had singled out the "rebellious negro"—the Maroon—for harsher punishments and offered greater incentives to catch them, but colonial whites never had the strength to control so many captives. In 1699, the assembly passed an Act for Raising Parties to Suppress Rebellious and Runaway Negroes. The law created no new powers, but it did draw attention to a threat of "fatal Consequences" if the rebels were "not timely suppressed." The law offered greater financial incentives to the white men who enlisted in such parties, with a month of service bringing six pounds to a captain, three pounds to a sergeant, and fifty shillings to enlisted men. And the parties could "plunder" at will, if they could manage it, among the small communities of escaped Africans who challenged the colonial monopoly on violence.[13]

The law had very little effect, and enslaved Africans had more reason to leave the plantations than ever before. In July 1702 the Yallahs planter Thomas Martyn wrote to Lord Carlisle of a drought that had left his cattle "almost dead" and his slaves near starvation. Moreover, five sugar plantations in Yallahs had been "destroyed by fier lately," in addition to "an abundance" of smaller farms. Named after the river that drained the Blue Mountains to the south, Yallahs was an established sugar district about twenty-five miles east of Kingston and within easy striking distance of the Windward Maroons. Indeed, in September Lieutenant Governor Peter Beckford reported to Whitehall that he had sent four parties against these Maroons, using the new law. One of the parties had come up against a band of three hundred men, whom Beckford claimed

were successfully routed by the much smaller force of whites after a
battle of five or six hours. The whites discovered their town in the
mountains and "well-planted" provision grounds estimated at a
hundred acres of land.[14]

These raids by the Windward Maroons marked a change in their
relation to the colony. They had lived in these mountains for several
generations, but the colony had grown and white settlements were
now closer to Maroon lands. The Windwards gathered salt, fish, and
turtle from Manchioneal Bay, which, in addition to hunting, brought
them into contact with the plantations then being built and new
sources of information about happenings around the island. The Old
Stander believed that the Windwards learned from the successes of
the new Maroon bands that had formed to the west, who accepted
fugitives and raided the plantations. The Windwards began to accept fugitive Africans into their towns, which made them stronger
by giving them greater access to the plantations. Newly freed Maroons maintained relationships with friends and countrymen who
remained on the plantations. The Maroons began to sell fruit, provisions from their grounds, and smoked wild hog in the Sunday markets near the plantations. They raided the small settlements for
manufactured goods, guns, and powder, but they also purchased
these items from slaves on the plantations, as well as from poor
whites. A manuscript map of the "settlements of the REBELLIOUS
NEGROES" drawn in 1730 shows two abandoned Maroon towns and
a third town with fifty-six buildings, signifying both the longevity
of this group and their organization at this moment. Eight buildings were drawn much larger than the others, and four of these were
uniformly circled by ten smaller structures. The organization of
"nations" can be seen in the arrangement of space.[15]

The slavers continued to bring more than 4,500 captive Africans
into Kingston Harbor every year. Most still departed from the Gold
Coast and Whydah, though significant numbers now left through
the Angola coast. In 1717, the Jamaica assembly passed a new slave
law that reflected the threats that planters saw in patterns of African
sociability and musical practice. Despite previous laws, whites had
failed to prohibit the assemblies of Africans, including many who
traveled from other plantations. And it had become apparent that Af-

ricans could "give Signals to each other at a considerable distance" with drums, horns, or various other "Instruments of Noise," including "barrels, goards, and boards." The assembly feared that such gatherings could "prove of fatal Consequence to this your Majesty's Island." Should any white man responsible for the oversight of Africans allow five or more to congregate, or allow them to make noise, the assembly would have him fined ten pounds of the island's currency. If any justice of the peace should be informed of such noise or congregation, he must issue the warrant to collect said fine, or be fined himself. If any officer of the militia should hear of such noise or congregation, then he must gather a force, enter the plantation, and suppress it. Though the law might be impossible for colonial whites to enforce to the letter, it did give them ample pretext to use organized force against any group of black men who came together. The whites suspected the culture of the slaves.[16]

The very next year, the assembly passed another law empowering the governor to raise parties that would pursue and suppress the "rebellious and runaway Negroes." The assembly realized that despite previous law, the Maroons had "formed themselves into several Bodies, and of late have very much increased." The new law of suppression replaced the monthly salaries for the men of the slave-catching parties with cash bounties of fifty pounds for every Maroon over the age of fourteen either killed or taken prisoner; any member of the party could collect this fee. Moreover, any hunter, or slave, who came upon and killed or captured a Maroon on his own could collect ten pounds and, if enslaved, gain his or her freedom. The law also empowered the slave-catching parties to slave among the Maroon towns, granting to the men "and their heirs, every Boy, Girl, or Pick-a-ninny which they shall so take under the Age of Fourteen." Planter-legislators knew that there were children born in mountains who had never known slavery, though they were Africans, were of slave parentage, and should thus be enslaved. The assembly must have assumed that Maroons over the age of fourteen would fight back and be killed. This new slave law incentivized slave catchers and aimed at the destruction of the Maroons.[17]

The colony's gravest threat during the 1720s came from the Windward Maroons of the Blue Mountains. Their towns were in the parishes of Saint Thomas in the East and Saint George, which had been granted by the Crown to various absentee landholders but remained practically unsettled. Colonial policy makers had long wanted to increase the number of whites on the island, both for security concerns and to work the plantations. In 1721 and 1722 the assembly passed legislation that compelled the sale of lands on which the quitrents had not been paid for thirty years, and offered grants of those lands to new settlers who agreed to settle within the year. A Protestant white could receive thirty acres, while a free black, mulatto, or Indian could receive twenty acres. Both types of grantees could receive five additional acres for every slave settled on their lands, so long as they established residence within six months. The assembly hoped that the increase in the white population encouraged by the law would "be a mighty discouragement to the rebellious and runaway Slaves" who already lived there.[18]

To settle these lands required pacifying the Maroons, and in August 1725 a new governor, the Duke of Portland, reported that colonial parties were constantly being sent out against the Maroons. The accounts show that these parties were only marginally effective, killing fifteen rebels in 1725, four in 1726, and eleven in 1727. Nevertheless, in August 1728 Governor Robert Hunter, who had arrived in 1727, reported that the new settlements behind Port Antonio were "going on with a good prospect" and further grants had been made not only to Jamaica's free inhabitants but also to "newcomers."[19]

When larger numbers of whites began to settle these lands, the Maroons found themselves cut off from the sea and hemmed in on all sides by the new settlers. And so they struck back with raids and banditry, bringing the island to a state of "continuall and open war."[20] In 1729 the House of Assembly asked Governor Hunter to raise one or more parties "of Numbers and Strength sufficient" to destroy the Maroon settlements in the Blue Mountains. At the same time, Hunter declared to Whitehall that because of the rebels in the mountains and the Spanish in Cuba, he could not guarantee the "safety of the Island, unless some Regular Troops were sent to Defend it." Hunter took care to point out how valuable the island colony had become. The planters had established four hundred sugar works on the island, which produced five thousand hogsheads of sugar, valued at £300,000.

The home government collected £65,000 in duties on this sugar, and the merchants collected £62,500 in freight charges alone. Rum and ginger brought in smaller but not insignificant revenues, and the island also produced cotton, indigo, pimiento allspice, and exotic woods such as ebony and lignum vitae. The slavers brought more than seven thousand captive Africans to the island every year, valued at £28 each; the annual revenues from these voyages brought more than £200,000 to the investors involved. Hunter wrote that all of this could be lost in the conflict with the Maroons.[21]

On January 7, 1730, six military transports arrived in Kingston Harbor with two regiments of men, nine hundred in all, after a seven-week voyage from Gibraltar. Governor Hunter immediately detached six companies of soldiers to go to Port Antonio with tents and six weeks' provisions for an expedition against the Maroons. He split the second regiment into many smaller detachments, sending them to disparate parts of the island, from Hanover Parish in the northwestern corner of the island to Port Antonio in the east. The new men began to die like flies. Colonel Townshend mused that many of the soldiers would never meet their comrades again. His company was two hundred miles from Captain Beaver's and a hundred miles from Captain Savage's. Some companies were stationed in districts where "there never was a Rebellious Negro heard of." An accounting of the dead taken on March 19 noted the deaths of six officers and so many "private men . . . the number I cannot mention."[22]

Hunter clearly used some of the troops at his command to defeat the Maroons, but he used just as many to maintain sugar production, which militarized governance of the slaves. Spreading troops around the island in small detachments sent a clear threat to Africans enslaved on the plantations and enabled sugar production to continue. Indeed, sugar production quadrupled over the first forty years of the eighteenth century, and even during the most intense years of war with the Maroons, the 1730s, sugar production remained stable.[23]

While most of the soldiers "pared their nails" on plantations where the Maroons posed no threat, a "grand party" of ninety-five men and

twenty-two enslaved porters sailed west from Port Antonio to String-
er's Penn at Plumtree Bay, where they launched the first of several
expeditions against the Windward Maroons. Under the command
of Captain Samuel Soaper, the expedition marched up into the mountains, sleeping one night at Major Hobby's plantation, followed by a
week of difficult marches through dense foliage on steep mountain
grades. On the fourth day they came upon a deserted town with ba-
nana and plantain groves. Soaper's men rested there for the night,
cut down the groves, and moved on. The party marched five more
days through the mountains, until June 6, when they saw the Maroon village in the valley below.[24]

The next day Soaper led his men down into the valley toward the
town. They sneaked through the bush to avoid detection and passed
"broad roads" that went up into the mountains, as well as provision
grounds where they saw people working the soil. Soaper climbed a
tree and saw the town farther below, situated in a river bottom less
than a mile away. Some of the men wanted to attack immediately,
but Soaper decided to lie quietly and await midnight, when they could
surround the town and attack at dawn. This was unwise. There were
children playing everywhere, and before night even fell, the party
heard, "Backra a-come, Backra a-come." Soaper and one of the men,
Nicholas Physham, went back up into the tree and saw the Maroon
men gathering arms, and a hundred women with heavy loads,
children in tow, fleeing up a mountain road on the other side of the
town. Soaper ordered a party to advance immediately toward the
town, but as they approached they soon found themselves at a sharp
precipice that dropped straight down to the valley floor. The party
had lost the element of surprise (if indeed they ever had it), so Soaper
ordered his men to stay there for the night. When night fell, the militiamen fired their guns and the Maroons started to beat their
drums.[25]

Soaper's delay gave the Maroons the element of surprise, for in
the night they surrounded the party. At dawn Soaper sent an advance
detachment of twenty men to scale the precipice, but they were immediately fired on when they reached the valley floor; some were
killed and others wounded. The remainder returned to the main
party, but they too were surrounded, and battle ensued. The Ma-

roons seemed to have ample powder and shot, so Soaper ordered one of the enslaved porters, a man named Quamina enslaved by Colonel William Nedham, the Speaker of the Assembly, to call out to the Maroons and offer terms. That Soaper chose Quamina for this role speaks to the likelihood of Coromantee leadership among the Windwards, as well as the cultural affinity between the Maroons and enslaved Akan. Soaper offered land and good relations with the whites if the Maroons would surrender and cease allowing runaways "to joyn them." But the Maroons just cursed him. Soaper heard reinforcements join the Maroons during the night, and the next morning the battle began again. Soaper's men had no choice but to retreat as best they could. Of the ninety-five who set out to destroy the Maroons' towns, only forty-six returned.

In the fall of 1731, Hunter reported "several partyes of rebel slaves" that had attacked the colony throughout the island. One raid on a small settlement in Saint David's on the southern slopes of the Blue Mountains had killed one slave and brought off another to join the rebels. Maroons in Saint James had killed two straggling soldiers and decapitated one of them. Another raid attacked the new barrack in the Blue Mountains, despite the presence of soldiers. They killed one slave who worked at the barrack, wounded another three, and "carried off" an enslaved woman. Growing numbers of slaves had run off from their plantations, including twenty from a Saint James plantation belonging to Colonel Nedham. These raids and accompanying escapes seemed designed not only to attack the whites but also to bolster Maroon numbers and convey a measure of power.[26]

The colony responded by raising more men, and this time they found surprising success. In the spring of 1732 two smaller parties led by Captain Thomas Peters and Captain Andrew Morrison marched along the same path to "the Great Negro Town" that Soaper had opened up the year before. The Maroons discovered them, of course, and set up an ambush outside their town that killed two soldiers and one enslaved porter. But the colonial party killed two Maroons and was able to follow the others into their town. Peters and Morrison were not impressed with their men, "a parcel of cowardly, obstinate, unable fellows," but the parties had found the Maroon town at a very weak moment, when most of their men were out on raids. Those who remained did not have the strength to defend the town, so they set it afire and escaped. The whites occupied the town and stayed in seven houses that had not burned. Peters reported to Governor Hunter that the town was much larger than he had expected. They had recently opened "a great deal of new ground" that had been well planted with cacao and plantains. In the months that followed, the colony built a sizable barrack in the town to maintain a permanent presence in the mountains that could be provisioned through a supply chain on the road that could now be completed from Port Antonio to the heart of Maroon country.[27]

The experiences of one group of Maroons dislodged from their homes can be glimpsed through the account of a woman from this group who was captured by a colonial party along with six children. She had been born in the mountains but spoke "good English," which suggests either that she was born among the Leewards, born on a plantation, or that the Windwards followed a similar policy with respect to language. Driven from their homes, these Maroons were starving and divided on what to do. They split into three groups and went their separate ways, one of them heading west into Saint James. They hoped to forage and raid at first, but they had also brought tools. This woman's group had formed a new settlement and begun to plant when they were found by the colonial party that captured her and the children.[28]

If the tenacity of this group shows how illusory a colonial victory could be, the journal of one Ebenezer Lambe, captain of a detachment of regulars, details the knowledge Maroons had developed on how to survive. Recorded in September 1732, Lambe's description of this town in the cockpits defies imagination. It consisted of thirty-five houses divided into apartments built on about an acre of land on a high plateau. To the north and south rose high, steep hills, each with a guardhouse built on top, and to the east and west dropped treacherous cliffs that could only be climbed with great difficulty. A path as wide as two men walking abreast led out of the town up one of these hills, but there must have been other ways to escape, for on the soldiers' approach to the town all the women and children escaped. The town's architecture reveals years, perhaps generations, of adjustment to these mountains, with skilled building that allowed for the privacy of individuals or families, as well as military defense.[29]

It is remarkable that Lambe's men even found this place. They picked up the track of the Maroons after several days of climbing steep cliffs and discovered the town by chance. After weathering a rainstorm under an outcropping of stone, Lambe heard Maroons "playing on the top of a high Hill over us." Lambe attempted surprise, but they were quickly discovered and exchanged shots with the Maroons, who taunted the whites that they would soon run away "like a parcel of white liver'd sons of bitches." Lambe ordered his men to keep up this banter while he brought some of his best soldiers up the hill toward the guardhouse. When the Maroons discovered this advance party, they picked up their guns and lances and cut ropes that held back "great stones," which went crashing down on the attackers. Luckily for Lambe and his men, a crook in the path allowed them to avoid the stones, and they were able to continue to scale the hill. These Maroons seemed to have very few balls, for a shot point-blank at Lambe upon his approach to the guardhouse did no harm. When the Maroons realized their defenses had been breached, "they blew the Callabash" horn and ran from the town. Lambe thought they had killed one fighter, but while they found a pool of blood, they discovered no body. The white men occupied the town, put sentries around the perimeter, and stayed in their houses that night.

While the law entitled Lambe's men to enslave whomever they took, their raid yielded no captives. But they found plenty of plunder. Lambe found no planted fields near this town, but his men took away forty bags of corn, plantain flour, and corn flour. They found jerked hog (dried for preservation), as well as hogs' feet for soups, dried beans, cacao, cassava, and China root (ginger), all of which Lambe supposed came from the Montego Bay market. They had also gathered thatch cabbage for the roofs of their homes, as well as wild yams. The Maroons left eight iron pots and a tin kettle Lambe recognized as having been taken from a Saint James party. There were "medicines proper for green wounds," blankets, earthenware, cedar bowls, pewter plates, dishes, silverware, looking glasses, hoes, axes, and numerous guns. And there were bags of tobacco and a "Curious Colom of their own staining," evidence of a spiritual life among these Africans that is difficult for us to see.[30]

Lambe's success against this Maroon town sheds a bright light on this military conflict. The town's extensive possessions show how deeply embedded the Maroons had become. These autonomous black societies, where African languages languages commingled with the emerging Jamaican patois of the island, had easy access to the growing local markets that formed around the sugar plantations and their African villages. Enslaved people bought and sold at these markets and the Maroons mingled among them, gaining material resources but also information from those still enslaved, to better coordinate their raids. To the east and the west, the colony raised force after force to send against the Maroons and gradually learned how to defeat them in battle. But such victories did not bring the end of war. Lambe never found a body. The Maroons he displaced simply disappeared into the hills and either coalesced with like-minded groups or founded new settlements. Theirs was a life of difficulties unimaginable to the modern mind. They could have never taken over the island, but they had secured their own freedom and would fight to sustain it.

Less than a year after these colonial victories, news arrived in Spanish Town of a great defeat. Jamaica had stationed troops in what colonists called the "Great Negroe Town" in the Blue Mountains, but on Friday, May 29, 1733, a large body of Maroons began to circle. They were said to be led by a man who had escaped from Colonel Nedham's plantation two years earlier. The Maroons came so close to the town that they could taunt its occupiers: "White man! Do you need any powder and shot? We have plenty for you!" Some called out to the slaves forced to work for the parties, asking after their "wives and acquaintances" still on the plantations. They bragged about "how well they live" away from the plantations and sought to persuade those still enslaved "not to fight for the white man." The Maroons also warned the whites that they had more forces coming. They laid low on Saturday and Sunday, but muskets cracked on Monday morning as the Maroons fired from all sides on the surrounded whites. By three o'clock that afternoon, colonial forces had abandoned the town.[31]

Stung by defeat, Governor Hunter immediately convened the House of Assembly to develop a plan to retrench. On July 6, 1733, the assembly wrote to Sir Chaloner Ogle, commander of His Majesty's fleet stationed in Jamaica, for assistance in raising two hundred men from the navy to march alongside another party of one hundred men that the assembly would raise. They feared "a general insurrection" of the slaves around the mountains and desperately needed a powerful force to finally "reduce the rebellious slaves."[32] Ogle responded promptly, and on August 21 a party of two hundred sailors marched from Port Antonio to the Breastworks, where they met a colonial party of fifty white men and fifty blacks, some armed as soldiers and others who worked as porters. The colonial party hired two guides to lead them up into the mountains, but as they descended into the valley toward the town, they faced a fierce ambush that killed one of the guides. The sailors fought back "with the utmost fury," and after an hour of gunfire the Maroons retreated. The surviving guide convinced the colonial party that they must leave the valley or be surrounded and utterly destroyed. Fearful that the man was right, the sailors ascended the hill to protect themselves. But they had been tricked. Under cover of night both the guide and all of the black porters abandoned the party, carrying all of the baggage with them. Fooled and defeated, the colonial party returned to Port Antonio.[33]

Maroon resurgence in the Blue Mountains illustrated a depth of resources that colonial officials had only begun to realize. The colonial parties claimed only one consolation after this embarrassing defeat: they had captured a Maroon. Identified as Seyrus, Sarra, or Ned, this rebel had joined the Maroons as an adult after his escape from the plantation of his owner, George Taylor. We do not know when he escaped or what role he had played in the recapture of the Great Negro Town, but in early August 1733 he had come down the mountain with three friends, Cuffy, Cudjoe, and Quamina, to Port Antonio to spy on the whites. These names are all Akan day names, further evidence of a Coromantee prominence among the Windward Maroons, and Seyrus named another Cudjoe, who had escaped from Colonel Nedham's plantation, as the headman of a Maroon party that had just sacked Hobby's plantation.[34]

As his interrogators turned the screws that punctured his thumbs, Seyrus explained how the Maroons got so much powder and shot. The Maroons had with them two white boys named John Dun (or Done) and Charles, runaways who had escaped from Blind Fletcher of Passage Fort. The boys could write and had forged passes in the name of Colonel Nedham for a man named Quashee, who went down to Kingston to a Jewish merchant named Jacob who had a shop on Church Street and would sell to him. Seyrus also explained plans to ambush any white party that marched against the Great Negro Town. One party of a hundred Maroons would sit on Carrion Crow Hill, which overlooked one path, while another would wait at Hobby's place. They would place a drum on the ridge above the town to mark the arrival of any white party. If the party looked too big, the drum would warn the women, who would burn the town and escape. But if the Maroons felt confident, the drums would sound a martial beat and the Maroons would fight.[35]

The colony would not send another party to take the Great Negro Town for more than a year. Governor Hunter realized the need for greater strategy in confronting their formidable foe, so he sent out smaller parties with the specific aim of destroying their sustenance. In September, Hunter sent one party to Hobby's plantation to drive out the band of Maroons they had learned about from Seyrus, and a second party with eight days' provisions and the sole task of cutting down the Maroons' "Great Plantain Walk." Throughout October and November, colonial parties ranged through the Blue Mountains, destroying provision grounds with "pretty good success." And in light of their recent defeats, Hunter finally convinced the assembly to build an additional barrack closer to the Maroon town, to project colonial power deeper into the mountains.[36]

Hunter also ordered the further interrogation of Seyrus, who now claimed to be Sarra, or Ned. The examiners learned that what they knew as the Great Negro Town was known to the Maroons as Nanny Town, named for the famous woman leader who is still venerated as the ancestress of the Windward Maroons and was made a National Hero of Jamaica in 1976. Seyrus said nothing about Nanny herself, but he did report that her town's three hundred men were "esteemed the best" fighters. A man named Cuffee led them now, and he could be identified by his "silver-lac'd hatt" and the "small sword" he wore. Governance in the town followed a strict military discipline. Men who committed a crime were shot; women were flogged. Men unskilled at war worked the provision grounds with the women, and their custom was to work one day and play the next. In addition to Nanny Town, the Windward Maroons had established Gay's, or Guy's, Town on the top of Carrion Crow Hill. The men of this town fought with lances and cutlasses rather than guns, and this town had more extensive provision grounds planted with cacao, sugarcane, plantain, melons, and corn. In both towns there were far more women and children than there were men.[37]

White colonists might have gained from this interrogation a clearer view of their enemy, but such intelligence brought little reward. The Maroons had become emboldened by their success, and those who remained enslaved began to doubt the power of their masters. On Christmas Eve, fearing insurrection during this dangerous holiday, Hunter wrote to Whitehall of a disturbing turn in the war— it had spread farther into the west. The parties in the Blue Mountains had undertaken regular patrols of the few avenues they controlled, which seemed to instill a temporary calm, but he now had reports from Hanover Parish, where a band of Maroons had attacked the plantation of one Knowles, a young absentee, and burned the works and all the cane fields while the slaves simply ran off.[38]

Over the next few weeks Hunter received further accounts of large-scale escapes. Twenty-two plantation slaves who had been recruited to work with the colonial parties had deserted them; forty Coromantees had left their plantations in Saint Thomas in the East and joined the rebels. And in the Blue Mountains a band of two hundred Maroons had attacked the Breastworks, where a colonial party was building another barrack. The colonists had been able to deflect this latest attack, but many slaves in the area had joined the rebels, leaving the planters in "great consternation." This dire situation prompted the council and assembly of the colony to write a desperate memorial to the Crown. "The Negroes in Rebellion" had proved impossible to subdue, despite countless "fruitless attempts." They were powerfully embedded in the "vast Rocky Mountains covered with thick woods," and the considerable taxes raised to support parties to fight them had become unbearably "burthensome" to the island's once-prosperous inhabitants. And the situation had worsened. "They now despise our power . . . openly appear in Arms & are daily increasing by the desertion of other Slaves." The Maroons encouraged the slaves to join them; a cultural "affinity" drew them together, but "above all the hopes of Freedom" had made the discipline of the slave plantation near impossible. The colony needed "aid and assistance" or they would be forced to "abandon the country or become victims of those merciless people."[39]

The protracted military conflict between colonial forces and the Maroons gained considerable attention in the London press. In April 1732 the *Historical Register* reprinted without comment an address of the Council of Jamaica to the King lamenting the sad state of the colony. While largely concerned with imperial trade policy, the council named the threats from "our rebellious slaves" to be the "most obvious and visible Causes of our Misfortunes." The council expressed its gratitude for the two independent companies of regular troops, but press reports during the next two years illustrated how powerful the Maroons had become. In June 1733, the *Gentleman's Magazine* reported that the Maroons had retaken from colonial forces their principal town in the mountains, and in November it noted the "sharp fight" with the sailors raised by Admiral Ogle. Over the course of the following year, London readers learned that the Maroons continued to increase in numbers, were governed by their own king, and were said to be supplied by the Spanish. Whites on the island were outnumbered almost nine to one, and Whitehall had sent to the island an additional force of British regulars, six independent companies drawn from the regiments stationed in Gibraltar.[40]

The news from Jamaica generated novel dimensions in the broadening debate over racial slavery. Quaker pamphleteers first advanced the moral critique of slavery in the late seventeenth century, and in the 1720s Whig writers began to develop a political-economic critique of slavery that emphasized the tendency in slave-based economies for wealth to become concentrated in a few hands. The Maroon war in Jamaica illustrated an additional line of antislavery argument—namely, that slavery caused rebellions that endangered the lives of free colonists and weakened the colony's military potential. These latter lines of argument led the Georgia House of Assembly to pass its famous ban on slaveholding in 1734. As "experience hath shewn" that settling colonies with "black slaves" limited the growth of the white population, which weakened the colony in times of war, the assembly ordered that the keeping of slaves be prohibited. The growth of slaveholding would expose the colony "to the insurrec-tions, tumults, and rebellions" that could lead to the colony's "utter ruin." The law did not rest on the moral critique of slavery, for it provided that runaway slaves from South Carolina be seized and returned to their masters. The law may have been antislavery, but its rationale was very different from the moral antislavery of the Quakers that would later flourish.[41]

Less than two years later, the Virginia planter William Byrd II saw the war in Jamaica as reason to ban the "unchristian traffic" of transporting enslaved Africans to the Americas. Byrd did not elabo-rate on the "unchristian" nature of slavery, but he did note that there were "mountains in Virginia too," where slave rebels could "do as much mischief as they do in Jamaica." He hoped that Parliament would ban the transatlantic slave trade, and he laid the blame for slavery on the "ravenous traders" who trafficked in slaves.[42]

Byrd's thinking may have been influenced by a remarkable debate in London magazines that stemmed from the Maroon war in Ja-maica. In January 1735, the *Prompter*, a London magazine, printed the address of one Moses Bon Sáam to the rebels in the mountains. Sáam's arguments struck antislavery chords that may have surprised readers, for he spoke in modern tones about human rights, and he spoke from the ground of resistance.[43]

Sáam might have been the invention of a radical white abolitionist, but his story and arguments gesture toward an abolitionism, even a black nationalism, that seems well ahead of its time. Sáam claimed to have once been enslaved, but sixteen years before, he had saved his master's life and been freed for the act. He gained an education during these years of freedom and realized that the power of the whites grew from their skill in the arts of war, not in some "wild imaginary Superiority." He condemned colonial slaveholders as "*Spoilers* of the *Work* of GOD, who dare make *Beasts* of human forms." He compared the "Majestic Glossiness" of the African to the "pale, sickly Whiteness" of their masters. Sáam acknowledged the legitimacy of the enslavement of the prisoners of war sold into Atlantic slavery, but why, he asked, should "the Children's Children of this wretch's children" be condemned to eternal slavery? To purchase one slave did not justify the enslavement of an entire "Race." Sáam had also discovered that he had been named after the Moses celebrated in the "white men's religion" as the savior of a "chosen Nation" who had delivered his people from "just such a *Slavery* as *Ours!*" Awakened by education and the anguished "shriekings" of his enslaved brethren, this Jamaican Moses had abandoned his colonial freedom to join the rebels in the mountains.[44]

Sáam made provocative arguments that found greater distribution through a reprinting in the *Gentleman's Magazine*, and they elicited a proslavery response from the Reverend Robert Robertson.[45] Born in the early 1680s, Robertson served as rector of Saint John's Church in Fig Tree Hill, Nevis. Robertson had defended colonial slaveholders once before, when Edmund Gibson, the Bishop of London, wrote two public letters to the West Indian planters, calling on them to aid the missionaries to the colonies in the terribly important conversion of their heathen African slaves. With defensive prose that reflected a deep frustration with his ministry, Robertson described a rebellious and brutalized, culturally alien slave population who were simply impossible to convert. Moreover, the whites sent to the West Indies consisted of "whores, rogues, vagrants, thieves, [and] sodomites" who set an awful example of Christian life for the slaves. For Robertson, to ask the handful of gentlemen colonists—namely, the masters and few ministers resident in the islands—to work harder at the conversion of slaves was at best a misinformed censure of valuable subjects to the King.[46]

Robertson wrote this first pamphlet from Nevis, but he must have returned to London thereafter, for his response to Sáam's address to the slaves appeared within a month of the latter's publication in the *Prompter*. Posing as Caribeus, "Chief of the Whites," Robertson sought to demonstrate the fallacy of Sáam's accusations of abuse. Colonial slaveholders, he argued, were "restrained from Cruelty, both by the Laws and by their own Interest." He condemned Sáam as an ungrateful servant who abused the "kind manumission" he had been granted. Robertson argued that Jamaica demanded an "easy servitude" far more humane than the *"native Slavery* to *savage Tyrants* of your own complexion" in Africa. He likened gentleman slaveholders to benevolent fathers of children, governing in accordance with the "tender Influence of Humanity." The English poor had lives far worse, he argued, mastered by *"grim Necessity"* rather than kind gentlemen. Robertson chastised those who had fled to the mountains and advised them to return to their "much injured Masters," who were ready with forgiveness. They should return to "honest Labour" and the "peaceful Blessings of domestick Life" it ensured.[47]

Robertson returned to his writing desk within the year for a more extended rebuttal. Exchanging the voice of Caribeus for that of a free and Christian black named John Talbot Campo-bell, Robertson tried to seize the same ground as Sáam with a "speech . . . to his Countrymen in the Mountains of Jamaica." Robertson invented a black character who resembled Sáam but cast blame for slavery on English slave trade merchants and the policy makers who supported them. He thus fostered the development of an intellectual defense of slavery that emphasized barbarous African wars, rapacious English merchants, and kind colonial slaveholders who saved their slaves from both.[48]

Campo-bell began with his wartime enslavement alongside his father and much of his family when he was a boy. Their African captors sold them to English merchants who clapped them in irons on a London slaver. One group of captive men rebelled, only to be slaughtered by the white sailors. Campo-bell thought it fortunate that the insurrection failed, or they would have all perished at sea with no whites to guide the ship. When they arrived in Jamaica, his master purchased him, along with his father and eight relatives, and brought him to his plantation. Campo-bell was a handsome boy, and his master decided to baptize and educate. He served as manservant to the master's eldest son during his education in England and his travels throughout the European continent. And having served so loyally and well, the master freed Campo-bell on his return to Jamaica.[49]

While he acknowledged the singularity of his own experience, Campo-bell argued that the life of any Jamaican slave was better than sure slaughter in the barbarous wars of Africa. Campo-bell did acknowledge that a few sugar planters had indeed "treated some of our Colour basely and barbarously," but these men were the exception, not the rule. The laws of the British sugar colonies were explicitly designed to obstruct such cruelty, for the English were not a cruel people. If the rebels in the mountains would submit, and reject the harangues of Sáam, they would find their lives "safer, easier, and happier than ever they can be in the Mountains." But Campo-bell, and indeed Robertson, suspected that Sáam and the rebels in the mountains protested slavery itself, and in this they shared much with those in England who censured the sugar planters. But if slavery were wrong—and Robertson held out the possibility that it was—then moral criticism should fall on the authors of the system, the African man-stealers and the English slavers who bought from them. The planters of the islands were honest souls who did not deserve the hatred of the rebels, or that of the antislavery writers at home.[50]

Such political debate over slavery would deepen in the coming generations, but in the 1730s the colony of Jamaica was caught in an intractable and debilitating military stalemate. In a memo penned for his patron, Prime Minister Sir Robert Walpole, in October 1734, Martin Bladen, one of the most informed imperial administrators, argued that the colony should end the war with the Maroons through a treaty for peace. He had clearly read a significant corpus of colonial correspondence, for he recited the litany of complaints forwarded by the several governors of Jamaica. The Crown had been "at great expense" to suppress this rebellion of slaves who "desert daily in great numbers" from the sugar plantations. The defeat of numerous parties rendered the white colonists "contemptible to the Negroes," who now believed they could take the island. Bladen recommended caution and a carefully considered plan. The governor of the colony should "make diligent inquiry" into why the colonists had failed so miserably in defeating these foes and make the necessary changes. Roads through the island needed to be cut;

barracks for troops needed to be built in every parish; and then the war needed to be taken to the rebels. Bladen did not believe the Maroons could be destroyed "entirely," but if the colonial forces could render these Africans "more tractable," then the colony should treat with them. Why not? The Spanish had done so throughout their empire with great success. "There is hardly a great Town in New Spain that has not a . . . Polanky, and their old Runaway Negroes thro' process of Time are become as good Subjects to the King of Spain" as any Spaniard. Bladen proposed a treaty that would grant the Maroons a remote section of land, that secured their acknowledgment of the colonial state, and that prohibited them from welcoming runaways from the plantations. Perhaps he felt the security of such a treaty would balance the indignity of granting a "general Amnesty" to such hardened enemies of the planters' regime.[51]

To treat with the Maroons appealed to imperial officials such as Bladen, but the Maroons continued to attack; they were not at all "tractable." Governor Hunter died before Bladen's essay could shape policy, and in early October 1734 a Maroon band descended the mountains into Saint George Parish and attacked John Broadgate's plantation, thought to be protected by Edwards Fort. The rebels burned the fort and the canes and attracted more recruits. The assembly met in the aftermath of this latest attack and agreed to establish martial law, which Hunter had been advocating since February. The new governor, John Ayscough, an established planter and member of the Jamaica Council, had stepped in as governor once before, in 1726, so he knew this conflict well. Ayscough declared martial law on October 23, 1734, which enabled the colony to draft six hundred men to form two additional parties that would march into the Blue Mountains. Moreover, six military transports arrived in Kingston Harbor in November, each with an independent company of a hundred troops. Ayscough sent the troops to the heart of the conflict in support of the parties. He stationed two companies in the barracks of Port Antonio, and the other four he divided up and "placed on the several plantations in St. Thomas in the East." Troops could instill order and maintain sugar production despite the Maroons.[52]

Such a massing of force boded ill for the Maroons, weakened as they were by the parties' destruction of their grounds. In December the newly raised colonial parties marched against Nanny Town following a now familiar route, one party clearing the ambushes and the second party following behind, which compelled the Maroons to retreat and again abandon their town.[53] They headed west as they had before, and by February 1735 a group of about 140 men, women, and children were spotted in Saint Ann. Ayscough sent smaller "flying parties" in pursuit of them, but despite their weakened condition, the Maroons evaded the parties, with the exception of "an Ebo named Cupid," who was said to have "escaped from them [the Maroons]." According to Cupid, they were headed to Saint Elizabeth, where they sought out John Cuffee, a leader of one of the Leeward bands. Led by one Quarantine (probably Quamina) and Colonel Nedham's Cuffee, these Maroons were starving and desperate. They lived off the land, raided plantations for food, and had killed four of their own men who no longer had the strength to keep up. They had weapons but little powder and carried their plantation tools, suggesting their aspiration to start a new settlement. Cupid reported that another band, led by Adou, had remained in the Blue Mountains. Nanny stayed with this group, which formed a new settlement but seems to have withdrawn from the war.[54]

This second seizure of Nanny Town seemed to present the opportunity that Bladen had described. The Board of Trade had recommended Bladen's policy to Governor Hunter before his death, and in the aftermath of victory, Governor Ayscough empowered one Mr. Granville, a lieutenant from one of the independent companies, "to capitulate with the rebels." Granville's orders instructed him to offer freedom and land to any rebel leader that he could approach. The results were quite mixed. One group warned Granville that "if he came to them again they would kill him." But another group, led by one Captain Goomer, offered to come in with his men, about forty or fifty strong, if granted amnesty. Goomer had been born among the Maroons, but he had come into conflict with Cudjoe, as well as with the colonial parties. He and his men had resorted to moving about constantly and, tired of such a life, Goomer embraced the opportunity to treat.[55]

Very few Maroons decided to treat, however, and Maroon attacks in the west continued to intensify. In May 1737, yet another temporary governor, the planter and former chief justice John Gregory, wrote to the Board of Trade that he saw no end to the conflict unless "we could bring them in by Treaty." He had recommended this solution to the assembly several times, he wrote, but few were yet inclined to such a desperate bid for peace.[56] For most Jamaican planters, to treat with the Maroons must have seemed the acknowledgment of defeat by an inferior foe—unthinkable. But a minority in the colony, including Governor Gregory, had come to believe that only a treaty would end this conflict. Another planter who shared this view was John Guthrie, a sugar planter from Westmoreland who owned about ninety slaves, a modest number in comparison with some of his neighbors. Soon after Cudjoe's Westmoreland attack, Gregory placed Guthrie in command of a party that had an unusual mandate: to seek information on and open communication with Cudjoe's people rather than fight them. Guthrie raised a small party of thirty-six men and placed one Lieutenant Chambers in command with very specific instructions. They were to seek out "the avenues to Capt. Cudjoe's Principal Settlement," but they were not to attempt a military engagement. If they could take a prisoner or two alive, that would be valuable, but they must "use them kindly." If they met up with any of Cudjoe's men, they were to "offer in [the governor's] name terms of accommodation" and a time and place to meet. If they were to discover one of Cudjoe's towns, they must not burn or plunder it.[57]

Like Ayscough, Gregory had lived with the Maroon conflict for many years, and he understood that such intelligence would be critical to any major offensive against the Leewards. The offensives waged by the Windwards had been bold and dangerous, but the Cockpit Country controlled by the Leewards lay at the center of sugar production, and it possessed a great concentration of the island's African population. The Blue Mountains spread into the parishes of Portland, Saint Thomas in the East, Saint David, Saint George, and Saint Andrews, a region of the island with more settlements than plantations that held about seventeen thousand enslaved Africans. In contrast, the Cockpit Country lay at the center of the sugar region, in the middle of the parishes of Saint James, Saint Ann, Clarendon, Saint Elizabeth, Westmoreland, and Hanover, where thirty-seven thousand enslaved Africans lived and worked, mostly in sugar. More was at stake in the war for the West.[58]

While Chambers gathered intelligence on the ground, the new governor of the island, Edward Trelawney, studied the correspondence of his predecessors. Trelawney had been offered the governorship in 1736, but he did not arrive on the island till April 1738.[59] In the interim, colonial administrators concerned with the Spanish threat against Georgia had proposed moving His Majesty's forces stationed in Jamaica to Georgia. Trelawney protested to the Duke of Newcastle that such a policy would "deliver the Island into the Hands of the Blacks." He cited a litany of desperate pleas from the Jamaica Assembly and attributed the survival of the colony to the six independent companies. He noted the recent insurrection in Antigua and warned of the "Dangerous Spirit of Liberty" among enslaved Africans throughout the sugar islands.[60]

Once established in Spanish Town, Trelawney visited the mountains and described the severe challenges of military service in Jamaica. "The great difficulty is not to beat, but to see the enemy." The Maroons could traverse "steep mountains & precipices" that were covered with woods so thick with "twisted & intangled" brush that a man had to hack at nature with a cutlass at each step. The weather brought "heavy piercing rains" that destroyed tents and rendered military protocols impossible to follow. Islanders called it "Bush-fighting."[61]

The Maroons who excelled at such war were a "great and," Trelawney was afraid, "a growing evil." They were spread in bands throughout the island, and not a day passed when they did not attack. And those enslaved on the plantations deserted to the rebels almost every day. The planters kept up "continual guards," but most could not afford the expense. Like his predecessors, Trelawney sent detachments of "four to ten or twelve soldiers" to individual plantations to assist the planters in managing their slaves, and while this "had some good effect," it could not be a permanent solution.[62]

The colonists who had fought in this war knew that it would be "impossible to reduce the Rebels by force." Among these men was Guthrie. Gregory must have introduced Guthrie to Trelawney soon after the new governor's arrival, for within a month of his taking residence on the island, Trelawney had a letter from Guthrie with intelligence on Cudjoe's town. Situated a "three days easy march from Little River in St. James Parish," Cudjoe's principal town was home to about a hundred men and a "great number" of women and children. There were several other Maroon towns in the region under Cudjoe's authority, but Guthrie knew little about these communities.[63]

By July 1738, Trelawney was ready to launch a major effort to establish a treaty with the Maroons. He presented his case to the Jamaica Council and recruited Guthrie to lead a party of two hundred volunteers, who would be joined by a smaller party of forty-two regular soldiers led by Francis Sadler. The parties recruited three former Maroons, Cuffee, Sambo, and Quashey, as guides to lead them to Cudjoe's town and gathered at William Hall's plantation Tryall, in Saint James parish near Montego Bay. The parties set out for Cudjoe's town on February 13, marching for two days in "fair weather" into the cockpits. They passed some old hunting huts and hog traps built by the Maroons and on the third day discovered a "plain path" that led toward the main town. On February 16 they came upon a group of Maroons working a provision ground, who spotted the party and raised an alarm. Guthrie and Sadler continued on but soon found themselves in "a small valley" that led toward a pass in the mountains. As the parties moved forward, the Maroons attacked from all sides, horns blowing. The parties lost one man and suffered two casualties in what had been a very brief fight, only fifteen minutes. But the pass they gained led only to another spacious provision ground surrounded by cockpits. It was late in the day, rain had begun to fall, and their guides told them a difficult mile remained before they would reach Cudjoe's town. So they remained in this place while Cudjoe prepared his defenses.[64]

The next morning their guides led them to "another Straight and Dangerous passage" that led to another provision ground, and once they passed through this, they faced "an ascent inexpressibly difficult" where the Maroons lay wait with another fierce ambush. The parties suffered three more casualties, but this time they marched into Cudjoe's town. According to James Knight, the Maroons knew many of the volunteers by name and there had been much banter and cursing. Guthrie also communicated his desire for peace, and Cudjoe sent word that he would meet with Guthrie in a secret place in the cockpits. Maroon escorts brought Guthrie there alone, and he and Cudjoe spoke for two hours. Guthrie offered terms for peace, stating that the Maroons should remain on this land if they would assist the colony against a foreign enemy and take up all future runaway slaves. But Cudjoe was unconvinced, or more likely he had to consult with others, for the men parted ways with no agreement. The Maroons hidden in the mountains began to fire down on the men who occupied their town. Guthrie ordered the town be set fire, and they retreated to the place where they had slept the night before.[65]

On the following morning the Maroons called for a second conference with Guthrie, attended not only by Cudjoe but also by another Maroon leader named Cuffee, as well as the "Captain of the Port Antonio Gang," who had arrived in the night with a hundred men. The presence of this man, and Cuffee, at the second conference resulted in an agreement between the Maroons and the colony. Guthrie wrote Trelawney immediately with news that the sides had agreed to wait ten days without hostilities while Guthrie awaited confirmation from the governor, and while Cudjoe no doubt held further deliberations with his captains.[66]

Trelawney called a nighttime meeting of the Jamaica Council as soon as he received Guthrie's news. He was thrilled by the parties' success. He sent orders to all the colonial parties to cease hostilities. He asked Guthrie to communicate to Cudjoe that he "had a good character of him" and would not hesitate to grant him freedom, posing as if he had this power. But most whites could not yet countenance granting freedom to those who had run away from their rightful masters. The council hammered out a series of resolutions to serve as the basis of a treaty, which included a clause that pardoned all rebels who had fled within the past two years, provided they returned to their masters, and to slavery. At best, Trelawney wrote, these runaways could be "employ'd as Slaves to the Public Service," but he did not consider manumitting them. He asked Guthrie to handle this point "very tenderly" and promised a meeting between the governor and Cudjoe in the near future.[67]

On March 1, 1739, at a camp near the burned-down town now named after Governor Trelawney, Captains Cudjoe, Accompong,

Johnny, Cuffee, and Quacow, leaders of the Leeward Maroons, met with Guthrie and Sadler, who represented the colony and the British Army, respectively. These men signed a treaty of fifteen clauses that ended a war as old as the colony itself. The Maroons would hereafter be considered "in a perfect state of freedom and Liberty." The treaty recognized Cudjoe's power over all the Leeward towns and established a line of descent in the case of his death. Cudjoe's towns would control 1,500 acres of the island in perpetuity, between Trelawney Town and the cockpits. They were free to plant their land with crops and raise herds, and they could sell their produce and meat in the colony's markets. Cudjoe and his men agreed to come to the aid of the colony if a foreign power were to attack the island, and they agreed to assist in the suppression of the other bands of Maroons, unless they too agreed to a treaty with similar terms. The Maroons would allow a white man to live in each of their towns, and they would send back runaway slaves who approached them in the future. But on the "tender" question of those who had joined the Maroons within the past two years, Cudjoe and his captains refused the Jamaica Council's demands. These men and women could choose to return to the enslavement of their white masters, but they could also choose to stay with the Maroons.[68]

As soon as Trelawney heard the treaty had been signed, he headed west in order to meet Captain Cudjoe and his men, and to develop a strategy to bring the Windward Maroons under treaty as well. After the final burning of Nanny Town, the Windwards had divided into several camps, one led by Nanny and at least one other in Saint George Parish under the leadership of Quao. One Windward captain (perhaps Quao) had attended an early meeting between Cudjoe, Guthrie, and Sadler, but the Windwards were not under Cudjoe's authority and so they did not agree to the treaty of March 1. Trelawney met with Cudjoe and his captains at Robert Bennet's plantation in Saint Ann and called on them to respect the terms of their new treaty and march with a colonial party against the Windwards. Cudjoe agreed and likely averted further bloodshed. He sent one of his brothers and fifty men with a colonial party led by Guthrie and Bennet. Cudjoe's men knew the terrain. They led the party to the Windward town of Quao, occupied the provision ground, sent word of their agreement with the colony, and encouraged Quao to agree to the same terms. And so, on June 23, 1739, the colony of Jamaica signed a treaty with Quao, a captain of the Windward Maroons in the Blue Mountains, ceding them land and gaining another unexpected ally in maintaining the political order of slavery.[69]

Nanny never signed a treaty, but she did secure land for her people and did come to an agreement with the colony. Nanny had wisely advised a tactical retreat after the second seizure of her town in 1735, but only some of the Windwards had followed her. Once the other Maroon towns had made their agreements with the colony, Nanny sent word that she too would come to terms on similar conditions. In August 1740, a clerk in Spanish Town entered into the official book of land patents a grant of five hundred acres in the Blue Mountains of Portland for "a certain Negro woman called Nanny and the people now residing with her." The legal authority to grant this land stemmed from the laws passed in the 1720s to people the "North-east Part of this Island." Ironically, the resistance Nanny led had contributed greatly to the passage of those acts. Nanny and her people agreed to pay an annual tax of one pound in Jamaican currency, to fight with the colony in the case of insurrection, and to support the residence of five white men on their land. So while Nanny never surrendered, the relationship of her town to the colony became much the same as that of the other Maroon towns throughout the island.[70]

The Jamaica House of Assembly passed laws that codified and revised these treaties signed on the battlefield. Each new law included the preamble "Whereas upon the late submission of . . . ," a phrase that was not true, a phrase to which the Maroon captains had not agreed.[71] With this sleight of hand the assembly established the Maroons as independent entities subject to the colony, rather than as sovereign entities unto themselves. And the assembly passed a further law that offered cold cash to the old fighters, to transform these slave rebels into slave catchers. The law ordered magistrates to pay Maroons three pounds for each runaway captured, money that would be collected from the owners. When these laws were passed, each community of Maroons numbered fewer than three hundred people; they were exhausted by war and had fought for three generations to

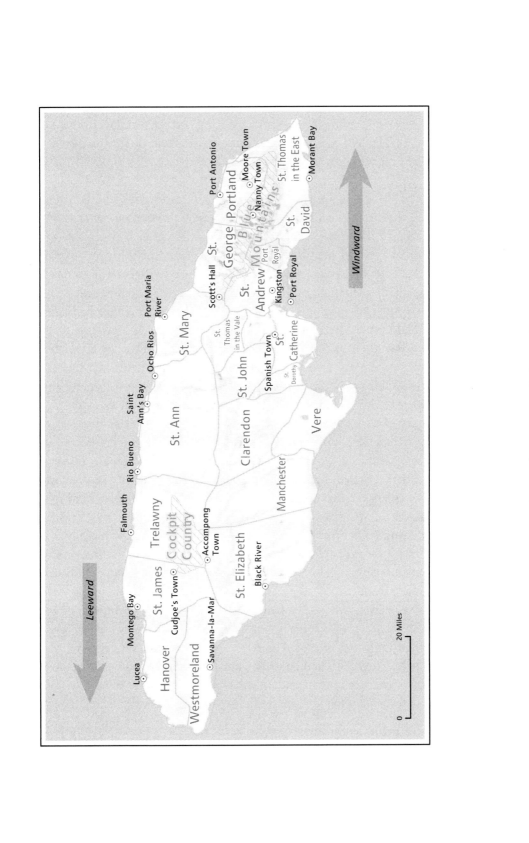

maintain the dignity of a life beyond slavery. The Jamaica Assembly had passed forty-four laws geared toward the elimination of these Maroons, spending £240,000 of the King's revenue in the effort. And for all of that, the planters had been forced to settle for treaties.[72]

After the treaties with the Maroons had been signed, the Board of Trade sent Governor Trelawney a series of questions about the condition of the island, which required him to gather considerable information about population, trade, agriculture, and the colony's state of defense. The Maroon wars had done great damage to the country, essentially depopulating large swaths of the island where small settlements had once been established. These settlers either had been killed by the Maroons or had left in fear, and their "settlements to this day are over run with Trees and Bushes." Trelawney estimated that more than two-thirds of the island remained uncultivated, whites were still hopelessly outnumbered by their black slaves, and the governor believed that the colony's only hope lay in attracting more white settlers. The assembly had designed "Barracking Laws" to attract such immigrants, whereby a barrack would be erected in each parish that would serve as the quarters for a company of forty soldiers and their officers. The parish vestries would make every effort to ensure that such barracks were established not on land that favored existing plantations but rather in undeveloped areas, thus attracting settlers who had the means to establish new plantations. These "Barrack Lands" would be granted to settlers at the rate of one hundred acres for every ten slaves and one white man established on the land.[73]

Such laws envisioned a familiar pattern of development with large-scale sugar production and the expectation of robust slave resistance. Only men of capital could afford to purchase ten slaves to build a new settlement, and the law embedded military force in the very infrastructure of the sugar frontier. Slave rebellions posed a serious risk for any capital investment in the colonial economy, which the assembly sought to allay by ensuring the proximity of a military force on which new planters could depend. Trelawney believed that if these laws were approved and actually enacted, then the island would be well peopled within "a very few years." Since news of the treaties had spread—and this had taken less than a year—sixteen white families from the Leeward Islands had come to Jamaica with their slaves and settled in Manchioneel, a good harbor but close to Nanny Town and previously subject to raids. No one, however, had settled in Norman's Valley in Saint James, near a proposed barrack that Trelawney believed contained better land. Norman's Valley lay eight miles inland and close to Cudjoe's towns, but there were few white settlements. That new migrants settled close to a port and none chose the good sugar land inland revealed the importance of security to the decisions new settlers made.[74]

Trelawney may have hoped these laws would be effective, but his personal correspondence suggests he had begun to think seriously about the political economy of the slave society he governed. In May 1741, before Trelawney had completed his report on the island, he wrote to his friend Henry Pelham, then lord of the Treasury, that he had begun to entertain "loose thoughts" about "abolishing slavery and putting the negroes upon some such foot[ing] as the ancient villeins of England." Trelawney had shared his ideas with Lord Monson as well, and perhaps others, and by June he wrote again to Pelham that his ideas were "more at heart than [Trelawney] could imagine."[75]

The Maroon treaties promised an era of peace on the island, and many whites invested considerable capital in new plantations and enslaved people to work them. By 1752, the seven parishes most affected by the Maroon wars had built new barracks. The parish of Saint James, where Trelawney hoped new settlers would go, built one of these barracks, and in subsequent years the parish economy exhibited the most dynamic growth on the island. In 1739 the parish remained undeveloped, with only eight plantations worked by 2,588 enslaved Africans who produced about 660 hogsheads of sugar each year. Neighboring Westmoreland, by contrast, had sixty-four plantations in 1739 that produced 5,450 hogsheads of sugar annually with 11,155 enslaved Africans. Thirty years later Saint James had surpassed Westmoreland to become the most productive and populous parish on the island. By 1768 colonists had established ninety-four sugar plantations in Saint James, worked by 14,500 enslaved Africans who produced about 11,000 hogsheads of sugar each year. More planters exploited more slaves more efficiently. But there had also been considerable expansion into other crops, for a third of the enslaved Africans of Saint James (7,229) worked on pens that raised stock and provisions to supply the plantations, or worked on smaller farms that produced cotton, ginger, or pimiento. Because of the treaties and the military barracks, the parish where most whites had been too frightened to settle in the 1730s had become a site for the most efficient exploitation of enslaved African labor.[76]

The transatlantic slave trade to Jamaica also grew, but only modestly, suggesting that the greatest factor in the island's economic growth during this period lay in enhanced security. During the twenty-year period after the signing of the Maroon treaties, the transatlantic slavers brought captives to Jamaica at the rate of about 7,200 every year, about 150,000 people total. The twenty-year period before the treaties saw about 6,500 African captives landed in Kingston by the slavers each year, 130,000 people in all. Sugar production doubled between 1739 and 1760, while the importation of enslaved labor increased by about 11 percent. The treaties had been effective indeed.[77]

While white Jamaicans marched heedlessly forward in the buying of slaves and the making of sugar, in 1745 about a dozen enslaved drivers in the parish of Saint John organized a conspiracy to rebel that probably stretched throughout this small inland parish. The planters discovered the conspiracy before the uprising began, but within months of these events a group of thirteen men and seven women enslaved in Kingston and Port Royal rebelled against their masters and marched into the mountains, where they sought "to live in the woods and be free." They killed several slave catchers, white and black, whom their masters sent after them, but it would take weeks of fighting and the enlistment of forty Maroons from Crawford Town before the rebels were surrounded and crushed. Governor Trelawney saw these developments as "small eruptions" that threatened to "endanger so much the whole body." How, he asked, could so few rebels put the entire colony on edge?[78]

The renewal of slave violence prompted Trelawney to elaborate his long-considered schemes for Jamaica, which he published anonymously as *An Essay concerning Slavery and the Danger Jamaica Is Exposed to from the Too Great Number of Slaves*. He had abandoned the idea to abolish slavery, but he clearly believed that slavery could not be defended on ethical grounds. Trelawney adopted an imagined dialogue between a military officer and a planter, which probably distilled many of his own conversations. He situated the officer alone with his books—Samuel von Pufendorf, John Locke, and the Bible among them—interrupted in his study by the planter. When the planter asked about the books, the officer admitted to being "a little crazy" but claimed that he intended to prove "that Slavery, as it is now practiced among us, is contrary to the Law of God and Nature." A long soliloquy followed that traced much of the ferment in European thinking about the legitimacy of slavery. Trelawney followed Pufendorf's discussion of the origins of slavery in (1) the forfeiture of liberty through desperate need, (2) enslavement as a punishment for crime, and (3) enslavement as the result of conquest in war. But anticipating the argument made by Baron Montesquieu in *L'Esprit de Lois* (1748), Trelawney argued that this third source of origin, widely known to be the most common source for enslaved Africans, could not be defended. Pufendorf had argued that slavery was the lawful continuation of war, and Locke had followed this line of thinking. The conqueror enslaved the conquered as the humane alternative to slaughter, and so slavery was right. But Trelawney observed that while killing was legitimate during battle, once "the combat is over," killing became wrong. Any victor in war who slaughtered his prisoners would be "reckon'd cruel and inhumane." Such a justification for slavery, therefore, could not stand.[79]

Trelawney grappled with the problem of slavery in the light of his own experience in Jamaica, but also through intellectual engagement with European authors. He even likened slavery in Jamaica to a fantastical story he attributed to Montesquieu's *Persian Letters* (1721), about savages who captured people in order to boil them into soap. How different were the planters, he asked, who "melt away through hard labor" the bodies of enslaved Africans to make sugar? Trelawney wrote with shock that "the generous Free Briton who knows the

Value of Liberty" would consider the enslavement of others. He even argued that the planters had caused the violent resistance of slaves by their brutal policies. But he stopped far short of abolitionism. Trelawney took the inconsistent position that while slavery could not be ethically defended, it had proved so profitable and valuable to empire that the institution required far better management than the current generation of white colonials had proved capable of providing.[80]

Trelawney saw the planters of Jamaica as so utterly deluded by their greed that they had endangered the colony. The poll tax of 1740 showed that the island's black population outnumbered the whites by a ratio of ten to one; some plantations had thirty black slaves for one white man. And while the slavers brought more enslaved Africans every year, "the *Whites* rather diminish." Where would this end? Did the planters really think that Africans were "not of the same Species with us, but that being of a different Mold and Nature, as well as Colour, they were made entirely for our Use?" Trelawney likened the planters to those who bought South Sea stock in the 1720s— they knew the high prices would collapse and gambled that they could sell before that happened. But the planters did not play with money alone; they risked the bloody wrath of the people they enslaved, who had risen up before and would do so again. He warned that if the planters did not reform their slave system, they would lose their lives and Great Britain would lose a valuable colony.[81]

Trelawney made three principal policy recommendations that he believed would enable the planters to sustainably manage their slaves. First and foremost, the transatlantic slave trade must be abolished by an act of Parliament. It would compel the colonists to encourage their slaves to reproduce and thus create a self-sustaining workforce. If the planters would give "a little linen" to every woman who became pregnant, and if they had "all the barren ones whipt upon a certain Day every Year," Trelawney believed the "Negro Ladies would yield better and at least keep up the present stock."[82]

His second policy recommendation proposed that enslaved people be entirely prohibited from either domestic labor in the home or any trade in the towns. Trelawney accepted the prevailing view that only black people could perform the drudgery of plantation labor in the tropics, and he argued from this point that all enslaved Africans should be limited to field labor. Eliminating slaves from the trades, and from the work of domestic servants, would send more black slaves to the plantations and open up this labor market to whites, which might rectify the island's dangerous demographic imbalance.[83]

Trelawney's third policy recommendation was that all planters be compelled to manumit the headmen of their estates to achieve a uniform proportion of ten or twelve enslaved people to one free man, be he white, brown, or black. The recent rebellion in Saint John Parish showed how dangerous it was to entrust enslaved men "with any Power." Trelawney saw that the drivers' power within the plantation had emboldened them to rebel against their own enslavement. The obvious solution was to promise these men freedom and twenty acres of land on the estate after seven years of service as driver. They would work cheerfully and efficiently and, once established as tenants, would be loyal servants to their patron. As freemen they would also have military obligations to the colonial state, to serve in the militia against a foreign enemy or to suppress the next insurrection. Trelawney likened such manumissions to the ancient myth of Jason's sowing of the hydra's teeth, which grew into so many soldiers. Trelawney's "black Sons of *Hydra*" would secure the island for generations to come. Like Martin Bladen in the midst of the Maroon wars, Trelawney turned to a Spanish practice—selective manumission—as a policy shift in the governance of slavery that would make the planters stronger.[84]

Trelawney was widely celebrated by the Jamaican elite when he retired from the island in 1752, but he never acknowledged his authorship of the *Essay concerning Slavery* and his ideas found little support. The transatlantic slave trade to Jamaica remained the largest branch of British slaving. British slavers now purchased captives in every coastal region of West and West Central Africa. From the end of the Maroon wars to 1760, captives from the Bight of Biafara and the Gold Coast each represented about 30 percent of the enslaved Africans arriving in Jamaica; smaller proportions arrived from Senegambia, the Windward Coast, the Bight of Benin, and West Central Africa.[85]

The Bight of Biafara had become the largest source of enslaved people for British slavers, but the stateless marketing system in the hinterland of the Bight of Biafara that drew captives down to the coast differed markedly from the slaving system of the Gold Coast. Asante developed into a formidable empire during this period, but its history was punctuated by several civil wars as once-conquered Akan states like Denkyira and Akyem continued to revolt. Dahomey remained the principal state in the hinterland of the Bight of Benin, but it became subject to Oyo, a kingdom to the north, and contributed far fewer captives to the transatlantic slave trade than in years past. In short, through the operation of the slave trade, Jamaica's African population was more multiethnic than it had ever been before. Men and women captured in the wars among the Akan states continued to be a significant presence in Jamaica, but they worked and lived alongside considerable numbers of people of different African heritage.[86]

The momentous rebellion of 1760 was an island-wide effort among the Coromantee to break their enslavement. Manuscript sources label the rebels Coromantee, contemporaries like Edward Long believed the rebellion to be the work of Coromantees, and the rebels clearly had considerable military experience. But a careful reconsideration of this rebellion also sheds light on the meaning of "Coromantee." The rebellion suggests that the coalescence of the Coromantee in Jamaica represented the decisions of diverse enslaved people rather than a cultural process inexorably linked to coastal origin in Africa. Not all Akan people embraced the Coromantee cause of radical rebellion, and some—perhaps many—people who were not Akan did join the rebellion. Coromantee roots may have been Akan, but Akan and Coromantee were not exchangeable identities. The Coromantee were an African people who emerged from the travails of Jamaican slavery.[87]

The rebellion began in the midst of the Seven Years' War when Jamaica's garrison of regular troops had been reduced by five companies of men who had been sent to the Mosquito Coast and to West Africa. The rebel leadership perceived this weakness, but the rebellion began prematurely on April 8, 1760, in the parish of Saint Mary in the north-central region of the island. That night about fifty rebels led by Tacky (a Fante name) raided Fort Haldane in Port Maria.[88] They killed the night watchman and "secured a great quantity of arms and ammunition." They then moved from plantation to plantation, killing sixteen whites in all and setting fire to the trash houses where the overseers stored the old, shredded cane to process the next crop. The rebels met with resistance from alert whites and several enslaved men who sided with the masters, and when they reached Esher plantation, owned by William Beckford, two enslaved men named Billy and Philip escaped the rebels and secured horses to ride into Spanish Town to alert the governor.[89]

Billy and Philip arrived in Spanish Town in the early afternoon, and by that evening Lieutenant Governor Henry Moore had mobilized colonial forces. Moore had plenty of troops at his command, as well as the enhanced power that comes with wartime readiness. He also had local roots. Moore came from a long-established planting family in Jamaica, and he owned a plantation in Saint Mary. He ordered four detachments of troops of three officers and sixty men to march to Saint Mary and to neighboring Saint John. Three detachments came from the Seventy-Fourth Regiment based in Spanish Town. They marched north on newly cut roads that passed through Liguanea. The fourth detachment came from the Forty-Ninth Regiment based in Kingston, and it too marched across the island. Moore knew that news of the rebellion would have already spread through informal networks among the enslaved, and the movement of troops sent a similar message. Moore also sent express messengers to the white superintendents of the Windward Maroons—Nanny Town, Crawford Town, and Scott's Hall—and called on the Maroons to adhere to the agreements of 1740. Finally, Moore called on the militia officers of Saint Mary's to mobilize their units. Surprisingly, many men refused to serve, despite the threat. So Moore imposed martial law to compel them, and by April 19 he could report to his council that the rebellion had been vanquished without any further losses in white lives.[90]

Within weeks of the apparent suppression of the Saint Mary's revolt, two "Coromantees" approached Cuffee, a man enslaved on John Ayscough's plantation in Saint Thomas Parish, and encouraged him to join a conspiracy planned for Manchioneal. The conspirators seem to have assumed that cultural affinity would protect them. Cuffee pretended to agree and so learned many details about the intended rebellion, but he shared this information with his mistress,

Mrs. Fuller, who informed the authorities. As parties of militia and Maroons were already on the march, this uprising never began. In December, the assembly granted Cuffee his freedom.[91]

But on May 25, 1760, a much larger rebellion broke out in Westmoreland Parish on the Maese Mure plantation of the absentee Arthur Forest. While contemporaries such as Long wrote that Coromantees had organized this rebellion as well, Westmoreland whites identified Apongo, or Wager, as the principal leader. Thomas Thistlewood, an overseer on nearby Egypt plantation, learned that Apongo had once been a very powerful man. He was reputed to have been a prince subject to Dahomey but had been kidnapped while hunting, enslaved, and sold to an English slaver who brought him to Jamaica. Apongo's story came indirectly from John Cope Sr., a rich Westmoreland planter and father of Thistlewood's first employer in Westmoreland. Cope had once served as the governor of Cape Coast Castle, and he knew Apongo from his time on the Gold Coast. Apongo had once visited Governor Cope as a man of great authority accompanied by a retinue of one hundred well-armed men. Cope later settled down as a Jamaican planter in Westmoreland, where he and Apongo met again. Cope had invited Apongo to dine with him several times, rich planter and enslaved prince at the same table. Apongo must have tried to secure his freedom through this unusual friendship, but for whatever reason this did not happen. It is not hard to imagine the rage of this man at his enslavement.[92]

Dahomey was not an Akan state, and Apongo was probably not Akan. But the military revolution that began among the Akan had spread east by the early eighteenth century to the coastal states of the Bight of Benin that became subject to Dahomey. Apongo would have been shaped by this military and social transformation. As a powerful man in West Africa, he had acquired the knowledge of war and the habits of command. He may or may not have identified as Coromantee, but he would have felt the camaraderie of former soldiers now enslaved.[93]

Apongo organized a rebellion among perhaps one thousand enslaved people from at least seven plantations in Westmoreland: Maese Mure, the Delve, Moorland, Campbellton, Fish River, New Hope, and Old Hope. Just after midnight on May 26, both Thistlewood and

Captain Robert Dinn, of the Seventy-Fourth Regiment stationed in Savanna la Mar, were roughly awakened to news that the slaves of Maese Mure had begun a revolt. Thomas Smith, overseer of Maese Mure, had been the first to die, along with three other whites of that plantation. Within the next few hours the rebels killed thirteen more whites and gathered recruits, arms, and provisions in preparation for a long struggle. Thistlewood immediately rode to Savanna la Mar to join his militia unit while Dinn raised his company of regulars and marched for Maese Mure. Martial law still reigned from the April rebellion, and colonial forces again began to mobilize.[94]

Lieutenant Governor Moore called on Admiral Charles Holmes for assistance in the movement of troops, for Westmoreland lay a great distance from Spanish Town. Moore ordered the mobilization of three more detachments of the Forty-Ninth Regiment, two of sixty men each to be sent to Westmoreland and a third of seventy-five men to be sent to Saint Elizabeth, where the planters feared the rebellion might spread. Holmes commanded His Majesty's ship *Harwick*, and the sloops *Port Royal* and *Viper*, to carry these men and provide them with any arms, ammunition, or provisions they would need. Holmes further commanded the marines of these ships, and as many seamen as could be raised, to fight alongside the regulars to suppress the rebellion, another four hundred men. The British Empire thus responded to this rebellion of Jamaica's slaves with a military force of almost six hundred trained soldiers and as many militia as the island society had.[95]

On May 29 the militia units of Westmoreland (though not including Thistlewood) suffered a strategic defeat against the rebels. Apongo and his rebels seized all the arms and ammunition these units carried and made their way north into the mountains. Over the next few days, the rebel camp grew. Women had been among the first rebels, and their numbers increased. The rebels built palisades and walls, some armed with cannon, around their camp in the mountains. And like the Maroons in previous decades, the rebels sent parties out to raid the plantations for provisions and more recruits.[96]

Colonial forces encircled Westmoreland, and the rebels had very little hope at all. Moore ordered the two companies of the Forty-Ninth Regiment stationed in Lucea and Montego Bay to join with all the militia units of Hanover and Saint James and march south across the island toward the rebel encampment. Meanwhile, the *Harwick*, *Port Royal*, and *Viper* arrived in Savanna la Mar on the May 30 and prepared to attack from the south. These troops were joined by the company of the Seventy-Fourth already stationed at Savanna la Mar, the militia units of Westmoreland, and two parties of Maroons from Trelawney Town and Accompong. In a coordinated offensive launched on June 2, colonial forces overwhelmed the rebels. They destroyed the fortifications, killed at least 130 people, and drove the rest into the woods. Surviving rebels organized themselves into smaller bands that continued to raid the plantations, sometimes for years thereafter.[97]

While the heart of the rebellion had been defeated, conspiracies continued to be detected across the island. In the Vale of Luidas in Saint John's Parish, Coromantee rebels approached Foster and Pembroke, two men enslaved by Assemblyman Charles Price, and attempted to recruit them to join a rebellion that would begin on June 24. But neither man would join. Foster was later said to be very influential among the Coromantees of the parish, and the planters feared that if he had joined the rebellion it would have been very difficult to suppress. The whites detected further conspiracies in Hanover, Saint John, Saint James, Clarendon, Saint Dorothy, and Saint Elizabeth, as well as an attempt to revive the insurrection in Saint Mary. Few details survive of these conspiracies, but the island-wide dimensions of this rebellion are clear.[98]

In Westmoreland, colonial forces began to bring captured rebels into Savannah la Mar, where many were tortured and some were gibbeted alive. Tacky had already been executed. Vengeful whites had severed his head and stuck it prominently aloft in Spanish Town, but Long wrote that Tacky's countrymen soon took it down, unwilling to tolerate such a spectacle. On May 28 a colonial party marched a group of captured rebels past Egypt plantation. Thistlewood counted twenty-one people, nineteen men and two women, and noticed that one of the rebels had his "hair shaved in the form of a Cap on his head." This man was said to be "one of their grandees," and Thistlewood later recalled that on the eve of rebellion some of Egypt's enslaved had shaved their heads in a similar fashion.[99]

Jamaican authorities did not record the accounts of tortured rebels as they would in later years, but it was during this period that Jamaican whites began to comprehend the island-wide dimensions of the conspiracy to destroy them. Thistlewood learned that Tacky's rebels in Saint Mary had acted too soon and upset the entire strategy. Apongo had planned the insurrection for Whitsuntide (Pentecost), a traditional holiday for the enslaved, but Tacky had started his rebellion fifty days earlier on Easter, also a holiday for the slaves. Moreover, in Kingston, rebels had staged a procession at the Spring Path graveyard in which the African man who led the procession carried a wooden sword decorated with parrot feathers. A slaving captain who had spent time in West Africa recognized the procession to be a declaration of war and alerted the authorities. Long later wrote that upon investigation, Kingston magistrates discovered that the Coromantees in Kingston had crowned a woman named Cubba as their queen. Enslaved by a Jewish widow named Rachel Cohen, Cubba may have had links to Coromantee leaders throughout the island. Kingston authorities sentenced her to be transported to Cuba, and John Swain, commander of the schooner *Mary*, had brought her there. But Cubba had somehow returned to Jamaica on the sloop *Catherine*, captained by James Daniel. An unnamed member of the assembly reported that she had been seen in Crooke Cove, a small harbor on the plantation of James Crooke, of Hanover, and then in the custody of the Hanover planter James Dawes. Cubba's movements suggest a woman with connections throughout the island, a set of relationships that facilitated her surprising ability to avoid punishment.[100]

Colonial forces captured Apongo during the second week of June and kept him prisoner till July 29, when the whites sentenced him to hang publicly for three days at Maese Mure plantation and then have his body burned.[101] Rebels remained at large, however, and on July 11 Captain Norwood Witter arrived in Westmoreland with orders to finalize the suppression. Witter replaced Lieutenant Colonel Spragge, who, according to Thistlewood, was prone to the sudden decapitation of any captured rebels, no questions asked. Spragge served with the regular forces and may have been new to the island, but Witter was a white Jamaican, born to a slaveholding family in Saint Elizabeth, who now had his own plantation of a hundred slaves in Saint James. For eight weeks, Witter established a base of operations on Moor- land plantation, where he lived "in a wretched hovel." He sent out parties that "killed and brought in a great number of the Rebels," and he learned from local people that many rebels were inclined to surrender if terms could be established that they not be tortured. Witter sought permission from Lieutenant Governor Moore to offer terms of amnesty for rebels who surrendered, and received approval for this policy on September 4. While the House of Assembly ulti- mately condemned Witter's leniency as "highly injurious to the honor" of the colony, his policy brought in 260 rebels who had re- mained in the woods, and it probably ended the rebellion.[102]

By December 1760 the rebellion in Jamaica was over, but as the Christmas holiday approached, whites on the island would not have felt that way. A holiday when the slaves usually had two or three days off, Christmas was feared by whites the most for the threat of insur- rection that it posed. Lieutenant Governor Moore ordered the mili- tias throughout the island to ride every night from the middle to the end of December.[103]

Meanwhile, Jamaica's legislators in the House of Assembly took a series of measures to reestablish the plantation order. First, they re- warded those enslaved men and women who had informed on or fought against the rebels. The assembly established a subcommittee to investigate these cases and on December 8 freed fifteen enslaved men and two enslaved women who had participated in the suppres- sion of the rebellion. Each received his or her freedom, a monetary reward, and a badge that read "Freedom, for being honest" on one side, and "By the country" on the other. The assembly also approved expenditures to compensate the masters of these honest slaves for the capital investments they lost.[104]

The assembly also developed two new laws they hoped would fore- stall the next rebellion. Passed during the third week of December, the assembly's legislation articulated an ideology of slaveholding, that of Jamaica's master class. These men had every intention to manage the colony with the same level of brutality that they always had. The planters knew very well that most Africans hated their enslavement. And over the past few months they had seen that Africans had the sophistication and numbers to pose a serious military threat to the plantation order. The sugar harvest of 1760 looked to be one of the largest in the island's history, and the planters would not give that up. In concert with the rewards for loyal slaves, the assembly's new laws illuminate a plan of order for the next generation.

As it was "necessary and expedient for the Security" of the colony, the assembly ordered the justices and vestry of every parish to either build a new barrack or repair and maintain an old barrack. Barracks had to be large enough to accommodate one company of His Majesty's forces. The parish vestries would also build "a proper Magazine" attached to each barrack, large enough to hold a "reasonable Quantity of gunpowder" and arms enough for the company of soldiers. The assembly empowered the vestries to decide on the exact location, to compel the sale of land if necessary, and to impose a new tax on all inhabitants to pay for these new barracks.[105]

The new law echoed Governor Trelawney's hopes for the laws of an earlier generation, but it contained no provisions for the establishment of new settlers. Previous legislation had done much of this work, evident in the development of parishes such as Saint James. But in the quieter years before 1760, when some hoped that the settlement with the Maroons had pacified the island, the barracks had fallen into disrepair. In the parish of Saint Mary, where the rebellion first began, the planters had already begun to act. The parish raised funds through subscription to rebuild Fort Haldane in Port Maria, which the rebels had damaged, and to build a new barrack at Oracabessa. The new barracking law pledged the assembly to repay all the subscribers, funds that the vestry would raise by imposing a new tax on all residents of Saint Mary.[106]

The new barracks ordered by the law were in less populated parishes such as Saint John and Saint Ann and in heavily populated sugar parishes that were inadequately defended. Clarendon, Westmoreland, and Saint James, for example, were all major sugar parishes with at least ten thousand enslaved Africans in each. Westmoreland and Saint James had barracks in the major ports of Savanna la Mar and Montego Bay, but in the sugar zone that stretched across all three parishes there were no barracks. The assembly ordered Clarendon Parish to establish a barrack in the Clarendon Mountains, Westmoreland in "the Leeward Part of the Parish" (inland), and Saint James at a place where the vestry thought it "convenient." The assembly thus ordered the construction of ten new barracks and the repair of seven old barracks to house the soldiers of the Forty-Ninth and Seventy-Fourth Regiments that had saved the island and would be needed again.[107]

A second law, "to remedy the Evils arising from irregular Assemblies of Slaves," which passed on December 18, ordered island whites to govern the slaves with greater vigilance. The law reiterated the importance of many long-established regulations, such as providing tickets for traveling slaves, prohibiting slaves from the use of weapons, and disrupting the assemblies of Africans, as well as the use of horns, drums, gourds, boards, and all the "Instruments of Noise" that had again proved to have "the most dangerous Consequences." But the new law also sought to instill new practices of surveillance over black life. Constables were ordered to attend all of the Sunday and holiday markets, or any "places of public resort" where Africans were known to assemble. Overseers were ordered to limit all the traditional holidays—Christmas, Easter, and Whitsuntide—to only one day instead of the customary two or three. And overseers were ordered to reside on the plantation during the traditional holidays, rather than retiring to white society in one of the island's towns as they usually did.[108]

But the most illuminating provision of the new law banned the practice of obeah, "the wicked art of Negroes." Whites had observed obeah before, but during their investigation of the rebellion, island whites had come to realize that "there are Slaves of both Sexes commonly known as Obeah Men and Obeah Women," who had acquired standing among island Africans because of the widespread belief in their "preternatural Faculties." Long later wrote that obeah men had been great instigators of the rebellion. Had the shaved heads among Thistlewood's slaves been indications of magic? What about the graveyard procession in Kingston? With this new slave law, the Jamaica House of Assembly admonished colonial whites to pay careful attention to the behavior of obeah practitioners, especially their use of "blood, feathers, parrots beaks, dogs teeth, alligators teeth, broken bottles, grave dirt, rum, egg-shells." Such materials became the ingredients of "witchcraft," and the skills of these men and women were dangerous. The planters had gained a measure of cultural understanding of black life on the island, which they used to augment their power to enslave.[109]

On December 31, 1760, Thistlewood recorded that he had issued 767 tickets to the slaves of Egypt plantation over the past six months. While Jamaica's masters would not follow all the new regulations, and obeah continues to be practiced in Jamaica today, the parish vestries did build the barracks. According to Governor Henry Lyttelton's report on the state of the colony for 1764, "every parish in the island" either had a barrack or was building one, as "posts for parties of His Majesty's troops, to secure the tranquility of the country."[110]

The rebellion of 1760 cost the colony £100,000 sterling, wrote Long, and it prompted the assembly to deepen its coercive powers, in both military strength and surveillance. The King's troops and the island's militia, now bolstered by the Maroons, had saved the island. Unlike in South Carolina, where the assembly sought to domesticate the planters' governance of their slaves, and even stopped the transatlantic slave trade after the rebellion at Stono, the planters of Jamaica continued to build up the colony as they always had, through a large, forced migration of captives from Africa and the militarization of slave governance that had been consistent throughout the colony's first century.[111]

By the planters' lights these policies were effective, as they resulted in a steady rise in sugar production. Despite the rebellion, 1760 marked the largest sugar harvest in the island's history—thirty-nine thousand tons—five times greater than the annual average of the century's first twenty-five years. By the 1770s this had become a typical harvest. The transatlantic slave trade fueled this growth with about eight thousand enslaved Africans shipped to the island every year during the 1760s, an annual average of two thousand more than the 1750s. The system worked.[112]

With the deep military support of the British Empire, the planters effectively controlled most of the Africans they enslaved on their sugar plantations, and as a result, they grew quite rich. While the black population of South Carolina, about thirty-nine thousand people at midcentury, had begun to grow naturally by 1770, surviving censuses from 1762 and 1769 create a sobering portrait of black life in Jamaica. Transatlantic slavers brought sixty thousand people to the island from 1761 to 1768, but the enslaved population increased by only twenty thousand. The normal operations of Jamaica's slave society extinguished forty thousand black lives in just six years. Add to this the twelve thousand people who died on the slavers before they reached the island, and it becomes time to stop and reflect.

CHAPTER 5

The Transformation of
Slavery's Politics

W<small>HEN THE RADICAL</small> Whig colonists who started the American
Revolution deployed the metaphor of slavery to embellish their critiques of imperial policy, they unwittingly fostered a transformation
in the politics of Atlantic slavery. Slavery has an ancient lineage as a
political metaphor, but the irony of slaveholders decrying enslavement quickly led to accusations of hypocrisy. These charges stemmed
in part from antislavery beliefs about the enslavement of Africans
that had been in gestation since the late seventeenth century. But
during the imperial crisis, organized slave resistance endowed antislavery argument with a sharp political edge. In London, this first
became evident in the momentous Somerset case of 1772, the cul-
mination of a series of cases brought by runaway slaves supported
by Britain's first abolitionist, Granville Sharp. As the crisis deepened,
political instability created opportunities for organized resistance in
both South Carolina and Jamaica, which black rebels exploited.
Through their actions during this Age of Revolution, slaves shaped
the course of events and redefined the meaning of a fight for liberty.

Distinctive politics of resistance shaped the slave societies of South
Carolina and Jamaica during the imperial crisis, and as a result, each
would emerge from the American Revolution in a very different
place. There were radical Whigs in both slaveholding classes, and

knowledgeable rebel leaders among the enslaved in each colony. But the planters had forged distinct regimes of oppression that shaped their respective roles in the imperial crisis. South Carolinian slave-holders had the latitude to become active players in the American Revolution; Jamaican slaveholders did not. The politics of slavery shaped the geography of the American Revolution. The concerns of slaveholders drove South Carolina out of the empire, but in Jamaica, those same concerns kept white colonists loyal. And looking forward, the transformation of slavery's politics would complicate the defense of slaveholding and create new opportunities for slave rebels in the generations that followed.

A small but cohesive black community had coalesced in London by the time Parliament and the colonial assemblies began having serious disagreements over the governance of empire. One anonymous Briton wrote to the *London Chronicle* in 1764 that "many thousands" of black people lived in London, the unfortunate result of the "folly which is become too fashionable of importing Negroes into this country for servants."[1] Sir John Fielding, justice of the peace for Mid-dlesex, Essex, and Surry counties, wrote that when black slaves ar-rived in England, they "put themselves on a footing with other ser-vants [and] become intoxicated with liberty." Many families who employed blacks as domestics had fired them, Fielding claimed, and once free, they "enter into Societies and make it their Business to corrupt and dissatisfy the Mind of every fresh black Servant that comes to England." They would convince newly arrived blacks that they could become free through baptism or marriage, even though the law stated otherwise. According to Fielding, most people believed emancipation did come in these ways, so that when a slaveholder tried to recover his or her property, "the mob" took the side of the black. And so the black population of London had become larger and bolder. Fielding even thought that slaves corrupted by English liberty were responsible for Caribbean insurrections.[2]

   Black Londoners did fight for their dignity, and they were correct that the status of slaves under English law was unclear. In 1729, At-torney General Sir Philip Yorke and the Solicitor General Charles

Talbot had jointly written an opinion that asserted the right of a slave owner to "legally compel" his or her slave to return to the colonies after a visit to Great Britain. But an authority so eminent as William Blackstone had declared in 1765 that "the spirit of liberty is so deeply implanted in our constitution, and rooted even in our very soil, that a slave or negro, the moment he lands in England, falls under the protection of the laws . . . and becomes *eo instanti* a freeman." Neither of these statements, however, had the power of precedent, the judgment of a court, and many continued to believe that baptism had liberating power. In 1762 Olaudah Equiano believed that because of his baptism three years earlier, his master, Michael Pascal, a lieutenant in the Royal Navy, had no right to sell him. Equiano "had heard a lawyer" tell his master that this was so, but when his master's vessel came alongside the *Charming Sally*, Pascal sold Equiano to her captain, James Doran. Equiano suffered ten more years of slavery.[3]

An apparently fortuitous encounter between Jonathan Strong and Granville Sharp in the early fall of 1765 began to transform the politics of slavery in England. Their meeting would lead to Sharp's emergence as Great Britain's pioneering abolitionist, but on that October day he was just visiting his brother William at his medical practice on Mincing Lane, where the doctor provided care for the dispossessed of London without charge. Strong had arrived in London as a slave from Barbados a few years earlier, brought by the attorney David Lisle. In a fit of unexplained rage, Lisle had pistol-whipped Strong and left him for dead. Someone found the brutalized man and brought him to Sharp's office.[4]

The brothers nursed Strong back to health and found him employment with an apothecary on Fenchurch Street. Two years later Lisle saw him at random on a London street and thought of the value he might draw from the black man's body. He drew up a bill of sale with the Jamaican planter James Kerr for thirty pounds, but Kerr, who understood the challenges of enslaving someone in London, would not pay until Strong was physically shackled on the ship. Lisle commissioned officers of the law to seize Strong and commit him to prison, but fortunately Strong managed to get a note to Granville Sharp alerting him to his plight. Sharp intervened by convincing the lord mayor of London, Sir Robert Kite, to consider the case. The interested parties met on September 18, 1765, and Kite decided that as Strong had not been accused of any crime, he would not enforce the arrest and declared Strong free to go.[5]

In the days that followed, Lisle challenged Sharp to a duel, which Sharp declined, and charged him with robbery, the theft of his slave Strong. Sharp could not find lawyers willing to challenge the opinion of Yorke and Talbot, so for the next two years he read deeply: the laws of England relating to villenage and slavery; Grotius on the history of slavery; cases relating to slaves in the United Kingdom; and the laws of slavery in the American colonies. Through this study Sharp developed an argument to disempower American slaveholders when they came to Great Britain. Circulated in manuscript and then published in 1769, Sharp argued "that Slavery is an innovation in England, contrary to the Spirit and intention of our present laws and constitution." Sharp's tract convinced Lisle's lawyers to pursue a settlement, but it also had ramifications for the future of slavery in the British Empire. In his analysis of the gross abuses allowed by colonial slave laws, Sharp could not help but critique "the *boasted liberty* of our American colonies." He wryly noted that the much-lamented "arbitrary power of despotic monarchies" differed little from the power that slavery created. The power of slaveholders "entirely subverts our most excellent constitution," Sharp wrote, "because liberty and slavery are so opposite to each other, that they cannot subsist in the same community." Black resistance to the indignities of slavery had drawn Sharp into a legal conflict with enormous ramifications. And when he realized this, Sharp tied the lived reality of racial slavery to the defense of liberty put forth by the radical Whig pamphlets of North America that were beginning to fuel an imperial conflict.[6]

Slavery had an important place in the worldview of these Whigs, who used it as a political metaphor that invoked the compelled submission of slaves to dramatize the denial of liberty. To be enslaved meant that an abusive power had forced its will on a free man. The metaphor did not suggest the physical brutality, the compulsory labor, or the forced poverty that black slaves suffered, though it did draw on their experiences. For colonial radicals like James Otis of Boston, a tax like the Sugar Act, imposed in 1764, could not be reconciled with "the rights of the colonists" because they were not represented in Parliament. The Assemblies could tax, but Parliament could not. The imposition of a tax in this manner robbed a man of his property, which "deprives me of my liberty and makes me a slave."[7]

Otis meant "freeborn *British white* subjects" when he personalized the impact of the Sugar Act. But like Granville Sharp, Otis also critiqued the enslavement of blacks. He wrote that all men, "white or black," were free according to the law of nature. "Does it follow that 'tis right to enslave a man because he is black?" he asked. Otis drew his antislavery argument from Baron Montesquieu's *L'Esprit de Lois* (1748), a witty critique of absolutist monarchy. But in 1764 Otis was unusual in yoking antislavery to the defense of colonial rights. He did so to embellish the enslavement of white colonials like himself, not to critique his fellow mainland colonists. We can see this in his clear identification of slaveholding with the "sugar islanders" of the West Indies already notorious for their brutality. Nowhere does he mention the slaveholding of Virginians, Carolinians, or New Englanders. Otis himself owned a small number of black slaves.[8]

Otis might have gone too far when he used this critique of racial slavery to embellish the popular charge that the colonists' relation to Parliament was "slavery." For several years thereafter, most Whig pamphleteers in the colonies did not weave antislavery into their critiques of the tyranny of Parliament, though they did continue to see themselves as "enslaved" by imperial policies.[9] Stephen Hopkins of Rhode Island likened the colonists to slaves in his *Rights of the Colonies Examined* (1765), and in 1768 after the Stamp Act crisis and the passage of the Townshend duties, the Quaker John Dickinson followed Otis's argument precisely in his widely read *Letters from a Farmer in Pennsylvania* (1768): "Those who are taxed without their own consent, expressed by themselves or their representatives, are slaves."[10] But these writers did not critique racial slavery as Otis had done. Proclamation of the antithesis between slavery and liberty might pose less of a threat in the northern colonial societies where fewer people were actually enslaved by law, but to the south, white colonists remained painfully aware that the black people they en-slaved could always become a threat that could devastate the colony. Radical Whigs in the southern colonies agreed with the main thrust of Otis's argument, but it is not hard to imagine their sense of ner-vous indignation upon reading his antislavery lines. Leading patriots sought to coordinate resistance against Parliament's unjust taxes among the colonies. They could ill afford to threaten their slave-holding compatriots.

The passage of the Stamp Act in March 1765 aroused even greater indignation in the colonies than the Sugar Act. In June the Massa-chusetts House of Representatives sent a circular letter to the main-land colonies, calling for a congress in New York to discuss the best manner of resistance to Parliament's latest outrage. Paying for the stamps would tax all commerce, draining valuable hard currency from a broad populace well beyond those who wrote pamphlets. The first popular resistance to the distribution of the stamps took place in Boston in August 1765 and quickly spread to Rhode Island, New Jersey, and New York. In October, when a ship rumored to be carrying the hated stamps entered Charleston Harbor, the Sons of Liberty erected a massive gallows and hung in effigy the figure of a stamp officer above the banner "Liberty and No Stamp Act." When the stamps did arrive ten days later, white mobs formed and the stamp agents had to take refuge in Fort Johnson on an island in the harbor. Colonial officials were impotent to govern for the next ten days. A mob of eighty men, their faces blackened with thick soot to drama-tize their enslavement, stormed the houses of gentlemen they believed had received stamps, including Henry Laurens. On October 28 the stamp agents resigned their offices and proclaimed that they would not sell the stamps.[11]

This defense of colonial liberty came at some cost to stability. In December the wife of a prominent merchant thought she heard dan-gerous talk among the slaves, and rumors spread that rebel slaves planned an insurrection that was to begin with a "massacre" of the whites on Christmas Eve. Lieutenant Governor William Bull Jr. called out the militia and ordered the patrols to ride for "fourteen days before and after Christmas Day." Laurens wrote that every white man in Charleston carried arms for a week. According to Laurens, the alarm began when a bold group of blacks took up the cry of "Liberty!" to the dread consternation of the whites who heard them. There was no general massacre, and Laurens believed the alarm to be without merit. But Governor Bull reported in January that there had been a mass escape of 107 slaves from rice plantations in Colleton County and that there were "several large Parties of Runaways still concealed in large Swamps."[12]

Christopher Gadsden had not been in Charleston for these events, though he was intimately involved. A wealthy merchant who had married into the planter elite, Gadsden was a leading radical in South Carolina and had a seat in the assembly. When the assembly agreed to send a delegation to the congress in New York, they elected Gadsden, along with Thomas Lynch and John Rutledge, to represent the colony. On October 31, 1765, the congress sent a list of strongly worded resolutions to the Crown that protested the injustice of the Stamp Act as a serious infringement on the liberties of His Majesty's subjects in America, but when Gadsden sat down to write his friend William Samuel Johnson in April 1766, neither Parliament nor the King had responded. "We are a very weak Province," Gadsden lamented, "and [the] great part of our weakness (though at the same time 'tis part of our riches) consists in having such a number of slaves amongst us." Gadsden worried that "slavery begets slavery," meaning that white Carolinians' fear of slave violence might render the colonists impotent against future parliamentary oppressions. He feared that South Carolina might be like "Jamaica and our West India islands" and succumb to Parliament's unconstitutional policies without complaint. This was not quite fair, for there had been Stamp Act riots in Saint Kitts and Antigua. But no slave society had witnessed black resistance of the kind seen in Charleston, and South Carolina had been the only colony south of the Mason-Dixon Line to send representatives to the congress in New York.[13]

The presentments of a grand jury that met in Charleston in October 1765 on the eve of the insurrection scare show why Gadsden had good reason to be concerned. Little had changed since the time of Johann Martin Bolzius; the colony's citizens continued to be negligent in the enforcement of their slave laws. Blacks still gathered "in great numbers" on Sundays in Charleston, and some were known to "make riots" well into the night. There were tippling houses that sold liquor to slaves and the country militias barely mustered. The patrols did not ride often enough and runaways roamed. The jury advised that a parochial tax be raised to maintain a permanent patrol, and its members believed that some runaways should be deemed outlaws and summarily executed when captured. White men did not carry arms to church as they should, and too many planters ignored the deficiency law, which left some settlements without a single white man to govern the large numbers of slaves sent to work them.[14]

The slave code of 1740 had generated a flexible system of social control that waxed and waned like the phases of the moon. In moments of white terror, as in December 1766, the patrols rode and men went armed. But when these insurrection scares passed, the laws fell into nonobservance. Masters earned more when they could hire out their slaves to work unmolested by patrols, and black men and women could again exploit the crevices of power to carve out a semblance of human dignity in their lives. The masters knew that slaves could also conspire to rebel in these moments of relative liberty, but in South Carolina white men were always ready to put in motion the powerful apparatus of oppression they had built.[15]

Gadsden's lamentations to Johnson in 1766 were private. South Carolinian slaveholders did not admit readily that slaves had power. But in 1769 Gadsden turned again to the metaphor of slavery to convince his constituents to sign nonimportation agreements. If we simply accept Parliament's authority to tax, Gadsden wrote, "we are as real Slaves as those we are permitted to command."[16] Gadsden trod dangerous ground. The enslaved of Charleston had already invoked "liberty" in their own right, and as they listened to their masters' hypocrisy, they thought of their own enslavement and how it could be undone. Slaveholders had to trust that the dynamism built into their system of coercive power would continue to hold.

Granville Sharp's activism and writings brought him considerable popularity in the black community of London. There is no better way to explain the series of runaway slaves who appealed for his assistance over the next few years. John Hylas came to Sharp in 1768

when a Barbadian slaveholder named Newton kidnapped his wife (who had been Newton's slave) and shipped her to Barbados. Sharp supported Hylas in suing Newton for her freedom and actually brought her back from slavery to London. In 1770 when the servants of the Banks family heard the cries of Thomas Lewis, an African reenslaved by Robert Stapylton of Chelsea, his former owner, they immediately sent for Sharp, who deployed a writ of habeas corpus to bring Lewis to court. And on December 3, 1771, when the Virginia slaveholder Charles Stewart attempted to reenslave James Somerset in the same manner, Sharp again secured a writ of habeas corpus to save Somerset from the ship and sue for his freedom.[17]

Both the case of Lewis and that of Somerset went to the King's Bench, where the Lord Chief Justice William Mansfield presided. Mansfield felt deeply conflicted about the legality of slavery in Great Britain. On the one hand, he felt great pressure from the enormous capital investments in the plantation system—the merchant houses, the colonial properties, the ships, and of course the slaves themselves—all of which rested on the legality of slave property. On the other hand, Mansfield considered unthinkable the proposition that colonial laws should have force in Great Britain. He had been quite outspoken on the contest between the North American colonies and Parliament, and in Mansfield's influential opinion there was no question that Parliament ruled the empire.[18]

Yet he knew very well that the laws respecting slavery in England were unclear, and Mansfield recommended settlements in such cases. He had presided over several, and in the case of Lewis, Mansfield used a technicality to free Lewis and dismiss the case. But in the case of Somerset, the West Indian planters and merchants in London pressured Stewart to pursue his rights in order to secure a judgment. Concerned by the emergence of "the Negro Cause," the West Indians had secured "a promise from Mr. Stewart . . . to have the point solemnly determined." Sharp secured five lawyers to present the antislavery case, and Stewart secured William Dunning, a prominent and experienced lawyer whose sympathies were not at all with slaveholders.[19]

Mansfield and his colleagues heard the case in the spring of 1772. Somerset's lawyers followed the lines of argument laid down by Sharp in his *Representation of the Injustice and Dangerous Tendency of Tolerating Slavery in England*, and Dunning performed terribly, greatly disappointing his supporters. Dunning disassociated himself from any support for slavery in his opening remarks; indeed, he had "much commendation" for the arguments of his opponents. He argued that slavery was legal in Great Britain based upon the ancient system of villenage, which, even though it had died out, established the legal precedent that supported the legitimacy of the racial slavery that had emerged in the colonies. Dunning attempted humor. He did not defend Stewart's right "to eat" Somerset like a cannibal; he only asked the court to recognize that the slave-master relation did not change upon arrival in Great Britain. Somerset's slave status originated in his enslavement in Africa, Dunning argued. Parliament had empowered the Royal African Company to trade in slaves and thus recognized the legitimacy of slave status. He likened the institution of slavery to that of marriage, which did not change when a person passed into a different kingdom. Like a traveling husband and wife whose marriage would be respected in all kingdoms, Stewart's ownership of Somerset should be respected when he passed from the colonies to Great Britain.[20]

Mansfield was unconvinced. He found it disagreeable to set the blacks of England free, but the weakness of Dunning's arguments forced his hand. "Slavery is so odious," Mansfield stated, "that nothing can be suffered to support it, but positive law." The British Parliament had never passed a law that recognized "so high an act of dominion" as Stewart claimed to hold over the body of Somerset. Mansfield regretted the "inconveniences" that might follow his decision, but nevertheless, he judged, "the black must be discharged."[21]

In the balconies of the court, black people who had attended these hearings "bowed with profound respect to the Judges" and celebrated "their recovery of the rights of human nature." That evening, at a public house in Westminster, one of the black societies sponsored a celebration of their victory attended by almost two hundred. Tickets for admission cost five shillings, and toasts were raised to "their brother Somerset" and to "Lord Mansfield's health." Leading black Londoners raised a subscription for Somerset for having nobly defended the "natural rights" of Africa's people. The good news spread across the Atlantic, inspiring black slaves with at least the hope of liberation. John Austin Finnie, a slaveholder in Virginia, believed that his runaway slaves Amy and Bacchus sought passage to Britain, "where they imagine they will be free." Gabriel Jones of Augusta, Georgia, wrote that his Bacchus also sought a vessel to Britain, "from the Knowledge he has of the late Determination of *Somerset's* Case."[22]

Mansfield's decision was actually quite narrow; black people continued to live as slaves in England for many years. But in the decade that brought Britain's imperial crisis, the Somerset decision subordinated the rights of colonial slaveholders to a belief in British liberty invoked by slaves and slaveholders alike. Black resistance to enslavement had pushed the antislavery argument before the King's Bench, and the slaveholders had demanded judgment. Mansfield's decision showed that antislavery beliefs could be endowed with judicial muscle in the British Empire. Independence might look better, in some regards, for slaveholders.[23]

Henry Laurens was in London during the opening arguments of the Somerset case, and in a letter to his friend John Gervais, he joked that if his slave had not just called him to supper, he would tell the "long and comical Story, of a Trial between a Mr. Stuart and his Black Man James Somerset, at King's Bench, for Liberty." Laurens left the city in late May to take his sons John and Henry Jr. to their school in Geneva, and by the time he returned to London on August 5, Somerset had been freed. Laurens later noted that Mansfield's decision suited "the times," but he wrote nothing else of substance about Somerset, nor did any other North American.[24]

Laurens's reaction to the Somerset case pales in comparison to the vituperative outburst of Edward Long of Jamaica. In the midst of writing his monumental three-volume *History of Jamaica* (1774), Long took time to pen the West Indian response. He wrote quickly; the announcement of his *Candid Reflections* appeared in the *London Chronicle* within a month of Mansfield's ruling. In the "advertisement" that opened his polemic, Long warned that Mansfield's name would "become more popular among all the *Quacoes* and *Quashebas* of *America*, than that of the patriot *Wilkes* . . . among the porter-swilling swains of St. Giles." Long elaborated his hostile racism through his scholarship on Jamaica, but this pamphlet's argument offered the colonial slaveholders' riposte to Mansfield's decision, and to Sharp's *Representation of the Injustice*.[25]

Long's work marked the opening salvo in the development of pro-slavery logic that would be most fully elaborated in later decades by American slaveholders such as John C. Calhoun of South Carolina.[26] The core of Long's argument lay in the long and legitimate history of African slavery in the British Empire. He put forth the climactic argument that whites could not do field labor in the tropics and explained how the Royal African Company had developed an English slave trade in response to this fact. This valuable commerce had contributed significantly to the wealth of the kingdom, especially after 1713 when the Crown secured the valuable Asiento contract with Spain. Long could not believe that Mansfield would undermine all of this in response to the writings of irresponsible persons who questioned "the right of property." If English law freed the blacks, it ought to at least "recompence" the masters for the financial losses sustained. Long predicted disastrous consequences. Mansfield's decision invited "*three hundred thousand blacks*" from the colonies to rebel and escape to Britain, the "land of Canaan," where by taking a single breath of air they gained the "rights of *free-born Britons*." The "lower class of women" would mingle and mate with these runaways; indeed, such women would mate with "horses and asses." The English nation would resemble "the *Portuguese* and *Moriscos* in complexion and baseness of mind," and in the colonies there would be nothing but insurrection once the news had spread.[27]

South Carolinian planters also responded to Somerset, but with far less sustained attention or vitriol. The *South Carolina Gazette* printed one news article on the case, which reflected Mansfield's legal reasoning but did not note his final judgment. An anonymous pamphlet by a "Back Settler" from South Carolina did warn that too much enthusiasm for freedom might pose a danger to the masters of slaves. Britons did not really want every person to enjoy *all* the rights of Britons, for such expansive notions of freedom would bring "the Ruin of many *American* Provinces, as well as the *West-India* Islands."

The allusion is clear, but it is subtle and short—one paragraph in thirty-six pages—nothing like the fiery prose of Long.[28]

North American slaveholders did not dwell on Somerset because they lived in a different moment of historical time from that inhabited by the West Indians. In North America, "slavery" still had as its most powerful meaning the tyranny that endangered the rights of free white men of property. Antislavery writers had begun to redefine the meaning of "slavery," but this shift did not yet threaten North American slaveholders. The difference in the responses of these planter classes was rooted in the political ground on which they stood. Black resistance posed a threat that Carolinians felt they could contain on their own, but black resistance in Jamaica rendered the planters dependent on the military garrison provided by their imperial masters. White Jamaicans had to fight antislavery as soon as it gained political salience because their relationship with the empire was critical to their survival. Carolinian masters did not share in this dependence. Antislavery views troubled them, but at this moment in history, they had greater concerns.

On December 31, 1773, the Jamaica Council and House of Assembly jointly resolved in a desperate petition to their "common parent and protector," King George III. The men who served these bodies were under "constant apprehension of the revolt of our Slaves." The Fiftieth and Sixtieth Regiments of the British Army, now the core of the island's garrison, were well under strength because of the tropical diseases that had always plagued new arrivals to the island. And the demographic imbalance between the white settlers and their slaves had reached "prodigious disproportion": fewer than sixteen thousand whites faced a hostile slave population of more than two hundred thousand, a ratio of one to thirteen. In the smaller settlements of the North Side, the white inhabitants were "in hourly Danger of Extirpation by their own Negroes." The assembly begged the Crown to send two warships to be permanently stationed in Port Antonio to protect the North Side settlements, to more than double the two regiments already on the island to a thousand men each, and to permanently station another regiment of the same size on the island.[29]

The assembly's request for reinforcements reveals a profound dependency on imperial power. The Jamaican petitioners emphasized their "longstanding loyalty and affection" for the Crown at a moment when the House of Assembly in South Carolina had refused to cooperate with its royal governor for four years. At the heart of Jamaican dependency lay the deepest of contradictions that plagued every slave society, that conflict between the imposition of a brutal slavery and the natural desire of every person to liberty. The politics of slaveholding revolved around maintaining social control despite this contradiction, and in Jamaica the key had long been military force provided by the empire.

No one articulated this better than Sir John Dalling, acting lieutenant governor in Jamaica from December 1772 until the arrival of the newly appointed Basil Keith in January 1774. In his remarkable "Observations on the present state of Jamaica," dated May 14, 1774, Dalling reflected on the social relations of an island society he had known for twelve years. Dalling arrived in the Caribbean as lieutenant colonel of the Forty-Third Regiment of Foot, which participated in the siege of Havana in 1762. After the war he settled in Jamaica and married Grace Pinnock, the eldest daughter of Phillip Pinnock, the planter patriarch of an old white Jamaican family, and Speaker in the colonial House of Assembly. Appointed acting governor in 1772 after the death of William Trelawney, Dalling wrote his "Observations" when he had been out of power for about six months.[30]

Like every governor who came to Jamaica, Dalling marveled at the "amazing disproportion" between the black slaves and island whites. But while governors past had simply relayed facts, Dalling paused. "Let us stop awhile and make some melancholy reflections on this truly alarming idea. Let us consider that to the distinctions which nature has made between the two Races of Men, our Laws have superadded others equally difficult to overcome, viz. Liberty to one and Slavery to the other." Dalling's ideas about racial distinctions paralleled those of Long and have persisted far too long, but his observations on human nature, and on the impact of slave law, remain insightful.

"A perpetual enmity must always subsist" between master and slave, he wrote, "which no policy, no time can eradicate. Let us likewise take into contemplation that inherent desire for all men to withdraw themselves from Pain, and equally to partake of the satisfactions of life." If these fundamental questions of human nature were considered, Dalling believed that white Jamaicans would see the "dreadful precipice" on which they stood. "This Country must one day or other (God knows how soon) be involved in the most dreadful of Human Calamities." Thus arose the need for three thousand troops, which Dalling endorsed, and the ships of war to bring troops quickly to the sites of combat when that dreadful day arrived.[31]

But in June 1774, the colony's agent in London, Stephen Fuller, wrote to the House of Assembly's committee of correspondence that their petition had been rejected. Fuller came from one of Jamaica's oldest planting families. He was the seventh son (the eighth child) of John Fuller and Elizabeth Rose. Elizabeth was the eldest daughter of Fulke Rose, a Jamaican planter who had served in the Assembly of 1683. John descended from Thomas Fuller, who had served on the Jamaica Council of 1671. Stephen's older brother Rose Fuller was one of England's most prominent West Indians. He had also married a planter's daughter, Ithamar Hill, whom he had met when sent to manage the family estates in the 1730s. Ithamar's father Richard Mill was a lawyer, probably in Spanish Town, and left 77 slaves in his estate at death. Rose combined the fortunes, made friends in Spanish Town, and went on to become very successful in Jamaica's colonial politics; he was appointed to the Jamaica Council, elected to the Jamaica House of Assembly, and later appointed Chief Justice for the colony. Rose Fuller returned to England in the 1750s and soon had a seat in Parliament, as a Member for New Romney, then Maidstone, and in 1768 for Rye, which he represented until his death in 1777.[32] Stephen Fuller most certainly had his brother's support to be agent; he also reported his own "large concerns" on the island. He became the colonial agent in 1764 and, through dedication and connections, became a leading figure in the Society of West India Merchants and Planters, an organization that dated to the early eighteenth century. Fuller could open doors at the highest levels of government and gain the attention of colonial officials, but on the eve of the American Revolution, he had failed.[33]

Fuller thought it unlikely that any force would be forthcoming until "the affairs upon the continent of N. America are all perfectly quiet and settled." The assembly had to protect the colony on its own. In the fall of 1774, the assembly passed a law that kept a patrol in every parish on constant guard. These patrols consisted of a white captain and sergeant in command of ten privates who could be white or free colored. These men were paid by the day by the colonial state. In an account of the colonial government's expenses for 1777, the cost of maintaining these patrols ran to £22,000 Jamaica currency—the single largest expense for that year and 37 percent of total expenditures—all dedicated to the control of runaway slaves. Almost more extraordinary is what happened next.[34]

Just four days after passing the new patrol law, the Jamaica House of Assembly passed a "Petition and Memorial" to the King that largely endorsed the arguments of radical Whigs in North America. The petition acknowledged the "incumbrance of more than two hundred thousand slaves" that would inhibit actual resistance, but the assembly embraced the most striking metaphor of the mainland patriots: that of slavery. In a conscious echo of the *Declaration and Resolves of the First Continental Congress* passed six weeks earlier, the Jamaica Assembly gave a sharp critique of the "plan almost carried into execution, for enslaving the Colonies." These were strong words from a colonial assembly that had just begged for protection, especially considering the well-known chain of events that led to the Continental Congress: Parliament's Tea Act, the Boston Tea Party, and what came to be known as the Intolerable Acts that closed the port of Boston. Radical Whig arguments advanced and acted on had led to violence and reprisals from the imperial authorities. It was a pattern that set a dangerous precedent for a fragile slave society dependent on imperial troops.[35]

The imperial struggle had a deep impact on colonial assemblymen accustomed to their power. Josiah Smith, a merchant in Charles Town, wrote proudly of the "brave Bostonians" who had defended their liberty, and the Jamaica Assembly, it seemed, felt the same. Jamaica had its share of radical Whigs, which Governor

Keith recognized as the "Kingston Party." These men were principally merchants and would have been hardest hit by the cessation of North American commerce agreed to by the First Continental Congress. While the sentiments expressed in the petition were no doubt genuine, the petition was a risky public effort to intervene in the imperial dispute between Parliament and the North American colonies.[36]

But the petition did not express the voice of a unified white Jamaica; on the contrary, its passage was only made possible by deft manipulation of the politics of slavery. The assembly passed this petition on December 28, the penultimate day of the legislative session, when the "Spanish Town Interest" had gone home. Almost entirely sugar planters, these were assemblymen with estates in disparate parts of the island whose fear of slave conspiracies during the Christmas holidays compelled them to return home before the end of business. Sessions of the assembly typically lasted until at least Christmas Eve or sometimes a few days later. Christmas also marked the beginning of the customary holidays for the slaves, "the time of the Year most dreaded for Insurrections and Rebellion." Planters liked to be home for the holidays, not for love of family and good cheer but to maintain order. The law expanding the patrols passed on December 24, but then the planters went home. The memorial and petition passed when only twenty-five of the forty-three members were even present, and a widely circulated newspaper account reported a vote of sixteen to nine. Jamaican whites were intimidated by their slaves, but the radical Whigs among them were well organized and acted despite these fears.[37]

The Earl of Dartmouth considered the petition almost "criminal" in its support for the North American patriots. A Virginia convention offered its "unfeigned thanks" to the Assembly of Jamaica for its "truly patriotic endeavors" in support of the colonists. North American newspapers from Massachusetts to Virginia noticed the Jamaica petition; some papers reprinted the entire text; and the radical printers William and Thomas Bradford published the petition as a pamphlet in both London and Philadelphia. Like their counterparts in South Carolina, white Jamaicans wanted "slavery" to be thought of as an encroachment on the liberties of propertied white men, but the fundamentally different regimes of slave control in these slave societies shaped the political ideology of these slaveholding classes in a distinctive fashion. The tangible threat of slave resistance made it impossible for whites in Jamaica to maintain the fiction of their own enslavement. Carolinians' ability to overwhelm slave resistance enabled this fiction to blossom in North America.[38]

In May 1775 the free black preacher David Margrett traveled to Charleston, where he stayed as the guest of one Patrick Hinds. Margrett had come from England in 1774 with a mission to preach to the slaves owned by the Countess of Huntingdon. A minister himself, Hinds had run afoul of Charles Town authorities for opening his doors to black preachers who had delivered "subversive" sermons to "large numbers of Negroes" that civil authorities considered dangerous. In his own sermon to an interracial audience, Margrett had reportedly taught that just as God had liberated the "Children of Israel from Egyptian Bondage," so too would he deliver "the Negroes from the power of their Masters." James Habersham, who managed Her Ladyship's affairs in Georgia, wrote that Margrett had been impudent with whites on the plantation, and with this preaching in Charles Town, his life was in danger. Habersham paid Margrett's passage out of the colony to save his life, but he chastised his English correspondent with clear overtones of colonial anger at the Somerset case. "We know these people better than you do," Habersham wrote. Margrett should never have been sent abroad, for whenever "these people should put their Feet in England . . . they get totally spoiled and ruined."[39]

Around the same time Margrett preached in Charles Town, a letter from England arrived that would prove to be a major catalyst for the military mobilization that supplanted British authority in South Carolina. Arthur Lee, a Virginian and close associate of Laurens who had authored several pamphlets defending the colonists and colonial slavery, wrote to Laurens that the Dartmouth administration had before it a "black plan" to instigate slave insurrections as a measure to cow the colonial rebellion. Laurens had achieved a powerful position that would enable him to deploy this information. After his return from London in December 1774, he stood in the January elections and won a seat to represent Charles Town in the First Provincial Congress, the body that replaced the colonial assembly. The congress appointed Laurens to the General Committee of Charles Town, which elected him to be its chair. Laurens immediately brought Lee's letter before the committee, which decided against sharing it with the Continental Congress in Philadelphia but resolved on May 11 that "the dread of instigated insurrections" justified the decision to mount a military resistance against British authority, a recommendation it would make to the Provincial Congress at its opening session in June. News of battles at Lexington and Concord had arrived, and the fear that the British would attack while the slaves rose in rebellion explains the intensity of white mobilization in South Carolina during the spring of 1775.[40]

The martial percussions of the drum and fife filled Charles Town, and every night "upwards of one hundred Men" joined the usual town watch "to guard against any hostile attempt that may be made by our domesticks." Perhaps referring to Margrett, Smith reported that the slaves had "been taught (by some designing Wretches) to believe they will be all sett free on the arrival of our New Governor." A rumor had spread that the governor's ship carried fourteen thousand stand of arms to distribute among the slaves, and the "impertinent behavior" among the enslaved rankled whites with dread. In one of its first measures, the Provincial Congress voted to raise two thousand men in regiments of horse and foot. The congress also created the Council of Safety, chaired by Laurens, which explored threats from slaves, Indians, and the British. In these critical weeks, South Carolinian planters created a new apparatus of government that replaced British authority, bolstered their military force, and enhanced their surveillance capacity to maintain order over a restive population of slaves in an imperial moment of political crisis.[41]

For black South Carolinians, the first months of June were terrifying. The Council of Safety had trials for several slaves suspected of plotting insurrections, and in a letter to his son John, now in London, Laurens wrote that the "most criminal" suspect was the pilot Thomas Jeremiah. Perhaps the wealthiest black man in Charles

Town, Jeremiah owned a fishing boat and the slaves to operate it, and he had long worked as a pilot guiding ships across the sandbar that stretched across the channel into Charleston Harbor. Two slaves, Jemmy and Sambo, implicated Jeremiah in organizing an insurrection to overthrow the whites. Jemmy testified that ten weeks earlier (early April), when talking at the fish market on Prioleau's Wharf, Jeremiah had asked him to deliver guns to one Dewar, a fugitive slave involved in the planned insurrection. Jeremiah would be "the Chief Command" of the insurrection and claimed to have plenty of powder, though not enough arms. Sambo seems to have worked for Jeremiah on his pilot boat, the small schooners that carried pilots out to large vessels at the harbor's mouth. He testified that about two months before, when working on Simmon's Wharf, Jeremiah had asked him if he knew "anything of the War that is coming." When Sambo replied that he did not, Jeremiah told him "yes, there is a great War coming soon [that would] help the poor Negroes." He instructed Sambo that when the war came, he should "set the Schooner on fire, jump on Shore and join the soldiers."[42]

While Jeremiah sat in jail, the Council of Safety received disturbing news from the Chehaw district in the upcountry. Thomas Hutchinson, a wealthy planter who had owned land in the area since the 1750s, wrote that he had learned of a slave conspiracy, arrested the ringleaders, and organized a slave court that executed some and flogged the others. Enforcement of the slave law had been efficient indeed, but Hutchinson enclosed the testimony of the slave Jemmy to alert them to the rumors that had spread. Jemmy named fifteen slaves as preachers who had been speaking to "Great crouds of Negroes" for the past two years. He had heard of an insurrection planned to take the country and kill all the whites. One preacher named George had explained that "the old King" had received a "Book from our Lord by which he was to Alter the World." But George II had failed to listen and "was now gone to Hell & in Punishmt." Now the "young King" had rediscovered the book and decided to "set the Negroes Free." According to Hutchinson, this story of the book came from John Burnet, a Scot who had been preaching to the slaves in the area for several years, had often been admonished for doing so, and was now sent to Charles Town to answer to the Council of Safety. Burnet acknowledged that he had in the past preached to slaves, but he claimed that he had stopped in 1773 when threatened by local slaveholders. The council believed Burnet's story and wrote to Hutchinson that he had been moved by "enthusiasm" rather than madness. The stories took on a life of their own, however, leading to rebellious talk, vigilance, and the deadly operation of a slave court.[43]

For South Carolinian patriots, the evidence of British influence on the slaves had become compelling indeed. The Somerset case, the preaching of Margrett, the rumors of liberation from the new governor, the prophecies from Chehaw, the mysterious insurrection scheme of Jeremiah, and slaves' general impudence in these uneasy days amounted to a train of revelations that demonstrated the prescience of Lee's warning of early May. The new governor from London, Lord William Campbell, arrived in the midst of these developments. In calmer times Campbell might have been welcomed by Carolinian planters, for he had married the daughter of one of their own, the beautiful young Sarah Izard, and bought a rice plantation, including eighty slaves to work it. But the Provincial Congress had already established its authority; Campbell was nothing but a "representative of Majesty."[44]

The council returned to the accusations against Jeremiah in mid-July and convened a slave court to consider his case. In the interim, the Reverend Robert Smith, the Anglican minister of Saint Phillips, the city's most prominent congregation, had begun to visit Jeremiah in prison. According to Campbell, Smith had come to believe in Jeremiah's innocence, describing him as a "modest" man who was "perfectly resigned" to his fate. Campbell decided to intervene. He spoke to one of the justices on the court about the "weakness of the evidence" and asked the judges and the attorney general, all royal officials, to consider the case. Campbell's attempt to intervene "raised such a Clamor amongst the People . . . [who] openly and loudly declared, if I granted the man a pardon they would hang him at my door." A colonial of "the first property," probably Laurens himself, wrote Campbell that an attempt to pardon Jeremiah would "raise a flame all the water in Cooper River would not extinguish."[45]

But Campbell persisted. Jemmy had retracted his confession before Reverend Smith, who declared Jeremiah entirely innocent.
Campbell asked Smith to attend the court, but when the reverend
proved unwilling, Campbell sent to Laurens an account of Jemmy's
retraction. Laurens received Campbell's letter while in session with
the General Committee, which "utterly refused" to consider it. "In the
Calamitous Situation of this Colony," Laurens replied, "under threats
of Insurrections, strong proofs of which the people are possessed of,
no wonder they are alarmed at the Sound of Pardon to a Man circum-
stanced in all respects as Jerry [Jeremiah] is." The court declared
Jeremiah guilty and sentenced him to be hanged by the neck until
dead on the following day, April 18, and his body to be burned to
ash on the workhouse green.[46] "I could not save him my Lord!"
wrote Governor Campbell to Lord Dartmouth. The man had been
"murdered" by cynical patriots who killed Jeremiah to legitimize
their claims of "instigated insurrections" that justified their usurpation of power from the Crown. Laurens, of course, was "fully satisfied that Jerry was guilty of a design & attempt to encourage our
Negroes to Rebellion and joining the King's Troops." Laurens questioned Campbell's motives, and it is easy to see why. Just a month
earlier, a British naval ship had carried off a black pilot like Jeremiah
after the captain had an altercation with the Council of Safety. If
Britain were to attack Charleston, they needed pilots to guide their
ships of war into the harbor. The British had attacked Boston already,
and white Carolinians certainly believed in "instigated insurrections" among their slaves. The last semblance of trust in the imperial relationship had been shattered, and a war for independence had
begun.[47]

The true intentions of Jeremiah remain shrouded in very thin evidence, but it is not difficult to imagine his involvement. His wealth
gave him prominence and respect, but it would never protect him
from the brutality of white dominion. In 1771, Jeremiah had become embroiled in a fight with Thomas Langen, a white ship captain, and a court had sentenced him to two hours in the stocks and
ten lashes. He had been pardoned by the governor, but such a fearful
episode must have grated him, and the governor's pleasure provided
little security for a self-made black man in eighteenth-century

Charles Town. The imperial crisis politicized slave resistance in ways that were both familiar and novel, reminiscent of the Anglo-Spanish rivalry of the 1730s but with new allies and opportunities. Jeremiah would have seen this with more clarity than most. Black people had little to gain from either the patriots or the British Empire, but they could take advantage of the conflict between them to strike a claim for their own liberty. Jeremiah had gambled all and lost his life, but he would not be alone.[48]

In June 1776, as North American patriots in Philadelphia considered declaring independence from the British Empire, a group of enslaved people in Hanover Parish, Jamaica, decided that another moment had arrived when they could rise up in rebellion and take the island from the whites. For black slaves in eighteenth-century Jamaica, they were older men, probably in their forties. They were the drivers, watchmen, and carpenters who worked the sugar plantations surrounding Lucea Bay. Some had been born in Africa and identified as Coromantees, Ibos, or Congos, but just as many had been born on the island and saw themselves as Creoles. The conspirators of 1776 worked across the lines of African identification to organize a "deeply laid" plot that terrified the whites and secured the colony's loyalty to the Crown. The Coromantee rebellion of 1760 was the recent past, and the conspirators of 1776 had probably been young men at the time. They may have seen the mistakes made during that rebellion and tried to learn from them.[49]

The conspirators knew enough about the colonial rebellion in North America to understand that it had weakened Jamaican whites. Governor Keith had learned in January that the Fiftieth Regiment would be transferred to North America, and in May seven companies of the Sixtieth Regiment departed for Pensacola. In early June, Keith ordered the companies of the Fiftieth Regiment to assemble at Fort Charlotte in Lucea Bay to board the transports for North America. And so the soldiers gathered their things from their country barracks and marched down the paths to Lucea Harbor, past the plantations, the provision grounds, and the thousands of slaves in Hanover Parish who worked them. As in the North American South, black people in Jamaica had developed a system of communication that effectively spread information among themselves. The slaves knew the soldiers were leaving, and they knew the whites were in "general consternation" about this moment of military weakness.[50]

The conspirators first met on June 9, a Sunday when the little town of Lucea filled up with the market women who walked down from their grounds with heavy loads of produce balanced on their heads. This was the slaves' milieu, and the conspirators met in the "open street" to organize their plot. They were one or two men from twenty of the surrounding estates, along with Daphnis of Pedro, the only woman among the principal leaders.[51] On the Baulk Estate lived Sam, king of the Coromantee, and Charles, king of the Creoles. Adam, second king of the Coromantee, lived on Richmond Estate, and Caesar, second king of the Creoles, lived at Cocoon. Prince, king of the Eboes, lived in the town of Lucea. A second tier of rebel leaders included Mingo of Batchelor's Hall and Quamina of Fatt Hogg Quarter, who would signal the beginning of the rebellion. January of Red Hill Pen in the hills would coordinate the rebellion toward Glasgow Estate in Westmoreland. Peter and Fisher, who lived on Point Estate across the bay from Fort Charlotte, would coordinate the rebellion with all the windward estates toward Montego Bay. And Blue Hole Harry of Spring Estate, five miles to the leeward of Lucea, would coordinate the rebellion among the people along the coast toward Green Island Harbor.[52]

The principal leaders met twice more, once in Lucea on June 23 and again on July 7 at Blue Hole Harry's house on Spring Estate. Both meetings were organized to recruit more people into the conspiracy from the estates a bit farther from Lucea. After the meeting of June 23, Peter of Point Estate visited seven estates: Hopewell, Barbican, Magotty, and Blue Hole along the coast; and Kew, Dundee, and Georgia along the Lucea East River. At some of these estates he found recruits willing to spread the conspiracy wider, such as Marriott at Dundee, who promised to recruit "his countrymen" from Retrieve, and Fisherman George of Blue Hole, who went to Tryal. The meeting at Blue Hole Harry's house was probably organized by Adam of Richmond. There he met the drivers from Cove, Harding

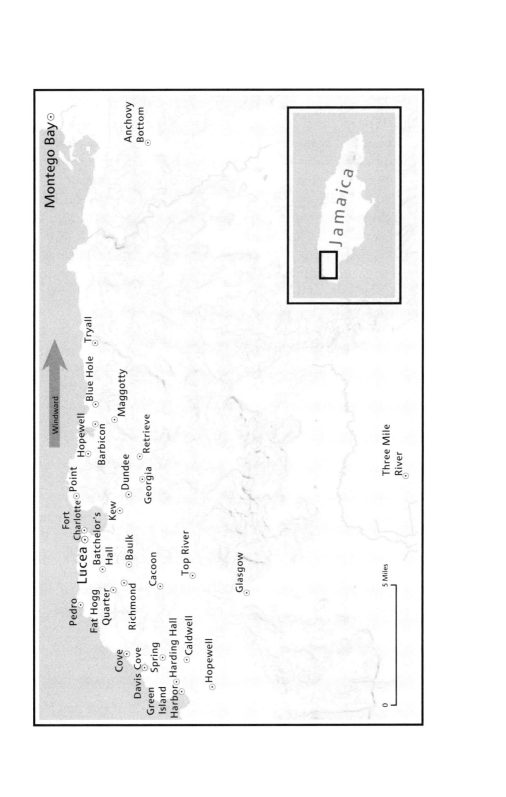

Montego Bay

Anchovy Bottom

Windward

Tryall

Blue Hole

Hopewell

Maggotty

Barbicon

Fort
Charlotte Point

Retrieve

Dundee

Georgia

Batchelor's
Hall

Kew

Lucea

Baulk

Pedro

Cacoon

Fat Hogg
Quarter

Top River

Richmond

Glasgow

Cove

Spring

Davis Cove

Harding Hall

Green
Island

Harbor Caldwell

Hopewell

Three Mile
River

Jamaica

5 Miles

0

Hall, and Caldwell Estates, along with Congo Leander, who also lived at Spring.[53]

When the appointed day arrived, Mingo would fire a gun at Batchelor's Hall to signal the rise. The cook Quamina of Fatt Hogg Quarter would answer with a second gunshot, to be answered by Adam at Richmond and Charles at the Baulk. These four contiguous plantations held more than eight hundred slaves all within a couple of miles of Lucea, and the estates visited by Adam and Peter held more than two thousand. The insurrection would spread like a ring of fire around Lucea Bay as the second-tier leaders put their people in motion. According to the list of estates assembled by the magistrates of Hanover after all the examinations were said and done, the conspiracy involved the people on twenty-eight more estates, more than five thousand people.[54]

But with their new patrol law, the whites were alert. On June 27 William Barnett, a member of the council from neighboring Saint James, learned of a conspiracy in Hanover connected to the imminent departure of the troops. Nine of the ten companies of the Fiftieth Regiment had already boarded the transports, and the tenth was en route. Barnett immediately relayed this news to Keith, who ordered the troops to remain on the island. But when he discussed the matter with the council, a majority dismissed the alarm, and the Fiftieth Regiment left on July 3.[55]

The conspirators no doubt learned about this moment of white panic, for nothing happened for about three weeks. They had planned to rise on a Monday after a final meeting in the market, but with white suspicions aroused, they decided to rise on Wednesday, July 17. That morning the overseer on Baulk Estate caught a slave removing the balls and powder from his pistols, and as he flogged him, the overseer "got hold of the Clew to the whole" and sent word to neighboring whites. The Hanover magistrates mobilized the foot and horse militia, and by the end of the day they had arrested Adam of Baulk along with about fifty others.[56]

By the frightened faces around him, Adam must have known that the whites had caught rebels in all the estates around Lucea Bay and along the coast to leeward. But he didn't see faces from the windward estates, nor did he see anyone from the hills. The magistrates put Adam under examination first, and he tried to mislead them. He told them he had been brought into the conspiracy by Leander of Spring Estate and told them of the meeting at Blue Hole Harry's, where he met the drivers of Davis's Cove, Harding Hall, and Caldwell Estates. Pressed further, Adam also told them that Leander had said that Coromantee Sam of Baulk Estate "promised to get hands from Fatt Hog Quarter, Cacoon, Top River, Richmond and Baulk Estates." And pressed still further, Adam admitted that he had known Sam before. Sam had complained of being "ill used by the overseer and that the hardships of Negroes were too great." We can presume that Adam's interrogation took place under the lash, and "the examination" reads that way, with a little information, then a little more, and still more. But Adam did not mention January of Red Hill, or Peter and Fisher of the Point, or the inland estates, or those to windward. Indeed, the millwright James Tucker later testified that around ten o'clock that evening a group of armed slaves passed through Jerusalem Estate in Westmoreland Parish, and by July 20, large groups of slaves from Glasgow, Pennants, and Three Mile River had left their plantations. January's people were on the march, and Adam could only hope that they would succeed.[57]

But the magistrates examined others whose testimony did not survive, and on July 19 they executed Congo Leander, Blue Hole Harry, Charles, Peter, Prince, and Quamina. They examined Sam on July 19 and were able to extort far more information from him than they had from Adam. Perhaps Sam felt he had nothing to lose; the whites knew too much and he might as well scare them deep. He told them of the estates to leeward and inland, and of January, Fisher, and Prince, who would lead their people. Finally seeing the enormity of the scheme, the magistrates sent an express to General John Palmer, commander of the remaining companies of the Sixtieth Regiment in Montego Bay, and begged him for troops. Palmer had learned of the conspiracy the day before and had already mobilized the Saint James militia to begin patrols. To support the magistrates, he sent a company of light infantry to Lucea by ship, which arrived at three o'clock that afternoon. He readied another company to depart in the morning, but he could spare no more, for the "infection has spread amongst our own Negroes." The patrols in Saint

James had captured many and begun to examine three prisoners from Anchovy Bottom, an estate several miles inland from Montego Bay that Sam never mentioned. Whites in the parish were "in the utmost consternation and in hourly expectation of some dreadfull catastrophe." He begged the governor to send a man-of-war with guns, powder, and men, for they were in desperate need.[58]

Late in the evening on July 19, Governor Keith in Spanish Town received an express from the Hanover magistrates with the examination of Adam enclosed. The magistrates believed a general insurrection was imminent, but when Keith presented this news to the council on July 22 and asked if they thought it wise to declare martial law, they thought not. Martial law entailed too many "inconveniences"—namely, the absence of all whites from the plantations and the consequent cessation of labor. But around noon on July 23, Keith received expresses from General Palmer and from General Cook in Saint Elizabeth, who offered further intelligence and the disturbing news that the Trelawney Town maroons were also implicated. That night Keith received a second express from the Hanover magistrates that included the examination of Sam. Half an hour after receiving this latest missive, Keith called a midnight meeting of the council and presented the latest news, and this time they agreed to call martial law. Admiral Gayton sent a man-of-war to Lucea; Keith ordered the remaining detachments of the Sixtieth Regiment to danger points throughout the island and placed an embargo against all shipping off the island, to keep as many white men in the ports as possible. And with martial law declared, white men throughout the island mustered with their units in every parish seat.[59]

With the entire apparatus of the colonial state thus mobilized and the major leaders of the rebellion either executed or incarcerated, the Jamaican rebels of 1776 had little hope of success. Two Maroons, Asherry and Billy, were tried by the court in Lucea, sessions that were attended by dozens of maroons; both were acquitted. The evidence against them proved weak, or perhaps the whites were afraid to prosecute.[60]

Trials of the conspirators in Hanover lasted until September 18, and of the 135 tried, 62 were acquitted. Seventeen were executed, 45 transported, and 11 subjected to severe and public corporal punishment. We know that Adam was gibbeted, but the details of the others' deaths have not survived. Jamaican whites were most alarmed by the involvement of Creoles, "who never before engaged in Rebellions, and in whose fidelity we had always most firmly relied."[61] In the aftermath of the conspiracy in Hanover, Jamaican whites had to face the insight of John Dalling. Slavery was not, as Edward Long had written, "the bond of fatherly love and affection on the one side, and filial reverence and obedience on the other." No, former governor Dalling wrote closer to truth and the conspirators acted on it— slavery was "perpetual enmity."[62]

James Otis's deployment of the antislavery argument in 1764 had dramatized the Whig claim that slavery resulted from parliamentary oppression, but since the publication of Otis's work, patriot writers had largely steered clear of linking the cause of the colonies to that of the slaves. Patriot sensitivity to slaveholders' fears muted antislavery expression, but extensive use of the slavery metaphor practically invited the observation that slaveholders decrying slavery were hypocrites. Widespread slaveholding throughout the colonies certainly hindered the antislavery critique from becoming pervasive, but in the development of the United States over the next ninety years, the consequences of antislavery's connection to the Revolution would be enormous.

In 1769, Benjamin Rush of Philadelphia, a preeminent physician and early partisan for independence, wrote privately to a French correspondent that "it would be useless for us to denounce the servitude to which the Parliament of Great Britain wishes to reduce us, while we continue to keep our fellow creatures in slavery just because their color is different from ours."[63] But that is precisely what happened. In 1773 Rush publicized his view with his *Address to the Inhabitants of the British Settlements in America, upon Slave Keeping*, which called upon "ye Advocates for American Liberty" to speak out against racial slavery. Rush did not accept the climactic arguments of planters from "the Sugar islands and South Carolina" that labor in the torrid zone required black slaves. And, as if in response to Gadsden's worry that slavery might beget slavery, Rush warned that "national crimes require national punishments."[64]

In 1774 the Baptist minister John Allen tied antislavery even closer to the patriot cause. Written after the passage of the Boston Port Act, Allen's *Watchman's Alarm to Lord N——h* deployed a familiar political print and an invocation of the biblical "watchman" to castigate Britain and warn Americans to repent of their slaveholding. The frontispiece to Allen's pamphlet delivered bitter political satire that built on the metaphor of slavery. Appearing first in the *London Magazine* and later as a broadsheet in Philadelphia, the image vividly portrays America as an Indian woman on the precipice of rape. In the original, she is pinioned from behind by Lord Mansfield and her dress has been ripped to her waist, exposing her breasts. Lord Sandwich, admiral of the Royal Navy, holds her ankles and peers up her dress with a nasty smile, and above her crouches Lord North, who pours "the taxed tea" down her throat as she vomits. Above them stands Britannia, an elegant white woman who turns away in sadness at the plight of her racialized daughter America, and to the right stands Lord Bute, his sword inscribed with "Military Law." Allen replaced Lord Mansfield with Alexander Wedderburn, who had drafted the Boston Port Act, and showed to those who could not see that British ministers raped America just as masters raped their slaves. For Allen the watchman, the Intolerable Acts that enslaved white Americans were divine retribution for American slavery. Abolish slavery and repent, he cried, "for what is a trifling three penny duty on tea in comparison to the inestimable blessing of liberty?"[65]

The writings of Rush and Allen represented an opinion that probably stood in the minority among white colonists, even in the colonies north of the Chesapeake. But the call for ideological consistency had a powerful attraction. The widely respected theologian Samuel Hopkins linked British tyranny to African slavery and white American hypocrisy, as did Thomas Paine in his first published essay in an American newspaper. Among Britons, Samuel Johnson's quotable query made the same point, "Why do we hear the loudest yelps for liberty among the drivers of negroes?" as did Granville Sharp's *Declaration of the People's Natural Right to a Share in the Legislature.*[66] But in the formal documents of the continental congresses that articulated the "imagined community" of American colonists then emerging from imperial crisis, the political metaphor of slavery found consistent expression while the delegates silenced antislavery argument. The "Declaration and Resolves of the First Continental Congress" declared that since the last war, Parliament had created "a system formed to enslave America." Nine months later the Second Continental Congress declared that Parliament's "inordinate passion" for power over the colonies had devolved into a policy of "enslaving these colonies by violence."[67]

When Thomas Jefferson attempted to write antislavery language into the Declaration of Independence, his colleagues deleted his carefully wrought prose. Jefferson had wanted to declare the transatlantic slave trade "a cruel war against human nature" imposed on the colonies by the British Crown. He had wanted to argue that the King's violation of the "sacred rights of life and liberty" of Africans had since devolved into the more recent policy of "exciting" those black men and women "to rise in arms among us." These black insurrectionists would "purchase that liberty of which [the King] deprived them, by murdering" the white colonists who were forced to buy them. With impenetrable logic, Jefferson wove the political metaphor of slavery, Gadsden's fear of slave violence, and Rush's antislavery into the same inconsistent argument.[68]

No record of the debates over Jefferson's draft has survived, but John Adams recalled that the delegates from South Carolina and Georgia insisted on cutting the antislavery language.[69] But the accusation that Britain planned to instigate insurrections remained. King George III, declared the Continental Congress, "has excited domestic insurrection among us, and has endeavored to bring on the inhabitants of our frontiers the merciless Indian savages." With such accusations, the Declaration of Independence echoed the preamble of the Constitution of South Carolina, adopted by the Provincial Congress three months earlier. South Carolinian patriots claimed that the King's officers had "excited domestic insurrections; proclaimed freedom to servants and slaves ... armed them against their masters; [and] instigated and encouraged the Indian nations to war against the colonies." So it was that the enslaved of South Carolina contributed to the movement for American independence. And by doing so, they endowed antislavery argument with a potent and lasting connection to the nation's violent struggle to exist.[70]

John Laurens found himself in Valley Forge, Pennsylvania, during the bitter winter of 1778, struggling alongside a Continental army that suffered from a lack of food, men, and morale. Laurens had returned from his studies in Europe nine months before and, through the influence of his father, had gained appointment as aide-de-camp to General George Washington. Ardently patriotic, Laurens corresponded regularly with his father throughout his time in Europe, so he was better informed than most. The Continental Congress had called on all the states to raise troops for their united defense, and Laurens knew that General James Varnum of Rhode Island had requested permission to raise a battalion of black troops. "Why not South Carolina?" thought Laurens, and so he made a proposal to his father.[71]

Despite his privileged upbringing as the son of a planter, John Laurens had adopted antislavery views. Moreover, in August 1776 when the spirit of independence blew strong, his father had declared in no uncertain terms, "I abhor Slavery." Like Jefferson, Henry Laurens blamed Great Britain for foisting slavery on the colonies, but he recognized that "the Laws and Customs of my Country" and the "avarice" of slaveholders, including himself, would be difficult to overcome. Henry estimated that the people he held enslaved would bring him £20,000 if he sold them, and yet he too had been taken by a need for consistency between action and the rhetoric of liberty. He did not know what to do with these ideas in the summer of 1776, and he asked for "advice & assistance." John approved right away, but not until the winter of 1778 did he propose a plan of action.[72]

"Instead of leaving me a fortune," John wrote, "cede me a number of your able bodied men Slaves" to join the Continental army as defenders of American liberty. Father and son could restore liberty to men who were "unjustly deprived of the Rights of Mankind," and they could renew the army's ranks to pursue the "sacred" war for liberty and independence.[73] The father hesitated. His antislavery ardor had cooled, and he had since been elected president of the Continental Congress. He did not reject the plan outright; rather, over the next couple of weeks, he dropped "hints" in casual conversations with fellow delegates, but he heard not a word of approval. Through a series of letters, father and son debated the merits of a "black Battalion," but as matters stood in the spring of 1778, Henry did not approve. The proposal was of great "magnitude"; only through the "Collective Wisdom of States" could such an idea be considered.[74]

Six months later the British gathered a considerable force in East Florida and prepared a massive offensive to take the war into Georgia and South Carolina. On February 17 John Laurens wrote his father that only "the black project" could save Carolina—their chance had arrived. Henry could triumph "over deep national prejudices, in favor of your Country and humanity at large," John wrote, and John himself would "transform the timid Slave into a firm defender of Liberty." Henry must have thought long and hard, but a few weeks later father and son put their plan into action. John set out for South Carolina via Philadelphia with a letter of introduction from Alexander Hamilton to John Jay (now president of the Continental Congress), while Henry proposed the idea to General Washington. Hamilton wrote that John Laurens hoped to raise as many as four black battalions. Slaves would be given "their freedom with their muskets," which would "animate their courage" and answer the "dictates of humanity." Hamilton believed the British would deploy the same tactic and it was better to strike first, but he also argued that liberating a few would "have a good influence on those who remain [enslaved], by opening a door to their emancipation." Henry Laurens reported to Washington that Carolina was "greatly distressed" and suggested that if he could personally "select" three thousand slaves to form into regiments, he could drive the British out of Georgia and subdue East Florida by the end of July.[75]

Before receiving Washington's reply, Henry Laurens pushed the Continental Congress to consider the defense of the southern states. South Carolina governor John Rutledge sent General Daniel Huger, of a prominent Lowcountry family, to report on the military situation. Huger testified to the severe lack of troops, which stemmed in part from the felt need of most white men "to remain at home to prevent insurrections among the negroes." On March 29, 1779, the Continental Congress passed resolutions that "recommended" the formation of new battalions raised from the slave populations of Georgia and South Carolina. These troops should be embodied under white officers, and slaveholders would be compensated at the rate of $1,000 per slave. At the war's end, these slaves would be freed, disarmed, and paid $50 for their service. Moreover, John Laurens would be promoted to lieutenant colonel, which empowered him to lead troops. The congressional resolutions gave authority to the ideas that had passed between the Laurens men and their close associates for the past year, but the critical word was "recommended." The state legislatures would have the last word. When Governor Rutledge brought the proposal to the legislature, the planters reacted "with horror" and only twelve delegates would support it. Gadsden wrote to Samuel Adams that Carolinians were "disgusted" by the Continental Congress's recommendation; most considered it a "dangerous and impolitic step."[76]

The British did not have such reservations. On June 30, 1779, in preparation for the southern campaign, General Henry Clinton proclaimed from his base in Philipsburg, New York, that slaves who deserted from the rebels would find "full security" behind British lines, where they could "follow . . . any Occupation which [they] shall think proper." It was not an act of emancipation, but black Carolinians would choose to interpret it as such.[77]

By April 1780, British camps were visible to the front lines of Charles Town's defenses, and on May 12 the city fell. Thousands of Carolinian blacks escaped to British lines with reasonable hope of gaining their freedom. White residents of the city lived under occupation for the remainder of the war, and the backcountry writhed in a relentless civil war that bloodied the land.[78]

When the absentee merchants and planters of Jamaica learned that France had declared war on Great Britain, in March 1778, they immediately petitioned the Crown for more troops. Despite the terrifying conspiracy of 1776, imperial demands in North America had drawn the island's garrison down to 560 regulars. In October, Governor Dalling learned that the French were massing troops in Saint-Domingue; invasion seemed imminent, so he declared martial law. The colonial state hired more than 1,200 slaves to work on the island fortifications, and almost four thousand free men, whites and free colored, mustered in their militia units.[79]

In the midst of this chaos, William Ricketts of Westmoreland found himself deeply impressed by the military discipline of the free colored men in the militia company he commanded. Ricketts had participated in the suppression of the Hanover conspiracy, and he was no doubt involved in similar work under martial law. In October Ricketts submitted petitions to both the Crown and the Jamaica House of Assembly, requesting a commission to raise a "proper regiment" of free colored troops to aid in the general defense of the island. This would be a considerable expansion of the responsibilities for a class of men the planters despised. A proper regiment would be under British pay, would wear the colors of a British soldier, and thus would gain status. Free colored men might expect more from the society they served after such an experience. Governor Dalling embraced the idea.[80]

In September 1778, as white Jamaicans watched the horizon uneasily for sails, France seized the little colony of Dominica in the eastern Caribbean. In London, so many Jamaican absentees were alarmed by the insecurity of their investments that Stephen Fuller hosted two meetings in his residence on Southampton Street near Covent Garden. These meetings produced a series of detailed resolutions that Fuller presented to Lord Germain on December 24, 1778. Fuller reminded Germain of the desperate and unanswered plea of 1773, which he appended, but made it clear that the security situation had worsened, especially considering the conspiracy of 1776. The racial imbalance had not changed, but troop levels were actually worse. From among the regulars, 137 men were bedridden with fevers, which reduced the active force on the island to 443 regulars with only sergeants to lead them. The Maroons, whom Jamaican whites had hitherto seen as allies against rebellious slaves, had shown during the Hanover conspiracy that they could not always be trusted. And the whites now knew from "melancholy experience" that they had dangerously miscalculated the sentiments of creole blacks. The absentees were also uncomfortable with Dalling's experiment with free colored troops. They were not impressed by the five hundred men who responded to Dalling's call; indeed, they dismissed them as "idle, debauched, distempered profligate wretches."[81]

The absentees wanted white troops from Britain, as many as the ministry could give them. In February, Fuller wrote with the excellent news that His Majesty had ordered the Liverpool regiment of 1,169 men and officers to depart for Jamaica. But in April, Spain declared its alliance with France against Great Britain, doubling the threat against Jamaica, which now faced invasion from Saint-Domingue and Cuba. In June Saint Vincent and Grenada fell to the French, and in August Dalling again declared martial law. Dalling also issued orders for the formation of two infantry companies of free colored Jamaicans, as well as a regiment of forty-eight free blacks, according to Ricketts's original proposal, who were paid as regulars and placed under military discipline. This was unprecedented in Jamaica but arguably justified by the threats the island faced. Nevertheless, at a meeting held at Fuller's residence in London, the absentees again balked at measures they considered "dangerous and delusive." Only white soldiers could be trusted to meet the island's security needs, and the absentees asked Germain to please send more.[82]

This time they were not forthcoming, but Germain left open the possibility that the absentees could raise a regiment if they paid for it themselves. Fuller presented this idea at a packed meeting held at the London Tavern on October 15. Fifty-five attendees with investments in Jamaica pledged £100 each to a subscription to provide bounties to men willing to serve in a new regiment destined for Jamaica. By the end of November they had raised more than £5,000 for the new regiment, and in December they began to advertise the bounties: six guineas for every man who joined immediately, five guineas for those who delayed six weeks, and so on. By August 1780, ten companies had been raised, a thousand men, but alas, on August 31, Fuller wrote to the assembly that seven of the ten companies had been taken at sea by the Spanish almost as soon as they had embarked. The remaining three would depart soon, and Germain promised that more men would be raised, but that would take time.[83]

On October 19, 1781, the British surrendered to General Washington at Yorktown, Virginia, a moment that most understand as the end of the American war for independence. Contemporaries did not see it as such, especially in Jamaica and South Carolina. For General Nathanael Greene of the Continental army, it appeared that the British were determined to keep the lower South. A Rhode Island Quaker, Greene had been appointed to the southern command in October 1780, and through a combination of brilliant military tactics and the susceptibility of newly arrived British soldiers to malaria, Greene's army had been able to narrow Britain's range of action to Charles Town and its immediate environs. The British had turned to the slave population as a critical source of labor in the maintenance of their position. They had begun to form regiments of blacks, presumably freed, and by January Greene reported to Governor Rutledge that they were well on their way to a force of three thousand. Greene recommended that Rutledge reconsider the plans long advocated by John and Henry Laurens. With such an augmentation of force, Greene believed that he could make an offensive and push the British out of Charleston. In February John Laurens made a final plea to the legislature to approve his plan, and while he gained twice as many supporters as in 1779, a large majority still could not countenance the arming of slaves. Rather, the assembly passed a law that granted bounties of one slave per year to white men willing to enlist. General Washington wrote to a dispirited John Laurens, "That spirit of freedom which at the commencement of this contest would have gladly sacrificed everything . . . has long since subsided."[84]

For people of the Caribbean, the British defeat at Yorktown meant that French forces would turn toward them. France warred against Britain for its own interests, and the most important prizes were in the Caribbean. On March 2, 1782, Jamaican governor Archibald Campbell called a council of war, and on March 3 he proposed to the legislature that they consider the arming of their slaves. Campbell's proposition resembled the Laurens scheme in every way except one: the slaves would not be freed. The assembly quickly replied that arming slaves was "an expedient too dangerous" to imagine. For most slaveholders of these societies, armed slaves posed the unthinkable threat.[85]

Campbell later wrote that he expected an attack of 30,000 troops with invasions from the north and south. He had fewer than 4,000 soldiers at his disposal, along with 800 seamen, and when he ordered martial law, 6,801 free Jamaicans mustered, including 1,714 free men of color. Their precarious situation did convince the assembly to finally approve the formation of free colored regiments. But Jamaica never had to face this invasion. On April 14, 1782, the very day that Ricketts repeated his proposals to the assembly, Admiral George Rodney won a decisive victory against the French fleet among the islets between Guadeloupe and Dominica known as Les Saintes. The French were en route to Jamaica. They carried siege artillery and fifty thousand pairs of fetters to reenslave the Jamaican blacks who would no doubt free themselves in the chaos of invasion. Rodney had saved the island, and he had probably saved slavery in Jamaica. The planters loved him for it, and the assembly raised funds for the larger-than-life sculpture of his likeness that still stands like a Roman centurion overlooking the now-abandoned Spanish Town Parade.[86]

But what if Rodney had lost? In an unpublished memoir on his plans to defend the island, Governor Campbell wrote that he would have armed the slaves. Every man in the militia, Campbell recalled, would bring with him "to the field one or more confidential slaves," armed with a gun and powder. These men would double the militia force, and "freedom was to have been the certain reward of their fidelity." At least 6,801 slaves would have been freed through Campbell's scheme. How many others would have freed themselves? A French invasion in 1782 might have initiated a wartime emancipation similar to that of Saint-Domingue in the 1790s, the American South in the 1860s, or Cuba in the 1870s. History may have unfolded quite differently if Rodney had lost.[87]

The war around Charles Town festered as the peace negotiators met in Paris to unwind the ties that bound Britain to the thirteen colonies. Greene did not trust the British, but he did not have the force to expel them from the city. The British sent out occasional parties beyond the city to forage for provisions, and Greene would send detachments against them. These were minor skirmishes with very little at stake, but on August 27, 1782, one of these battles took the life of John Laurens, a tragic loss as he was only twenty-seven. His father mourned in London. He had just been released from the Tower of London, where he had been imprisoned after being captured on the high seas en route to Holland, where the Continental Congress had sent him to negotiate a loan. In the interim Congress had appointed Laurens to be one of the peace negotiators, along with Benjamin Franklin and John Jay, but he did not join them until November. Laurens added only one phrase to the treaty, that the British would agree, as they disembarked from North America, to leave behind whatever "Negroes or other property" they had acquired during the occupation.[88]

That would not happen. In August 1782 Lieutenant General Alexander Leslie gave the orders to begin preparations for the evacuation of Charles Town. Thousands of slaves had run to British lines during the war, and they had worked for the army in numerous ways. But British policies toward black slaves had been strictly military; there had never been an antislavery commitment. British officers and men began to sell the black men and women who had worked for them to the departing loyalists, who registered them on the ships as their lawful property. Cassandra Pybus has documented the evacuation of 6,940 black Carolinians by the time the evacuation was complete in December 1782. Of these, perhaps 1,200 departed as free people, the remainder as slaves. They left for numerous locations in the British Empire: East Florida, Saint Lucia, Nova Scotia, New York, and England, and almost 5,000 went to Jamaica. South Carolina lost about 25,000 slaves during the war. Many certainly died of disease and from the war itself. But as many as 10,000 departed with the British, during the clandestine slave trade that went on during the occupation, and in the evacuation of 1782.[89]

Those loyalists and their slaves who came to Jamaica arrived in a society in the midst of devastation by a different force: nature. Rodney might have saved the island from the French, but beginning in 1780, five hurricanes struck the island, followed by a severe drought that lasted until 1787. The hurricanes destroyed countless provision grounds, and as the Revolution had disrupted commerce between the island and North America, from where food had arrived for so long, dreadful famines resulted that killed between fifteen thousand and twenty-four thousand slaves. The war's end found both societies devastated, war-weary, and deeply uncertain about the future.[90]

Black resistance had long sounded alarms to slaveholders and the masters of empire, but when radical Whig pamphleteers invoked the inhumanity of enslavement to dramatize their own protests against imperial taxation, the deeper indignity of racial slavery emerged as a political question in its own right. Black people seized on this moment when the terms of liberty appeared uncertain, and they found white allies, men and women shaped by the rise of antislavery beliefs. The cases black Londoners pushed before Lord Mansfield demanded a resolution of the question of slavery's legality. And when the West Indian planters encouraged Charles Stewart to push for his rights, Lord Mansfield demonstrated the subordination of the colonies by curtailing the rights of slaveholders in the metropole. The Somerset case did not contribute to the causes of the American Revolution. If it had, North Americans would have written a lot more than they did. But Somerset did endow antislavery ideas with rich political salience, and as the imperial crisis deepened, antislavery calls rang louder.[91]

The fact that Edward Long devoted considerable time and intellectual energy to combating antislavery while Henry Laurens did not reveals the distinct politics of slavery in these otherwise similar slave societies. Jamaica's dependence on Great Britain lay not only in the considerable need for military support but also in the power of metropolitan opinion. Intellectual life among whites was richer in South Carolina than in Jamaica. Thinkers like Long did most of their writing as absentees in London; indeed, the celebrated petition of the Jamaica House of Assembly appeared in North American newspapers and as a pamphlet in London and Philadelphia, but no Jamaican printer fixed its type on a press. Radical Whig ideology had emerged in both societies, but in Jamaica only a minority of the tiny white minority embraced it. In South Carolina, the adherence to radical Whig beliefs ran deep, despite the antislavery implications of this thought.

The political differences in the leadership of these slaveholding classes stemmed in part from their very different systems of slave control, which were in turn shaped by starkly different demographics. White Carolinians were a minority representing about 40 percent of the population. But there were enough white men to secure slavery in this society through a resilient culture of white solidarity that generated a flexible system of slave control based on internal strength and an alert white citizenry. Whites in Jamaica were a minority of less than 10 percent, a ratio they had never been able to change. Jamaican whites shared many qualities with their South Carolinian counterparts—racial solidarity, brutality, and an alert militia—but their small number encouraged slave rebels and bred dependence in Jamaica on the military garrison. The assembly paid these men, who came from the British Isles. But most of these soldiers died and had to be replaced, a destructive and costly cycle of death. And few of those who survived became committed to the island's deeply violent colonial society.

The structural differences between these slave societies help to explain the distinct possibilities for militant organization among the enslaved of each. Thousands of black slaves in Jamaica saw white people only rarely. The Sunday markets throughout the island created semiautonomous spaces for black Jamaican communities, including the Maroons who visited these markets. These spaces allowed for the organization of conspiracies in moments like 1776. Enslaved blacks in South Carolina had fewer opportunities. They did have provision grounds, and enslaved women oversaw the commerce in the food markets of Charles Town and the other ports. But these slave-controlled markets were not as pervasive in South Carolina as they were in Jamaica, thus the availability of time away from white observation was more limited, the organizational possibilities stunted in comparison.

The Revolutionary War pushed individuals from both planter classes to consider the arming of slaves to meet pressing military needs, but only in South Carolina were these proposals accompanied by an antislavery agenda. The loose dedication to radical Whig ideology in Jamaica never generated the aspiration for consistency between thought and action. Those Whigs in the Assembly of 1774 declaimed the "slavery" of white colonists with language as strong as that of the North Americans, but there was never a Jamaican Laurens. The antislavery of Henry and John Laurens is astonishing. Unlike the British in North America or Governor Campbell in Jamaica, the antislavery dimension remained important in each iteration of the Laurens' proposal to arm black slaves. That a wealthy slaveholder like Henry Laurens could even consider the abolition of slavery highlights the radicalism of the American Revolution. But the failures of his and John's proposal highlight the deep conservatism that slaveholding had engrained among this society's elite. South Carolinian slaveholders like Gadsden embraced republican values, but there were limits. Proposals to abolish slavery fell dead to slaveholder intransigence.

The Jamaican and South Carolinian proposals to arm slaves suggest a genesis of political abolitionism. An organized abolitionist movement would first emerge in Great Britain, best explained as a response to Britain's loss of the North American colonies.[92] Yet in the proposals to arm slaves in South Carolina, we can see antislavery ideas attached to a political movement that some hoped would end slavery. In 1779 William Whipple of New Hampshire expressed great satisfaction that should the black regiments be raised, it would "lay a foundation for the Abolition of Slavery in America." After the debate on John Laurens's final proposal in the South Carolina legislature in 1782, the backcountry planter Aedanus Burke wrote with great concern that he suspected that "the northern people . . . secretly wish for a general Emancipation."[93]

Burke's elision of Laurens's Carolinian pedigree notwithstanding, his comment reveals a transformation in the politics of slavery fostered by the imperial crisis and the throes of revolutionary war. The American Revolution had pushed antislavery argument from the pages of philosophers to the pamphlets of politicians, and endowed slave resistance with a novel validity that intensified the ancient struggle between the masters and the slaves.

CHAPTER 6

The Slaveholders Retrench

THE LAST GENERATION of the eighteenth century witnessed bewildering events in the politics of slavery that seemed to promise the unraveling of a world. Like a one-two punch, the emergence of radical abolitionism in the 1780s and the Haitian Revolution of the 1790s forced slaveholders to find their balance and deflect unprecedented threats from above and below that would test their political skills in moments of great weakness.

In May 1787, in Great Britain and in the United States, the struggle over Atlantic slavery took on a new dimension as white men with power and antislavery views began to act toward the abolition of racial slavery. Among the delegates of the new American states who arrived in Philadelphia during that month to frame a new plan of government were men of antislavery convictions who wanted racial slavery to wither and die so that revolutionary rhetoric might become reality. In London on May 22, twelve men met in a printer's shop to form the Society for Effecting the Abolition of the Slave Trade (later known simply as the London Committee). Like their North American counterparts, the members of this group hoped that slavery would soon end, but tactically, they chose to levy their assault on the transatlantic slave trade. A couple of weeks later, William Wilberforce, one of their number and member of Parliament (MP) for Hull, made his first formal proposals to consider the abolition of the slave trade with Africa. The struggle over slavery in the highest seats of power had begun.[1]

Political compromise trumped moral principle in 1787, and slaveholders retained great power. But in August 1791, on the central plain of French Saint-Domingue, began the world-historic slave rebellion that extinguished one class of slaveholders and posed an existential threat to all the rest. African-born slaves and their descendants in Saint-Domingue exploited the revolutionary divide in France and its empire and struck for their own liberation. Their actions inspired enslaved peoples throughout the Atlantic World. Rebels in many Atlantic slave societies, including Jamaica and South Carolina, developed conspiracies, and some led insurrections. While none of these militant actions sustained the violent intensity or the duration of the Haitian Revolution, slave violence in the wake of Haiti showed how the liberating ethos of the age inspired men and women of every status and origin.[2]

The resistance of slaves had always challenged the power of the planters, but in this era of the Haitian Revolution, resistance was reinforced by abolitionist agitation. The American Revolution had divided the Anglo-Atlantic World of slavery, but in their respective political milieus, Jamaican and South Carolinian slaveholders still had much in common. They championed the defense of slavery against abolitionist pressure, and they crushed the resistance of those they enslaved. Both planter classes developed new commodities—coffee and cotton—which promised a new era of wealth and slavery at the dawn of the nineteenth century. In response to abolitionism and the Haitian Revolution, the slaveholders retrenched.

When Thomas Clarkson mapped out the intellectual eddies and rivers that fed into the great sea of modern abolitionism, he left out Ignatius Sancho, the black writer of critical importance to Clarkson's own career.[3] Born on a slave ship bound for Cartagena in 1729 and orphaned as an infant, Sancho acquired his Christian name from the Spanish Jesuit who baptized him and his surname from the three English sisters who bought him but did not like him and named him after the portly fool in Cervantes's *Don Quixote*. Fortunately, the

young man caught the eye of the second Duke of Montagu, who resided in Blackheath; the duke took a liking to Sancho, taught him
to read, and gave him domestic employment. Sancho prospered in
England, becoming a prominent member of the black community
in London that supported James Somerset. Sancho wrote music; he
worked in the theater, where he met the famous actor David Gar-
rick; and Londoners of all ranks visited his grocer's shop. Sancho
married a white woman of West Indian descent, Anne, with whom
he raised five children. But he was best known for his letters, one
especially to the celebrated novelist Laurence Sterne in 1766 that
gave the lie to Edward Long's insulting portrayal of black people.[4]

"I am one of those people whom the vulgar and illiberal call Negroes," Sancho wrote to Sterne. He expressed deep gratitude for
Sterne's condemnation of slavery in his *Tristram Shandy* (1766) and
lamented that so few writers dared to do so. When Sterne's letters
were published after his death in 1772, periodicals such as the *Edinburgh Magazine*, *Gentleman's Magazine*, and the *Monthly Miscellany*
highlighted Sancho's letter, as well as Sterne's gracious response, in
their reviews of the work.[5] *Gentleman's Magazine* noticed Sancho's
death in 1780, making him the first black Briton to receive such
recognition, and Miss F. Crewe, one of Sancho's correspondents,
painstakingly collected his letters and had them published in two volumes to widespread acclaim. By 1784 the volumes had been through
four editions, and Sancho's son William printed a fifth in 1803. The
Critical Review celebrated the letters as proof that "the untutored African may possess abilities equal to those of an European."[6]

Sancho's letters inspired Peter Peckard, the vice-chancellor of
Cambridge University, who in 1785 set the exam question that made
Thomas Clarkson famous. Sancho's influence on Peckard can be seen
in the latter's sermon, *Piety, Benevolence, and Loyalty, Recommended*,
which he published in 1784 just months before his appointment as
vice-chancellor. Peckard told the story of Sancho's life and drew from
Sancho's letter to the London bookseller Jack Wingrave to describe
the slave trade in West Africa, that "abominable traffic of the Christians for Slaves." Peckard was quite thorough in his antislavery
stance. He condemned color prejudice, slavery, and the slave trade
as "against the light of nature and the accumulated evidence of

divine Revelation." Parliament and all Britons, he argued, should be ashamed that all of this horror had the support of their laws.[7]

Every year the students of Cambridge participated in a contest in Latin composition, and in 1785 Vice-Chancellor Peckard posed the following question: "Is it right to make slaves of others against their will?" The award-winning essay that Clarkson wrote launched his career as the bête noire of slaveholders for the next half century. Research lit the fire of advocacy in Clarkson's soul, and in the years that followed he expanded the composition and published it as *An Essay on the Slavery and Commerce of the Human Species* (1787). Clarkson read all of the antislavery writers we have encountered before, including Baron Montesquieu and Granville Sharp, but the most influential author Clarkson read was James Ramsay.[8]

Ramsay was a longtime resident of Saint Kitts. His *Essay on the Treatment and Conversion of African Slaves* (1784) advanced a trenchant critique of West Indian slavery centered on a comparison of the slave codes in the French and British West Indies. It was savvy political argument to unfavorably contrast slavery in Britain's colonies with the slavery of Britons' archenemy, and it allowed Ramsay to demonstrate the particular barbarity of British West Indian slavery. He highlighted the various protections for slaves embedded in the French Code Noir that were noticeably absent from the British West Indian codes. The Code Noir required French slaveholders to provide their slaves with established allowances of food and clothing; it prohibited masters from mutilating their slaves; and it stated that enslaved people in the French colonies could appeal to the intendants, who were required to guarantee the rights of slaves. The Code Noir also required the purchasers of newly arrived Africans to notify a Catholic priest, who took on the responsibility of religious instruction for every enslaved African. In contrast, Ramsay lamented, not a single law in the British West Indies secured "the least humane treatment" for England's slaves. English slaves were often naked and hungry, and a slave in Britain's sugar islands could be "hacked to pieces with a cutlass" for stealing a piece of cane. Not a clause in the British colonial codes would offer the slightest protection.[9]

Ramsay's idealistic view of French West Indian slavery notwithstanding, the potency of his argument inspired nine proslavery responses by 1787, and the legal foundation of his argument would structure the debate over slavery in the British Empire. Clarkson embraced Ramsay's emphasis on the weakness of the British colonial slave codes. Britain's slaves were "beaten and tortured at discretion . . . badly clothed . . . miserably fed . . . without a single law to protect them." He cited the brutality of Jamaica as particularly harsh and challenged the planters to account for the inconsistencies between their legislation and the norms of "civilized nations." West Indian apologists claimed that their laws were informed by experience, but what, Clarkson demanded, explained "that long catalog of offences, which you punish, [that] no people but yourselves take cognizance of at all?" And what of the law that "authorizes murder? That tempts an unoffended person to kill the slave, that abhors and flies your service?"[10]

Clarkson referred to several clauses of Jamaica's 1696 slave code that were still in effect in 1785. Whites could legally kill a slave for striking a white person or just imagining the death of a white person. Whites could kill any slave who refused to submit to punishment when caught stealing or simply being off the plantation at night. Even if a white person "wantonly or bloody mindedly" killed a black person, the white could not be punished until he or she did this twice. And the law provided compensation for the owners of slaves killed in accordance with the slave code, lest economic incentives discourage full enforcement of the law. Clarkson did not exaggerate when he made such accusations.[11]

Jamaicans had not responded to Ramsay's *Essay* in 1784. Their public stance toward abolitionist writings had been one of "silent contempt" until Wilberforce submitted his proposals to abolish the slave trade to the House of Commons in May 1787. During the following year the London Committee coordinated a campaign that brought more than one hundred antislavery petitions to Parliament from institutions and communities throughout Great Britain. The first Jamaican contribution to the debate, the absentee Gilbert Francklyn's *Answer to the Rev. Mr. Clarkson's Essay*, did not appear until 1789, but in fact, Jamaican slaveholders had been quite active in responding to the abolitionist assault. Once it became clear that antislavery writings were gaining a positive reception in Great Britain—and sympathetic coverage of antislavery publications by *Gentleman's Magazine*, the *Monthly Review*, and the *Scots Magazine* demonstrated this—Jamaicans on either side of the Atlantic responded with complementary strategies that would ultimately blunt the abolitionist assault on their slave system.[12]

Stephen Fuller organized the proslavery defense in London. He organized a series of meetings of the Society of West India Merchants and Planters to coordinate the lobbying response to the abolitionists, but he also deployed the fear of slave violence. The threat of rebellion was always fundamental to Jamaican governance, and the memories of the Hanover conspiracy remained quite fresh. In January 1788, just two weeks before the Board of Trade began to take evidence on the African slave trade, Fuller penned a letter to Lord Hawkesbury, president of the board, that warned of a slave rebellion if the abolitionists were to continue their agitation. Fuller warned Hawkesbury to order all of the colonial governors in the West Indies to be sure the militias were armed and the regular troops prepared to respond to threats from the slaves. In Jamaica, Fuller noted, there were "upwards of 200,000 slaves and only between 12,000 and 13,000 whites," a frightful proportion. The "domestic slaves," Fuller explained, "read all the public prints and instantly communicate any intelligence respecting themselves to their fellow slaves employed in the field." If the slaves learned of their "friends" in England raising large sums of money on their behalf, they might "strike whilst the iron is hot" and liberate themselves. Fuller hoped that Hawkesbury could "prevent this matter from being agitated at all in Parliament" and reminded him that a "great number" of His Majesty's subjects had made considerable investments in the sugar colonies based on the present system of commerce. Nevertheless, in February 1788 the Board of Trade took under its consideration the "present state of the Africa trade." The board would take reams of testimony from captains, sailors, and slaveholders on the nature of the transatlantic slave trade, as well as slavery in the Caribbean.[13]

Fuller no doubt expected this result. Wilberforce had the support of Prime Minster William Pitt, and in May *Gentleman's Magazine* reported Pitt's motion to recognize antislavery petitions submitted to Parliament. Some of the most prominent MPs, Whigs and Tories, supported Pitt's motion, including the Tory Edmund Burke and the Whig Charles James Fox. Only one MP, Richard Pennant (Lord Penrhyn), a Tory and an absentee planter from Jamaica, rose to defend his fellow slaveholders. By the end of 1788 more than one hundred petitions calling for the abolition of the slave trade had arrived in London.[14]

As the abolitionists coordinated strategies in London, active measures to defend the slave system were also under way in Jamaica. The House of Assembly began to build a case that the abolitionists were "ill-informed scribblers" who libeled honorable British subjects whose commerce was of great value to the empire.[15] The assembly took the first step in October 1787 when it met to reconsider its slave code. Ramsay and Clarkson had paid particular attention to these laws, which had clearly become a liability. The assemblymen did their work quickly, passing a new code just two months later that came to be known as the Consolidated Act. The new act repealed the seventeenth-century code with a new set of laws that presented a system of governance far gentler than its predecessors. The first several clauses appealed to the "humanity" of the planters. They required the provision of adequate land for their slaves' provision grounds; care for slaves who were old or sick; and "proper and sufficient" clothing for all slaves. The new laws prohibited the mutilation of slaves and prescribed death for any person duly convicted of "wantonly" killing a slave. It remained legal to kill a slave who struck a white person or imagined the killing of a white person, and the legislature continued to give whites considerable power to maintain control over the black population. But the new laws did appear to respond to the abolitionist critique.[16]

Stephen Fuller had the new law printed widely and abstracted as a pamphlet with some curious emendations that suggest their intent as propaganda. On the title page for the entire Consolidated Act, which sold for two shillings as a pamphlet (though MPs received it gratis), Fuller presented the new laws as the "essential regulations of the JAMAICA CODE NOIR," suggesting that the new laws brought colonial governance in line with the more humane regulations of the

French. And in a very brief abstract of the new law, printed as a short pamphlet in 1791, a clause was added guaranteeing religious instruction to the slaves. This clause does not appear in the text of the Consolidated Act. In an almost point-by-point fashion, the Assembly had passed new laws to undermine the charges of cruelty advanced by Ramsay and Clarkson.[17]

These formal representations of the new slave laws appeared alongside a series of commentaries by prominent Jamaicans, as well as the House of Assembly, that offered a progressive narrative to frame the evolution of West Indian slavery. Francklyn and Bryan Edwards argued that the abolitionists based their portrayal of Jamaican society on histories and laws that reflected a bygone era, not their own time. They cited the history by Hans Sloane, who wrote about Jamaica when its inhabitants were "a very unpolished, uncivilized race." The planters in Sloane's Jamaica had arrived as Oliver Cromwell's soldiers; they were planters and pirates, entirely unlike the "rising generation of West Indians, nursed in the bosom of peace" with refined manners and "humane sentiments." Both men claimed that slave rebellions were no longer a threat due to the growth in the creole slave population and the amelioration of the laws, and Francklyn went so far as to predict a gradual abolition of slavery through the increase in manumissions by benevolent white Jamaicans.[18]

Complementing this tale, the Jamaica House of Assembly commissioned two reports to challenge the accusation of tyranny. Published by Fuller as a single pamphlet in 1789, the *Two Reports from the Committee of the Honourable House of Assembly of Jamaica* were originally commissioned in the fall of 1788. The assembly claimed to have no responsibility for the slave trade, which they described as "purely a British trade" that did not concern them. On the charges of cruelty, however, the assembly sought to demonstrate that in fact "the negroes in this island are under the protection of lenient and salutary laws." They expressed astonishment that "respectable bodies of men" in Britain had accepted abolitionist allegations. The assembly acknowledged that seventeenth-century laws had persisted into their own time, but in 1784, they claimed, there were so many calls for "improvements and amendments . . . for giving further protection and security to slaves" that the assembly sought the opinions of planters throughout the island for a thorough revision of the laws. In the following years, "pressing business" had postponed this effort until October 1787, when the revision was completed.[19]

This was a fiction. The Jamaica Assembly that met in October 1784 did establish a committee to revise laws that would soon expire, but the assembly's journals do not mention the Act for the Better Order and Government of Slaves.[20] The *Two Reports* were rather part of a robust campaign on the part of West Indian slaveholders to blunt the first abolitionist effort of 1788. Unfortunately, it worked. The abolitionists wrote dozens of pamphlets condemning West Indian slavery and the African trade that supported it. The Board of Trade hearings on the slave trade lasted two years and brought much evidence to light of the abuses that pervaded the entire slave system. A second abolitionist petition drive, in 1792, brought 519 petitions to Parliament from all parts of Britain. But the West Indian slaveholders defended themselves ably in print, and the *Two Reports* purported to show that the Jamaica Assembly had been in step with the humane intentions of the abolitionists. The abolitionists, they argued, were naïve. Wilberforce brought motions to abolish the slave trade twice, in 1791 and 1792, and both times they were defeated. The only legislative accomplishment the abolitionists could show after eight years of agitation was the passage in the Commons of a toothless resolution to consider the abolition of the slave trade in 1796. And the Lords rejected it. West Indian slaveholders, led in large part by the Jamaicans, had met their opponents in the court of public opinion, and in the legislatures, and they had soundly defeated them.[21]

In his award-winning essay, Clarkson noted with great pleasure the increased practice in North America of manumitting slaves and employing "free men" on the plantations. Perhaps he had in mind Virginia, where a 1782 law broadened the possibilities of manumission for about fifteen years. Some Virginia slaveholders did manumit their slaves for antislavery reasons, but Clarkson would have found far more encouraging developments north of the Chesapeake. African Americans had begun to send antislavery petitions to the state legislatures in the 1770s, and white abolitionists formed the Pennsylvania

Abolition Society and the New York Manumission Society in 1784 and 1785, respectively. Some states even began to act against slavery. The Vermont Constitution of 1777 abolished slavery outright, and in 1780 the Pennsylvania legislature passed a gradual abolition law; Rhode Island and Connecticut would do the same in 1784. In 1781 the Massachusetts slave Quok Walker sued for his freedom, and in 1783 the state supreme court declared slavery incompatible with the Massachusetts Constitution. Such developments attest to the strength of antislavery opinion in the northeastern states, but they also reflect a political landscape of state autonomy that did not reflect the national context.[22]

South Carolina's newspapers did not print any notice of the northern abolitions. But in October 1785, the *Charleston Evening Gazette* did report that the ancient university in Cambridge had made Negro slavery the subject of a Latin composition contest that had attracted "no less than two hundred essays." The anonymous correspondent did not name Clarkson, but the writer did note that the winning author intended to publish his essay in English, and that numerous religious societies—Presbyterians, Baptists, and Independents—had begun to consider steps to discourage the transatlantic slave trade. "This business is likely to proceed," the writer warned, as respectable men were taking interest in the question.[23]

This news from Britain came at a time when the South Carolina legislature was in the midst of a debate over its own slave trade. The Revolutionary War had devastated the economy, and Carolina suffered along with the rest of the United States. Contemporaries estimated that between twenty thousand and twenty-five thousand slaves had escaped, died, or left with the British in 1782, leaving countless plantations bereft of labor. Moreover, by the 1780s thousands of whites from the upper South and Mid-Atlantic states had migrated to the Carolina backcountry, where they settled on lands that had been wrested from the Cherokee during the Revolutionary War. These new settlers adopted slavery with relative ease, creating a new demand for slaves at the same time that the managers of Lowcountry rice estates sought to repopulate their gangs.[24]

Carolina's slave trade had ceased entirely in 1776, but early in 1783 Carolinian merchants began to outfit slavers for the African coast.

In December, the *Polly*, owned by John Vesey and Company, arrived in Charleston with ninety-four Africans, and by the end of the next year more than five thousand Africans were forcefully transported to Carolinian ports; most of the slavers were British, and most of the Africans departed from Gold Coast ports. By March 1787, when the state legislature banned the trade, almost ten thousand Africans had arrived and been sold into Carolinian slavery.[25]

The debate over South Carolina's slave trade began soon after the commerce itself. As early as February 1783 some legislators began to argue that the trade should be banned or highly taxed. Many Carolinians were deeply in debt to British merchants, who had gained permission to remain in Charleston after the British evacuation. Proponents of a slave trade ban argued that planters spent too much on newly enslaved Africans. For Lowcountry representatives like Edward Rutledge and Ralph Izard, this resulted in too much debt and a painful limitation of credit. For petitioners in backcountry Camden, the slave trade "drained us of our cash and prevented the increase of population and growth of manufactures." These were different visions of political economy with the same solution. Delegates against the ban argued that black slaves were the "raw materials" of the Carolinian economy because their labor produced the staples that fueled commerce and brought new lands into production. Slaves were not "luxuries"; they were essential to Carolina's export economy, and the problems of indebtedness were only temporary. Proponents acknowledged the fundamental principles of this argument, and they always imagined reopening the trade when economic conditions improved. But the postwar economic depression had created an unusual situation. By March 1787 those legislators in favor of the ban prevailed. Each side of this vote represented a cross section of South Carolina, with votes from Charleston, the Lowcountry, and the backcountry on either side of the aisle. But in the final vote, the underrepresented backcountry voted thirty-three to twenty in opposition to the ban. Almost four thousand Africans had been imported since the debate had begun. Planters from the Lowcountry, wealthier and better connected, had bought enough slaves to rebuild their plantations while aspiring planters of the backcountry sought more and more enslaved Africans. The Camden petition represented a minority backcountry opinion, but in alliance with the Lowcountry, they banned the Carolinian slave trade for the next seventeen years.[26]

South Carolina's slave trade debate was about political economy. The terms of debate treated enslaved Africans as investments, and as capable hands with strong backs. But the remarkable coincidence of the Carolina debate with the northern abolitions and the onset of antislavery agitation in Great Britain attracted comment that Carolina's newspapers did not neglect. In April 1785, for example, the *South Carolina Gazette* reprinted a letter from a "gentleman of Philadelphia" who lamented the efforts in South Carolina's Assembly to defend the "cruel and oppressive trade to Africa." The following week, the *South Carolina Weekly Gazette* reprinted an excerpt from Richard Price's *Observations on the Importance of the American Revolution* (1784) entitled "Of the Negro Trade and Slavery," which castigated the African trade as "shocking to humanity, cruel, wicked, and diabolical." Price, a prominent English supporter of the American Revolution, expressed his confidence that the United States "are entering into measures for discountenancing [the slave trade], and for abolishing the odious slavery which it has introduced." He acknowledged that abolition might take time but hoped that it would be done with "as much speed" as possible.[27]

Attention to the humanitarian debate over slavery continued the next year when the *Charleston Morning Post* printed an extract from the anonymous *Cursory Remarks upon the Reverend Mr. Ramsay's Essay on the Treatment and Conversion of Negroes*, recently printed in London. The *Post* recommended the pamphlet as a "formidable" reply to the "reprehensible passages of Mr. Ramsay's book." The lengthy extract described the humane treatment of slaves in the West Indies, from portraits of toddlers well clothed and fed thrice daily, to a bucolic description of a young slave family with a tidy house, extensive gardens, a pig and two dogs, goats, poultry, and the leisure to maintain these "riches." The great slavery debate that began in Britain had arrived in South Carolina.[28]

Slave ships arrived in the harbor with cargos of enchained Africans. Ambitious planters from the backcountry visited brisk slave markets and the rice magnates sent their proxies to do the same. Merchants and lawyers trudged daily to the courts to secure unpaid

debts, and runaways languished in the workhouse. Amid this ca-
cophony of slavery, the legislature debated the management of a
trade in people that modulated the flow of capital and labor in this
export economy. And in the newspapers, the occasional article suggested that prominent men were now taking seriously the moral dimensions of this entire world.

The same legislature that suspended the slave trade sent four slaveholders to Philadelphia to represent South Carolina in the convention called to consider a new constitution for the United States of
America: John Rutledge, Charles Cotesworth Pinckney, his cousin
Charles Pinckney, and Pierce Butler. Rutledge and both Pinckneys
were trained in the law, and all four had served in the state legislature. Each of these men possessed sizable fortunes in land and slaves.
All hailed from the Lowcountry elite that had dominated Carolinian
politics since the early eighteenth century, and three of the four had
been members of the Carolina legislature during its slave trade debates. But more importantly, South Carolina sent the delegation most
distinguished among the states for their collective service in the Revolutionary War. Rutledge was governor during the entire war, and
Butler served as his adjutant general. Charles Pinckney, the youn-
gest delegate to the convention, had served in the state militia, seen
action during the assault on Charleston, and been held prisoner in
British military brigs. And with the exception of George Washington, who sat silently during the debates, Brigadier General
Charles Cotesworth Pinckney had achieved the highest rank in the
Continental army of all the delegates present in Philadelphia. As a
group, the South Carolina delegation embodied most completely the
personal sacrifices the Revolutionary War had entailed. No one arriving in Philadelphia during the spring of 1787 had a better understanding of the political economy of slavery protected by the Revolution, and no one was more invested in defending it.[29]

In Philadelphia the South Carolina delegation faced men who had
starkly different views on the future of slavery in North America.
Many northerners had hoped that the Revolution would bring the
end of slavery. In the northern states, Great Britain, and even

Virginia, some had begun to act on antislavery beliefs, through activism and / or the passage of legislation that gradually abolished or ameliorated slavery. But at the Constitutional Convention in Philadelphia, antislavery came into conflict with the Carolinians, men who had no moral qualms regarding slavery. Arguments over slavery became the sharp edge that tested diverse visions of governance in the young American republic.[30]

Slavery took on a central role in the debates beginning in June when the delegates took up the question of apportionment in the House of Representatives. A principal tenet of the republican ideology shared by most delegates held that national sovereignty derived from the will of "the people." But many delegates, including the South Carolinians, thought wealth should be the principle consideration when it came to the question of who would govern. To marry these concepts took great energy, oratory, and conciliation among the delegates. Inevitably, it required the discussion of slavery.[31]

All delegates agreed that those enslaved were people, but for the delegates from South Carolina, the people enslaved were the single most important measure of wealth. This truth held for the other slaveholding delegations as well, but the South Carolinians were most sensitive to the slaveholding interest. On June 11, James Wilson of Pennsylvania proposed that the congressional representation from each state be "in proportion to the whole number of white & other free Citizens & inhabitants of every age sex & condition including those bound to service for a term of years and three fifths of all other persons . . . except Indians not paying taxes." Charles Pinckney seconded the motion, and for the next month the delegates became embroiled in debate over how to count, or whether to count, slaves.[32]

The question of counting slaves had frustrated the Continental Congress in 1777 when it was attempting to assess the tax bill of the several states in support of the war effort. The concept of a ratio had emerged from those debates, but mired in disagreement, the congress had taxed land instead. In 1783 the federal Congress in New York again proposed population as the basis of taxation, worked out through the "federal ratio" of counting the population of free citizens, plus three-fifths of the slaves from each state, to assess a state's tax bill. The states had never ratified this proposal, but it was gener-

ally understood among the delegates in Philadelphia, and the young
Charles Pinckney made it part of his plan of government, which he
circulated among the delegates in May 1787.[33]

Vigorous debate on the three-fifths provision began on July 11
when Butler and Charles Cotesworth Pinckney attacked the proportion as unfair to the slaveholding states. They wanted black slaves to
be "included . . . equally with Whites," for as Butler argued, black
slaves were as productive of wealth as free white laborers, and "in a
Government . . . instituted principally for the protection of property," slaves must be included. South Carolina stood alone on this
issue. George Mason of Virginia agreed as to the value of slaves, but
for the purposes of representation he could never "regard them as
equal to freemen." Likewise, Gouvernor Morris of Pennsylvania
stated that his white constituents would "revolt at the idea of being
put on a footing with slaves." Wilson also thought that white Penn-
sylvanians would feel "disgust" at the representation for slaves; nevertheless, he pushed for "the necessity of compromise." But Morris
went further. To count slaves for the power of slaveholders would
encourage the transatlantic slave trade, which Morris considered a
violation of "human nature." It was the first clear expression of antislavery views among the delegates. No one followed Morris at this
point, but a line had been crossed.[34]

On the following day, Butler and Pinckney repeated their demand
that black slaves be counted equally, and Pinckney expressed his
"alarm" at Morris's remarks "concerning the Negroes." William
Davie of North Carolina accused "some gentlemen" of seeking to
deny the southern states of their fair share of representation and
threatened that his state would "never confederate" on anything less
than the three-fifths ratio. Antislavery men held their tongues, and,
realizing that the project of creating a stronger national government
would otherwise fail, the delegates agreed to the three-fifths ratio.[35]

On July 13, Edmund Randolph of Virginia moved that the three-
fifths provision be applied toward the assessment of the representation of any new state. Morris was first to reply. Known for his oratory, Morris observed that the debate of July 12 had led him into a
"deep meditation." He thought it best at this juncture to "candidly
state" that a distinction had emerged in the Union between the

northern and southern sections. If this fissure could not be overcome, he asked, why not "at once take a friendly leave of each other"? There would be "no end of demands for security" of one section or another. New Englanders could demand security for their fishery just as southern slaveholders now pressed for their "peculiar objects." And in the future, delegates from the "interior country" would have their own demands. How would union work?

Pierce Butler responded, "The security the Southn. States want is that their negroes may not be taken from them which some gentlemen within or without doors, have a very good mind to do." Slaveholders demanded protection. At this point in the debates, Morris was the only delegate to condemn slavery in moral terms. He had brought antislavery beliefs into the convention, alarming the South Carolinians.[36]

Morris and Butler stepped back from the breach, and on July 16 the delegates agreed to the report that embodied all of the resolutions they had debated since May. Historians have long believed that news from the federal Congress in New York, which passed the Northwest Ordinance on July 13—the very day Morris and Butler squared off—played an important role in the critical vote of July 16. The ordinance settled the pattern of governance for the as yet unorganized northwestern territory. Its final article banned slaveholding from this entire region, which made the Ohio River into a continuation of the border between the slaveholding states and the nonslaveholding states initially created when the Pennsylvania legislature passed gradual abolition legislation in 1780. Critically, the article that banned slavery included a fugitive slave clause designed to enforce this border, which was later incorporated into the Federal Constitution without debate. Passage of the ordinance secured a future for the expansion of both sections into the west and demonstrated to the delegates that compromise on this intractable issue was possible.[37]

For the next ten days the delegates discussed the executive branch, the courts, and state representation in the Senate, and by the end of the day on July 23 most issues appeared settled. Elbridge Gerry moved that a committee be formed to draft a constitution for final approval of the convention, but before the vote, Charles Cotesworth Pinckney had one last comment: "that if the Committee should fail to insert some security to the Southern States agst. an emancipation of slaves and taxes on exports," he would be bound to vote against it. The Northwest Ordinance may have been comforting, but it was not enough. As if in response, the delegates made John Rutledge of South Carolina chair of the committee; the other members included one slaveholder, Edmund Randolph of Virginia, and three nonslaveholders: James Wilson of Pennsylvania, Nathaniel Gorham of Massachusetts, and Oliver Ellsworth of Connecticut, all moderate men in favor of sectional compromise. In short, the committee included one of the strongest proslavery voices and moderates; antislavery opinion went unrepresented.[38]

The convention granted Rutledge's Committee of Detail (as it came to be known) the power to formulate into a single text all of the resolutions that the convention had passed over the preceding three months. The document that these men produced answered all of Pinckney's concerns and went considerably further in the protection of slavery. It provided that immigration could not be limited, a protection for the transatlantic slave trade, and it did not tax exports, upon which the planters depended. Rufus King of New York pointed out the enormous concessions made to slaveholders. He reminded the convention that the "great objects" of a federal government would be to defend the country against "foreign invasion" and "internal sedition." The protections extended to slaveholders weakened the nation on both counts and absolved staple-producing slaveholders from contributing to the national defense. "If slaves are to be imported," asked King, "shall not the exports produced by their labor supply a revenue the better to enable the Gen[eral] Gov[ernment] to defend their Masters?" King identified in plain language each of the weak points of a political economy based on slavery. More slaves from Africa left the southern states susceptible to rebellion, and while bolstering the southern slave population did have the potential to increase exports, it seemed unfair that the general government would protect slaveholders from the slaves and not tax them for the added expense.[39]

Antislavery delegates let loose. Roger Sherman of Connecticut denounced the slave trade as "iniquitous." Morris moved to revisit the question of representation and delivered an impassioned speech on the supremacy of free labor. "Compare the free regions of the Middle

States . . . with the barren wastes . . . of the other States having slaves." The "rich and noble cultivation" of the eastern states changed dramatically when one crossed into New York and New Jersey, where "the effects of the institution become visible." Passing again into Pennsylvania, "every criterion of superior improvement" became evident, and then "southwardly . . . every step you take thro' the great regions of slaves presents a desert increasing with . . . ye proportion of these wretched beings." How, he asked, could this convention consider slaves in representation? "Are they men? Then make them Citizens & let them vote? Are they property? Why then is no other property included? The Houses in this City (Phila.) are worth more than all the wretched slaves which cover the rice swamps of South Carolina." Stirring words indeed. But when it came down to a vote, most of the delegates, even the majority of the Pennsylvania delegation, did not wish to revisit the question of representation.[40]

Luther Martin of Maryland spoke against the slave trade two weeks later. He sought to prohibit or heavily tax the importation of slaves and declared the trade "inconsistent with the principles of the revolution and dishonorable to the American character." Martin repeated the concern voiced by King that the slave trade enhanced the threat of insurrection. Rutledge responded. He disclaimed any concern with insurrections and even offered to absolve the other states from any obligation to suppress them. But Rutledge went further than the question of security. He argued to exclude "Religion & humanity" altogether from the debate. "Interest alone is the governing principle with Nations—the true question," Rutledge warned, was whether the "southern states" would stay in the Union. Charles Pinckney concurred. South Carolina could never agree to a new constitution that "prohibits the slave trade. In every proposed extension of the powers of Congress, that state has expressly . . . excepted that of meddling with the importation of negroes."[41]

Rutledge and Pinckney had drawn the line even clearer, which raised the ire of George Mason of Virginia. "This infernal traffic originated in the avarice of British merchants," Mason claimed, and if South Carolina and Georgia retained the liberty to import Africans, the western lands "will fill . . . with slaves" and "bring the judgment of heaven upon the country." Mason voiced most of the antislavery arguments that would be heard for the next seventy years: slavery discouraged manufactures; it impoverished the value of labor; it turned masters into petty tyrants; and if South Carolina and Georgia had their way, slavery would discourage white migration into the western lands. Mason argued that the "Genl. Govt. should have the power to prevent the increase of slavery."[42]

Again, the Carolinians responded with clear determination. The younger Pinckney began, citing the "example of all the world" against the notion that slavery was wrong. "Greece, Rome & the other antient states . . . France, England, Holland & the other modern states," all had slaves and none had even considered abolition. The elder Pinckney observed quite candidly the material interests that divided the slaveholding regions on this question. In Virginia, banning the trade would increase the "value" of slaves, which enriched the Virginia planters and raised costs in South Carolina and Georgia, where the planters "cannot do without slaves." The planters of the Lowcountry needed to be able to import captive Africans to bolster their labor force that remained diminished from the Revolutionary War. Carolinians would not move from this stance. Such aggressive posturing did not entirely stifle antislavery expression, but more speakers began to point toward a national compromise, and Morris suggested that an agreement could be forged between lower South slaveholders and the commercial interests of the northern states. The convention turned over the question to a committee with one representative from each state, which in turn put forth an amendment that would allow the trade until 1800. During the debate on this provision, it was Charles Cotesworth Pinckney who called for the date to be pushed back to 1808, the date that appeared in the final document.[43]

The Constitution ultimately ratified during 1788 offered a multitude of protections for slaveholders, most of which had been won through the efforts of the delegation from South Carolina. Through the three-fifths clause, slaveholders were guaranteed disproportional representation as lawmakers, and their right to import enslaved Africans could not be reconsidered for another twenty years. The Constitution obligated the federal government to deploy military force against slave insurrections and obliged the nonslaveholding states to return fugitive slaves to their masters. Despite the rhetoric of antislavery that had been so compelling during the Revolution, and voiced with such passion during the debates at the convention, North American slaveholders had never been in a stronger position. The South Carolinians had repeatedly threatened to withdraw from the Union if their property in slaves were not protected. And while delegates like Mason and Morris spoke with eloquent urgency, at the end of the day their vision of the future lost.

On the eve of the Haitian Revolution, then, slaveholders from Jamaica and South Carolina had played critical roles in obstructing the political impact of antislavery opinion. Jamaica's long-established lobbying network had been effective, and the propaganda efforts of writers like Gilbert Francklyn and Bryan Edwards laid a foundation for proslavery argument that would prove extremely useful to later generations of slaveholders. In Philadelphia, when antislavery beliefs clashed with the desire to create a stronger union, antislavery lost. During the First Federal Congress of 1790, one lonely petition from the Pennsylvania Abolition Society, albeit signed by Benjamin Franklin, inspired fierce denunciation from the representatives from Georgia and South Carolina. Thomas Tucker of South Carolina argued that Congress "had no authority under the Constitution" to do anything more with the slave trade other than to tax it. When debate continued, both James Jackson of Georgia and William Smith of South Carolina warned their fellow members that they played with the fire of "insurrection" if they discussed the issue further. Congressional leaders attempted to establish a "gag rule" to blunt the discussion of slavery, and while their efforts failed, sharp lines of division on the question of slavery were now quite clear. In stark contrast, British antislavery had transformed dramatically from a set of ideas into a potent political force rooted in a social movement that appealed to significant constituencies in Parliament and in the public. Antislavery tactics in the United States remained the work of a small group of dedicated activists until the late 1820s.[44]

The threat of slave insurrection also played a different role. When Americans raised the issue, Butler quickly dismissed it and even claimed that his state would not need the military assistance the final Constitution allowed. And during the debates over the antislavery petition in 1790, insurrection was a minor issue. In stark contrast,

Stephen Fuller raised the alarm of insurrection immediately, as soon as the agitation began. While both sides may have been posturing for political effect, their relative strength would be severely tested in the decade to come.

In August 1791 slave rebels in French Saint-Domingue began the most radical revolution in the history of the Atlantic World. These slave rebels, most of them African-born, saw that the Revolution of 1789 in France had wrought political division among their oppressors, and they rose up to break their chains. The Assembly of Saint-Domingue quickly realized the enormity of the insurrection and called on "neighboring powers" to come to their assistance in the name of "humanity and their respective interests." By early December more than 160,000 slaves had joined the revolt, killed more than six hundred whites, and "reduced to ashes" some three hundred plantations. The terrified members of the assembly blamed "philosophy" for their plight.[45]

"When we recollect how nearly similar the situation of the southern states and St. Domingo are in the possession of slaves," wrote Governor Charles Pinckney of South Carolina to the Assembly of Saint-Domingue, "we cannot but sensibly feel for your situation." Pinckney expressed his confidence that the French colonists would have "decided success" against the rebels, which he hoped would set "an example to prevent similar insurrections in other countries." He explained that the United States Constitution barred the states from extending assistance to foreign powers, but after a second request for aid in December, accompanied by even more gruesome details of "blood and desolation," the South Carolina legislature agreed unanimously to extend a loan of £3,000 to the besieged planters, despite the Constitution. In New York, the Washington administration advanced the French colonists $726,000, drawn from the United States' war debt still owed to France. In Jamaica—less than a day's sail from these scenes of black rebellion—the plea from Saint-Domingue sparked disagreement between wealthy planters such as Bryan Edwards, who favored a loan of £100,000, and the majority of white Jamaicans, who were principally concerned with their own self-preservation. Ultimately, the Jamaica Assembly sent only a few ships with provisions.[46]

News of the great insurrection traveled along less formal channels with the scores of terrified migrants who fled the violence and found refuge in every Atlantic port. In Jamaica the slaves sang songs about the "Mingo Nigras"—the blacks of Saint-Domingue—who signified the latent power black slaves possessed. News traveled more slowly to South Carolina, and while enslaved Carolinians surely knew about the rebellion, there is little evidence that they acted in response to these events before 1793. For its most rebellious contemporaries, the Haitian Revolution established a precedent to be followed, and for at least the next hundred years, the Haitian Revolution inspired the black peoples of the Americas with the example of slavery overthrown.[47]

Enslaved people in Jamaica responded to the insurrection in Saint-Domingue almost instantly. They advanced conspiracies that were probably long established, but perhaps inevitably, the planters learned of them. In November 1791 Lieutenant Governor Adam Williamson reported that every parish vestry on the island had organized a "committee of secrecy and safety" to investigate conspiracies among the slaves, and that each vestry had requested additional arms for their respective militias. The colonial council of war met on November 30 and voted to declare martial law to begin on December 10, well before the onset of the Christmas holiday, when "the Blacks are very outrageous."[48]

Evidence from the reports of the committees of secrecy and safety from the parishes of Saint James, Saint Ann, and Trelawney illuminates a widespread conspiracy among the slaves in western Jamaica that might have been quite destructive. Sugar planters had developed these parishes fairly recently, over the past thirty years, and the western port of Montego Bay had only recently become an important destination for transatlantic slavers. Situated along an important shipping lane that went past French Saint-Domingue and out into the Atlantic, Montego Bay had become a cosmopolitan port town saturated with news. This is where a black man named Philip, described as Spanish, was caught buying unusually large amounts of gunpowder. According to Philip's own testimony, he had bought the powder on behalf of Jack, a slave hired out to one Gobay, a Jewish merchant. Jack worked as a peddler. He had an arrangement with Gobay by which Jack would carry merchandise to the plantations and their slave villages, sell the wares, and keep one-eighth of the profits for himself. The committee suspected that Jack had been distributing gunpowder throughout the countryside for several weeks.[49]

Duncan, a Coromantee slave owned by one Mr. Mounsey, testified that he had learned from the enslaved man Guy that "the Negroes to windward say St. Domingo had risen and killed the Boccaras [whites] and taken the country." Duncan acknowledged that he planned to join the insurrection in Jamaica, which had been set to begin during the Christmas holiday. The slaves of Westmoreland were to rise first, followed by those in Saint James, and if the Maroons joined them, nothing would have saved the whites. The committee heard a report that a Negro from Saint Mary had bought three dozen cutlasses at a store in Saint Ann; that several enslaved blacksmiths had been observed working "during the usual time allowed for dinner," making cutlasses. When one Mr. Stirlin of Hamden had recently taken the road to Montego Bay, he was disturbed by the sight of several hundred black men, all of them with "cutlasses, apparently large and new." Mr. Hudson, a white carpenter, found evidence on Fairfax Estate that pistol balls had been made during his absence. A young girl enslaved on Scarlett Hall Estate, upon being whipped, said, "Very well, no more than two weeks for you." This was two weeks before Christmas.[50]

But white Jamaicans were ready. Lieutenant Governor Williamson had at his command a garrison of about 1,800 regular troops. He responded quickly to the parish vestries with a distribution of seven thousand stand of arms with ammunition. He sent detachments of regulars, thirty men under an officer, by warship to Savanna la Mar, Montego Bay, Oracabessa, and Morant Bay, and he sent a fifth detachment to march from Spanish Town into Clarendon, a heavily populated sugar parish. Williamson still had at his disposal more than 1,600 troops stationed in Kingston and Spanish Town.[51] Moreover, martial law required every white man from the age of fifteen to sixty to report with arms to militia duty. The business of the entire island came to a halt. No work proceeded on the plantations because, in the absence of whites, the people enslaved did what they wanted. More than 8,000 white Jamaicans mustered in the parish seats throughout the island during the Christmas season of 1791. They stayed in the local taverns of these little towns for about a month, and in the opinion of one Portland planter, this amassing of white men served "to show . . . our strength" to the blacks who might be inspired by the rebellion in Saint-Domingue.[52]

The display of white power during the Christmas holiday of 1791 had the intended effect; the slaves did not rise. But it had been a terrifying time for Jamaican whites. In November 1791, as rumors of conspiracy swirled but before the committees of secrecy and safety had completed their interrogations, the assembly sent an anxious petition to Stephen Fuller to be presented to the king. They beseeched their "August and Impartial Father" to consider the "apprehensions and the terrors which now surround us." Island whites, along with the profitable sugar economy and the revenue it generated, "solely depend" on the protection granted by His Majesty. The French in Saint-Domingue now suffered, the petition argued, from "the dreadfull effects of those wild and enthusiastic doctrines" propounded by the abolitionists. Jamaican slaves now had the "precedent of the triumph of savage Anarchy," and white Jamaicans feared that the scenes of "horror and confusion" would visit their island as well. The assembly asked for a regiment of three hundred light dragoons "for the internal service of the island," the augmentation of the island's four regiments from four hundred to seven hundred men each, and a regiment of cavalry, for which the assembly pledged to provide horses, arms, and barracks. But this was not all. His Majesty must "decidedly discourage the further Discussion of the Slave Trade in Parliament." The petition rightly observed that abolitionist oratory often condemned slavery as well as the slave trade, despite the strategic parliamentary focus on the slave trade alone. "The Negroes cannot, or will not make any such distinction." Abolitionist agitation would surely inspire slave rebellion. The politics of resistance had become transformed.[53]

While the Crown did not grant the assembly all it wanted, two additional regiments from Halifax, Nova Scotia, were sent to Jamaica in September 1792, and for the first time in its history Jamaica had a regiment of 150 cavalry (though not the 300 the assembly requested). These troops might have saved the whole system in 1795 when war did break out on the island. In August, when the magistrates of Trelawney had two members of the Trelawney Town Maroons flogged, the young men of that town waged war on the colony. Diplomacy failed and a council of war imposed martial law, but the fighting lasted for nine months. After the Maroon surrender, bands of runaway slaves who had taken advantage of the war remained at large, terrorizing the smaller settlements. But never did the Jamaican slaves rise up in the manner of the rebels in Saint-Domingue—not yet. Most saw the odds against them and waited; that level of rebellion would be the work of a later generation.[54]

While blacks conspired and whites panicked in Jamaica, white Carolinians celebrated the revolution in France and black Carolinians bided their time. Governor Pinckney did forward his correspondence with Saint-Domingue to the state assembly and called for stronger "militia and patrol laws" to check any rebellious movements among the slaves. But white Carolinians were far more impressed by the French Revolution than by the insurrection in Saint-Domingue. Many saw the events in France as a transatlantic second chapter in the revolution they had begun in 1776, and despite the Assembly of Saint-Domingue's condemnation of "philosophy," the *Charleston City Gazette* printed the entire text of Thomas Paine's *Rights of Man*. "What we now see in the world," wrote Paine, "from the revolutions of America and France, are a renovation of the natural order of things." When Citizen Edmond Genêt visited the United States in 1793 as a representative of the National Assembly, he arrived first in Charleston, where he was widely celebrated.[55]

But in the summer of 1793 a convergence of developments made white Carolinians deeply concerned that revolution might upset the order of things in ways dangerous and unthinkable to white slaveholders. In June the most elegant city of Saint-Domingue, Cap-Français, burned to the ground when vicious fighting broke out between French sailors led by General François-Thomas Galbaud and the revolutionary regiments loyal to Civil Commissioner Léger-Félicité Sonthanax. Sonthonax also had the support of the colony's free blacks, and he declared the immediate abolition of slavery in the city to bolster his forces, and as the city burned, hundreds of refugees—white and black—fled the island. Many arrived in Charleston with terrifying tales of insurrection and mayhem.[56]

Contemporary estimates ranged from three hundred to six hundred white refugees and as many blacks and mulattoes whose legal status had become uncertain. Charlestonians welcomed the refugees and raised significant amounts of money for their support. But on August 14, 1793, Governor William Moultrie received letters from Lieutenant Governor James Wood of Virginia suggesting the development of a widespread conspiracy that stretched from Richmond to Charleston. Authorities in Yorktown, Virginia, had found a letter that they believed to have been misplaced by one Gawan, a black preacher who had passed through town on the way to Norfolk. Addressed to the "secret keeper" of Norfolk from the "secret keeper" of Richmond, the letter told of a conspiracy long planned. They had collected five hundred guns and heard from "our friend in Charleston" that six thousand men were organized and a source of powder found. The killing would begin when they heard again from Charleston. "Have good heart, fight brave," the conspirator wrote, "and we will get free." Thomas Newton, a militia commander from Norfolk, wrote that "two hundred or more Negroes" from Cap-Français then residing in Norfolk compounded the threat of insurrection. They were in "great danger." Two days after receiving these letters, Governor Moultrie placed the militia on alert and ordered regular patrols throughout the Charleston district "to suppress every large meeting of Negroes." Patrol leaders were ordered to be vigilant to any "tendency of the Negroes to revolt" and to search slaves' quarters for arms and ammunition.[57]

Despite these measures (or perhaps because of them), rumors of insurrectionary plots began to circulate in Charleston. In early September a white mob broke into the home of Peter Mathews, a free black butcher who had petitioned the assembly on the rights of Charleston's free blacks, in search of a cache of arms they never did find. Later in the same month one Captain Paul, whose ship had anchored in Charleston Harbor, overheard a group of blacks say that the whites "had not many soldiers" and that they need not fear them. Pierce Butler, then in Philadelphia, received reports in October and November of insurrections in the Carolinas that he attributed to the "rights of man."[58]

In early October 1793 two more ships arrived from Saint-Domingue carrying refugees, black and white, from Cap-Français. Concerned white citizens called a meeting to determine a new policy toward the refugees, and in its formal resolutions, the committee requested that Governor Moultrie keep the ships under the guns of Fort Johnson until the committee itself had interviewed the passengers to account for their political views. Most importantly, "the negroes and people of color" should on no account be allowed "to land in any part of the state."[59]

When the governor arrived at his office on the morning of October 10, a letter signed "A Black" had been left for him. The writer claimed to be "in the secret" yet concerned with the bloodshed that others planned. He warned the governor that there were "enemies to the Northward as well" and that he should not be concerned with Frenchmen alone. Military readiness and patrols throughout the state should be maintained till "after the 10th January at least." A free black, the writer feared for his own life lest he be caught as an informer. And while he acknowledged the scorn so many Charlestonians felt toward him, he still felt "love [for] a people among whom I have been all my life." Because he remained anonymous, we have no reason to believe this man benefited from the information he shared, and his letter suggests that the conspiracy was real.[60]

On October 17, Governor Moultrie issued an order commanding "all free negroes and persons of color, who have arrived within twelve months from any other place, to depart . . . within TEN DAYS." And in November the City of Charleston strengthened its slave code by banning assemblies of any more than seven male slaves, with the now ironic exception of funerals.[61]

The Haitian Revolution and the discovery of the secret conspiracy contributed to the development of a mind-set deeply suspicious of the antislavery dimensions of republican ideals that were still so important to white Carolinians. In a series of unpublished letters under the pseudonym Rusticus, the war veteran, planter, and later historian Alexander Garden warned his fellow Carolinians to be vigilant in curbing the influence of revolutionary developments that had proved quite destructive. Written in the summer of 1794 in the wake of the formal abolition of slavery by the National Convention of France, Garden wrote of the transformation in politics that their Jamaican counterparts already understood. Garden had discovered "a paper published by one of our own citizens" that advanced the French doctrine that "our Negroes are equally with ourselves entitled to the blessings of liberty." This idea—the abolitionist argument— had "transformed . . . the negroes [of Saint-Domingue] into so many Heroes," who now trampled in victory over "the disciplined armies" of Europe. Garden had no doubt that "there are many among our Slaves, who from the possession of superior advantages of improvement, can clearly conceive & readily explain to the more ignorant of their Class, the full force of this dangerous doctrine." Before this moment, Garden argued, "the ignorance of our Slaves" had been slaveholders' greatest source of security. Slaves were taught from their "earliest infancy" that whites were superior. But if they were taught otherwise, he feared, "the milder feelings of their nature will be lost . . . and before long, Revenge & Liberty will" take their place. Garden's specific recommendation was to expel all the blacks from Saint-Domingue, without exception, but his letters hold a deeper import. They indicate a recognition that the governance of a slave society had transformed into a multidimensional struggle in which abolitionism and slave resistance were interconnected forces that posed an existential threat to the entire slave-holding world.[62]

Garden's concerns no doubt deepened as the cycle of suspected conspiracy and reaction continued. In the late 1790s, as hostilities began with France in what became the Quasi War, the evidence mounted that slaves in Carolina were testing their chains with much coordination. In November 1797 authorities in Charleston discovered an extensive plot attributed to "French Negroes," led by the slaves Figaro and John Louis, to murder the whites in the churches on Christmas Day, blow up the magazines, and raise an insurrection. A slave court found the ringleaders guilty of treason and sentenced them to hang the next day directly across from the Lower Market, so Charleston's slaves could witness the vengeful spectacle. A petition signed by ninety-nine of Charleston's finest citizens demanded that a permanent guard of fifty infantry and twenty-five horsemen be established in Charleston, that every nonwhite French person be summarily deported from the state, and that even stronger laws be passed and enforced against the entry of black people into South Carolina, whether they were slave or free and regardless of where they came from.[63]

And the threats of slave violence did not end. In September 1799, William Read, who had served on the slave court that condemned Figaro and John Louis, wrote his brother Jacob that ten slaves in Charleston who had been caught in a conspiracy were now "weekly punished and rigidly confined." Read suspected others were involved and prayed for the Lord's deliverance from "ploting slaves." In February 1800, Read, whose overseer had lost control of the slaves at Read's Ricehope plantation, saw in news reports from Jamaica another "instance of the destructive lava" that flowed from Saint-Domingue. Isaac Sasportas, a French Jewish merchant from Saint-Domingue with relations in Charleston, had been caught organizing a slave insurrection in Jamaica. The *South Carolina State Gazette* carried news of the plot and of Sasportas's public execution, commenting, "We sincerely hope his fate will be a lesson to those who have come among us on the same errand."[64]

In September 1800, upon hearing of the slave rebellion led by Gabriel in Richmond, Virginia, Governor John Drayton of South Carolina ordered strict enforcement of the slave code. In the last legislative session of that year, the state legislature passed a set of laws to bolster security. Responding to the Charleston petitioners of 1797, the first law stiffened the restrictions and increased the fines on those who would bring nonwhite people into the state of South Carolina. A second law barred the assemblage of slaves or free people of color, even if whites were present, for any reason whatsoever, including religious services. It ordered patrols to break up such meetings if found, and protected patrollers from any lawsuits brought "on account of such acts as may be done" in the breaking up of illicit meetings. The law strengthened the regulations on slave patrols, including fines for those who failed to serve and a mandate for patrol captains to properly organize their units into detachments, each with "a proper officer," to better establish control over the slaves. It reintroduced a deficiency law quite similar to that of Jamaica, requiring slaveholders of ten slaves to hire at least one overseer capable of riding patrol. In September 1802, when rumors spread that a French ship carrying incendiaries had been sighted, five hundred militiamen mobilized under Brigadier General Peter Horry and marched to the coast. The Haitian Revolution heightened resistance among the slaves and simultaneously triggered a powerful white reaction, and as in Jamaica, the slaves of South Carolina did not rebel.[65]

In light of their successful defense of slavery, it should not be surprising that slaveholders in both Jamaica and South Carolina had every confidence that their property in human beings remained secure. This confidence can be seen in the economic expansion of both regions. In Jamaica the growth of slavery first appeared in a significant increase in the number of captive Africans arriving each year. The five-year period beginning in 1790 saw an average of eighteen thousand Africans entering Jamaican ports each year, an average annual increase of ten thousand people from the five years before 1790. Newly enslaved Africans provided labor for a significant expansion of Jamaican sugar production, as well as the development of a new staple crop, coffee. Between 1791 and 1804, Jamaica planters established sixty-three additional sugar plantations; between 1793 and 1799, they established eighty-one new coffee estates. By 1807, Jamaica produced more than half of British sugar; and while coffee remained secondary, Jamaica's crop of 1814 accounted for 30 percent of global exports.[66]

With respect to the slave trade, the most powerful Carolinians of the Lowcountry were far less enthusiastic about importing Africans than their Jamaican counterparts. Despite their forceful defense at the Constitutional Convention of the right to import slaves, Lowcountry planters were satisfied with the number of slaves they owned and fearful of importing Africans because of the turmoil caused by

Haiti. In the underrepresented backcountry, however, the development of short-staple cotton created a new class of aspiring slaveholders who demanded that the transatlantic slave trade be reopened so they could purchase inexpensive Africans. In 1793, South Carolina planters produced less than one hundred thousand pounds of cotton, but with the development of the cotton gin this number soared to eight million pounds by 1801. And yet, a vote in the General Assembly to reopen the transatlantic slave trade in 1802 failed by a vote of eighty-six to eleven.[67]

The tide turned the very next year with the Louisiana Purchase. The victories of Toussaint Louverture's Haitian army had foiled Napoleon's vision for a renewed American empire, enabling the Jefferson administration to maneuver for the purchase of the Louisiana Territory. Three weeks after Carolinians learned of the purchase, Governor James Richardson called on the General Assembly to reopen the transatlantic slave trade, and on December 6, 1803, the state senate voted fifty-five to forty-six to reopen the transatlantic slave trade. The sectionalism of earlier battles remained, but Lowcountry support for reopening had increased dramatically, creating the sectional coalition within the state that secured the overthrow of the old ban. The new law continued to prohibit the entrance of black people from the Caribbean, especially those who had ever resided in the French West Indies, enslaved or free. But captive Africans from the slave systems of Africa could again be brought to the docks of Charleston and there be sold.[68]

The most perceptive Lowcountry political leaders recognized that the expansion of slavery benefited their long-term political interests as slaveholders, even if they remained uneasy about the introduction of more Africans. Because of the three-fifths clause, more African slaves meant more slaveholders, more slaveholding states, and greater influence in the federal Congress. And perhaps because insurrection had not spread northward from the Caribbean, they felt secure enough in the forceful measures they had taken to make a calculated risk. From 1804 to 1808, when the slave trade closed, South Carolinians imported almost forty-seven thousand enslaved Africans, more than in any other five-year period in the history of this slave society. While some of these people went to the upcountry cotton regions, a substantial number were brought straight to Louisiana.[69]

The emergence of political abolitionism and the existential threat posed by the Haitian Revolution fostered distinct evolutions in the political economies of slavery in Jamaica and South Carolina. Antislavery emerged as a political force in Great Britain and the United States at the same moment, but while South Carolinians could now defend their interests against their antislavery peers as equals, Jamaicans continued to depend on the old imperial lobbying system. South Carolinian slaveholders possessed equal representation with South Carolina's partner states in the federal government. In contrast, their Jamaican counterparts depended on intermediaries. Stephen Fuller did thwart antislavery action in 1788, but his political position was no stronger with this victory and he could not inhibit the growth of antislavery sentiment. Carolinians not only guaranteed their right to import newly enslaved Africans for another twenty years, they also ensured the incommensurate power for slaveholders as a political class through the three-fifths clause.

At the convention in Philadelphia, South Carolinians confronted antislavery with the far more privileged value of national union, which they threatened to undo if slavery were not protected. Jamaicans were compelled to develop the proslavery argument, which was not convincing to a British public that prized the abstract concept of "liberty" despite the nation's long history of encouraging slavery. Abolitionism emerged in an era of nationalism, and abolitionists sought to bind moral concerns to the interests of the nation, widely embraced as a moral entity. Because of their wartime sacrifice to independence, and the constitutional position they had achieved, Carolinian slaveholders were in a better position to meet the abolitionist challenge.

Both planter classes used the terror of the Haitian Revolution against those who hoped to see an end to slavery. With a formula that would become central to the Anglo-Atlantic proslavery agenda, the Jamaican planter-historian Bryan Edwards argued in 1793 that the "origin" of the slave rebellion in Saint-Domingue "was not the strong and irresistible impulse of human nature, groaning under oppression." Rather, the slaves of Saint-Domingue "were driven . . .

reluctantly driven—by the vile machinations of men calling themselves philosophers."[70] To varying degrees, Fuller of Jamaica and
William Smith of South Carolina had made this argument in response to abolitionist agitation before the rebellion in Saint-
Domingue, to blunt agitation. But when the enslaved Africans of
Saint-Domingue rose up in 1791, and rebel leaders in Jamaica and
South Carolina initiated conspiracies, slaveholders perceived a dangerous development. Not only did they need to stay keenly alert to
the resistance of those they enslaved, which had always been the case,
slaveholders now had an additional challenge—to counter the abolitionist agitation coming from the free zones of the Atlantic World
that encouraged the resistance of the peoples enslaved.

Because of national independence and the Constitution, South
Carolinians were in a far more powerful position to adjust to this
transformation in the politics of slavery than were their Jamaican
counterparts. The Jamaica Assembly had to plead for more troops
and beg the King's ministers to stifle the abolitionists. In contrast,
South Carolinian slaveholders could count on the white majority that
now represented 57 percent of the state's population and a slaveholding ethos that compelled rapid mobilization in the face of the
threat from below, as evidenced in 1802. And South Carolinian slaveholders had the constitutional compact, which all the states had
agreed on, that provided assurance in the very structure of the federal government that the rights of slaveholders would be well represented. The West Indians were still colonists, they had nothing like
the Constitution to preserve their power against an ascendant
abolitionism.

This relative strength of Carolinian slaveholders was not immediately apparent. The Jamaican economy boomed in the 1790s and
the old Jamaican lobbying network had secured more troops and a
delay to antislavery agitation that encouraged those who had invested
in the slave economy. But in 1807 political abolitionists achieved the
abolition of the transatlantic slave trade throughout the Anglophone
Atlantic. Slave trade abolition was a defeat for slaveholders in both
places, but white Jamaicans would never again achieve their former
status of power and wealth. White Carolinians would. In the United
States slave trade abolition was the resolution of a constitutional

compromise that resulted in no clear winner. Lower South representatives voted against the ban, and though defeated, they hardly
faced an ascendant abolitionism. White Jamaicans did. Slave trade
abolition represented for thousands of Britons a national moral accomplishment, and the West Indian interest was powerless to change
this belief. British abolitionism became more radical and powerful
while American abolitionism remained comparatively quiet, margin-
alized within mainstream politics by the political power of the
slaveholding states.[71]

The slaveholders of Jamaica and South Carolina orchestrated a retrenchment of power at the turn of the eighteenth century, but the
structural differences in their politics made their paths diverge
sharply in the decades that followed. These planter classes stood in
distinct moments of historical time.[72] The next generation of Jamaicans would witness the demise of the colonial system of slavery they
had known for almost two hundred years. South Carolinians would
pioneer in the creation of a "second slavery" in the United States.
The first Atlantic slavery had its origins in the Portuguese Atlantic
of the sixteenth century. This slavery ended violently in French
Saint-Domingue, but it ended gradually in the northern United
States, Spanish America, and the British Caribbean. This second
slavery stemmed from the strong demand for tropical goods in the
Atlantic markets, as well as the concerted political efforts of slaveholders to reconsolidate slavery in the aftermath of Haiti. It exploded
throughout the cotton lands of the American South, the sugar zones
of Cuba, and the coffee plantations of southeastern Brazil. In the
United States, South Carolinians led the effort to silence the abolitionists and suppress the organized resistance of the slaves. National
cotton production rose; a sugar industry developed along the lower
Mississippi valley; rice production continued apace; and an interstate
slave trade that devastated black communities in the upper South fueled the powerful economic expansion that made the United States
an Atlantic power.[73]

The limited geography of Britain's Caribbean colonies would
not have supported the same magnitude of expansion as the American South. But if not for the weakening political position of Jamaican
slaveholders, who had led the West Indian interest for a century,

slavery would no doubt have persisted much longer in the British Caribbean. West Indian slaveholders could not suppress the abolitionists in the metropole, nor could they stem the influence of liberating ideas that emboldened enslaved men and women to rebel. Slavery in the British Caribbean survived the abolition of the slave trade for only one more generation. In terrible contrast, slavery in the United States expanded at the base of the most lucrative branch of American commercial agriculture. Slavery was the lethal reality for three more generations of African Americans. It would only by destroyed by a brutal civil war.

CHAPTER 7

The Political Significance
of Slave Resistance

THE AGE OF REVOLUTION so transformed the politics of slavery that within a single generation after the abolition of the African slave trade, the volatile combination of organized slave resistance and abolitionist agitation initiated divergent paths in the histories of Jamaica and South Carolina.

There were more slave rebellions in the first three decades of the nineteenth century than during any like period in Atlantic history. Most enslaved people in of the American South and the British Caribbean were now born in the Americas. They were born into societies forged by a racial slavery that had always inspired resistance. There were more African-born people in Jamaica than in South Carolina, but among the enslaved of both societies there were significant numbers of creoles, the descendants of Africans. Many had English surnames and most had come of age in the Americas, not Africa. They were conversant with the language and politics of the whites. They could see the moments of their masters' weakness, and they knew their own strength. Significantly, they had the example of Haiti.

Likewise, the masters of this era were born into their mastery. They had inherited land and slaves and been raised in cultures of unquestioned white supremacy, shaped by the laws of slavery that their forebears had developed for over eight generations. But they were the first to confront radical abolitionists. Antislavery rumblings had begun in the days of their fathers, who had answered them deftly, losing access to the transatlantic trade in slaves but maintaining their right to hold slaves. British abolitionism became a movement, with a following broad and deep. In the United States, however, the founding generation suppressed antislavery in favor of national unity. Antislavery activists in the United States persisted in their work, but they faced greater obstructions than their British counterparts, and an abolitionist movement did not emerge until the 1830s.

Powerful abolitionist forces in Great Britain made for more frequent slave rebellions in the Caribbean. The confluence of these radical efforts—slave rebels and abolitionists—brought Parliament's law to end slavery in 1834. A different scenario took place in the United States, specifically in South Carolina, where the master class perceived the threat of abolitionism earlier than did slaveholders from other regions of the South, and acted forcefully to forestall it. The politics of resistance generated opposite histories on either side of the Atlantic Ocean: the abolition of slavery in the British Empire, and the rise of the American planter class.

John Moultrie saw himself as a benevolent slaveholder. He owned a rice plantation on the Pee Dee River in the South Carolina Lowcountry, along with the slaves who lived there and produced its rice crop. Moultrie received a healthy remittance most years from the sale of that rice crop, and he did not see himself as the oppressor of slaves. He descended from an old Carolina family whose roots stretched back to the early eighteenth century. He was an absentee planter and resided in Aston Hall, near Shropshire, a country village in the hinterlands of Liverpool, the old center of the transatlantic slave trade.

When his grandfather died and Moultrie became a slaveholder, he reflected, "My duty [was] to take care of them and feel an interest in their welfare & humane treatment." He had always ordered his agents in South Carolina, Hughes and Fife, to be sure that "my people are housed & comfortable." Perhaps because of these beliefs, it took Moultrie some time to comprehend the significance of the news of slave conspiracy in Charleston during the summer of 1822. In a letter to his brother-in-law, Isaac Ball, a Charleston merchant who also hailed from an old planting family, Moultrie expressed relief that this "second St. Domingo business" had been "providentially discovered." He hoped his people had not been involved.[1]

Moultrie returned to the conspiracy just a month later in his next letter to Ball. "In these times of emancipation, freedom, and liberality," he gravely wrote, "you Gentlemen freeholders in the Southern States will be in constant apprehensions & terror will keep you on the constant alert, which will take off much of the enjoyment of life." He closed this letter with a prayer: "May the Almighty protect you & evermore mightily defend you all from their machinations with the Blacks of St. Domingo."[2]

Through Moultrie's understanding of his slaveholding, its jarring contrast with his fear of rebellion, and his ominous prayer for changing times, we catch a glimpse of the new politics of slavery. Moultrie wrote from England, where the old abolitionists William Wilberforce and Thomas Clarkson had just published pamphlets heralding precisely what Moultrie feared: emancipation, freedom, and liberality. Like Moultrie, the abolitionists spoke of the "welfare & humane treatment" of those enslaved, but they had a different end in mind—the abolition of slavery itself. Whereas Moultrie and other paternalists saw the humane treatment of the slaves as a useful, moral means of managing them, the abolitionist pamphlets of 1823 marked a new agenda for British abolitionism. No longer willing to wait for the closing of the transatlantic slave trade to soften the brutality of Caribbean slavery over time, reformers now demanded an immediate amelioration of the conditions of slavery, through law and regulation. The abolitionist goal for such amelioration was to prepare the enslaved for freedom, which would come soon, though no one was yet clear as to precisely when.[3]

Moultrie's situation was somewhat unique. His property lay in the southern United States, but he lived in Great Britain. And as a slaveholder, Moultrie would have known too well the story of Barbados. Just seven years ago, Wilberforce had advocated for a registry of slaves in the West Indian colonies. Abolitionists had reports of a clandestine slave trade and believed a registry would facilitate the end of this illicit trade. Vigorous debate followed, and the act of Parliament that resulted established a registrar in each West Indian colony, an appointed office.[4]

This parliamentary interference in local governance outraged the colonial assemblies, and throughout the West Indies white colonists held meetings of protest that passed angry resolutions. Among those enslaved in the villages of Barbados, rumors began that the rumblings of this political struggle between their masters and Parliament heralded their own emancipation, which would come at Christmas. Black people knew about Wilberforce, and though most could not read his words, they did know that he was an influential white man who was an ally to them. When Christmas came and went and their masters denied them their due emancipation, rebel leaders on the plantations, mostly skilled men and women, organized a revolt to gain control of the island and thereby force their emancipation. As the rebel leader Robert stated before his execution, "That was the way they did it in St. Domingo."[5]

The rebellion began at eight o'clock in the evening on Easter Sunday in the parish of Saint Philip and spread quickly into the adjoining parishes of Christ Church, Saint John, and Saint George. Colonial repression was terrible and swift, with the imposition of martial law, a full mobilization of the island's local militia, and the deployment of British regulars. Colonial forces killed at least fifty rebels during the fighting, and troops often executed captured rebels right there in the field. Trials ensued, which led to the execution of 144 more people in the weeks that followed. Few whites lost their lives, but the property damage was immense. White colonists placed the blame squarely on the abolitionists.[6]

Now Moultrie saw the same thing happening in the United States, where his friends and property were at great risk—thus his prayer.

On December 20, 1819, the freshman congressman James Tallmadge of Poughkeepsie, New York, rose in his seat to propose an amendment to the Missouri Territory's application to be the twenty-third state of the Union. Missouri's leaders had proposed that the new state would support the right to hold slaves, but Tallmadge, who had previously attempted to bar slavery from Illinois, wanted statehood to come under far different terms. He wanted the children of those currently enslaved in the territory to be emancipated by law at the age of twenty-five, as well as a bar against the "further introduction of slavery" into the new state. In short, Tallmadge proposed that in exchange for statehood, Missouri must begin the process of gradual emancipation under way in the northern states since 1780.[7]

Tallmadge found the support of seventy-nine congressmen and his amendment passed the House. While it did not pass in the Senate, the House vote appeared to be a stunning expression of antislavery will within the US government. The debate had publicly aired a fierce clash of beliefs about American slavery. At the heart of this debate lay the political struggle over the future of slavery that had occurred during the Constitutional Convention. Congress had debated slavery numerous times, most momentously in 1807 when it banned Americans from the transatlantic slave trade. Yet ever since 1790, as the northern abolitions continued, and as cotton, sugar, and slavery pushed the spread of American civilization into the southwest, Congress had admitted new states to the Union in careful equilibrium. Through the years, the number of nonslaveholding states remained equal to the number of slaveholding states. The debate over Missouri threatened that balance.[8]

The most prominent antislavery voice in 1819 belonged to Senator Rufus King of New York. King had spoken against slavery during the constitutional debates thirty-two years earlier, and he had continued to do so for his entire career. In 1819 King gave two speeches in support of Tallmadge's amendment when it came before the Senate. When the bill failed and the Senate adjourned, King polished his speeches and had them printed as a pamphlet, first in New York City and later in Philadelphia. King argued foremost that the extension of slavery into Missouri would deepen the unfair benefit that the Constitution granted to slaveholders through the operation of the three-fifths clause. Slavery would also depress the economy of Missouri by inhibiting the development of manufactures there, and slavery would weaken the new state in time of war by keeping its young men at home to guard against rebellious slaves. King did not make a case for the immorality of slavery, but he did put himself at the forefront of the northern movement to curtail the western expansion of slavery. Throughout the northern states, public meetings of citizens passed resolutions that endorsed the arguments of Senator King.[9]

Such excitement ensured that the debate over slavery would resume when Congress reconvened, and in February 1820, Senator William Smith of South Carolina delivered an ardent defense of slavery that moved far beyond the arguments made by the Jamaicans Edward Long and Bryan Edwards.[10] A Lowcountry lawyer, Smith won his seat in the Senate in 1816, and he had established himself as that body's foremost proponent of states'-rights ideology. Those who believed in the supremacy of states' rights held that each individual state of the Union possessed the authority to refuse compliance with a law of the federal government. States'-rights ideology would soon find its champion in John C. Calhoun, the ambitious and brilliant upcountry cotton planter of Fort Hill, South Carolina, who would soon emerge as the state's preeminent political figure. But in 1820 Calhoun served as secretary of war under President James Monroe, and he was not yet concerned that the power of the federal government might be used against slavery.[11]

Incensed by the "most opprobrious epithets . . . lavished upon those who hold slaves," Smith disparaged the "convenient humanity" of his northern colleagues who condemned racial slavery from positions of complete hypocrisy. The abolition of slavery by the northern states, he claimed, had been for profit, not humanity, as northern slaveholders had sold their people in into the southern markets to planters glad to buy them. He reminded the Senate that all of the states except Massachusetts held slaves at the moment of the nation's founding, and that the Constitution created by those states did not endow the central government with the power to regulate slavery; that power remained with the states. But Smith turned also to history and human nature to defend the property of his constituents. The Greeks and Romans, during "the most enlightened periods of those republics," held slaves. The Spartans, who best exhibited "pure democracy," held slaves. And nowhere did the Holy Bible condemn the holding of slaves.[12]

Abolitionists played with fire when they raised the question of slavery, Smith warned, but they would not succeed against the benevolence of southern slavery. There were many in the North, claimed Smith, who believed that southern slaveholders lived "in a constant danger from an insurrection" of the slaves. On the contrary, he claimed, American slaves "are so domesticated, or so kindly treated by their masters" that abolitionist agitation "cannot excite one among twenty to insurrection."[13]

Smith even challenged the authority of the esteemed Thomas Jefferson, now eighty-two years old, still writing letters from retirement. Antislavery writers loved to trumpet Jefferson's lines in his *Notes on the State of Virginia*, which Smith quoted for the Senate to ponder: "The whole commerce between master and slave is a perpetual exercise of the most boisterous passions. Our children see this, and learn to imitate it. I tremble for my country, when I reflect that God is just. The Almighty has no attribute which can take side with us in such a contest." Smith paid tribute to the "venerable patriot" of Virginia, but on this question of slavery, as the Senate reporter wrote, "he did not hesitate to contradict him in the most unequivocal terms." The relationship between master and slave involved no "boisterous hostility," claimed Smith. Rather, "the whole commerce between master and slave is patriarchal." Black and white children "eat together, they play together" on the plantations of the South. "Their affections are often times so strongly formed in early life" that by maturity, even when one is master and the other slave, "there is nothing but the shadow of slavery left." Jefferson had written for a foreigner forty years ago. His description of slavery effused from "a young and ardent mind" that his "riper years have corrected." Smith rightly pointed out that Jefferson had never abandoned slaveholding.[14]

The deep gulf between the views of King and Smith illustrates the intractable problem of slavery in the early American republic. Whites throughout the country, from Florida to Ohio to Maine, would have agreed on the basic principle of white racial superiority, but the range of opinion on slavery itself, as a practice and a form of property, ranged widely. As Americans tried to comprehend the meaning of this intense debate in the spring of 1820, William DeSaussure mingled with the leading whites of Columbia, South Carolina, the state capital in the piedmont. He was surprised to hear Carolinians declare, upon reading the speeches of King, that there was "no more safety to the Southern States in the Union." DeSaussure shared this conversation with his friend and ally Calhoun, then residing in Washington, D.C., and unable to hear the political chatter in Columbia. Calhoun acknowledged that "we should prefer disunion . . . to the consequences of emancipation," but he did not think this would happen. The men who think this grossly exaggerate southern weakness, he cautioned. King's words gave "great offence," but he believed the New Yorker's sentiments to be "very exceptional." The real object of Tallmadge, King, and their supporters was "political power and preeminence," Calhoun explained. He too was outraged by their slanders, but Calhoun thought that the only reason northerners deployed antislavery was to "excite dangerous feelings" in order to win the political contest, "not to endanger our property in slaves." Calhoun did not yet see antislavery as a threat.[15]

It did not take long for the newspapers of New York and Washington, D.C., to reach the editors of Charleston, South Carolina. The United States Postal Service Act of 1792 allowed all editors of newspapers to exchange their own papers for the newspapers of other cities, with no postal charge. Newspapers were carried throughout the country as a public service of the federal government. It was brilliant legislation that facilitated the flow of information, so critical to national cohesion and economic development.[16] But information helped to upset the status quo. In Charleston news of the debates about slavery found fertile ground in radical circles of the black community, some enslaved and some free, whose members were trapped in the midst of a terrifying expansion of slavery, as well as a tightening of the small freedoms they enjoyed as people in a city. News of the debate over Missouri came alongside intensified repression.

Black Charlestonians received their news about the nation and the world from the black seamen who worked the ships that plied the North American coast between Charleston and northern cities like Philadelphia, New York, and Boston. These men were not enslaved; they were often literate and cosmopolitan through their various travels, and as black men in a world where racial slavery reigned, most were committed to its abolition. When they arrived in a southern port like Charleston, they worked alongside and social-ized with the black men and women, enslaved and free, who worked on the docks and in the shops and taverns where sailors stayed during their time in port. The Missouri debates, which lasted two years, were the subject of hushed conversation in the taverns and alleyways, the black spaces of the city beyond the docks.[17]

Charleston had thrived on a vigorous trade in rice and cotton. South Carolina's cotton production had increased by 46 percent since 1800, and while rice production had fallen, it still fueled a signifi-cant commerce that in a short time would grow. The greatest por-tion of these crops moved north in ships to Philadelphia or New York out of Charleston. Black Carolinians performed most of the labor in this bulky commerce, not only laboring on the plantations' fields but also bringing the harvest to market, usually by boat; loading ships; and performing much of the artisanal work—the carpentry, coo-perage, and metalwork that kept everything moving. There were also people in chains traveling on ships that went farther south, as merchandise for the slave markets of Savannah or New Orleans. Information traveled through the intertwined routines of labor that, through cotton, rice, and slavery, linked enslaved people of the slaveholding states to the abolitionism that had germinated up north.[18]

Charlestonian blacks made up half of the city's population, and most were enslaved. There were about 1,500 black people in the city who had gained their freedom, about 10 percent of the urban popu-lation but less than 2 percent of the black people in the state. The free black population had increased faster than either slaves or whites during the first three decades of the nineteenth century, a pattern in common with the urban North, then in the midst of gradual abo-lition. Because of the language of South Carolinian law, however, free blacks in the state were generally subject to the same constraints as enslaved people, and most had some family still enslaved. The law marked race rather than status as the most salient factor of civil life.[19]

Gradual emancipation in the northern states had been a very dif-ficult process for black people. In the aftermath of slavery, most were poor, and most had migrated to urban areas, where they found security and comfort in black communities. Some did prosper, and leading members of these communities had organized benevolent societies, and educational societies, to help each other cope with the poverty and the intense racism that followed emancipation. African Americans began to organize their own churches, most prominently in Philadelphia, where Richard Allen and Absalom Jones established the first African Methodist Episcopal church in 1792. They also developed a politics that demanded inclusion in the American polity, participants in its democracy and beneficiaries of the hope that many still held in republican ideals. Prominent black men such as Prince Hall, James Forten, Allen, and Jones wrote pamphlets and delivered political addresses to mixed-race audiences, while black women did the work of "building free black communities." In Boston, Philadelphia, and New York the black community staged public celebrations of the abolition of the transatlantic slave trade, perhaps the only signal of hope in the republic's short history. African Americans did have white abolitionist allies in the North, but they were few in number and often ostracized from the white American mainstream.[20]

Black people in Charleston were embedded in an expanding slave system that overshadowed their lives, yet many engaged in the same black institution building that was taking place in the North, especially in the churches. As in the British Caribbean, the largest Christian congregations of blacks in Charleston were Baptists and Methodists. During the eighteenth century, missionaries to the colonial slave societies from these denominations adopted the evangelization strategy first pioneered by the Moravians. Missionaries selected especially pious slaves as "deacons" responsible for converting the Africans among whom they worked and lived. As congregations grew, each would have small classes of enslaved members led by a deacon. There were also church trials, run by slaves, which adjudicated disputes among church members and punished those found guilty of backsliding from the faith. Enslaved deacons developed leadership skills through the churches, which derived from teaching the mysteries of faith. What "the faith" meant was a matter of interpretation. The white authorities of most churches held that the Christian slave rightly served the Christian master, and that the slave should respect the worldly power of the masters, just as believers respected the divine power of God. Black deacons might see the faith in a different light. Methodists and Baptists practiced this evangelical methodology throughout the slaveholding societies of the Anglo-Atlantic, wherever there were missionaries willing to serve. The practice had radical implications for black Christianity, in the American South and the British Caribbean. It allowed black deacons considerable autonomy, despite the theology of subservience, for white ministers did not oversee every meeting of the slaves.[21]

By 1815 the majority of the congregation at the Trinity Methodist Episcopal Church was of African descent. Most were enslaved, and many had become deacons with their own classes of converts. When in that year white church officials looked into reported irregularities in the expenditure of funds by the deacons and discovered that funds had been used for manumissions, the white church authorities changed the rules for black members of the church. Henceforth, black church members could only count monies, or hold church trials, in the presence of a white minister who would be in charge of the proceeding. Offended by this change in policy, a group of black church members sent Morris Brown, a free black bootmaker and lay preacher who had once been imprisoned for helping enslaved friends buy their freedom, to travel north with Henry Drayton, a former slave and church member, to meet with Allen and Jones about establishing an African Methodist Episcopal church in Charleston. Brown and Drayton may well have attended the convention of African Methodist Episcopal churches that convened in April of that year in Philadelphia, which included delegations from Maryland, Delaware, Pennsylvania, and New Jersey. Whether or not they mingled with these men, Brown returned in 1817 an ordained pastor in his own right. He and his supporters established in Charleston the African Church on Anson Street. A total of 4,346 members of the Charleston Methodist Church departed and joined the African Church. The church grew so rapidly that it established a second church on Cow Alley in Hampstead, a predominantly black neighborhood close to the markets.[22]

Such a bold display of black autonomy brought white repression. In June 1818 the Charleston city guard arrested 140 members of the church for violation of the city curfew at nightfall for blacks. The state court sentenced Brown and four of his fellow ministers to either transportation from the state or a month's imprisonment. Eight other ministers had to either pay fines or leave the state. Then, in October 1820 a meeting of the Grand Jury of Charleston, a body of leading white men who periodically assessed the state of the city, noted the "great grievance" among the white inhabitants that free blacks and mulattoes had settled in Charleston from other places. The blacks had increased their proportion in the city, and through their "idle habits," set a terrible example for the slaves. They were "a growing evil," and the jury called on the state legislature to address the problem.[23]

On December 20, 1820, just in time to obstruct any hoped-for Christmas manumissions, the State of South Carolina passed the Act to Restrain the Emancipation of Slaves, and to Prevent Free Persons of Color from Entering into this State. The law explicitly addressed "the great and rapid increase of free negroes and mulattoes in this State, by migration and emancipation," which the legislature sought to curtail. The new law made manumission very difficult. Masters who wanted to manumit a slave now had to make a personal request to the state legislature for each individual act of manumission. The exchange of money and freedom papers between master and slave would no longer suffice. And if any free person of color came into the state of South Carolina and stayed more than fifteen days, any white person could arrest said black person and bring him or her before a justice of the peace, to be examined and expelled from the state. The law protected black sailors, so important to commerce, but it fined any ship captain who knowingly brought a free black to Charleston and did not take said free black with him upon his ship's departure. And, suggestive of the new politics of slavery, the final clause of the law addressed the threat of "any written or printed paper" that might be distributed by some designing agitator with "intent to disturb the peace or security of [the state] . . . in relation to the slaves of the people of this State." The debates over Missouri, alongside recent displays of black assertion in public life, caused South Carolina's legislators to heed the warnings of Rusticus.[24]

The law of 1820 landed a severe blow on the prospects of black Carolinians. For more than a century it had been possible for enslaved men and women to gain their freedom, either by cultivating the good graces of a master or by saving a portion of every small pittance they received until they amassed the price of their bodies on the market. Then, if they had family members enslaved, they could save their money and purchase their freedom. Now, they had to raise the money, go before the state legislature, and convince its members to pass a law to free this person. What had already been difficult now seemed insurmountable.

This oppressive new law came in the midst of the hopeful news from Washington about the debates over slavery, and in Charleston a small group of black radicals began to organize for rebellion. By most accounts, the idea to revolt began with Denmark Vesey, a free black carpenter of about fifty-three years of age. Born in Africa, sold into the Atlantic market, and enslaved to the ship captain Joseph Vesey until 1800 when he purchased his freedom, Denmark Vesey had already lived a singular life for an enslaved man. He worked at sea for many years with his master, and some said that he had been enslaved in Saint-Domingue as well, before its revolution. He had lived in Charleston since 1783, when Captain Vesey had settled there and opened up a chandler's shop, supplying ships with all necessary hardware. Denmark worked as an assistant in the shop, where he would have occasionally received a small pittance. In 1799 the young man bought a lottery ticket and, incredibly, he won $1,500. Captain Vesey charged him $600 for the return of his body, more than the price of a prime field hand.[25]

Vesey's winnings purchased his freedom, but the master of his wife and children refused to sell them. The new freedman probably used some of the money to apprentice himself to a master carpenter, a status he ultimately achieved himself. After mastering his trade, Vesey rented a small house on Bull Street, turned its front room into a workshop, and gained himself a reputation as an industrious worker and an astute businessman. He maintained relationships with Captain Vesey and his son Joseph, necessary white patrons for any free black man in this slave society. When he was not engaged with work, Vesey read the Bible, and he read the newspapers.[26]

On the afternoon of May 30, 1822, an enslaved cook named Peter, a man in his fifties, walked over to the Bull Street office of Intendant James Hamilton with a letter from his master, John Prioleau, a planter and rice factor who lived on Meeting Street. Peter had a story about a conspiracy among the slaves of Charleston to rise. Hamilton acted quickly. The son of a wealthy rice planter, he understood the gravity of such information. He immediately convened the city council and sent officers to arrest William Paul, the enslaved man who had tried to recruit Peter.[27]

It had begun as a casual conversation between two men on the Market Wharf in Charleston, a black man and a brown man, both of them enslaved. Paul asked Peter if he "knew that something serious is about to take place," that many of them had organized, "determined to shake off our bondage." Would Peter join them? Peter demurred at such talk and stopped the conversation. Paul might have shared even more details, making every effort to convince Peter.[28]

When Peter told his master, Prioleau, what he knew, Prioleau sent the cook to Hamilton, who questioned him, and Peter gave up the name of Paul. Hamilton had Paul arrested and interrogated, probably flogged as well, until he gave up two further names: Mingo Harth and Peter Poyas, who were also arrested and interrogated. These men were higher up in Vesey's circle of conspirators, and both had the sense of purpose to keep their cool and say nothing. Hamilton released the men, but he kept Paul imprisoned and stayed alert.[29]

About two weeks later, on June 14, 1822, George Wilson, a blacksmith and deacon in the African Church, told his master what he knew. Like Peter, Wilson had been unwilling to join the conspiracy. He had been approached by two black men from the class he taught at the African Church, Rolla, a domestic slave in the home of Governor Thomas Bennett, and Joe, owned by the widow Mary La Roche. Vesey had recruited Rolla early in the planning, and Rolla had recruited his friend Joe. Together the men approached Wilson. He was a logical choice to recruit, for most of Vesey's circle of conspirators were involved in the African Church. But Wilson wept when he heard their plans. You will not succeed, Wilson warned them, do not follow through with this rebellion. The planning has gone too far, Rolla said, and he warned Wilson to get out of town on the designated night to avoid getting caught up in the violence. Wilson agonized over the information, but ultimately he told his master, who, like Prioleau, shared the news with Intendant Hamilton.[30]

This time Hamilton went immediately to Governor Bennett. Bennett hesitated to believe that one of his trusted domestics was involved in a conspiracy, but he sensed enough smoke in the stories he heard to investigate. He ordered the militia captains to gather at Intendant Hamilton's house to spread the alarm. Word spread to the conspirators that white officials had learned of their plans, and they too met, in Vesey's house. Everyone saw, and heard from the countryside, that the patrols were very active. The timing for revolt was not right.

On June 18 Hamilton sent officers to arrest ten more black men named by the slaves that his men had captured. As the interrogations deepened, Hamilton began to see the dimensions of the conspiracy. He asked Lionel H. Kennedy and Thomas Parker, two Charlestonian lawyers, to form a court in accordance with South Carolina's Negro Act of 1740. Kennedy and Parker invited five freeholders to join them on the court: William Drayton, Nathaniel Heyward, James Reid Pringle, James Legare, and Robert J. Turnbull, prominent Charleston residents and slaveholders all.[31]

The court sat the next day. Hamilton began the proceedings by detailing whom he had arrested, why, and when. Then the interrogations began. For more than a month, until July 26, the court learned of this vast conspiracy among the blacks of Charleston to revolt against the entire system of slavery, murder the men who ruled it, and escape in ships to Haiti, which would assist and welcome them. In a letter describing their plans, written after two weeks of interrogations, Hamilton told a friend that the rebels had a bold plan with "fine military tact and admirable combination." Three columns of rebels were to have marched on the city center: one from James Island across the Ashley River, the other two from the north and west.

They would seize the arsenal, murder the white men as they stepped out of doors, and set forty fires throughout the city to signal the slaves in the countryside. The rebels were said to have lists that had nine thousand names on them of black men from the countryside around Charleston, enslaved and free, ready to arm themselves and storm the city when they saw the fires.[32]

Much like the conspirators in Barbados in 1816, the Charleston rebels not only said what they planned to do, they also explained why they acted. Vesey's recruitment of Rolla, which the latter described for the court on June 25, illustrates the curt vibrancy of this dangerous moment in 1822. "On one occasion he asked me what news," Rolla told the court. "I told him none," but Vesey replied, "We are made free but the White people here won't let us be so . . . the only way is to raise up & fight the Whites." Rolla was interested. He went to one of the meetings at Vesey's house, which was full of people, none of them white. Vesey had spoken, and Rolla remembered the plan as first presented to the group. On the night of the rebellion, they would first seize the guardhouse, arm themselves from the city arsenal, and then "rise up and fight for our liberties against the whites." Vesey had read from the book of Exodus and told the story to those gathered of how "the Children of Israel were delivered out of Egypt from bondage." The rebel Jack Purcell testified that Vesey read the newspapers aloud and even read from a copy of a speech by Rufus King. Vesey described King as "the black man's friend," who had declared his intention to "speak, write, and publish pamphlets against slavery . . . until the Southern states consented to emancipate their slaves."[33]

Rolla recruited Joe La Roche in much the same manner. Several months earlier, Joe told the court, Rolla had asked him if he "would join with him in slaying the Whites." The men were good friends. They shared meals together and were in the same class at the African Church. Joe asked for some time to think about it, and Rolla agreed. Joe wrestled at first with God's injunction that "we must not kill." But Rolla laughed and called him coward. Rolla told him what he had learned at Vesey's meetings, that "our Legislature had set them free & our people here would not let us be so—that St. Domingo & Africa would come over & cut up the White people." Joe

was still unsure. "It could not succeed," he said. "Our parents for generations back had been slaves & we had better be contented." But
ultimately, Joe did come around to Rolla's way of thinking.[34]

The court also heard from witnesses who heard Vesey defend his
creed in public spaces. Benjamin Ford, a white boy of only fifteen or
sixteen who worked at a shop near Vesey's house, testified that Vesey
often came into the shop, where his "general conversation was about
religion, which he would apply to Slavery." Vesey condemned the
"hardships of the blacks" and the laws so "rigid & strict & that the
blacks had not their rights." At the "creation of the World," Vesey
would say, "all men had equal rights, blacks as well as Whites."[35]

Hamilton had been listening to the interrogations of black men
for five weeks on July 3, 1822, the day before the national holiday that
in Charleston could well turn dangerous. He took a moment of relative calm to write to his friend Charles Harris, a Charleston resident
and former mayor of Savannah. Hamilton had a clear opinion of the
conspiracy they had discovered and why it had happened. He had
overseen the hanging of six conspirators the day before, including
Vesey. He acknowledged that while the "causes" of the conspiracy
might have come from the "suffering unavoidable incident to a state
of slavery," the energy for rebellion had come from "religious fanat-
icism." All of the "ring leaders of the conspiracy [were] Class leaders
or Deacons," Hamilton wrote. The planters were saved by "the fidelity of a favorite slave to his Master." He was confident that the
measures so far taken ensured safety for whites, and that the Court
of Magistrates and Freeholders had "conducted its deliberations with
humanity." But Hamilton noted with grave resignation that the
rebels hanged yesterday "had met their fate with the heroic fortitude
of Martyrs." In the coming weeks the court would sentence twenty-
nine more black men to swing from the gallows in the public square
of Charleston. Northern newspapers condemned the brutality.[36]

The ideology of resistance evident in the traces of conversation
recorded by the court reveals an elaboration of the politics of resistance for the generation born in the Age of Revolution. There was
nothing new about a hatred for slavery or an embrace of violence to
rise up against the whites. But here we have the words of these rebels,
who took heart in the speeches of King, found inspiration in the sto-

ries they knew from the Christian Bible, and were connected to the
Africans still among them through a racial identity. These were novel
dimensions of radical thought among slaves that reflected the creolization of resistance. It no longer mattered where rebels had been
born or what ethnicity they claimed; what mattered now was how
they thought about slavery.

The debates in Congress over the future of slavery had become
the soil in which rumors grew that Congress had abolished slavery,
that Carolina whites wrongly denied them freedom. The rebels did
not have the facts correct, but their belief that black people possessed
rights, that their enslavement was wrongful, and that they had the
right to rise up in violence against those who had violated them for
generations would have great relevance in the unfolding of American history. Yet at the same time, the power of slaveholders had
deepened. This was evident in the quick, forceful response of Intendant Hamilton, the justices and freeholders who served on the slave
court, and the systematic trials of accused rebels, which were the
work of a seasoned planter class. But unlike the records of past interrogations, which sat obscurely in offices and archives until historians
explored them, both Hamilton and the court had their proceedings published so that all the reading world could see that they had
behaved both honorably and within the law. The growth of antislavery sentiment in the country, and the turmoil it had caused
during the debacle over Missouri, meant that the planters had to defend to the outside world their right to enslave, and to manage their
slaves as they saw fit.

During the spring of 1823, less than a year after the tumult in
Charleston, George Hibbert of Jamaica learned that William Wilberforce had given notice in Parliament that he would soon initiate
"proceedings, having in view a liberation from Slavery of the Slaves
in our Colonies." Hibbert had dedicated his entire life to West Indian commerce. His uncle Thomas was Kingston's greatest merchant
and when George came of age in 1780, he moved with £1,500 from
the family home in Manchester to London, where he joined a West
India merchant house as a junior partner. He eventually established

his own firm and rose to such prominence in the trade that in 1799 he spearheaded the project to establish the West India Docks. Wealth translated into political power and he gained a seat in the House of Commons, representing Seaford, an old West Indian seat, in 1806. He spoke and published against the abolition of the slave trade but soon retired from Parliament. Yet Hibbert stayed very involved in West Indian concerns, and in 1813 he began to represent the Assembly of Jamaica in London, a post he held until 1826.[37]

Hibbert quickly secured a meeting with Colonial Secretary Lord Bathurst, who assured Hibbert that His Majesty's ministers understood very well that British laws protected slave property. That did not mean, however, that the "slaves and their progeny are to remain in a state of slavery forever." British slaveholders needed to ponder "a time . . . when [the slaves] or their posterity may by gradual means and without injuring the property of their Masters, be liberated." Bathurst had several specific suggestions himself for the immediate amelioration of slavery, such as freeing infants born now but compelling them to work for their mother's master until they reached a certain age. Or perhaps all slaves could be given one day off in addition to Sunday, so that they could work for money and save toward their price of manumission. Similar laws operated in the northern United States and in Spanish America.[38]

Hibbert responded to Bathurst's speculations in a manner similar to that of his predecessor, Stephen Fuller, when he faced the abolitionists in 1788. With only a bit more subtlety, Hibbert warned of the "dreadful effects" that might arise from "new projects" in the colonies that might be "grossly misunderstood" by the slaves. Better to pass no legislation at all, Hibbert argued, not only to avoid misunderstandings but also because the slaves were improving in character every day. That was the aim, was it not? The end of the transatlantic slave trade meant that more of the planters' slaves were now Creoles, "habituated to our language and regulations, and . . . fitted for exercising without hazard new duties and privileges." Hibbert had condemned the abolition of the trade, but he now held that the end of the African trade had benevolent effects in the West Indies. The abolition of the slave trade had fulfilled the nation's antislavery mission. The sanctity of private property protected colonial slavery itself, which every year was becoming more humane. Protests notwithstanding, Hibbert knew at this point that West Indian slaveholders would soon come under serious political pressure. He did not bother to send the Assembly "all the Pamphlets which the Press has poured forth upon the subject of Slavery." Some could be ignored, "but the effect of all of them must ere long be shown in the proceedings of Parliament."[39]

For the next month Hibbert and his colleagues in London, merchants and absentee planters, worked methodically to build an opposition to the abolitionists. They revived the West India Committee, more than two hundred men, planters and merchants resident in London and invested in the Caribbean trade. On the evening of April 25, a meeting of this group passed a pair of resolutions that expressed their position. The committee viewed "with the greatest alarm" the intentions of the abolitionists in Parliament, which were "liable to be both misrepresented and misunderstood." As Barbados had shown, outright rebellion could result.[40] They sought not to obstruct inquiries into the well-being of their slaves, but they wanted to make it absolutely clear that "the right of the Master to the labour of the slave (subject always to the liberal maintenance and proper care of him) is a Right recognized by British Law." If Parliament interfered with these rights, slaveholders possessed "the same title to compensation . . . as is admitted in every other case of interference, with private property for a public purpose." Absentees wanted to make this point of compensation very clear; of greatest importance were their investments.[41]

The West India Committee also established a subcommittee that met with His Majesty's ministers to discuss specific reforms in the management of slaves. This smaller group resolved on five areas of life among the enslaved that should fundamentally change. First, Sundays, which had developed into the traditional market day throughout the islands, should become days of worship. The slaves were to worship in established Episcopal and Presbyterian churches. To facilitate the work of religion, masters needed to give their slaves one more day for themselves so that they could work their provision grounds and hold their weekly markets. The committee also recommended three specific modifications in the way masters disciplined their slaves: they must no longer flog in the field as "a stimulus to labor"; they shall no longer flog women at all; and they shall keep a book to record any whippings inflicted. The proposed regulations allowed masters to inflict whippings, but they must have another white man present, and in lieu of a white man, a free person of color. The book must record the name of the slave, a witness of the infraction, the infraction itself, and the number of lashes inflicted, and books must be sworn to at every quarter of the year before the parish vestries. Finally, the subcommittee recommended granting to enslaved men who were married the right to hold property that could be inherited by a wife or children. Clearly designed in response to abolitionist critiques of West Indian slavery, these proposed regulations were going to be very hard to impose on West Indian masters, who were not at all accustomed to considering the humanity of the black people they enslaved.[42]

As the subcommittee discussed amelioration, Hibbert and the other agents of the West Indian colonies lobbied to obstruct the abolitionists. On May 3 they petitioned the Colonial Office, expressing "the great alarm we feel concerning the vital interests of our Constituents." They argued that the forthcoming debate posed "extreme danger" to an enormous amount of private property, as well as thousands of lives in the colonies. They reminded the government of their long-established loyalty and insisted on their right to "full compensation" in the event of a change in the law. Six days later Hibbert shared the latest developments. He and others had met with His Majesty's ministers, who had privately stated their opposition to "anything like a Parliamentary pledge to emancipation" but were equally clear that "emancipation must be contemplated." The ministers had agreed to the principle of compensation, though the details remained unclear, and the agents had requested "a reinforcement of Troop, [which] would become necessary in all the West India Garrisons, to guard against any movement which the agitation of this question might occasion."[43]

Hibbert knew by early May that the government would actively consider the question of emancipation. He knew that His Majesty's ministers planned to adopt measures that would render emancipation "gradual and safe" and knew that the debate in Parliament would begin very soon. Hibbert believed that the planters should stand their ground on the legality of their property in slaves, which would provide the argument for compensation. But they must embrace the recommended changes in the manner that masters governed slaves. Hibbert wrote that abolitionism was a powerful force in British society that would force His Majesty's ministers to act. He would be correct. Before abolitionists in Parliament had even launched the formal debate, Hibbert seemed to know that slaveholders in Britain's Caribbean colonies would have to give up their property in slaves. If you have to witness emancipation, he argued, far better to control the process than to have it imposed.[44]

On May 15, 1823, Thomas Fowell Buxton rose from his seat in Parliament to present the long-anticipated motion that "the state of Slavery is repugnant to the principles of the British constitution, and of the Christian religion, and that it ought to be gradually abolished throughout the British colonies." Buxton did not advocate immediate abolition. Rather, he sought to implement regulations that would "by slow degrees, and in the course of years," fit the slave for freedom. Most of his colleagues agreed. By the end of the day, Parliament had passed the resolutions that imagined an amelioration of slavery guided by "effectual and decisive measures" to be crafted by the colonial governments. These would be attentive to the property rights of slaveholders, but with the aim of preparing the people long enslaved for "participation in those civil rights and privileges which are enjoyed by other classes of His Majesty's subjects."[45]

A few days later an unknown scribbler working for the West India Committee wrote a "most explicit and impressive" account of the dire political situation in London, to be shared with the colonial assemblies.[46] A growing portion of Great Britain's limited voting public held the view that colonial slavery in the West Indies had to be improved. This belief could be heard not only from "the enthusiasts" but also from "the sober-minded and dispassionate portion of Politicians." These men believed that the colonial legislatures were not capable of developing regulations that would humanize slavery. Many believed that the colonial legislatures had been "temporizing" with the British public ever since the abolition of the slave trade.[47]

"To remove such a prejudice against the West Indian local governments" should be central to the response of the colonies to this encroachment of parliamentary authority, the committee argued. Due to competition from Brazil and Cuba, the state of the markets for West Indian produce had been very difficult, and it had left the colonies politically weak. Island whites should recognize that the colonies might soon be fiscally required to seek public relief for their debts. The colonies would need a good public image. The abolitionists had "greater means of influence on the Public mind" than did the absentees, and "All Ministers must be more or less dependent on public opinion."[48]

The absentees recommended conformity. They advised their colonial counterparts to conform "to the Spirit of the Resolutions of the House of Commons" by crafting new laws that would improve "the condition" of those they enslaved. They should do this now. Reform was coming from above, the absentees warned. It was "manifestly essential to public tranquility . . . that the Negroes should look up to those who have immediate authority over them, and not to the British Parliament, British Government, or British Public, as their Protectors." The mastery of slaves had become more difficult in this modern age of information and activists. The absentees understood the challenging tactics of slaveholding, but unlike colonial planters in the Caribbean, they also understood the palpable influence of abolitionism in Britain. If the colonial Assemblies failed to pass legislation that satisfied public feeling on slavery, they would face "constant and angry discussions in the House of Commons" that would certainly threaten "the safety of the Colonies." Reform would come to the Caribbean; the question was, Who would control the process?[49]

Once Parliament had spoken, colonial officials in Whitehall busied themselves with communicating imperial policy to the West Indian colonies. It was decided that Demerara, one of Britain's most recent imperial possessions, would be the first West Indian colony where the new regulations on slavery would be implemented. A fertile strip of the Caribbean coast of South America, the colony of Demerara was established by the Dutch in the seventeenth century, and it had only been under British authority for twenty years. Britons had settled there in significant numbers after the American Revolution, and by the 1820s Anglophone colonists were the majority of whites, alongside numerous Dutch, French, and Danes. A regular slave trade to the colony began in 1796, and British slavers brought sixty-six thousand enslaved Africans to Demerara before the trade ended in 1807. The fertile colony changed hands six times among Europe's empires during the Napoleonic Wars, but in 1803 Britain established Demerara as a colony governed directly by the Crown.[50]

In May 1823 Colonial Secretary Lord Bathurst penned a letter to Governor John Murray of Demerara, a longtime West Indian planter who owned an estate in the colony, that informed him of Parliament's resolutions and suggested specific reforms in the management of slaves that should begin immediately. The flogging of enslaved women should be immediately prohibited, and drivers in the field should be prohibited from using the whip "as a stimulus to labor." The ban on flogging women came as a direct order from the King, but Bathurst left it to the colony's Court of Policy, an appointed body of resident planters, to determine the legal mechanism for banning the whip from the fields. Bathurst acknowledged that the punishment of flogging might still be necessary, but as the absentees had suggested, flogging "should be subject to defined regulations and restrictions."[51]

Bathurst sent a copy of this letter to the governors of the older colonies with Assemblies. He asked them to use their influence among the great men of the colony to recommend the adoption of new laws that conformed to Parliament's resolutions at the next session of the Assembly. And significantly, he included another dispatch, marked "secret and confidential," that reflected his concern with the prospect of rebellion. "In the event of any misunderstanding" on the part of the slaves, Bathurst provided the governors with a "Proclamation," which warned that all reforms would be "rendered utterly abortive" in the event of any "general misconduct" among the slaves. Implicitly addressed to the slaves themselves, the secret proclamation

reflects the presumption of organized resistance in the wake of antislavery discussion. Colonial officials had learned a lesson from the
rebellion in Barbados.[52]

Governor Murray received Bathurst's dispatch on July 7, 1823, and
proceeded to ignore it. He waited two weeks to convene the Court of
Policy, and when it did meet, they decided nothing. At their next
meeting, in early August, the court begrudgingly agreed to the proposed reforms but made no public announcement of this decision.[53]

Yet many in the colony talked openly about Parliament's resolutions and Bathurst's dispatch, and, perhaps inevitably, the slaves
learned of it too. As in Barbados and Charleston, news of abolitionist
activism became the soil in which rumors grew that emancipation
was imminent. Rumors spread of "new laws" from England that some
believed abolished slavery. Others held that the new laws gave them
three days a week to themselves. Many came to believe that the King
had acted in their favor, but that whites in the colony were denying
them the boon. Some remembered the "Barbadoes War," when there
had been talk of freedom, revolt had ensued, and many had been
killed. Some Caribbeans believed in the righteousness of a violent
uprising, while others remembered the brutal fighting, the hangings
of black bodies, and asked, Why go there again? But the rumors that
spread in Demerara during the summer of 1823 created a moment
for the radicals to act.[54]

At six o'clock in the evening on August 15, 1823, rebels on Success
plantation led by Jack Gladstone started an insurrection with horns
blowing and drums beating. As in Charleston, many rebels were connected to the Bethel Chapel, a Methodist congregation among the
slaves founded by English missionaries earlier in the century. Gladstone and his father, Quamina, had considered the meaning of the
"new laws" for several weeks before Jack acted, but they had not
agreed on strategy. The father had been born in Africa, most likely
among the Akan of the Gold Coast hinterland, and brought to the
colony as a boy. In 1808 he had joined the Methodist Bethel Chapel,
then run by the Reverend John Wray, and had risen to first deacon
under the guidance of the Reverend John Smith, who replaced Wray
in 1817. A young man of perhaps thirty, Jack Gladstone had been
born in the colony, and he too had served as a deacon in the Bethel

Chapel. But the son had rebelled against the discipline of the chapel and was no longer a deacon. He nevertheless attended services there regularly, and it was through these meetings, especially the gatherings after services, that the "new laws" and their meaning were widely discussed, and the rebellion planned.[55]

Quamina wanted to delay the use of force, but Jack wanted to act now. Black people outnumbered the whites of Demerara by an enormous proportion, and the rebels used these numbers to their advantage. On plantation after plantation along the east coast of the colony, between Georgetown and the Mahaica River, the slaves surrounded the plantation great houses, seized the whites and put them in the stocks, and then ransacked the buildings for arms and ammunition. For two days, the rebels upended the world of masters and slaves. They flogged white men, ate the food they hoarded, and drank from their wine cellars. The rebellion spread throughout much of the colony and ultimately involved between nine thousand and twelve thousand slaves from sixty east coast plantations. Wilberforce, Clarkson, Hibbert, and Bathurst had all worried about this outcome of Parliament's deliberations—and it had arrived.[56]

Repression came quickly and severely. Governor Murray encountered a body of rebels on his way home from dinner on the night after the rebellion began. When he asked them what they wanted, they responded, "Our rights," and when he told them that reforms had indeed been ordered but that he could only enact them if they lay down their arms, the rebels refused. Murray rode off quickly for Georgetown, where he convened his council and ordered a detachment of regular troops to the east coast. He declared martial law the following morning, called out the militia, and formed two companies of five hundred men. The regulars were already moving from plantation to plantation seeking out rebels, and the militia marched down the coast toward the river on the following day. Numerous firefights broke out between the soldiers and the rebels, but as the rebels were poorly armed, if at all, and generally untrained, they often fled after an exchange of gunfire. When soldiers or militia caught rebels in the field, they often executed them summarily. By the time the fighting was over, colonial forces had left 255 black bodies dead on the ground; very few whites lost their lives.

It was only then that Governor Murray issued a proclamation announcing the intended ban on the flogging of women and the use of the whip in the fields. But his proclamation included the authorized threat to abort all reforms because of the rebellion. Trials of suspected rebels began under martial law on August 25 and continued for five months. Colonial authorities interrogated the captured rebels and slowly uncovered the layers of plot and rumor that had swirled through the colony for so many weeks. They discovered talk of the "new laws" and the connections to the Bethel Chapel, to Quamina and Jack Gladstone, and to the Reverend John Smith. They began formal executions immediately and ultimately left thirty-five black bodies hanging from gallows on the plantations as "an example" to the rest. Demerara authorities tried Smith under martial law, to punish the man that the planters believed was responsible for the rebellion. The rebellion and its bloody suppression had certainly attracted the attention of the British press, but the trial of Smith inspired a great antislavery backlash in Great Britain, for although he was acquitted, he died in prison before his trial closed, becoming a "martyr" for the antislavery cause.[57]

When Hibbert heard the news, he immediately requested more troops for Jamaica. The island had a regular garrison of about 2,300 troops, but 167 men had died from a "great sickness" that had visited the island over the past six months. "Experience has shown," he wrote, "that Plots of Insurrection may be deeply laid and effectually concealed until ripe for execution." His constituents badly needed "a respectable military force in or before the Christmas holidays."[58]

Parliament's resolutions profoundly destabilized the West Indian status quo. Back in May, just ten days after the House of Commons had spoken, and about a month before Jack Gladstone launched the insurrection in Demerara, the free people of color in Kingston, Jamaica, staged a public meeting that demanded an expansion of their civil rights. "When it is even in contemplation to grant manumission to slaves," they argued, it was certainly time to admit "the free colored inhabitants of Jamaica [into] the full participation of the rights of British subjects in common with their European brethren."[59]

Free people of color in Kingston had been organizing since January to develop a plan to pursue their rights. They were a far larger group than their counterparts in South Carolina, a little more than half of the island's free population of seventy thousand people, though a distinct minority to the enslaved population of three hundred thousand. Most free people of color were "absolutely poor," wrote one observer, but there were four hundred rich planters among them, and almost six thousand were in "fair circumstances." Most lived in Kingston, Spanish Town, and the smaller port towns around the island, but there were free people of color in the country as well.[60]

In the family history of every free person of color, no matter his or her standing in society, was an enslaved African mother who gave birth to the child of a white man. Enslaved black women, especially domestic workers, were often raped by white men, either their own masters or his friends. It also became colonial practice among many white men in early Jamaica to live openly with black or a brown woman, free or enslaved, as a mistress. White men in Jamaica would not usually marry brown or black women legally, which meant they had no legal obligation toward the children that came from these relationships. But fathers' feelings differed toward the children. Some abandoned their children to slavery, which meant that there were "mulattoes" among the slaves, even while most free people of color were also mulattoes, or of even lighter complexion. Other white fathers provided education and even some inheritance to their children with black women, and some of the male children became rich planters. Only a relative few received the inheritance, but white people thought brown people smarter and more capable than black people, due to their white blood. This belief structured the labor force, as more opportunity opened for brown people to make decent livings as artisans, or merchants, or even freeholders growing coffee or pimiento.[61]

Economic opportunity for brown people coexisted with a systematic privileging of whites in civil life. The petitioners identified "that imaginary distinctive line" that divided free society in Jamaica and oppressed "the colored people." Jamaican law only recognized "musteefines" (people four degrees from African ancestry) as "white" and thus deserving of full participation in the rights of a British subject. Regardless of wealth or sophistication, a man had to be of fully white parentage, or the child of a mustee and a white, to be considered a British subject. If a man were the son of a mustee and a mustee, he could not be considered a British subject; if that of a mulatto and a quadroon, not a British subject, and so on.[62]

The rights denied to free coloreds by this legal distinction were considerable. They could not vote for members of the House of Assembly; they could not sit on juries; they could not participate in the local vestries, which both collected taxes and organized the militia. And any farmer or planter who owned slaves but was not musteefine could not count himself or his family as "white" in the annual assessment of "the deficiency." This annual tax descended in law from the fine imposed by the seventeenth-century slave acts on slaveholders who operated large plantations with few white men. Originally designed to encourage white migration to the island, the fine developed into an annual tax, assessed by the parish vestries, and an important source of revenue for the colonial government. Each pen or plantation that did not meet the standards of the law, and most did not, paid a fine that came to be known as "the deficiency." The free colored planters who owned slaves but could not count themselves as "white" paid more, per head, than their white neighbors did.[63]

These were not radical demands, especially considering the position that colored people held within free Jamaican society. In 1813 the published returns of the island militia showed that free men of color made up almost half of the rank and file, and about 40 percent of its officers. Prominent white Jamaicans such as Governor Edward Trelawney, Edward Long, and Bryan Edwards had long argued that the free coloreds should be favored and cultivated as a military force against the slaves; these numbers suggested that this had happened. This information had inspired petitioning and a loosening of the law by the Assembly, allowing free coloreds to pursue a wider array of professions, such as that of sea captain. But the legal impediments to the most successful among the free coloreds had remained.[64]

In July 1823 the prominent free colored leader Richard Hill, who would later serve in the House of Assembly, wrote to the English abolitionist William Allen seeking his support in the free colored cause. Free coloreds had mobilized in Dominica, Grenada, Saint Kitts, and Saint Lucia as well, and the Colonial Office had already received several petitions making similar demands. Hill condemned colonial whites as "complexional misanthropes" who came "to sap the vitals of the country." They had made themselves wealthy and powerful while the coloreds remained "poor and wretched." Two free colored leaders, Sympson and Scholar, wrote to the London lawyer Richard Wilson, a brown man who grew up in the Leewards but now worked in the metropole, to promote the petitions of West Indian free coloreds. They expressed a deep loyalty to the Crown, which hitherto rendered them unwilling to take up arms against "a system so Tyrannical" as operated on the islands. They may not have indicted slavery itself with these words, but they condemned the racial assumptions that slavery rested on, and they challenged the status quo. Sympson and Scholar pointedly observed to Wilson that the free coloreds possessed "a great Physical Superiority" on the island, which they could use in "one energetic effort [to] overthrow and destroy."[65]

The relationship between whites and the most accomplished free coloreds had grown very tense. On October 7, 1823, the Duke of Manchester sent magistrates to arrest two free colored men, Louis Lecesne and Edward Escoffery, prosperous shopkeepers who had come under the suspicion of the Kingston police. As Manchester later told the story, the police suspected Lecesne and Escoffery of being "aliens of dangerous description" and thereby subject to deportation. Both men had French names and were known to be of Haitian parentage, and some said that they maintained dangerous connections with Haiti. Lecesne and Escoffery were not without supporters, and the latter filed a writ of habeas corpus and delayed the men's deportation. But allies of the police in the House of Assembly created a "Secret Committee" of nine members who investigated the charges. They convinced Manchester to reissue the arrest order, which he did on November 28, this time deporting the men to Jacmel, Haiti. They immediately sent petitions to London, protesting their deportation and demanding restitution of their rights.[66]

The swirl of accusations surrounding Lecesne and Escoffery took place in the context of widespread recrimination among island

slaveholders concerning Parliament's resolutions, now intensified
by the news from Demerara. Both the Colonial Office and the West
India Committee had wanted a carefully orchestrated deliberative
process among the white colonists in the old colonies, whereby
leading men would facilitate the passage of ameliorative legislation. Yet by May 1823, "literal copies" of Lord Bathurst's letter to
Manchester were in "general circulation" throughout the island,
and the planters had staged meetings of protest.[67]

On September 15, 1823, the magistrates and vestrymen of Saint
Ann Parish in Jamaica convened a meeting of freeholders at the
courthouse in Ocho Rios to consider "the critical situation" of the
colony as a result of the machinations of the "African Society."
The freeholders, some of whom were undoubtedly free men of color,
believed that Parliament's resolutions were a "breach of sacred trust"
between the colonies and the home government. They called on the
colonial Assembly to resist Parliament's encroachments on "our
Properties, our rights, our Liberty, and our Constitution." They accused members of Parliament of being "led away by passion" toward
"overheated schemes" that posed an enormous danger to colonial
lives and property. The freeholders argued that their property had
been "acquired by our ancestors and our own industry" under the
explicit protection of British law. If their rights to this property were
to be extinguished, they deserved to be compensated.

The freeholders of Saint Ann thus echoed the West India Committee's now familiar argument, but in a startling final resolution,
the freeholders boldly rejected the leadership of the committee. "It
is with real grief that we observe" the recent resolutions of the West
India Committee, the freeholders resolved. The committee was a society of men whom they had once seen as "Fellows in affliction," but
the freeholders of Saint Ann now condemned their "error in judgement," which revealed an astounding "ignorance of our real situation." The West India Committee had resolved at least twice in
recent months to embrace the concept of gradual abolition. Resident planters did not take kindly to the notion of accepting the
reality of gradual emancipation. It was one thing to observe emancipation from afar and collect compensation for the government's
forcible liquidation of your assets. But it was another thing to live

through emancipation, cheek by jowl with the people you and your fathers had enslaved.[68]

G. T. Gilbert, an overseer on the New Yarmouth Estate in Vere Parish, had the temerity to write directly to Manchester about "the present crisis of affairs." The proposed reforms to slavery had "created sentiments the most hostile to His Majesty's Government" that Gilbert likened to "the independents" of Spanish South America. The rebellion in Demerara showed "how cautious" government needed to be with the governance of slaves. Imperial policy had failed badly. "A lapse of ages" should pass "before the Negro can ever participate of the blessings of Freedom," Gilbert wrote, and "the very name of the African must cease to exist in their memories." Gilbert believed that the "internal policy of our laws" had kept Jamaica's slaves as "quiet spectators" during the recent years of war and rebellion. Let them remain "happy in their stations," he wrote, and he prayed to God that "the present tranquility may not be interrupted by scenes too dreadful to reflect upon."[69]

The Christmas holiday passed without incident, but in early January 1824, rebels on Frontier Estate in Saint Mary Parish destroyed the buildings on their estate in an effort to instigate a broader rebellion. Lord Manchester called out the militia and issued the proclamation that Bathurst had provided back in May. Rapid mobilization of freeholders suppressed the rebellion quickly and it did not spread beyond Frontier. Local magistrates hanged the rebel leaders as soon as they were caught, but freeholders in the region suspected something more extensive and investigations continued into February.[70]

The planters staged trials followed by public floggings. These terrible displays unfolded not only in Saint Mary Parish, where the rebellion started and quickly fizzled, but also in neighboring Saint George, and in Saint James farther west. There had been no missionaries involved, and the only detail Manchester included in his report to Bathurst was of an obeah man responsible for it all. He had "deluded" his followers into thinking they were "invulnerable," which emboldened them to rise up. Perhaps. Manchester's portrayal of the conspiracy rests on the colonial trope of savage Africans duped into rebellion by a wizard of the dark arts. In a postscript he appended to this report, Manchester implicated the free colored Lecesne, only

recently deported. Suspected rebels had revealed the man's involvement, and while this evidence from the mouths of slaves could not
be admitted in court against the free Lecesne, Manchester believed
it was true.[71]

Some might have thought the danger had passed, but in June 1824
a larger rebellion broke out in Saint James. Late at night on June 13,
Colonel A. Campbell of His Majesty's forces stationed at Halfpoint,
Saint James Parish, learned of a fire on the Alexandria Estate. He
sent a small company of twenty men to investigate. At one o'clock in
the afternoon on the next day, Campbell received a letter from the
company's leader, who had learned some details of the revolt from
the driver at Golden Grove plantation. Some of the enslaved men
on his plantation had "broken open the prisoners house" and taken
all the arms that were kept there. The driver accused the slaves of
Argyle plantation of setting fire to the "Negro Houses" of Alexandria plantation, an act that must have seemed like local vengeance.
But at the same time Campbell learned from a local man that the
Accompong Maroons were the "instigators of this rebellion." Campbell had examined a free colored planter in the region, Richard
Hemmings, who told the story that his slave woman told him.[72]

The night before, the woman had come down to Hemmings and
asked him if he "had heard that the Negroes were going to rise."
Hemmings told her the rumor was "pure nonsense," but the woman
knew of recent unusual events. Seven of "Mr. Malcolm's Negroes"
had gone into the hills of Saint Elizabeth to meet the Accompong
Maroons. "Have not you heard that they have been whipping one or
two at Montego Bay?" the woman had asked Hemmings, speaking
of the Maroons.[73]

The woman had concrete intelligence. The slaves at Dundee had
agreed to join the uprising; they planned to start by firing the trash
houses at Alexandria plantation. She also knew that two of "Mr. Hall's
estates in St. James had promised to join" the revolt, but she did not
know the names of the plantations. Then, just that morning, Hemmings had been walking down the road when he saw one of his men
and jested with him "why he was not at work sooner." Was he running
off to join the Maroons? But the man had stopped Hemmings and
asked him which road he was going. Down to Argyle "through the

short cut," Hemmings had replied. Do not go that way, the man had said; "a great force of them" was gathered there, the rebels from Malcolm's and a body of men from Accompong. As Hemmings continued on his way, he ran into John Clarke, a slave from Malcolm's, who spoke to him in a "surly tone."[74]

Moreover, an "anonymous letter" had been sent to one of the militia officers in Savanna la Mar, the principal port of Westmoreland Parish, which disclosed a "projected massacre of the White Inhabitants in St. Elizabeth and Westmoreland." The writer claimed to know of this plot because he was a member of a "secret society" that had organized the massacre and bound him by oath "not to divulge their plan." A portion of the Westmoreland regiment "was not to be depended upon," and the letter described in careful detail the enslaved rebels involved in the plot and to which plantation they belonged.[75]

Such intelligence was enough to call out a military response, so on the following morning Sir John Keane left Kingston on the *Hassar* frigate with a division of the Ninety-Second Regiment and a detachment from the Royal Artillery. They arrived in Savanna la Mar, Westmoreland, that afternoon. The troops marched out to Argyle, Alexandria, and Golden Grove plantations. Two rebels killed themselves immediately, and the soldiers made about twenty arrests. Keane ordered the remaining captives to be interrogated before local magistrates. When these men were "satisfied of their innocence," they were sent back to their plantations. But it did not end there. Local investigations continued into mid-July. The freeholders of Westmoreland organized trials that lasted three days, and on July 17 they staged the executions of six rebels on Argyle plantation, four on Golden Grove plantation, and two more executions in the town of Lucea. Manchester's informants told him that the executed men were "very audacious." Some had even tried to intervene in the executions. One of the rebels from Golden Grove said that "the War had only begun," and one of the Argyle rebels had reportedly said, on his deathbed, that while he now "saw it was vain to contend against the power of the White Inhabitants he was satisfied that he was at that moment Free." Manchester reported that "a very general impression existed throughout the island amongst the Slave Population, that they are entitled to their Freedom." The rapid deployment of significant military force had been effective, Manchester wrote, but the "spirit" of revolt had not been quelled.[76]

Like the Missouri debates in the United States Congress, Parliament's resolutions of 1823 inspired rage and fear among the masters and hope for those enslaved. Black radicals seized the opportunity to mobilize rebellion, though nowhere did they have the power to achieve their aims. Similar mobilizations in moments of the masters' weakness had occurred in Stono and western Jamaica during the eighteenth century, in Charleston and Lucea Bay during the American Revolution, most dramatically in French Saint-Domingue, and then in Richmond, Virginia, in 1800. In the 1820s, however, these moments of slaveholders' political weakness were caused by abolitionist agitation, not by imperial conflict. Organized resistance became more common than ever before—Barbados, Charleston, Demerara, and Jamaica—all during a decade of sustained abolitionist agitation. Moreover, the evident division among the slaveholders of Britain's empire, who were divided by both space and perspective, would become increasingly significant as abolitionism deepened. The West India Committee in London could perceive the influence of abolitionism and had adopted a resistant but compromising stance. Their foremost concern was financial compensation in the event of a change in the law of slave property. In contrast, the freeholders of Saint Ann expressed impotent rage at their cousins' compromise. They were presciently fearful of organized rebellion from those they enslaved. The political dynamic in South Carolina would be quite different.

One year after the hangings in Charleston ended, a group of prominent planters began to meet and discuss an institutional response to the conspiracy of the previous summer that appeared so dangerous and vast. They called themselves the South Carolina Association and announced in the *Charleston Courier* that their first official meeting would be at Saint Andrew's Hall on July 24, 1823. The association's purpose would be to correct a dangerous turn in South Carolina,

made evident by the terrible conspiracy and subsequent developments, whereby civil officials had begun to allow "the daily violation, or evasion of the laws, made to regulate the conduct of our coloured population." The formation of the association was a public
event accompanied by some protest about the potential abuse of
power by such an extralegal organization, but by far more support
than critique. In November 1824 the association submitted a petition to the state senate that announced their purpose, their reasoning,
and their membership. The association had the petition printed as a
broadside, with a long list of the names of the 334 men who had organized to protect their slave society from the dangers of the modern
world.[77]

More than half the members of the association were wealthy
planters or big merchants who resided in Charleston. Some hailed
from prestigious planting families that had held slaves for generations.
They were Balls, Pinckneys, Heywards, Laurenses, Legares, Man-
igaults, Middletons, and Wraggs. They depended on the perpetuation
of the slave system for their status and wealth and felt personally
threatened by the slave conspiracy. Five members, including the
association president Keating Simons, held slaves who had been implicated by the court. Four had served on the court and four had
authored pamphlets in response to the conspiracy. The historian
David Ramsay signed his name, as did the author of the prescient
Rusticus essays, Alexander Garden. Former senator William Smith
affixed his as well. Yet a significant proportion of these men
were not planters. Forty-four artisans signed their names to the petition, alongside twenty shopkeepers, eighteen physicians, sixteen
clerks, and fourteen lawyers. The formation of the association signified a mobilization of South Carolina's slaveholding class, and its
broad membership illustrates the hegemonic power of the slaveholding ethos among Carolina whites.[78]

The association's petition warned that the state's police controls
of the free black population did not protect the state from the
dangers of abolitionist influence. It was a remarkable statement of
racial fear. Less than a year earlier, the state legislature had passed
the Act for the Better Regulation and Government of Free Negroes, which considerably strengthened the law of 1820 that had

enraged Denmark Vesey. Free black men now had to pay an annual tax of fifty dollars to remain in the state. They also needed to retain a white "guardian" who would attest to their character in writing. Any free person of color who left the state and returned could be subject to flogging or even enslavement. And while the law of 1820 law had excepted black seamen from its strictures, the 1822 law ordered the imprisonment of every black sailor who entered any South Carolina port. Ship captains were required to pay for the maintenance of these prisoners and fined $1,000 if they failed to take them upon embarkation from the port. Yet even such draconian measures had proved inadequate against escalating abolitionist activity.[79]

Members of the association had monitored the enforcement of this law and found it woefully lacking. According to their research, 154 black sailors had entered Charleston's port in the past two months alone, 118 from the northern states, 15 from the West Indies, and 21 from Europe. Sometimes the entire crew of a ship was black, as they had seen on recent ships from New York and Boston. These men endangered the state through "the moral contagion of their pernicious principles and opinions." They carried the ideas of "the Abolition Societies of the North," which had become more ambitious. In previous years, these societies had limited their aims to a particular state, but they now had national, even international, ambitions. The petition cited the memorials of the free people of color in Grenada, Antigua, Saint Kitts, and Jamaica. It recounted the rebellion in Demerara and the rumors in Barbados that warranted the unbelievable proclamation that slavery had not ended. These foreboding developments were "attributable altogether to the proceedings of the African Associations in London, and to the influence of Mr. WILBERFORCE in Parliament." The only solution, the association argued, was to "prevent ANY FREE COLOURED PERSON FROM ANY PART OF THE WORLD *ever entering again into the limits of the State of South-Carolina*, by LAND OR BY WATER."[80] The state of South Carolina had to adjust to "the new relations in which we stand to the rest of the world." Abolitionism posed a greater threat than it ever had, but South Carolina had passed from a state of colonial dependency to a "sovereign state." As such, the legislature possessed the power "to resort to any measures which may menace our prosperity as a Slave-holding State."[81]

The association's reasoning drew from an intellectual ferment in South Carolina that generated numerous pamphlets seeking to justify racial slavery. The conspiracy in Charleston, which slaveholders uniformly believed had been inspired by the Missouri debates, prompted the masters of slaves not only to greater repression but also to the intellectual defense of slaveholding that would place this planter class at the vanguard of modern slaveholding. Association member Edwin Holland described the gentle treatment and light workload of the typical plantation, which he paired with detailed accounts of the numerous slave rebellions in Carolina history. Black slaves were the "Jacobins of the country," he wrote, despite masters' benevolence, which justified the rigid discipline that shocked ignorant northerners. The Baptist reverend Richard Furman and the Episcopalian minister Frederick Dalcho developed scriptural defenses of slavery to blunt the Christian foundation of antislavery thought. A most arresting voice belonged to Robert J. Turnbull, who in 1827 penned a series of essays for the *Charleston Mercury*, under the pseudonym Brutus, that explained for readers with alarming prose "The Crisis" that slaveholders faced in this era of ascendant abolitionism.[82]

Dedicated to the "People of the Plantation States," Turnbull elaborated on the states'-rights arguments cultivated by Senator Smith. He began where the association had closed its petition, with the question of state power. The federal Constitution, he argued, had arisen from the need of the states to organize commerce and to unite them in common defense, nothing more. Turnbull looked askance at projects such as the building of national roads and canals, or tariffs to support domestic manufactures. It was not that such national policies were inherently dangerous, but they introduced federal power into the states beyond the bounds established by the Constitution, and this power could be quite dangerous. He did not accept the notion that such federal efforts promoted "the general welfare" of the American people and were therefore constitutional. The powers of the federal government were external, not internal, and any interpretation that recognized federal power within the states was a dangerous "*Usurpation*" of the powers of the states.[83]

In this historical moment, the slaveholding states had to guard against the encroachments of federal power because of abolitionists

and the example of the British Caribbean. The American Colonization Society was for Turnbull nothing more than an abolitionist society. Earlier that year the society had petitioned Congress for
funds to support its enterprise. South Carolina senators Smith and
Robert Hayne had successfully fought the petition, but what if, Turnbull asked, Congress were to construe colonization as in the "general welfare" of the United States? And what if, in fifteen or twenty
years, the colonization of free blacks were to give way to the argument that the "gradual emancipation" of America's slaves would contribute to the "general welfare" of the American people? Some
might say that this was an "extreme case," wrote Turnbull. No, he
replied, it was not extreme; rather, it was "probable." Recall the "fire-
brand resolutions" of Rufus King. They were mere "pioneers" to
more radical propositions. Thus, "resistance" must be organized
now.[84]

Turnbull drew this insight from the recent history of abolitionism
in Britain. "When Mr. Wilberforce first brought forward his bill for
the abolition of the slave trade, he was even *more cautious* than the
Colonization Society." Turnbull believed that it had always been
Wilberforce's aspiration to abolish slavery itself, but in the 1780s
he found few followers. Yet Wilberforce had a "mighty subject" in
the idea of British liberty and, consequently, abolitionism grew. Now
the West Indian colonists were in a deplorable state. Parliament's
discussions of West Indian slavery had "caused" the insurrections
that had stricken the islands. The colonists' property had depreci-
ated, and some had lost their lives. The same could happen in the
United States, but it did not have to. "They are weak colonists. But
WE have the POWER. . . . We are Sovereign and Independent States."
The moment Congress moved to ameliorate the condition of the
slaves, South Carolina must act, even "at the hazard of DISSOLVING
THE UNION."[85]

Turnbull's attention to Caribbean developments indicates the centrality of transatlantic influence at this moment in the history of Atlantic slavery. Carolinian planters may have been responding to
northern antislavery, but northern antislavery only looked dangerous

because of the precedent of British abolitionism. The antislavery of the American Colonization Society was tepid in comparison to that of the London Society for the Mitigation and Gradual Abolition of Slavery, popularly known as the Anti-Slavery Society. Colonizationists wanted to foster the emigration of free blacks from the southern states, and to support slaveholders who wanted to manumit their slaves, so long as those freed would depart the South. A minority saw these measures as gradually eroding slavery, but the leadership of the society, prominent men such as Supreme Court Justice Bushrod Washington, the war hero Andrew Jackson, and Secretary of State Henry Clay, sought to consolidate slavery by removing the danger of free blacks. Most African Americans in the North roundly rejected the American Colonization Society.[86]

In stark contrast, British abolitionists had taken in stride the violence of Caribbean slave rebellions, which they saw as abundant evidence that slavery itself was badly in need of reform. During the fall of 1823 and extending throughout the following year, Thomas Clarkson traveled throughout Great Britain on behalf of the Anti-Slavery Society. He lectured in numerous towns and villages where local activists often organized new abolitionist societies and petition campaigns in the wake of his visits. For Clarkson, the insurrections in Demerara and Jamaica were "neither new, nor extraordinary, nor unexpected." These insurrections stemmed from the dehumanization of slavery itself. He did not believe that Parliament's resolutions had caused the rebellions; there were always rebels plotting. But he did entertain the idea of missionary influence. Suppose, Clarkson asked, that a missionary dedicated to the promotion of his faith encountered every Sunday his enslaved congregants, underfed and exhausted, with open stripes on their backs from the overseer's whip. Should we be surprised that compassion aroused indignation and an incautious "vent of feelings?" Such understandable outrage may well have "inflamed the minds" of the Demerara rebels, but slavery itself remained the "original cause of the rebellion." Clarkson's travels reprised his lecture tour of 1788, and by 1825 there were 250 branches of the Anti-Slavery Society throughout Great Britain, which had sent 777 petitions to Parliament seeking the reform of West Indian slavery.[87]

British abolitionists also flooded the reading public with dozens
of pamphlets and scores of newspaper articles about colonial slavery.
The Anti-Slavery Society began to publish the *Anti-Slavery Monthly
Reporter* in 1825. The *Edinburgh Review* regularly printed articles fa-
vorable to abolition. The *Scots Magazine, Gentleman's Magazine*, and
the *Monthly Review* also supported abolition, though with less ardor.
The Society of West India Merchants and Planters responded in kind
with the *West India Reporter*, founded in 1827. The society also planted
proslavery articles in the mainstream press, paying the editors to do
so. Proslavery writers such as George W. Bridges and Augustus
Beaumont, both of Jamaica, wrote vitriolic pieces attacking the abolitionists, denigrating blacks, and defending the planters as lawful,
loyal men. After 1823, scribblers in Great Britain spilled more ink
on the question of slavery than ever before.[88]

For many abolitionists, however, especially those new to the movement, there was very little evidence that the gradualist agenda of
the Anti-Slavery Society had been effective. Some of the colonies had
passed laws to ameliorate slavery, but Jamaica had not, and the newspapers still carried stories about the gross abuses of enslaved people.
In an 1824 pamphlet that went through three editions, the Quaker
schoolteacher Elizabeth Heyrick argued that Britain's abolitionists
should abandon gradualism and instead demand the "immediate"
abolition of slavery. Slavery implicated all Britons, Heyrick wrote.
"The West Indian planter and the people of this country stand in
the same moral relation to each other, as the thief and the receiver
of stolen goods." The sugar, molasses, rum, and cotton that Britons
purchased every day rewarded the slaveholder. Abolitionist words
were mere "cant" in the face of the marketplace.[89]

Heyrick pushed for more direct action, now. Like Clarkson, she
believed the violence of slave rebels to be the inevitable consequence
of slavery itself, and the punishments perpetrated by slaveholders to
be barbarous. Her radicalism reflected the growing influence of
women within the movement. Antislavery women such as the poet
and philanthropist Hannah More had long been involved in British
abolitionism, but not as members of the Anti-Slavery Society. This
began to change in 1825 when a group of women met in the home of
Lucy Townshend in Birmingham, England, to form the Female So-

ciety for Birmingham, which pledged to arouse public indignation about colonial slavery. Women's antislavery societies proliferated, sometimes in coordination with the male societies, sometimes not. Beyond expanding the role of women in public discourse, the Female Society of Birmingham developed the most significant tactic in transatlantic abolitionism, the paid lecturer. Modeled on a similar tactic used by the Bible societies that had taken root earlier in the century, in 1829 the Female Society hired the Reverend Doctor John Philip, a Congregational missionary who had worked in the Cape of Good Hope, to travel throughout Great Britain and give antislavery lectures. Two years later a group of young men within the Anti-Slavery Society formed a subcommittee called the Agency Committee, which was committed to immediatism and intent on using this new tactic. They hired six lecturers to travel the countryside and raise antislavery consciousness. By the end of 1831, there were more than 1,200 antislavery societies in Great Britain, which sent almost two thousand petitions to Parliament demanding the immediate abolition of colonial slavery. It was the largest petition drive in the history of abolitionism—indeed, in the history of Great Britain.[90]

By June 1831 Colonial Secretary Viscount Goderich had received numerous missives from the Caribbean by authors fearful of "the excitement which prevails in the minds of the slaves." He was unsure of the details but not of the danger, and citing the Demerara insurrection of 1823, Goderich authorized the colonial governors to reissue the Royal Proclamation of 1824, reminding the slaves to obey the laws of slavery. West Indian slaveholders were also deeply alarmed, and in Jamaica leading planters called meetings in all the parishes to discuss the threats they faced. The meetings passed resolutions that Jamaica governor Somerset Lowery, the Earl of Belmore, described as "violent and intemperate." They emphasized the lawfulness of property in slaves, guaranteed by the empire for two hundred years, and demanded compensation if emancipation were to come. They decried the "mad and irresponsible party denominated Saints" and accused His Majesty's ministers of "criminal credulity" for accepting abolitionist claims as truth. Some predicted "servile war," and most established committees of correspondence to coordinate strategy with the other parishes. Assemblyman Beaumont

even penned a pamphlet that declared Parliament impotent to legis-
late for the colonies. Abolitionist influence in Parliament had created a dire situation, he argued, "similar to that of the Colonies of
North America in 1775." Indeed, Goderich already knew from one
Mr. G. Jones that "feelers" had been extended "from the Jamaica
planters to the Government of America U.S. as to taking that Island
under its care." Reform Parliament and give the colonies representation, Beaumont demanded, or acknowledge our independence.[91]

Free men of color held separate meetings that condemned the abolitionists, and some colored men participated in the meetings of
white planters. Their struggle for equal civil rights had accomplished
its goal the year before when the Jamaica House of Assembly had
abolished racial distinctions among free colonists. On the question
of slavery, however, the free people of color were divided. Many followed the lead of Edward Jordan, champion of the civil rights movement and editor of the *Jamaica Watchman and Free Press*, who bravely
supported emancipation even while living in Kingston. Yet others
were planters and identified as such. "It is not our intention," a
meeting of brown men in Buff Bay resolved, "to consent to emancipate our slaves independently of the white population, for our interests are so united and interwoven, that any disunion on this subject
would endanger the whole."[92]

The resolutions of these meetings appeared in the island newspapers throughout the summer of 1831 and, as in Barbados, Demerara,
and Charleston, became the substance for rumors that the slaves
were free and Jamaican whites kept them wrongly enslaved. Leaders
among the enslaved had planned to rebel for years, ever since what
they now called the "Argyle War" of 1824. Every year they had
planned to rise in October or December, but they had not felt the
confidence to mobilize until Christmas of 1831, after the abolitionist
petition drive and the planter meetings.[93]

Organized resistance began on a Friday morning, December 16,
when the head driver on Salt Spring Estate in Hanover Parish refused to flog an enslaved woman on the orders of their overseer,
James Grignon, who had already flogged the woman once for stealing
sugarcane. The woman was the driver's wife. The other drivers supported him, and Grignon sent for the authorities in Montego Bay.

Two magistrates rode mules out to the estate and tried to arrest the drivers, but a large group of women and men met the magistrates in the road, beat them, took their pistols and mules, and sent them walking back bloodied to the city with word that the slaves would do no work after New Year's Day. The magistrates responded with a detachment of militia to the estate, fifty armed men, but when they reached Salt Spring it was empty. Everyone black had absconded into the hills, nowhere to be found.[94]

Three days later, on Monday night in the market in Montego Bay, a free black woman named Elizabeth Ball, dressed all in white, harangued a group of black men who had come down from the mountains. "You no hear it da the newspaper say you are all free," she said, "why don't you fight the white people, the same as the Argyle people . . . take the bill and the machete . . . fight them as fast as you catch them you must chop them and cut them up." Few free blacks participated in the rebellion, but Ball had family members enslaved. That she dressed in white suggests a Baptist faith, as that is what converts wore during the powerful baptism ceremony. While the Methodist deacons Quamina and Jack Gladstone had been the preeminent organizers of the Demerara rebels, and so many Charleston rebels worshiped in the African Methodist church, in Jamaica the Baptist deacons Samuel Sharpe, George Taylor, Thomas Dove, and Robert Gardner acted as the principal architects of rebellion in the West. These men were older artisans and class leaders associated with Thomas Burchell's Baptist mission in Montego Bay. They could read and write and, because of their position in the church, could often travel freely to visit class members to help them in their faith. They used these freedoms to organize rebellion.[95]

According to the missionary Henry Bleby, who had extensive interviews with Sharpe in prison once the rebellion had been quashed, the rebel strategy drew more from the strike tactics of industrial workers than from the methods of slave rebels of the past. In the months before the rebellion, Sharpe traveled to numerous estates around Montego Bay, preaching to small groups and telling them of the planned rebellion. He swore them on "the book," most likely a Bible, called on them to refuse to work when the overseers called them back to the fields after Christmas. Like workers in the mines and mills of Great Britain during the same period, the black Jamaicans planned a general strike to protest their enslavement. Those who testified at Sharpe's trial made no mention of armed insurrection, but the violent language Ball used in the marketplace that evening, well before Christmas, suggests that the rebels knew very well that their plans to take their freedom would turn violent.[96]

We find similar plans made by the rebel leaders in Portland: Solomon Atkinson, the forty-nine-year-old Creole and head carpenter at Fairy Hill Estate; Richard Buckley, a thirty-eight-year-old cooper at Fairfield Estate; and Frederick Fisher, a sixty-five-year-old African and head cooper at Fairy Hill. All of these men were class leaders, or "rulers," in the Native Baptist chapel at Fairy Hill. They had organized their rebellion toward the end of summer. The Portland rebels built houses hidden in the bush in a place called Cum Cum Sa Hill, where they could retreat once the rebellion turned violent. The leaders gathered at the chapel on Christmas night, drank wine, tipped some on the ground to honor the ancestors, and swore to each other that if the whites did not give them freedom, they would take it. The similarity of these plans, at opposite ends of the island, 150 miles from each other, testifies to the breadth of this rebellion, the potency of the rumor of emancipation, and the organizational prowess of the enslaved creole leadership.[97]

It took almost a week before news of the conflict at Salt Spring reached Governor Belmore in Spanish Town. On Thursday morning, December 22, Belmore sent letters to all the parish custodes advising them of the conflict, which he thought a mere "local excitement." He warned them nevertheless to be alert for the holiday and distributed printed copies of the royal proclamation to the slaves, to be read aloud on all the plantations. But the rebellion had already begun. On Friday morning rebels on the York Estate in Trelawney set fire to the cane trash houses and threatened to kill the resident whites. That same day Belmore received a letter from Portland from authorities who had learned of the rebels' plans. Belmore ordered ships to carry companies of regulars to Port Antonio, Montego Bay, and Black River. On Sunday, Christmas Day, Colonel George Lawson of the

Saint James regiment learned from the overseer of Moor Park Estate that the slaves had told him they would not work after Christmas, and if the whites tried to force them, they would set fire to everything and fight. On Monday the custos of Trelawney learned that the slaves on the Green Park and Orange Valley Estates, more than a thousand men and women, had declared they would no longer work. By Tuesday evening, the authorities in Montego Bay could see at least six fires burning in the hills around the port. Whites were pouring into Montego Bay seeking protection. Both the island militia and the regulars had begun to move. But enslaved people throughout the island believed that the King's troops would not fight them, for they had been freed; the proclamation was a lie.[98]

Jamaica's rebels in 1831 had developed a sophisticated theology of resistance and an organizational capacity that encompassed the entire island. The rebellion destroyed astonishing amounts of property, mostly the sugar works and canefields that made this slavery modern. These rebels did not have the martial skills of their Coromantee forebears. Only a minority among them had been born in Africa, and many of these had arrived in Jamaica as children. When troops confronted rebels and fired, the rebels usually fled. Belmore declared martial law on December 30, and although Montego Bay was in "the greatest confusion and panic" when Sir Willoughby Cotton arrived there on New Year's Day, his offer of pardon to all but the ringleaders brought most people back to the estates. By January 5 Cotton notified Belmore that "tranquility" had returned.[99]

The masters' tranquility, perhaps, but for those enslaved the torture ensued. Trials of captured rebels began under martial law and continued into February. Once martial law ended, the parish vestries organized courts of magistrates and freeholders, much as they had in Charleston, to investigate the breadth of the rebellion. Trials took place in Saint James, Saint Thomas in the East, Hanover, Westmoreland, Saint Elizabeth, Portland, Trelawney, Saint Thomas in the Vale, and Manchester. Elizabeth Ball suffered twenty-four lashes followed by six months' solitary confinement. George Shaw of the Great Valley Estate in Hanover, who had pillaged the plantation stores during the chaos of rebellion, was shot. Phoebe of the Moco plantation in Saint Elizabeth, who had fed some rebels passing through, suffered hard labor in the workhouse. Samuel Sharpe, George Taylor, Thomas Dove, and Robert Gardner were hanged at the gallows in Montego Bay. Solomon Atkinson and Richard Buckley were hanged in the marketplace in Port Antonio, and Buckley's head was severed, to be fixed prominently at Fairfield Estate. Frederick Fisher received 150 lashes.[100]

The masters' vengeance did not end with the slaves. On February 6 the day after the end of martial law, a mob of white and free colored men gathered at Thomas Burchell's chapel in Montego Bay and tore it to the ground. The next day, mobs destroyed Baptist and Methodist chapels in Falmouth, Stewart Town, Lucea, Savanna la Mar, Ridgeland, Brown's Town, and Rio Bueno. Parish magistrates arrested numerous missionaries, including William Knibb, the Baptist pastor at Falmouth and Savanna la Mar. A mob stormed the home of Henry Bleby and tarred and feathered him in front of his family. The Reverend George W. Bridges, now the rector in Saint Ann, founded the Colonial Church Union in this moment, a paramilitary organization dedicated to driving the missionaries from the island. By the end of March there were chapters of the Colonial Church Union in eleven parishes and the newly arrived Governor, Constantine Henry, the Earl of Mulgrave, reported that "almost the whole community is made up of only different degrees of opposition to the authority of the King's Government." Jamaican planters now faced their own "crisis" of political weakness.[101]

The tumult in Jamaica marked the onset of a remarkable historical conjuncture in Britain's empire that would lead to abolition. News of the insurrection, its brutal suppression, and especially the planters' assault on the missionaries arrived in Great Britain in the midst of great political ferment. The question of parliamentary reform, which had percolated for decades, had become the most pressing issue in Parliament and the press, while the abolitionist mobilization that had fostered the rumors of emancipation continued. The importance of reform to the abolitionist agenda lay in a very simple reality: votes. As the West Indians had correctly asserted since the Somerset decision, property in slaves had enjoyed the protection of British law for

many generations. Britons had invested millions of sterling in enslaved people, as well as the estates and the entire system of colonial
commerce that had evolved around the consumption of tropical commodities. The legitimacy of slave property lay at the heart of this
enterprise, and it would be a profoundly radical act to declare this
property illegitimate.

Yet, by design, Parliament represented Great Britain's men of
wealth, men who were unlikely to undermine any form of property.
Since the thirteenth century, representation in Parliament had been
based on the borough, a community enfranchised by the Crown to
send a member to Parliament. Men of property from the borough
could stand for election to Parliament. How much property changed
occasionally, but it was always beyond the means of most men. Moreover, economic change, especially industrialization, had so transformed the demographic geography of Great Britain that the ancient
system of boroughs in no way represented the British people, or even
the British elite. There were "rotten boroughs" and "pocket boroughs" that rarely changed hands and sometimes stayed in the same
family for generations. West Indian absentees held some of these
seats, but most importantly, the industrial centers where abolitionism
had taken hold, places like Birmingham and Manchester, were hardly
represented.[102]

On May 24, 1832, the Marquis of Chandos, a Jamaican absentee,
rose in his seat in Parliament to present a petition composed at a
meeting of the West India Committee, praying for relief. Hurricanes
had recently struck several of the colonies, and Jamaica, of course,
had suffered enormous damage at the hands of its insurrectionists.
Sir Adolphus Dalrymple rose in support of the colonies. He celebrated
their impressive investment in chapels for the religious instruction
of slaves and condemned the member for Weymouth, Thomas
Fowell Buxton, for his "scandalous stories" of slavery in the colonies,
which were grossly exaggerated.

Buxton had two petitions to present, but he also made a motion
to form a select committee to consider "the extinction of slavery
throughout the British dominions." He responded forcefully to
Dalrymple with the story of the chapels in Jamaica destroyed by
mobs of slaveholders, and asked pointedly, "Did anyone doubt that

a crisis was coming which would leave them no alternative but an immediate concession of freedom to the slaves, or a dreadful attempt to extort it through the horrors of a servile war?" Buxton drew on the authority not of Wilberforce but of Thomas Jefferson, who trembled for his country when he recalled that "God is just."[103]

Lord Althorp, chancellor of the Exchequer, sought to soften Buxton's resolution with an amendment that alluded to the resolutions of 1823, thus maintaining a gradualist stance. Buxton disagreed. The West Indian legislatures had taken nine years to change their laws, and as they had not done so, it was time for stronger measures. Sir Robert Peel warned the House of the dangers of history. How often had dangerous talk in London led to insurrection in the Caribbean? asked Peel. Establishing such a committee was reckless. The abolitionist Stephen Lushington replied that insurrection would surely come if the slaves had to look to the island legislatures for their freedom, for it would never come. The Jamaica Assembly agent William Burge, also the member for Eye, recounted the example of Saint-Domingue, where the declaration of the National Assembly of France, combined with the work of the Amis des Noirs, had visited that rich and splendid colony with "scenes of horror." The insurrection in Jamaica had moved members to the rhetorical edge. At stake was the charge of the committee, and when the votes were counted, Buxton and his supporters had lost, but not by much. They had gained 90 votes to 163 for Althorp's amendment. The committee was formed with a gradualist mandate, but a significant minority of members wanted more. It was a sign of things to come.[104]

The discussion of slavery ebbed for the rest of the session as the committee heard testimony and Parliament took up the question of reform. In June 1832 the Reform Bill passed. Elections for the first reformed Parliament were set for December, and the Anti-Slavery Society stood poised to act. Soon after the Reform bill passed, the Reverend William Knibb arrived from Jamaica, sent for by the Baptist Missionary Society to explain the dramatic happenings in Jamaica since the great insurrection. Knibb spent the next six months touring the country, speaking about slavery and contributing to the work of the Agency Committee. The West India Committee followed suit, hiring two lecturers, Peter Borthwick and one Mr. Franklin. These men actually studied the tactics of the abolitionist lecturers and deployed them for the slaveholders, for a fee. Borthwick kept it up for nine months, and savvy marketers staged public debates featuring Borthwick and Knibb, which attracted crowds in the thousands. All of this agitation took place in the period before the general election of 1832, and abolitionists pressed candidates to pledge themselves to immediate abolition or risk losing the abolitionist vote. The abolition of slavery thus became the first modern issue campaign, clearly designed to pack the next Parliament with the votes necessary to achieve the extinction of colonial slavery.[105]

And it worked, though not as the abolitionists hoped it might, and certainly not the way enslaved people had imagined. Officials within the Colonial Office began to draft a plan for emancipation in the fall of 1832, and Parliament debated the ministry's plan for more than a year. The final bill, which became law on August 1, 1834, declared slavery abolished. Overseers could no longer flog workers in the field, and, most importantly, people could no longer be bought and sold. But those enslaved became "apprentices," obliged to work for their former masters for forty hours a week without pay. The Colonial Office would appoint special magistrates to adjudicate disputes between the planters and the laborers, replacing the slave courts. And, most offensive to the abolitionists, the planters received what they had long lobbied for: compensation for their lost investments. Over the next several years, the Exchequer of Great Britain disbursed £20,000,000 in payments to those who had once owned slaves. Payments were based on the average market value of prime slaves, by island, for the last ten years of slavery. The laws of slavery always undermined human dignity, even at the onset of freedom.[106]

For the planters of South Carolina, the events across the Atlantic confirmed the drastic difference made by the sovereign power of their state. Insurrection had struck the South as well, in Southampton, Virginia, in August 1831, but in contrast to the impact of Jamaica's Baptist War, the Southampton insurrection marked the historical conjuncture that would lead to the most forceful defense of racial slavery the world would ever know.

The slave revolt in Virginia erupted in the wake of the circulation of radical writings from the black abolitionist David Walker and the white abolitionist William Lloyd Garrison. Both men were immediatists in the mold of Elizabeth Heyrick, and while Garrison had denounced violence, Walker had not. Nat Turner and his rebels killed sixty-one white people, including women and children, in sparsely populated Southampton County in a matter of hours. In South Carolina rumors spread that a black army approached from Virginia. Several slaves in Marion County, which sat on the North Carolina border, voiced their eagerness to join them. Benjamin Holt, Edward Whealen, and John Ervin, leading planters in the district, organized a company of thirty men to ride armed each night during the excitement. In Abbeville District on the state's western border with Georgia, planters believed they uncovered a conspiracy and executed a man named Ned. His master, Robert Cunningham, had owned Ned since childhood and was astonished by his disloyalty.[107]

South Carolina governor James Hamilton did not think there was substance to these rumors, but he nevertheless seized the opportunity to propose a strengthening of the state's military defenses against future insurrectionists. In a message to the legislature in December 1831, Hamilton recommended the establishment of a company of dragoons in every upcountry district in the state, as well as three companies in each of the Lowcountry districts, where the enslaved population was much larger. Modeled on the response of the planters of Marion, Hamilton described companies of thirty armed men, funded by the state, which would drill once a month in front of the district courthouse and be ready to mobilize in response to any movement among the slaves.[108]

For Hamilton, the military reorganization of the state's internal defenses was necessary because of the Southampton revolt. He had corresponded with the governor of Virginia, who believed that the revolt had been "excited by incendiary newspapers" and pamphlets from the northern states, which had circulated freely. Hamilton knew that such publications circulated in South Carolina as well. He himself had been sent a copy of the *Liberator*, the radical newspaper published in Boston by Garrison. The governor of Georgia had recently complained about these publications to the governor of Massachusetts, who acknowledged their impropriety but protested that the writers had broken no laws. Hamilton saw in this situation "the extraordinary fact that, in a peaceful and united confederacy of states, we may have to submit to Acts of hostility . . . from the Citizens of one of its members." The conspiracy in Charleston, the rebellions in the British Caribbean, and the Southampton revolt all taught slaveholders that the circulation of abolitionist material in a slave society was an act of war. Turnbull's warnings had never seemed so prescient.[109]

Military force represented only one dimension of the power necessary to maintain slavery in the face of abolitionism. As Senator Smith and Turnbull had warned, the expansive views of federal power had dangerous potential for slaveholders. Prominent politicians such as Henry Clay of Kentucky and Daniel Webster of Massachusetts argued for these expansive powers as justification for the "American System" of tariffs, internal improvements, and a national bank. They also believed in the colonization of free blacks as an encouragement to manumission. The ideology of states' rights had only deepened in popularity in South Carolina since Turnbull's pamphlet and was now known as nullification, or the right of a state to nullify an act of the federal government. John C. Calhoun had privately embraced nullification in 1827, but he kept his views quiet, probably because of his ambitions for the presidency. Hamilton had worked to popularize nullification through the States Rights and Free Trade Association, which emphasized the impact of federal tariffs on southern agriculture. The tariff on imported manufactured goods protected northern industries and made the cost of living higher for those who depended on imports. Hamilton was a skillful organizer, and association meetings were social occasions for a cross section of white Carolinians, from the planter to the poor farmer. The association carried Hamilton to the Governor's Mansion in 1830. But as Calhoun privately observed, it was concern for "the peculiar domestick institution" of the South that energized the movement and gave it its urgency and rhetorical edge.[110]

In the state elections of 1832 the Nullifiers won clear majorities in the state house. Governor Hamilton immediately called for a nullification convention, which met in November 1832 and resolved "to redeem ourselves from the state of Colonial vassalage" to the federal government. The West Indian example could not have been clearer. The convention warned that "the time must come when the people . . . will rise up in their might and release themselves from this thraldom, by one of those violent convulsions, whereby society is uprooted from its foundations, and the edict of Reform is written in Blood." But much like the Colonial Church Union in Jamaica, the Nullifiers failed. Similar movements did not develop elsewhere in the South, and President Andrew Jackson, a slaveholder himself who hated abolitionists, asserted forcefully the supremacy of federal power over the states.[111]

Moreover, abolitionism seemed to thrive and radicalize, especially after Great Britain abolished slavery in 1833. Beginning with the effort of black abolitionists in Philadelphia, Boston, and New York to discredit the American Colonization Society, radical abolitionism began to spread. The first meeting of the American Anti-Slavery Society took place in December 1833, in black-owned Adelphi Hall in Philadelphia, just months after King William IV had signed Great Britain's Slavery Abolition Act. Garrison penned the society's "Declaration of Sentiments," which boldly pronounced the same immediatist agenda that had motivated British abolitionism. By 1836 there were more than five hundred local antislavery societies affiliated with the society, most of them in Ohio, New York, and Massachusetts. The American movement adopted many of the same tactics that British abolitionists had deployed, including the employment of sixty paid agents on lecture tours and the presentation of thousands of petitions to Congress. But most white American detested the abolitionists and in many cities white mobs attacked their meetings. But that did not silence them.[112]

On February 6, 1837, Calhoun rose on the Senate floor to address the crisis at hand. A mass of petitions from abolitionist societies sat on the table, and Calhoun picked two of them at random and had them read by the secretary. The language was no doubt strong. Calhoun wondered how the senators from twelve of the "sovereign states" of this Union were to "sit here in silence" and allow such attacks. He was not at all satisfied with the current treatment of these petitions—to acknowledge them but then leave them on the table un-

considered. In this republic that he served, to acknowledge a petition of the people was to give it legitimacy, and if the Senate were to
give these petitions legitimacy, then it must entrust them to a committee for deliberation. Yet in Calhoun's view, "the subject is beyond
the jurisdiction of Congress"; the Senate had "no right to touch it."
The federal Constitution had settled the problem of slavery, Calhoun
argued, and the question of its legitimacy should not be raised again.
He believed that most northerners were not abolitionists, but he
feared for the next generation. The demand for the abolition of
slavery would only grow, he predicted, if the "disease" of abolitionism
were not checked. "Abolition and Union cannot coexist. As a friend
of the Union I openly proclaim it, and the sooner it is known the
better."[113]

The South could never give up racial slavery. "It cannot be sub-
verted without drenching the country in blood, and extirpating one
or other of the races." This would be a great tragedy, said Calhoun,
for despite the false calumny of the abolitionist societies, racial slavery
had made valuable contributions to humanity. The "black race of
Central Africa" had never achieved such a high standard of civilization
as had the enslaved population of the South. They had disembarked
from the slave ships in a "low, degraded, and savage" condition, but
the peculiar slavery of the North American South had civilized
them. Calhoun acknowledged that southerners were not as wealthy
as the men of the North, but southern society had produced many
men of talent who had made important contributions to the young
republic. Southern society was good. "I hold that in the present state
of civilization, where two races of different origin, and distinguished by color, and other physical differences, as well as intellectual, are brought together, the relation now existing between the two
is, instead of an evil, a good—a positive good."[114]

Calhoun could not see the inconsistency between the phantasm
of a bloody race war and the paternalistic relations between master
and slave that he and John Moultrie imagined from their studies. Racial attitudes blinded both men. The proslavery argument Calhoun
advanced on the floor of the United States Senate, grounded in racial thinking as it was, laid the intellectual foundation for a powerful
slaveholding class that would dominate American politics for another

generation. The southern economy expanded apace with that of the industrializing North, generating enormous wealth in the hands of a few men who stood large on America's political stage. Calhoun died in 1850, and by 1860 the slaveholders of the American South held four million African Americans enslaved, a lawful crime still justified by the myths of racial difference and a benevolent slavery. But proslavery argument never convinced enough of the white North to curb the expansion of antislavery views. When the election of 1860 brought a man to the presidency who believed slavery was wrong, who led a party willing to act on the evils of slavery, the planters of South Carolina led the South out of the Union. The war that came was not the race war Calhoun imagined, but it did obliterate the power of the master and it did free the people once enslaved.[115]

The politics of resistance shaped the development of racial slavery in every society of the Atlantic World. The histories of Jamaica and South Carolina represent distinct versions of this central theme in Atlantic history. These slave societies emerged from the same historical moment and shared a legal genealogy born of the expansion of England's seventeenth-century empire. But differences in geography, indigenous power, and the unequal profitability of sugar and rice generated distinctive systems of slavery. As these slave societies evolved, their different characteristics created distinct political dynamics between the masters and the slaves, which led the planter-legislators of these colonies to construct very different systems of social control to make slavery pay. Thus, when the American Revolution brought antislavery ideas from the libraries of the well read into the tumble of the everyday, enslaved people and their masters, in Jamaica and South Carolina, occupied distinct positions of political advantage to pursue their interests in the tumultuous Age of Revolution. Slaveholders retrenched and held their own for another generation in both places, but the expansive geography of North America, and South Carolina's powerful position within the early republican United States, made its slaveholders far more powerful than their Jamaican counterparts, who remained dependent colonists.

The consequences of distinct politics of slavery can be seen in the Atlantic geography of racial slavery in 1834. The Haitian Revolution had destroyed France's most profitable colony, but Napoleon had reimposed slavery in Martinique and Guadeloupe, where it persisted until abolished by the radical government of 1848. The independence movements of Spanish America tied republicanism to antislavery, and Argentina, Colombia, Chile, and Mexico gradually abolished slavery beginning in the 1810s. In the English-speaking Atlantic, two political divisions created three different regions: the northern states of the American Union, where the state legislatures abolished slavery through gradual abolition laws; the US South, where slavery thrived; and Great Britain's Caribbean colonies, where Parliament had imposed gradual abolition. British abolition gave encouragement to abolitionists throughout the Atlantic World. It had, in the words of Frederick Douglass, "made the name of England known in and loved in every slave cabin, from the Potomac to the Rio Grande." But the persistence of racial slavery in the American republic gave the institution international legitimacy until the destruction of the Confederacy in 1865. The transatlantic slave trade to Brazil thrived until 1850, and slavers visited Cuba as late as 1867. These modern slavers, many of them sailing under the flag of the United States, brought more than eight hundred thousand captive Africans into the plantation order. Racial slavery itself lasted until 1886 in Cuba and 1888 in Brazil, and various slaveries persist today. Slavery does not die on its own; the masters' power has to be destroyed before the people enslaved can begin to heal.[116]

Notes

Abbreviations

AHR	*American Historical Review*
BNA	British National Archives, Kew, England.
Burnard database	Database of Jamaican Inventories in the Jamaica National Archives, Spanish Town, Jamaica. Compiled by Trevor Burnard, 2010; in possession of the author.
CO	Colonial Office Records, British National Archives, Kew, UK.
CSP	*Calendar of State Papers, Colonial Series, America and the West Indies*, 45 vols. ed. W. Noel Sainsbury, J.W. Fortescue, and Cecil Headlam (London: Her Majesty's Stationery Office, 1860-1994).
Fuller Letterbooks	Stephen Fuller Letterbooks, John J. Burns Library, Boston College, Chestnut Hill, Mass.
GM	*Gentleman's Magazine*
HL	Henry Laurens
JAJ	*Journals of the Assembly of Jamaica*, 14 vols. (Saint Jago de la Vega, Jamaica, 1811-1829).
JBMHS	*Journal of the Barbados Museum and Historical Society*
JCHA	*Journal of the Commons House of Assembly of South Carolina*
JL	John Laurens
JNA	Jamaica National Archives, Spanish Town, Jamaica.
NLJ	National Library of Jamaica, Kingston, Jamaica.
PHL	*The Papers of Henry Laurens*, 16 vols., ed. Philip Hamer, George C. Rogers Jr., David R. Chesnutt, and C. James Taylor (Columbia: University of South Carolina Press, 1976).
SCDAH	South Carolina Department of Archives and History, Columbia, South Carolina.
SCHGM	*South Carolina Historical and Genealogical Magazine*
SCHM	*South Carolina Historical Magazine*

SC Trans./   *Records in the British Public Record Office Relating to South*
  microfilm   *Carolina, 1663–1782*, 36 vols. (Columbia: South Carolina
               Department of Archives and History, 1971).
SC Transcripts *Records in the British Public Record Office Relating to South*
               Carolina: 1663–[1710], 5 vols. ed. A.S. Salley, Jr. (Atlanta,
               Ga.: printed for the Historical Commission of South
               Carolina by Foote and Davies, 1928-1947).
Voyages   David Eltis et al., Voyages: The Transatlantic Slave Trade
               Database, http://www.slavevoyages.org
WMQ   *William and Mary Quarterly*, 3rd Series.

PROLOGUE   At the Heart of Slavery

Epigraphs: Elsa V. Goveia, "The West Indian Slave Laws of the 18th Century," in Douglas Hall, Elsa V. Goveia, and F. Roy Augier, eds. *Chapters in Caribbean History* 2 (Barbados: Caribbean Universities Press, 1970), 9; David Brion Davis, *The Problem of Slavery in the Age of Revolution, 1770–1823* (1975; repr., New York: Oxford University Press, 1999), 49.

1. David Brion Davis, "At the Heart of Slavery," in *In the Image of God: Religion, Moral Values, and Our Heritage of Slavery* (New Haven, Conn.: Yale University Press, 2001), 123–136.

2. David Brion Davis, *The Problem of Slavery in Western Culture* (1966; repr., New York: Oxford University Press, 1988); Seymour Drescher, *Capitalism and Antislavery: British Mobilization in Comparative Perspective* (New York: Oxford University Press, 1987); James Brewer Stewart, *Holy Warriors: The Abolitionists and American Slavery*, rev. ed. (New York: Hill and Wang, 1997); Manisha Sinha, *The Slave's Cause: A History of Abolition* (New Haven, Conn.: Yale University Press, 2016). I have adopted the "generation" as a meaningful measure of historical time from Ira Berlin, *Many Thousands Gone: The First Two Centuries of Slavery in North America* (Cambridge, Mass.: Belknap Press of Harvard University Press, 1998).

3. A rich historiography on the relationship between slavery and the law begins with Frank Tannenbaum, *Slave and Citizen: The Negro in the Americas* (New York: Vintage Books, 1946), and is further developed in the following studies: Stanley Elkins, *Slavery: A Problem in American Institutional and Intellectual Life* (Chicago: University of Chicago Press, 1959), 25, 63-80; Davis, *Problem of Slavery in Western Culture*, chap. 7; Goveia, "West Indian Slave Laws," 9-53; Alan Watson, *Slave Law in the Americas* (Athens: University of Georgia Press, 1989); Thomas D. Morris, *Southern Slavery and the Law, 1619–1860* (Chapel Hill: University of North Carolina Press, 1996); and Christopher Tomlins, *Freedom Bound: Law, Labor, and Civic Identity in Colonizing English America, 1580–1865* (New York: Cambridge University Press, 2010).

4. The comparative approach to the history of slavery also begins with Tannenbaum's *Slave and Citizen*. Works that influenced the conceptualization of this book include Herbert Klein, *Slavery in the Americas: A Comparative Study of Virginia and Cuba* (Chicago: University of Chicago Press, 1967); Carl Degler,

Neither Black Nor White: Slavery and Race Relations in Brazil and the United States (Madison: University of Wisconsin Press, 1971); George Fredrickson, *White Supremacy: A Comparative Study in American and South African History* (New York: Oxford University Press, 1981) and *Black Liberation: A Comparative History of Black Ideologies in the United States and South Africa History* (New York: Oxford University Press, 1995); Peter Kolchin, *Unfree Labor: American Slavery and Russian Serfdom* (Cambridge, Mass.: Harvard University Press, 1987); Michael Mullin, *Africa in America: Slave Acculturation and Resistance in the American South and the British Caribbean, 1736–1831* (Urbana: University of Illinois Press, 1992); Philip Morgan, *Slave Counterpoint: Black Culture in the Eighteenth-Century Chesapeake and Lowcountry* (Chapel Hill: University of North Carolina Press for the Omohundro Institute, 1998); Camilla Townsend, *Tales of Two Cities: Race and Economic Culture in Early Republican North and South America: Guayaquil, Ecuador, and Baltimore, Maryland* (Austin: University of Texas Press, 2000); Enrico Dal Lago, *Agrarian Elites: American Slaveholders and Southern Italian Landowners, 1815–1861* (Baton Rouge: Louisiana State University Press, 2005); Rebecca Scott, *Degrees of Freedom: Louisiana and Cuba after Slavery* (Cambridge, Mass.: Harvard University Press, 2005); and Richard S. Dunn, *A Tale of Two Plantations: Slave Life and Labor in Jamaica and Virginia* (Cambridge, Mass.: Harvard University Press, 2014).

5. Raymond A. Bauer and Alice H. Bauer, "Day-to-Day Resistance to Slavery," *Journal of Negro History* 27 (October 1942): 388–419; Michael Craton, *Testing the Chains: Resistance to Slavery in the British West Indies* (Ithaca, N.Y.: Cornell University Press, 1982), 14; Eric Hobsbawm, "From Social History to the History of Society," in *Essays in Social History*, ed. W. Flinn and T. C. Smout (Oxford: Oxford University Press, 1974), 17 (previously published in *Daedalus* 100 [Winter 1971]: 20–45). The literature on everyday resistance, and the related debate about enslaved agency, is too vast to list here; influential studies include Walter Johnson, *Soul by Soul: Life inside the Antebellum Slave Market* (Cambridge, Mass.: Harvard University Press, 1999); Stephanie Camp, *Closer to Freedom: Enslaved Women and Everyday Resistance in the Plantation South* (Chapel Hill: University of North Carolina Press, 2004); and Walter Johnson, "On Agency," *Journal of Social History* 37 (2003): 113–124.

6. Important works on the political significance of slave resistance that have shaped this study begin with C. L. R. James, *The Black Jacobins: Toussaint L'Ouverture and the San Domingo Revolution* (1938; repr., New York: Vintage Books, 1963); Mary Turner, *Slaves and Missionaries: The Disintegration of Jamaican Slave Society, 1787–1834* (1982; repr., Kingston, Jamaica, UWI Press, 1998); James Oakes, "The Political Significance of Slave Resistance," *History Workshop Journal* 22, no. 1 (1986): 89–107; Emilia Viotti da Costa, *Crowns of Glory, Tears of Blood: The Demerara Slave Rebellion of 1823* (New York: Oxford University Press, 1994); Steven Hahn, *A Nation under Our Feet: Black Political Struggles in the Rural South from Slavery to the Great Migration* (Cambridge, Mass.: Harvard University Press 2003); and Vincent Brown, *The Reaper's Garden: Death and Power in the World of Atlantic Slavery* (Cambridge, Mass.: Harvard University Press, 2008).

7. Marc Bloch, "A Contribution towards a Comparative History of European Societies," in *Land and Work in Medieval Europe: Selected Papers*, trans.

J. E. Anderson (London: Routledge, 1966), 44–81; Peter Kolchin, *A Sphinx on the American Land: The Nineteenth-Century South in Comparative Perspective* (Baton Rouge: Louisiana State University Press, 2003), 74–75; George M. Fredrickson, *The Comparative Imagination: On the History of Racism, Nationalism, and Social Movements* (Berkeley: University of California Press, 2000); Fernand Braudel, "History and the Social Sciences: The *Longue Durée*" (1958), trans. Immanuel Wallerstein, *Review* (Fernand Braudel Center) 32, no. 2 (2009): 173; Dale Tomich, "The Order of Historical Time: The *Longue Durée* and Microhistory," in *The* Longue Durée *and World-Systems Analysis*, ed. Richard E. Lee (Albany, N.Y.: SUNY Press, 2012), 10. On historical time see Reinhart Koselleck, "Representation, Event, and Structure," in Koselleck, *Futures Past: On the Semantics of Historical Time*, trans. Keith Tribe (Cambridge, Mass.: MIT Press, 1985), 105-115.

8. Trevor Burnard, *Planters, Merchants and Slaves: Plantation Societies in British America, 1650–1820* (Chicago: University of Chicago Press, 2015).

9. R. M. Bent and Enid L. Bent-Golding, *A Complete Geography of Jamaica* (London: Collins, 1966); Robert M. Weir, *Colonial South Carolina: A History* (1983; repr. Columbia: University of South Carolina Press, 1997), 33–47; Matthew Mulcahy, *Hurricanes and Society in the British Greater Caribbean, 1624–1783* (Baltimore, Md.: Johns Hopkins University Press, 2006).

10. Carl Ortwin Sauer, *The Early Spanish Main* (Berkeley: University of California Press, 1969), 51–52, 82, 180–181; Francisco Morales Padrón, *Spanish Jamaica*, trans. Patrick Bryan (1952; Kingston, Jamaica,: UWI Press, 2003), 31; Frank Cundall and Joseph L. Pietersz, *Jamaica under the Spaniards, Abstracted from the Archives of Seville* (Kingston: Institute of Jamaica, 1919), 34; Irving Rouse, *The Tainos: Rise and Decline of the People Who Greeted Columbus* (New Haven, Conn.: Yale University Press, 1992), 7; Andres Resendez, *The Other Slavery: The Uncovered Story of Indian Enslavement in America* (Boston: Houghton Mifflin, 2016), 13–45.

11. J. Leitch Wright Jr., *The Only Land They Knew: The Tragic Story of the American Indians in the Old South* (New York: Free Press, 1981); Alejandra Dubcovsky, *Informed Power: Communication in the Early American South* (Cambridge, Mass.: Harvard University Press, 2016), 11–41; Peter H. Wood, "The Changing Population of the Colonial South: An Overview by Race and Region, 1685–1790," in *Powhaten's Mantle: Indians in the Colonial Southeast*, ed. Peter H. Wood et al. (Lincoln: University of Nebraska Press, 1989), 38; Russell Thornton, "Demographic History," in *Handbook of North American Indians: Northeast*, ed. Raymond D. Fogelson (Washington, D.C.: Smithsonian Institution, 2004), 48–52; Jerald T. Milanich, "Timucua," in Fogelson, 227; John E. Worth, "Guale" and "Yamasee," in Fogelson, 244, 252; Gene Waddell, "Cusabo," in Fogelson, 263; Blair A. Rudes et al., "Catawba and Neighboring Groups," in Fogelson, 309; Bonnie G. McEwan, "Apalachee and Neighboring Groups," in Fogelson, 675.

12. Peter Wood, *Black Majority: Negroes in Colonial South Carolina from 1670 through the Stono Rebellion* (New York: W. W. Norton, 1974), 13–24; Richard Dunn, *Sugar and Slaves: The Rise of the Planter Class in the English West Indies, 1624–1713* (1972; repr., Chapel Hill: University of North Carolina Press for

the Omohundro Institute, 2000); Jennifer L. Morgan, *Laboring Women: Repro-duction and Gender in New World Slavery* (Philadelphia: University of Pennsylvania Press, 2004), 77–87; David Barry Gaspar, "With a Rod of Iron: Barbados Slave Laws as a Model for Jamaica, South Carolina, and Antigua, 1661–1697," in *Crossing Boundaries: Comparative History of Black People in Diaspora*, ed. Darlene Clark Hine and Jacqueline McLeod (Bloomington: Indiana University Press, 1999), 343–366; Edward B. Rugemer, "The Development of Mastery and Race in the Comprehensive Slave Codes of the Greater Caribbean during the Seventeenth Century," *William and Mary Quarterly* (hereafter *WMQ*) 70 (July 2013): 429–458.

13. Trevor Burnard, "'Prodigious Riches': The Wealth of Jamaica before the American Revolution," *Economic History Review* 54, no. 3 (August 2001): 506–524; Alice Hanson Jones, *Wealth of a Nation to Be: The American Colonies on the Eve of Revolution* (New York: Columbia University Press, 1980), 379–380; Ray A. Kea, *Settlements, Trade, and Polities in the Seventeenth-Century Gold Coast* (Baltimore, Md.: Johns Hopkins University Press, 1982); Craton, *Testing the Chains*; Trevor Burnard, *Mastery, Tyranny, and Desire: Thomas Thistlewood and His Slaves in the Anglo-Jamaican World* (Chapel Hill: University of North Carolina Press, 2004); Mavis Campbell, *The Maroons of Jamaica, 1655–1796: A History of Resistance, Collaboration and Betrayal* (Granby, Mass.: Bergin & Garvey, 1988). Alan Taylor explores a similar dynamic in his *Internal Enemy: Slavery and War in Virginia, 1772-1832* (New York: W. W. Norton, 2013).

14. Alan Gallay, *The Indian Slave Trade: The Rise of the English Empire in the American South, 1670–1717* (New Haven, Conn.: Yale University Press, 2002); William L. Ramsey, *The Yamasee War: A Study of Culture, Economy, and Conflict in the Colonial South* (Lincoln: University of Nebraska Press, 2008); Dubcovsky, *Informed Power*, 161–173; Philip Morgan, *Slave Counterpoint*, 284–296. The notion of "domesticating" slavery was first articulated by Willie Lee Rose in "The Domestication of Domestic Slavery," in *Slavery and Freedom*, ed. William W. Freehling (New York: Oxford University Press, 1982), 18–36. See also Jeffrey R. Young, *Domesticating Slavery: The Master Class in Georgia and South Carolina, 1670–1837* (Chapel Hill: University of North Carolina Press, 1999).

15. Davis, *Problem of Slavery in the Age of Revolution*, 84–163; Jack P. Greene, "'Slavery or Independence': Some Reflections on the Relationship among Liberty, Black Bondage, and Equality in Revolutionary South Carolina," in *Imperatives, Behaviors, and Identities: Essays in Early American Cultural History* (Charlottesville: University of Virginia Press, 1992), 268–289; Andrew Jackson O'Shaughnessy, *An Empire Divided: The American Revolution and the British Caribbean* (Philadelphia: University of Pennsylvania Press, 2000); Robert Olwell, *Masters, Slaves, and Subjects: The Culture of Power in the South Carolina Low Country, 1740–1790* (Ithaca, N.Y.: Cornell University Press, 1998).

16. Christopher Leslie Brown, *Moral Capital: Foundations of British Abolitionism* (Chapel Hill: University of North Carolina Press for the Omohundro Institute, 2006); David Geggus, "Jamaica and the Saint-Domingue Slave Revolt, 1791–1793," *The Americas* 38 (October 1981): 219–233; George D. Terry, "A Study of the Impact of the French Revolution and the Insurrections in

Saint-Domingue upon South Carolina: 1790–1805" (MA thesis, University of South Carolina, 1975); Dale Tomich, "The Second Slavery," in *Through the Prism of Slavery: Labor, Capital, and World Economy* (Lanham, Md.: Rowman and Littlefield, 2004), 56–71; Anthony Kaye, "The Second Slavery: Modernity in the Nineteenth-Century South and the Atlantic World," *Journal of Southern History* 75 (August 2009): 627–634.

17. David Brion Davis, "The Emergence of Immediatism in British and American Antislavery Thought," in *From Homicide to Slavery: Studies in American Culture* (New York, 1986), 245–246 (previously published in *Mississippi Valley Historical Review* 49, no. 2 [September 1962]: 209–230); Sinha, *Slave's Cause*, 103–105.

18. Edward B. Rugemer, *The Problem of Emancipation: The Caribbean Roots of the American Civil War* (Baton Rouge: Louisiana State University Press, 2008), 42–142; Sinha, *Slave's Cause*, 1; Gelien Matthews, *Caribbean Slave Revolts and the British Abolitionist Movement* (Baton Rouge: University of Louisiana Press, 2006); Claudius Fergus, *Revolutionary Emancipation: Slavery and Abolitionism in the West Indies* (Baton Rouge: Louisiana State University Press, 2013); William Freehling, *Prelude to Civil War: The Nullification Controversy in South Carolina, 1816–1836* (New York: Harper & Row, 1965); Lacy Ford, *Origins of Southern Radicalism: The South Carolina Upcountry, 1800–1860* (New York, 1988), 1–144; Manisha Sinha, *The Counter-revolution of Slavery: Politics and Ideology in Antebellum South Carolina* (Chapel Hill: University of North Carolina Press, 2000).

CHAPTER 1   England's First Slave Society, Barbados

1. Winthrop Jordan, *White over Black: American Attitudes toward the Negro, 1550–1812* (Chapel Hill: University of North Carolina Press for the Omohundro Institute, 1968), 44–91; Robin Blackburn, *The Making of New World Slavery: From the Baroque to the Modern, 1492–1800* (London: Verso, 1997), 250–256. The numbers on the transatlantic slave trade used in this study come from the estimates presented in David Eltis et al., Voyages: The Transatlantic Slave Trade Database, accessed May 22, 2015, http://www.slavevoyages.org/voyage/search (hereafter Voyages). The adoption of racial slavery in Providence Island in the 1630s was an important precedent for Barbados, but as the Providence colony failed, England's racial slavery developed first in Barbados; see Karen Ordahl Kupperman, *Providence Island, 1630–1641: The Other Puritan Colony* (New York: Cambridge University Press, 1993).

2. David Eltis, *The Rise of African Slavery in the Americas* (New York: Cambridge University Press, 2000), 193–204; Stuart B. Schwartz, *Tropical Babylons: Sugar and the Making of the Atlantic World* (Chapel Hill: University of North Carolina Press, 2004).

3. David Brion Davis, *The Problem of Slavery in Western Culture* (1966; repr., New York: Oxford University Press, 1988), 169–170.

4. A. J. R. Russell-Wood, "Iberian Expansion and the Issue of Black Slavery: Changing Portuguese Attitudes, 1440–1770," *AHR* 83, no. 1 (Feb-

ruary 1978): 16, 18–19; David Brion Davis, *Inhuman Bondage: The Rise and Fall of Slavery in the New World* (New York, 2006), 82; Stuart Schwartz, *Sugar Plantations in the Formation of Brazilian Society: Bahia, 1550–1835* (New York: Cambridge University Press, 1985), 3–27, 65–66.

5. John William Blake, trans. and ed., *Europeans in West Africa, 1450–1560: Documents* (London: The Hakluyt Society, 1942), 263, 295–297, 299; Elizabeth Donnan, ed., *Documents Illustrative of the History of the Slave Trade to America*, vol. 1 of 4, *1441–1700* (Washington, D.C.: Carnegie Institution, 1930), 44–72.

6. T. Bentley Duncan, *Atlantic Islands: Madeira, the Azores and Cape Verdes in Seventeenth-Century Commerce and Navigation* (Chicago: University of Chicago Press, 1972), 55; Peter C. Mancall, *Hakluyt's Promise: An Elizabethan's Obsession for an English America* (New Haven, Conn.: Yale University Press, 2007).

7. Robert Brenner, *Merchants and Revolution: Commercial Change, Political Conflict, and London's Overseas Traders, 1550–1653* (Princeton, N.J.: Princeton University Press, 1993), 3, 13–14, 122; J. W. Blake, "The Farm of the Guinea Trade," in *Essays in British and Irish History*, ed. H. A. Cronne et al. (London: F. Muller, 1949), 90–91, 95, 103; R. Porter, "The Crispe Family and the African Trade in the Seventeenth Century," *Journal of African History* 9 (1968): 59–61, 64.

8. Philip Curtin, *Rise and Fall of the Plantation Complex: Essays in Atlantic History* (New York: Cambridge University Press, 1990), 3–28.

9. Porter, "Crispe Family," 61–64.

10. Porter, 64–68; Brenner, *Merchants and Revolution*, 115.

11. Carl Bridenbaugh and Roberta Bridenbaugh, *No Peace beyond the Line: The English in the Caribbean, 1624–1690* (New York: Oxford University Press, 1972), 32; Vincent Harlow, *A History of Barbados, 1625–1685* (Oxford: Clarendon Press, 1926), 4; Charles Andrews, *The Colonial Period of American History*, 4 vols. (New Haven, Conn., Yale University Press, 1936), 2:246.

12. Brenner, *Merchants and Revolution*, 118, 184; Edmund S. Morgan, *American Slavery, American Freedom: The Ordeal of Colonial Virginia* (New York: W. W. Norton, 1975), 90, 105.

13. Brenner, *Merchants and Revolution*, 127.

14. Winthrop letters published in N. Darnell Davis, *The Cavaliers and Roundheads of Barbados, 1650–1652* (Georgetown, British Guiana: Argosy Press, 1887), 32–36.

15. Brenner, *Merchants and Revolution*, 129; Russell R. Menard, *Sweet Negotiations: Sugar, Slavery, and Plantation Agriculture in Early Barbados* (Charlottesville: University of Virginia Press, 2006), 18.

16. James Dering to Edward Dering, July 20, 1640, published as "A Letter from Barbados in 1640," *Journal of the Barbados Museum and Historical Society* (hereafter *JBMHS*) 27 (August 1960): 192–193.

17. Hilary Beckles, "Plantation Production and White 'Proto-slavery': White Indentured Servants and the Colonisation of the English West Indies, 1624–1645," *The Americas* 41 (January 1985): 21–45; Menard, *Sweet Negotiations*, 11–28.

18. [William Duke], *Memoirs of the First Settlement of the Island of Barbados* (London, 1743), 20. On the Indians enslaved on Barbados, see Jerome S. Handler, "The Amerindian Slave Population of Barbados in the Seventeenth and Early Eighteenth Centuries," *Caribbean Studies* 8 (January 1969): 38–47.

19. Gary A. Puckrein, *Little England: Plantation Society and Anglo-Barbadian Politics, 1627–1700* (New York: New York University Press, 1984), 31.

20. Jerome Handler and Lon Shelby, eds., "A Seventeenth Century Commentary on Labor and Military Problems in Barbados," *JBMHS* 34 (March 1973): 118.

21. Menard, *Sweet Negotiations*, 34. See also the richly detailed social histories of early Barbados by Simon P. Newman, *A New World of Labor: The Development of Plantation Slavery in the British Atlantic* (Philadelphia: University of Pennsylvania Press, 2013), and Jenny Shaw, *Everyday Life in the Early English Caribbean* (Athens: University of Georgia Press, 2013).

22. Brenner, *Merchants and Revolution*, 191; Voyages.

23. Richard Ligon, *A True & Exact History of the Island of Barbados* (London, 1657), 52; Menard, *Sweet Negotiations*, 17.

24. Puckrein, *Little England*, 25, 65; Brenner, *Merchants and Revolution*, 164–165, 191; Menard, *Sweet Negotiations*, 67.

25. Ligon, *True & Exact History*, 90–91; Dunn, *Sugar and Slaves*, 191–196. See also Peter Thompson, "Henry Drax's Instructions on the Management of a Seventeenth-Century Barbadian Sugar Plantation," *WMQ* 66 (July 2009): 565–604.

26. "A Brief Description of the Ilande of Barbados," in *Colonising Expeditions to the West Indies and Guiana, 1623–1667*, ed. Vincent Harlow (London: The Hakluyt Society, 1925), 44.

27. Ligon, *True & Exact History*, 44, Jerome S. Handler, ed. "Father Antoine Biet's Visit to Barbados in 1654," *JBMHS* 32 (May 1967): 68.

28. Handler, "Biet's Visit," 66–67.

29. John Berkenhead to John Thurloe, February 17, 1654, in *A Collection of the State Papers of John Thurloe*, 7 vols., ed. Thomas Birch (London, 1742), 3:159; Neville C. Connel, ed., "An Account of Barbados in 1654 [Extracted from Henry Whistler's Journal of the West India Expedition, under Date 1654, Sloane MS 3926 British Museum]," *JBMHS* 5 (August 1938): 184–185.

30. Jennifer L. Morgan, *Laboring Women: Reproduction and Gender in New World Slavery* (Philadelphia: University of Pennsylvania Press, 2004); Menard, *Sweet Negotiations*, 44.

31. Menard, *Sweet Negotiations*, 25.

32. Bridenbaugh and Bridenbaugh, *No Peace beyond the Line*, 131; William S. Powell, *The Proprietors of South Carolina* (Raleigh, N.C.: Carolina Charter Tercentenary Commission, 1963), 47; *Oxford Dictionary of National Biography Online*, s.v. "Modyford, Sir Thomas, First Baronet," by Nuala Zahedieh, accessed October 22, 2009, https://doi.org/10.1093/ref:odnb/18871.

33. Ligon, *True & Exact History*, 57–58.

34. Bridenbaugh and Bridenbaugh, *No Peace beyond the Line*, 108; Beauchamp Plantagenet, *A Description of the Province of New Albion* (1648), in *Tracts*

and Other Papers Relating Principally to the Origin, Settlement, and Progress of the Colonies in North America, from the Discovery of the Country to the Year 1776, ed. Peter Force (repr., Gloucester, Mass.: Peter Smith, 1963), 5.

35. [John Jennings], comp., *Acts and Statutes of the Island of Barbados* (London, 1654), 17, 28, 81.

36. Alfred D. Chandler, "The Expansion of Barbados," *JBMHS* 13 (1946): 108.

37. Ligon, *True & Exact History*, 45–46; Puckrein, *Little England*, 109.

38. Robert H. Schomburgk, *The History of Barbados: Comprising a Geographical and Statistical Description of the Island, a Sketch of the Historical Events since the Settlement, and an Account of its Geology and Natural Productions* (London, 1848), 269, 283–284; Puckrein, *Little England*, 111–113.

39. [Duke], *Memoirs of the First Settlement*, 29; [Jennings], *Acts and Statutes*, 176. The first law of slavery, the Act concerning Negroes, passed in 1644, but the text has not survived and Jennings did not record it; see Richard Hall, ed., *Acts Passed in the Island of Barbados from 1643 to 1762* (London, 1764), 450. Jerome Handler helped me contextualize this volume.

40. Rugemer, "Development of Mastery and Race,"432–433.

41. [Jennings], *Acts and Statutes*, 17, 20, 38.

42. [Jennings], 17, 18, 19, 28, 33, 79.

43. *Act to Restrain the Wandring of Servants and Negros*, in [Jennings], 62, 147.

44. "To prevent the injurious keeping of Run-away Negroes," in [Jennings], 43–44.

45. Hilary Beckles, "A 'Riotous and Unruly Lot': Irish Indentured Servants and Freemen in the English West Indies, 1644–1713," *WMQ* 47 (October 1990): 506–507; *Oxford English Dictionary Online*, s.v. "Barbados," accessed June 7, 2010, http://www.oed.com/view/Entry/15375?rskey=Z7TswR&result=1&isAdvanced=false#eid. The first use of this term in print seems to have been in 1655.

46. *England's Slavery or Barbados Merchandize* (London, 1659), 4–5.

47. Beckles, "'Riotous and Unruly,'" 515–516.

48. Charles Andrews, *British Committees, Commissions, and Councils of Trade and Plantations, 1622–1675* (Baltimore, Md.: The Johns Hopkins University Press, 1908), 62–67. See also Abigail L. Swingen, *Competing Visions of Empire: Labor, Slavery, and the Origins of the British Atlantic Empire* (New Haven, Conn.: Yale University Press, 2015), esp. chap. 3.

49. Andrews, *British Committees*, 67–68.

50. "An Act for the good governing of Servants, and ordaining the Rights between Masters and Servants" (hereafter Barbados Servant Act, 1661), in Hall, *Acts Passed*, 35–42; "An Act for the better ordering and governing of Negroes" (hereafter Barbados Slave Act, 1661). Most of the law's provisions have been reprinted in Stanley Engerman, Seymour Drescher, and Robert Paquette, eds., *Slavery* (New York: Oxford University Press, 2001), 105–113. I have also consulted copies of the original manuscript in the British National Archives, Kew, UK, CO 30/2/16–26, which were kindly provided to me by Stanley Engerman.

51. Barbados Servant Act, 1661, preamble, in Hall, *Acts Passed*, 35; Barbados Slave Act, 1661, preamble, in Engerman, Drescher, and Paquette, *Slavery*, 105.

52. Alan Watson, *Slave Law in the Americas* (Athens: University of Georgia Press, 1989), 40–62.

53. Barbados Servant Act, 1661, clauses 1, 9, 10, 11, 14, in Hall, *Acts Passed*, 35, 37–40.

54. Barbados Slave Act, 1661, clause 14, CO 30/2/22.

55. Barbados Slave Act, 1661, clause 1, in Engerman, Drescher, and Paquette, *Slavery*, 106. Other examples of the use of informers include the order that overseers search the slave quarters twice a week for runaways; overseers who neglected this duty, if informed on, were fined one hundred pounds of sugar per offense, to be split between the public and the informer. See Engerman, Drescher, and Paquette, *Slavery*, 107.

56. Barbados Servant Act, 1661, clause 9, in Hall, *Acts Passed*, 37–38; Barbados Slave Act, 1661, clause 6, in Engerman, Drescher, and Paquette, *Slavery*, 107. Clauses 5, 7, 8, 9, 10, 12, and 13 of the Slave Act also relate to runaways; clauses 5, 7, 12, and 13 are reprinted in Engerman, Drescher, and Paquette, *Slavery*, 107–110; clauses 8, 9, and 10 are not in Engerman et al.; see CO 30/2/19–20.

57. See the classic analysis of this process in Morgan, *American Slavery, American Freedom*, 327–331.

58. Barbados Slave Act, 1661, clauses 17, 18, in Engerman, Drescher, and Paquette, *Slavery*, 110–111.

59. Barbados Slave Act, 1661, clause 2, in Engerman, Drescher, and Paquette, *Slavery*, 106; Barbados Servant Act, 1661, clause 4, in Hall, *Acts Passed*, 36.

60. Bradley J. Nicholson, "Legal Borrowing and the Origins of Slave Law in the British Colonies," *American Journal of Legal History* 38 (1994): 38–54; the relevant statutes include 27 Hen. VIII, c. 25 (1535) and 39 Eliz. c. 4 (1597). On animalization and racial slavery, see David Brion Davis, *The Problem of Slavery in the Age of Emancipation* (New York: Alfred A.Knopf, 2014), 3–44.

61. "Item" and "An Act for Punishing Offences, Committed on the Sabbath Day," in [Jennings], *Acts and Statutes*, 28, 79.

62. Barbados Servant Act, 1661, clause 12, in Hall, *Acts Passed*, 39; Barbados Slave Act, 1661, clause 20, in Engerman, Drescher, and Paquette, *Slavery*, 111–112.

63. *Oxford English Dictionary Online*, s.vv. "brutish" and "uncertain," accessed November 4, 2009, http://www.oed.com/view/Entry/24026?redirected From= brutish#eid; http://www.oed.com/view/Entry/210207?rskey=5ythAP& result=1&isAdvanced= false#eid; Deirdre Jackson, *Lion* (London: Reaktion Books, 2010), 76; George M. Fredrickson, *Racism: A Short History* (Princeton, N.J.: Princeton University Press, 2002), 9.

64. Gov. Wm. Ld. Willoughby to the Privy Council, December 16, 1667, in *Calendar of State Papers, Colonial Series, America and the West Indies* (hereafter *CSP*), vol. 5 of 45, *1661–1668*, ed. W. Noel Sainsbury (London: Her Majesty's Stationery Office, 1880), 108–109, 133.

CHAPTER 2   Animate Capital

1. Alan Watson, *Slave Law in the Americas* (Athens: University of Georgia Press, 1989), 40–90; Malick Ghachem, *The Old Regime and the Haitian Revolution* (New York: Cambridge University Press, 2012), 43–76.

2. See the important new histories of the Western Design by Carla Pestana, *The English Conquest of Jamaica: Oliver Cromwell's Bid for Empire* (Cambridge, Mass.: Harvard University Press, 2017); and Kristen Block, *Ordinary Lives in the Early Caribbean: Religion, Colonial Competition, and the Politics of Profit* (Athens: University of Georgia Press, 2012), 119–133.

3. Wm. Goodson to the Navy Commissioners, March 13, 1656, Wm. Godfrey to Robt. Blackborne, April 30, 1656, and Edward D'Oyley to Comm. of the Admiralty, February 1, 1660, in *CSP*, vol. 9, *1675–1676*, ed. W. Noel Sainsbury (London: Her Majesty's Stationery Office, 1893), 108–109, 133. My understanding of the Jamaican Maroons is informed by ethnohistorical work on North America; see Stephan A. Kowalewski, "Coalescent Societies," in *Light on the Path: The Anthropology and History of the Southeastern Indians*, ed. Thomas J. Pluckhahn and Robbie Etheridge (Tuscaloosa: University of Alabama Press, 2006), 94–122.

4. Cornelius Burough to Robt. Blackborne, April 10, 1660, and Cornelius Burough to [Comm. of the Admiralty], May 27, 1660, in *CSP*, 9:133–134, 136–137; Edmund S. Morgan, *American Slavery, American Freedom: The Ordeal of Colonial Virginia* (New York, 1975), 10–13.

5. Trevor Burnard, "European Migration to Jamaica, 1655–1780," *WMQ*, 3rd ser., 53 (1996): 770–772; Charles Andrews, *The Colonial Period of American History*, 4 vols. (New Haven, Conn.: Yale University Press, 1937), 3:13; J. R. McNeil, *Mosquito Empires: Ecology and War in the Greater Caribbean, 1620–1914* (New York: Cambridge University Press, 2010), 97–104.

6. Russell R. Menard, *Sweet Negotiations: Sugar, Slavery, and Plantation Agriculture in Early Barbados* (Charlottesville: University of Virginia Press, 2006), 113; *Journals of the Assembly of Jamaica* (1663–1826; hereafter *JAJ*), vol. 1 of 14, *From January the 20th, 1663–4, . . . to April the 20th, 1709 . . .* (Saint Jago de la Vega, Jamaica, 1811), 1–3. The text for "An Act for the better ordering and governing of Negro Slaves" is only available in manuscript in the British National Archives (hereafter BNA), Kew, UK, Colonial Office Records (hereafter CO), vol. 39, fols. 66–69. This act will hereafter be referred to as the Jamaica Slave Act, 1664. I would like to thank Vincent Brown for providing me with a copy of this manuscript.

7. Wm. Dalyson to Robt. Blackborne, February 22, 1660, and April 11, 1660, in *CSP*, 9:134–135.

8. Richard Sheridan, *Sugar and Slavery: An Economic History of the British West Indies, 1623–1775* (Baltimore, Md.: Johns Hopkins University Press, 1973), 211–212.

9. Voyages; "Observations on the Present State of Jamaica by M. Cranfield," December 14, 1675, in *CSP*, 9:314; Burnard, "European Migration," 771–772.

10. John Style to Wm. Morice, January 1, 1669, in *CSP*, vol. 7, *1669–1674*, ed. W. Noel Sainsbury (London: Her Majesty's Stationery Office, 1889), 5.

11. Minutes of the Council of Jamaica, May 2, 1670, and John Style to the Sec. of State, May 2, 1670, in *CSP*, 7:64–65. The "North Side" was the undeveloped region along the northern coast of the island.

12. Jamaica Council minutes, September 26, 1672, and January 8, 1673, MS 60, vol. 3, pp. 11, 16, National Library of Jamaica, Kingston (hereafter NLJ).

13. Minutes of the Council of Jamaica, June 9, 1672, in *CSP*, 7:365.

14. Minutes of the Council of Jamaica, September 3, 1675, in *CSP*, 9:274; Jonathan Atkins to Joseph Williamson, October 3, 1675, in *CSP*, 9:294; *Great Newes from the Barbadoes; Or, a True and Faithful Account of the Grand Conspiracy of the Negroes againſt the English* (London, 1676), 9–13. Also see Michael Craton, *Testing the Chains: Resistance to Slavery in the British West Indies* (Ithaca, N.Y.: Cornell University Press, 1982), 105–111; and Hilary Beckles, *Black Rebellion in Barbados: The Struggle against Slavery, 1627–1838* (Bridgetown, Barbados: Antilles Publications, 1984), 30–42.

15. The significance of African history in the formation of American slave societies has generated a rich historiographic debate that began with Melville J. Herskovits, *The Myth of the Negro Past* (1941, repr. Boston: Beacon Press, 1958); and has been further developed in: John W. Blassingame, *The Slave Community: Plantation Life in the Antebellum South*, rev. ed (New York, 1978), 3-104; Sterling Stuckey, *Slave Culture: Nationalist Theory and the Foundations of Black America* (New York: Oxford University Press, 1987); John Thornton, *Africa and Africans in the Making of the Atlantic World, 1400–1800*, 2nd ed. (New York: Cambridge University Press, 1998); Michael A. Gomez, *Exchanging Our Country Marks: The Transformation of African Identities in the Colonial and Antebellum South* (Chapel Hill: University of North Carolina Press, 1998); Judith Carney, Black Rice: The African Origins of Rice Cultivation in the Americas (Cambridge, Mass.: Harvard University Press, 2001); and Gwendolyn Midlo Hall, *Slavery and African Ethnicities in the Americas: Restoring the Link*s (Chapel Hill: University of North Carolina Press, 2005).

16. The names listed here are Anglicizations of Akan day names that appear in English sources; see, for example, "List of Negroes & other Slaves on Nutts River Plantation, [Jamaica] . . . 1 December 1789," Egerton 2134, British Library, London. For different views on the significance of slave names, see Jerome S. Handler and JoAnn Jacoby, "Slave Names and Naming in Barbados, 1650–1830," *WMQ* 53 (October 1996): 685–728; Trevor Burnard, "Slave Naming Patterns: Onomastics and the Taxonomy of Race in Eighteenth-Century Jamaica," *Journal of Interdisciplinary History* 31 (Winter 2001): 325–346.

17. Barbara K. Kopytoff, "The Maroons of Jamaica: An Ethnohistorical Study of Incomplete Polities, 1655–1905" (PhD diss., University of Pennsylvania, 1973), 52n11; Jonathan Atkins to Joseph Williamson, October 3, 1675, in *CSP*, 9:294; Voyages. Important works on the Coromantee include John Thornton, "The Coromantees: An African Cultural Group in Colonial North America and the Caribbean," *Journal of Caribbean History* 32 (1998): 161–178; Kwasi Konadu, *The Akan Diaspora in the Americas* (New York: Oxford Univer-

sity Press, 2010); Walter Rucker, *Gold Coast Diasporas: Identity, Culture, and Power* (Bloomington: Indiana University Press, 2015); and Vincent Brown, "The Atlantic Odyssey of an African Insurrection" (paper presented to the Race and Slavery Workshop, Yale University, January 24, 2018).

18. Ivor Wilks, "Wangara, Akan, and Portuguese in the Fifteenth and Sixteenth Centuries" and "Land, Labor, Gold, and the Forest Kingdom of Asante: A Model of Early Change," in *Forests of Gold: Essays on the Akan and the Kingdom of Asante* (Athens: Ohio University Press, 1993), esp. 77, 96. See also Peter Shinnie, "Early Asante: Is Wilks Right?," in *The Cloth of Many Colored Silks: Papers on History and Society Ghanaian and Islamic in Honor of Ivor Wilks*, ed. John Hunwick and Nancy Lawler (Evanston, Ill.: Northwestern University Press, 1996), 195–203. On the seventeenth-century Gold Coast, see Ivor Wilks, *Akwamu 1640–1750: A Study of the Rise and Fall of a West African Empire* (Trondheim, Norway: Department of History, Norwegian University of Science and Technology, 2001); Ray A. Kea, *Settlements, Trade, and Polities in the Seventeenth-Century Gold Coast* (Baltimore, Md.: Johns Hopkins University Press, 1982); and Ivor Wilks, "The Golden Stool and the Elephant Tail: Wealth in Asante," in *Forests of Gold*, 144.

19. Kea, *Settlements, Trade, and Polities*, 130–164; William Bosman, *A New and Accurate Description of the Coast of Guinea* (1705; repr., London, 1967), 183. That Akans were influential in American rebellions has been suggested by Ray A. Kea in "'When I Die, I Shall Return to My Own Land': An 'Amina' Slave Rebellion in the Danish West Indies, 1733–1734," in Hunwick and Lawler, *Cloth of Many Colored Silks*, 159–194. My argument follows Craton, *Testing the Chains*, 99–104.

20. Minutes of the Council of Jamaica, September 3, 1675, in *CSP*, 9:274.

21. "Anonymous History of the Revolted Negroes," Add. MSS 12431, British Library, London, and James Knight, "History of Jamaica," Add. MSS 12419, British Library, both reproduced on microfilm in *Materials on the History of Jamaica in the Edward Long Papers* (Wakefield, UK: Microform Academic Publishers, 2006), reels 6, 8; minutes of the Council of Jamaica, December 15, 1675, in *CSP*, 9:315; Journal of the Council of Jamaica, January 23, 1676, in *CSP*, 9:339.

22. Larry Gragg, *Quaker Community on Barbados: Challenging the Culture of the Planter Class* (Columbia: University of Missouri Press, 2009), 53–55; "Complaint and Request of the People Called Quakers," July 6, 1676, in *CSP*, 9:426; "An Act to prevent the people called Quakers from Bringing Negroes to their Meetings," in Richard Hall, *Acts Passed in the Island of Barbados from 1643 to 1762* (London, 1764), 97–28.

23. "Memorandum by the Bishop of London concerning the Church in Barbadoes," [August 28, 1680], in *CSP*, vol. 10, *1677–1680*, ed. W. Noel Sainsbury and J. W. Fortescue (London: Her Majesty's Stationery Office, 1896), 590; Journal of the Lords of Trade and Plantations, October 8, 1680, in *CSP*, 10:611. See also Richard Dutton's speech to the Assembly of Barbados, March 30, 1681, in *CSP*, vol. 11, *1681–1685*, ed. J. W. Fortescue (London: Her Majesty's Stationery Office, 1898), 24–25.

24. Journal of the Lords of Trade and Plantations, May 30, 1676, in *CSP*, 9:394.

25. "An Act for Regulating Servants," in *Acts of Assembly, Passed in the Island of Jamaica, From 1681, to 1737, Inclusive*, comp. John Baskett (London, 1738), 2, 4. In 1661, the Barbados Assembly had ordered all freeholders who owned more than twenty acres of land to keep "one Christian servant" for every twenty acres of land owned; see Barbados Slave Act, 1661, clause 22, in *Slavery*, ed. Stanley Engerman, Seymour Drescher, and Robert Paquette (New York: Oxford University Press, 2001), 112.

26. Edmund Morgan, *American Slavery, American Freedom*, 327–331.

27. "Act for Regulating Servants," in Baskett, *Acts of Assembly*, 2.

28. On the historiography regarding the origins of "white," see Edward B. Rugemer, "The Development of Mastery and Race in the Comprehensive Slave Codes of the Greater Caribbean during the Seventeenth Century," *WMQ* 70 (July 2013): 446n62.

29. [John Jennings], comp., *Acts and Statutes of the Island of Barbados* (London, 1654), 20; "An Account of the Carybee Islands," [May 12, 1669], William Blathwayt Papers, BL 368, Huntington Library, San Marino, Calif.; *JAJ*, 1:7; Sir Thomas Lynch to Lord Cornbury, March 29, 1672, Papers Relating to the West Indies, 1654–1682, Add. MS 11410, British Library, London; A. S. Salley Jr., ed., *Records in the British Public Record Office Relating to South Carolina: 1663–[1710]* (hereafter SC Transcripts), vol. 1 of 5, *1663–1684* (Atlanta, Ga.: printed for the Historical Commission of South Carolina by Foote and Davies, 1928), 38; "Account of Passengers, Servants, and Slaves Brought to Jamaica," March 25, 1679, in *CSP*, 10:344.

30. Lords of Trade and Plantations to Gov. Thomas Lynch, February 17, 1683, in *CSP*, 11:386; *JAJ*, 1:65.

31. For the membership of the 1683 Assembly, see *JAJ*, 1:64–78. For further information on these men, see Walter Augustus Feurtado, *Official and Other Personages of Jamaica, from 1655 to 1790* (Kingston, Jamaica: W. A. Feurtado's Sons, 1896).

32. "An Act for the Better Ordering of Slaves," in *The Laws of Jamaica, Passed by the Assembly, and Confirmed by his Majesty in Council, April 17, 1684* (London, 1684), 147 (hereafter Jamaica Slave Act, 1684).

33. Burnard, "European Migration," 772.

34. Voyages; David Buisseret, ed., *Jamaica in 1687: The Taylor Manuscript at the National Library of Jamaica* (Kingston, Jamaica: University of the West Indies Press, 2008), 276; Richard Dunn, *Sugar and Slaves: The Rise of the Planter Class in the English West Indies, 1624–1713* (1972; repr., Chapel Hill: University of North Carolina Press for the Omohundro Institute, 2000), 217, 260.

35. Barbados Slave Act, 1661, clause 1, in Engerman, Drescher, and Paquette, *Slavery*, 106; Jamaica Slave Act, 1684, 140.

36. Jamaica Slave Act, 1684, 140–141; David Brion Davis, *The Problem of Slavery in Western Culture* (1966; repr., New York: Oxford University Press, 1988), 98–102.

37. Jamaica Slave Act, 1684, 141, 144, 148.

38. Barbados Slave Act, 1661, preamble, in Engerman, Drescher, and Paquette, *Slavery*, 105.

39. "An Act declaring the Negro Slaves of this Island to be Real Estates," in Richard Hall, *Acts Passed*, 64–65.

40. Claire Priest, "Creating an American Property Law: Alienability and Its Limits in American History," *Harvard Law Review* 120 (December 2006): 398–407, 413; "Act declaring the Negro Slaves of this Island to be Real Estates" and "A Declarative Act upon the Act making Negroes Real Estate," in Richard Hall, *Acts Passed*, 64, 93–94.

41. Jamaica Slave Act, 1684, 140. On the importance of credit to the transatlantic slave trade, see Jacob M. Price, "Credit in the Slave Trade and Plantation Economies," in *Slavery and the Rise of the Atlantic System*, ed. Barbara L. Solow (New York: Cambridge University Press, Cambridge, UK, 1991), 293–340.

42. William Blackstone, *Commentaries on the Laws of England*, vol. 2 of 4 (Oxford: Clarendon, 1766), 389–391. On animalization and racial slavery, see David Brion Davis, *The Problem of Slavery in the Age of Emancipation* (New York: Alfred A. Knopf, 2014), 3–44.

43. Blackstone, *Commentaries*, 2:391–393.

44. Andrews, *Colonial Period*, 3:183–185; Wesley Frank Craven, *The Southern Colonies in the Seventeenth Century, 1607–1689* (Baton Rouge: Louisiana State University Press, 1949), 321; Robert M. Weir, *Colonial South Carolina: A History* (1983, repr. Columbia: University of South Carolina Press, 1997), 48–49. William S. Powell, *The Proprietors of Carolina* (Raleigh, N.C.: Carolina Charter Tercentenary Commission, 1963), 12–49; Warren M. Billings, *Sir William Berkeley and the Forging of Colonial Virginia* (Baton Rouge: University of Louisiana State University, 2004), 142, 156–158.

45. Langdon Cheves, ed., *The Shaftesbury Papers and Other Records Relating to Carolina and the First Settlement on the Ashley River prior to the Year 1676* (1897; repr., Charleston: South Carolina Historical Society, 2010), 10–11, 44; Alexander S. Salley, ed., *Narratives of Early Carolina, 1650–1708* (New York, 1911), 37.

46. Richard Waterhouse, *A New World Gentry: The Making of a Merchant and Planter Class in South Carolina, 1670–1770* (Charleston, S.C.: History Press, 2005), 22–24.

47. The text of the first draft of the Fundamental Constitutions is in *North Carolina Charters and Constitutions, 1578–1698* (Raleigh, N.C.: Carolina Charter Tercentenary Commission, 1963), 132–152. On some recent historiography, see Rugemer, "Development of Mastery and Race," 451n80.

48. Salley, *Narratives*, 114–119; Alan Gallay, *The Indian Slave Trade: The Rise of the English Empire in the American South, 1670–1717* (New Haven, Conn.: Yale University Press, 2002), 7, 10.

49. Maureen Meyers, "From Refugees to Slave Traders: The Transformation of the Westo Indians," in *Mapping the Mississippian Shatter Zone: The Colonial Indian Slave Trade and Regional Instability in the American South*, ed. Robbie

Ethridge and Sheri M. Shuck-Hall (Lincoln: University of Nebraska Press, 2009), 90–95.

50. Alexander Moore, ed., *Nairne's Muskhogean Journals: The 1708 Expedition to the Mississippi River* (Jackson: University of Mississippi Press, 1988), 34, 43; Orlando Patterson, *Slavery and Social Death: A Comparative Study* (Cambridge, Mass.: Harvard University Press, 1982), 106–115; Christina Snyder, *Slavery in Indian Country: The Changing Face of Captivity in Early America* (Cambridge, Mass., 2010), 47–49; Brett Rushforth, *Bonds of Alliance: Indigenous and Atlantic Slaveries in New France* (Chapel Hill: University of North Carolina Press for the Omohundro Institute, 2012), 3–9.

51. On slaving, see Joseph Miller, *The Problem of Slavery as History* (New Haven, Conn.: Yale University Press, 2012).

52. Henry Woodward to Sir John Yeamans, September 10, 1670, and Stephen Bull to Lord Shaftesbury, September 12, 1670, in Cheves, *Shaftesbury Papers*, 187, 194.

53. Salley, *Narratives*, 105.

54. Lord Shaftesbury to Sir John Yeamans, April 10, 1671, and Lord Shaftesbury to Henry Woodward, April 10, 1671, in Cheves, *Shaftesbury Papers*, 314–316; "Proprietors Instructions to Governor Joseph West," [May 1674], in SC Transcripts, 1:26.

55. Shaftesbury to Joseph West, May 23, 1674, in Cheves, *Shaftesbury Papers*, 446–447; Verner W. Crane, *The Southern Frontier, 1670–1732* (1929; repr., Tuscaloosa: University of Alabama Press, 2004), 18.

56. Instructions for Henry Woodward, May 23, 1674, and Lord Shaftesbury to Joseph West, May 23, 1674, in Cheves, *Shaftesbury Papers*, 446–447; Alexander S. Salley, ed., *Journal of the Grand Council of South Carolina, August 25, 1671–June 24, 1680* (Columbia, S.C.: Historical Commission of South Carolina, 1907), 63–64.

57. Henry Woodward to Lord Shaftesbury, December 31, 1674, in Cheves, *Shaftesbury Papers*, 456–462.

58. Henry Woodward to Lord Shaftesbury, December 31, 1674.

59. Proprietors to Gov. Joseph West, April 10, 1677, in SC Transcripts, 1:59; Eric E. Bowne, "'Carryinge Awaye Their Corne and Children': The Effects of Westo Slave Raids on the Indians of the Lower South," in Ethridge and Shuck-Hall, *Mapping the Mississippian Shatter Zone*, 104–114.

60. Memorial of the Lords Proprietor, October 22, 1677, in SC Transcripts, 1:60; Salley, *Journal of the Grand Council*, 82.

61. Salley, *Journal of the Grand Council*, 83–85.

62. M. Eugene Sirmans, *Colonial South Carolina: A Political History, 1663–1763* (Chapel Hill: University of North Carolina Press for the Omohundro Instiute, 1966), 17–18, 27.

63. Lords Proprietors to the Governor and Council, February 21, 1680, and September 30, 1680, in SC Transcripts, 1:104–105, 255–257; Crane, *Southern Frontier*, 19–21; Matthew H. Jennings, "Violence in a Shattered World," in Ethridge and Shuck-Hall, *Mapping the Mississippian Shatter Zone*, 286.

64. Lord Shaftesbury to John Yeamans, [May 1670], in Cheves, *Shaftesbury Papers*, 164; Richard Waterhouse, "England, the Caribbean, and the Settlement of Carolina," *American Studies* 9 (1975): 259–281.

65. This and the following paragraphs are based on an analysis of all of the warrants for lands claiming Negroes, transcribed in Alexander S. Salley, ed., *Warrants for Lands in South Carolina*, 3 vols. (Columbia, S.C.: Historical Commission of South Carolina, 1910–1915), vol. 1, *1672–1679* (1910), 52–54, 60–61, 72, 82, 84, 87, 89, 110, 112–113; vol. 2, *1680–1692* (1911), 55–56, 61, 70, 76–77, 86, 98, 101, 109, 133, 147–148, 152–153, 163, 165, 168, 176, 182, 185–187, 195, 205, 212, 215; vol. 3, *1692–1711* (1915), 46.

66. Philip Morgan, *Slave Counterpoint: Black Culture in the Eighteenth-Century Chesapeake and Lowcountry* (Chapel Hill: University of North Carolina Press for the Omohundro Institute, 1998), 82–83; Jennifer L. Morgan, *Laboring Women: Reproduction and Gender in New World Slavery* (Philadelphia: University of Pennsylvania Press, 2004), 78–83.

67. Salley, *Warrants for Lands*, 2:109.

68. Salley, 2:212, 3:46.

69. *American National Biography Online*, s.v. "Johnson, Nathaniel," by Alexander Moore, accessed November 15, 2009, https://doi.org/10.1093/anb/9780198606697.article.0100457; Salley, *Warrants for Lands*, 2:107, 116.

70. Sir Nathaniel Johnson to Lords of Trade and Plantations, April 20, 1689, in *CSP*, vol. 13, *1689–1692*, ed. J. W. Fortescue (London: Her Majesty's Stationery Office, 1901), 25–29; Dunn, *Sugar and Slaves*, 133–134; Steve Pincus, *1688: The First Modern Revolution* (New Haven, Conn., Yale University Press, 2009).

71. Mabel L. Webber, ed., "Letters from John Stewart to William Dunlop [April 27, 1690]," *South Carolina Historical and Genealogical Magazine* (hereafter *SCHGM*) 32 (January 1931): 6–7, 16–17, 22–23.

72. J. G. Dunlop, "William Dunlop's Mission to St. Augustine in 1688," *SCHGM* 34 (January 1933): 20; Jane Landers, "Gracia Real de Santa Teresa de Mose: A Free Black Town in Spanish Colonial Florida," *AHR* 95 (February 1990): 13–14; Crane, *Southern Frontier*, 30–31; Edward Randolph to the Board of Trade, March 16, 1699, in Salley, *Narratives*, 204–206.

73. Landers, "Gracia Real de Santa Teresa de Mose," 14n29.

74. Landers, 14n29.

75. Dunlop, "William Dunlop's Mission," 3–4, 25; Landers, "Gracia Real de Santa Teresa de Mose," 13, 14n29.

76. Sirmans, *Colonial South Carolina*, 46–50; Weir, *Colonial South Carolina*, 67–68.

77. "An Act for the Better Ordering of Slaves," in *The Statutes at Large of South Carolina*, ed. Thomas Cooper and David J. McCord, vol. 7 of 10, *Acts Relating to Charleston, Courts, Slaves, and Rivers*, ed. David J. McCord (Columbia, S.C.: printed by A. S. Johnston, 1840), 343–347; Rugemer, "Development of Mastery and Race," 430, 452–453; David Barry Gaspar, "With a Rod of Iron: Barbados Slave Laws as a Model for Jamaica, South Carolina, and

Antigua, 1661–1697," in *Crossing Boundaries: Comparative History of Black People in Diaspora*, ed. Darlene Clark Hine and Jacqueline McLeod (Bloomington: Indiana University Press, 1999), 343–366.

78. Salley, *Warrants for Lands*, 2:215.

79. Sirmans, *Colonial South Carolina*, 46–50; Dunn, *Sugar and Slaves*, 162–163; membership of the 1696 Assembly drawn from Feurtado, *Official and Other Personages of Jamaica*.

80. Burnard, "European Migration," 772; Voyages.

81. "An Act for the Better Ordering of Slaves," 1696, in *Acts of the General Assembly*, vol. 6, March 2–16, 1696 (Governor Archdale's Laws), fol. 60, South Carolina Department of Archives and History, Columbia, S.C. (hereafter 1696 South Carolina Slave Act); "An Act for the better Order and Government of Slaves," in Baskett, *Acts of Assembly*, 81 (hereafter 1696 Jamaica Slave Act).

82. 1696 Jamaica Slave Act, 73.

83. Lt. Gov. Molesworth to William Blathwayt, August 29, 1685, in *CSP*, vol. 12, *1685–1688*, ed. J. W. Fortescue (London: Her Majesty's Stationery Office, 1899), 82–85; "Anonymous History of the Revolted Negroes," fol. 69; Knight, "History of Jamaica," Add. MSS 12418, fol. 132; Dunn, *Sugar and Slaves*, 260–261; Voyages.

84. Knight, "History of Jamaica," Add. MSS 12418, fol. 142, and Add. MSS 12419, fol. 96; 1696 Jamaica Slave Act, 73; Earl of Inchiquin to the Lords of Trade, August 31, 1690, in *CSP*, 13:315–317; Jamaica Council minutes, February 22, 1692, vol. 11, NLJ; Dunn, *Sugar and Slaves*, 261.

85. 1696 Jamaica Slave Act, 73, 79.

86. 1696 Jamaica Slave Act, 73, 76, 79.

87. 1696 South Carolina Slave Act, fol. 60.

88. 1696 South Carolina Slave Act, fol. 62.

89. Buisseret, *Jamaica in 1687*, 275–276; Winthrop Jordan, *White over Black: American Attitudes toward the Negro, 1550–1812* (Chapel Hill: University of North Carolina Press for the Omohundro Institute, 1968), 155–156.

90. Quoted in Jane Landers, *Black Society in Spanish Florida* (Urbana: University of Illinois Press, 1999), 25.

91. Stuart B. Schwartz, *Sugar Plantations in the Formation of Brazilian Society: Bahia, 1550–1835* (New York: Cambridge University Press, 1985), xiv,, 98–131; Ira Berlin, *Many Thousands Gone: The First Two Centuries of Slavery in North America* (Cambridge, Mass.: Harvard University Press, 1998), 5; Philip Morgan, *Slave Counterpoint*, xxi, n10. Morgan also provides further examples of slaveholders treating their slaves as cattle; see *Slave Counterpoint*, 271.

92. Quoted in Gary S. Dunbar, "Colonial Carolina Cowpens," *Agricultural History* 35 (July 1961): 127–128.

93. Peter Wood, *Black Majority: Negroes in Colonial South Carolina from 1670 through the Stono Rebellion* (New York: Alfred A. Knopf, 1974), 30–33.

94. Davis, *Problem of Slavery in Western Culture*, 56; Keith Bradley, *Slaves and Masters in the Roman Empire: A Study in Social Control* (New York: Oxford University Press, 1987), 128; Bernard Lewis, *Race and Slavery in the Middle East: An Historical Inquiry* (New York: Oxford University Press, 1990), 52;

Frederick Bowser, *The African Slave in Colonial Peru, 1524–1650* (Stanford, Calif.: Stanford University Press, 1974), 155, 196–197; Colin Palmer, *Slaves of the White God: Blacks in Mexico, 1570–1650* (Cambridge, Mass.: Harvard University Press, 1976), 123; David Brion Davis, *Inhuman Bondage: The Rise and Fall of Slavery in the New World* (New York: Oxford University Press, 2006), 33, 68–69.

95. Jordan, *White over Black*, 44; Robin Blackburn, *The Making of New World Slavery: From the Baroque to the Modern, 1492–1800* (London: Verso, 1997), 250–256.

CHAPTER 3   The Domestication of Slavery in South Carolina

1. "A Report of the Governor and Council, 1708," in H. Roy Merrens, ed., *The Colonial South Carolina Scene: Contemporary Views, 1697–1774* (Columbia: University of South Carolina Press, 1977), 33.

2. "Report of the Governor," 33; Denise I. Bossy, "Godin & Co.: Charleston Merchants and the Indian Trade, 1674–1715," *South Carolina Historical Magazine* (hereafter *SCHM*) 114 (April 2013): 96–131.

3. "Report of the Governor," 32; Ira Berlin, *Many Thousands Gone: The First Two Centuries of Slavery in North America* (Cambridge, Mass.: Belknap Press of Harvard University Press, 1998), 370; Trevor Burnard, "European Migration to Jamaica, 1655–1780," *WMQ*, 3rd ser., 53 (1996): 771–772.

4. "Report of the Governor," 32.

5. "An Act for the Encouragement of the Importation of White Servants," in *The Statutes at Large of South Carolina*, ed. Thomas Cooper and David J. McCord, vol. 2, *Acts from 1682 to 1716*, ed. Thomas Cooper (Columbia, S.C.: printed by A. S. Johnston, 1837), 153–156.

6. R. Ferguson, *Present State of Carolina* (London, 1682), 5; "An Act for Raising and Enlisting Slaves," in Cooper and McCord, *Statutes at Large of South Carolina*, vol. 7, *Acts Relating to Charleston, Courts, Slaves, and Rivers*, ed. David J. McCord (Columbia, S.C.: printed by A. S. Johnston, 1840), 348, 350; "Report of the Governor," 32.

7. "An Act to Settle a Patroll," in Cooper and McCord, *Statutes at Large of South Carolina*, 2:254–255.

8. "Report of the Governor," 34; Peter H. Wood, "The Changing Population of the Colonial South: An Overview by Race and Region, 1685–1790," in *Powhatan's Mantle: Indians in the Colonial Southeast*, ed. Peter H. Wood et al. (Lincoln: University of Nebraska Press, 1989), 38.

9. Matthew H. Jennings, "Violence in a Shattered World," in *Mapping the Mississippian Shatter Zone: The Colonial Indian Slave Trade and Regional Instability in the American South*, ed. Robbie Ethridge and Sheri M. Shuck-Hall (Lincoln: University of Nebraska Press, 2009), 285–286; "An Act to Limit the Bounds of the Yamasee Settlement, to Prevent Persons from Disturbing Them with Their Stocks, and to Remove Such as Are Settled," in Cooper and McCord, *Statutes at Large of South Carolina*, 2:317–318; see also Map 2, p. 104.

10. J. Leitch Wright Jr., *The Only Land They Knew: The Tragic Story of the American Indians in the Old South* (New York: Free Press, 1981), 150; Alexander

Moore, ed., *Nairne's Muskhogean Journals: The 1708 Expedition to the Mississippi River* (Jackson: University of Mississippi Press, 1988), 47; Peter C. Mancall, *Deadly Medicine: Indians and Alcohol in Early America* (Ithaca, N.Y.: Cornell University Press, 1995).

11. Verner W. Crane, *The Southern Frontier, 1670–1732* (1929; repr., Tuscaloosa: University of Alabama Press, 2004), 56–57.

12. Crane, 73–74.

13. Crane, 78–80; Christina Snyder, *Slavery in Indian Country: The Changing Face of Captivity in Early America* (Cambridge, Mass.: Harvard University Press, 2010), 74; Wright, *Only Land They Knew*, 147; Moore, *Nairne's Muskhogean Journals*, 75. Historian Alan Gallay has estimated that between twenty-four thousand and fifty-one thousand enslaved Indians were shipped out of Charles Town in the years before 1715; *The Indian Slave Trade: The Rise of the English Empire in the American South, 1670–1717* (New Haven, Conn.: Yale University Press, 2002), 299.

14. Alexander S. Salley, ed., *Warrants for Lands in South Carolina*, vol. 3, *1692–1711* (Columbia, S.C.: Historical Commission of South Carolina, 1915), 152; Gallay, *Indian Slave Trade*, 156–164.

15. Gallay, *Indian Slave Trade*, 164; Moore, *Nairne's Muskhogean Journals*, 43.

16. Gallay, *Indian Slave Trade*, 164–170.

17. An Act for Regulating the Indian Trade and Making it Safe to the Publick, in Cooper and McCord, *Statutes at Large of South Carolina*, 2:309–316 (quotes on 309).

18. Thomas Nairne to the Earl of Sunderland, October 16, 1708, deposition of Francis Oldfield, June 26, 1708, and deposition of Janet Tibbs (undated). Papers of Charles Spencer, 3rd Earl of Sunderland, Huntington Library, San Marino, Calif.; Gallay, *Indian Slave Trade*, 222.

19. [Thomas Nairne], *A Letter from South Carolina* (London, 1710), 8, 10, 12–13, 15–17.

20. [Nairne], 31–32, 44.

21. [Nairne], 18.

22. [Nairne], 52–53.

23. Letters of Edward Hyrne, in Merrens, ed., *Colonial South Carolina Scene*, 17–19; Walter Edgar, ed., *Biographical Directory of the South Carolina House of Representatives*, vol. 2 of 5, *The Commons House of Assembly, 1692–1775*, ed. Walter Edgar and N. Louise Bailey (Columbia: University of South Carolina Press, 1977), 350–353; Pauline M. Loven, "Hyrne Family Letters, 1699–1757," *SCHM* 102 (January 2001): 27–46.

24. "Rice Exported from South Carolina and Georgia: 1698–1790," in *Historical Statistics of the United States Online*, millennial ed., ed. Susan Carter et al. (Cambridge: Cambridge University Press, 2006), https://hsus.cambridge.org/HSUSWeb/search/searchessaypdf.do?id= Eg1160-1165; Elizabeth Donnan, ed., *Documents Illustrative of the History of the Slave Trade to America*, vol. 4 of 4, *The Border Colonies and the Southern Colonies* (Washington, D.C.: Carnegie Institution, 1935), 243, 255; on the politics of the monopoly see William A. Pettigrew,

Freedom's debt: The Royal African Company and the Politics of the Atlantic Slave Trade, 1672–1752 (Chapel Hill: University of North Carolina Press, 2013).

25. Voyages.

26. Voyages; minutes of the Committee of Goods, August 15, 1704, October 28, 1704, October 27, 1705, October 12, 1706, Treasury Office (T) 70/130, fols. 20, 29, 40, 58–59, British National Archives, Kew, UK. Jamineau invested in seven more voyages, but all were destined for the Caribbean, where, presumably, the profits were more ensured. I'd like to thank Anne Ruderman for these references to Jamineau.

27. Voyages; Richard Splatt to Samuel Barons, July 20, 1720 (and marginal notations), CO 5/382, fol. 66, British National Archives, Kew, UK.

28. Nigel Tattersfield, *The Forgotten Trade: comprising the log of the Daniel and Henry of 1700 and accounts of slave trade from the minor ports of England, 1698–1725* (London: J. Cape, 1991), 291–293; Anne Ruderman, "Supplying the Slave Trade: How Europeans Met African Demand for European Manufactured Products, Commodities and Re-exports, 1670–1790" (PhD diss., Yale University, 2016), 155–191.

29. St. Julien R. Childs, ed., "A Letter Written in 1711 by Mary Stafford to Her Kinswoman in England," *South Carolina Historical Magazine* 81 (January 1980): 4; Frank Klingberg, ed., *The Carolina Chronicle of Dr. Francis Le Jau* (Berkeley: University of California Press, 1956), 52, 55.

30. "An Act for the Better Ordering and Governing of Negroes and Slaves," [1712], in Cooper and McCord, *Statutes at Large of South Carolina*, 7:352–365. For an earlier revision of the slave code, see L. H. Roper, "The 1701 'Act for the Better Ordering of Slaves': Reconsidering the History of Slavery in Proprietary South Carolina," *WMQ* 64 (April 2007): 395–418.

31. [Edwin C. Holland], *A Refutation of the Calumnies Circulated against the Southern & Western States, respecting the Institution and Existence of Slavery* (Charleston, 1822), 64–65. Holland was principally concerned with the Charleston conspiracy of 1822, but he did considerable archival research for the history of insurrections at the core of this pamphlet.

32. "An Act for the Governing of Negroes," in *Acts Passed in the Island of Barbados from 1643 to 1762*, ed. Richard Hall (London, 1764), 116. In 1727, in response to slave stealers from Martinique and elsewhere, the Barbados Assembly followed South Carolina's lead by threatening slave stealers with execution; see "An Act to Prevent the Vessels That Trade Here, to and from Martinico or Elsewhere, from Carrying Off Negro, Indian, or Mulatto Slaves," in Hall, 283–284.

33. "Act for the Better Ordering and Governing of Negroes," [1712], 357, 359–360.

34. "Act for the Better Ordering and Governing of Negroes," [1712], 355; "An Additional Act to an Act Entitled 'An Act for the Better Ordering and Governing of Negroes and Slaves,'" in Cooper and McCord, *Statutes at Large of South Carolina*, 7:366; "Act for the Governing of Negroes," in Hall, *Acts Passed*, 116.

35. "Act for the Better Ordering and Governing of Negroes," [1712], 354; "Additional Act," 368; Philip Morgan, *Slave Counterpoint: Black Culture in the Eighteenth-Century Chesapeake and Lowcountry* (Chapel Hill: University of North Carolina Press for the Omohundro Institute, 1998), 186. These laws were not taken from Barbados.

36. Gallay, *Indian Slave Trade*, 259–314.

37. Le Jau to the Secretary, February 20, 1712, in Klingberg, *Carolina Chronicle*, 108–109.

38. Le Jau to the Secretary, February 20, 1712, 109.

39. Le Jau to the Secretary, August 30, 1712, February 23, 1713, and January 22, 1714, in Klingberg, *Carolina Chronicle*, 121, 129, 137. On the New York conspiracy, see Jill Lepore, *New York Burning: Liberty, Slavery, and Conspiracy in Eighteenth-Century Manhattan* (New York: Alfred A. Knopf, 2005).

40. W. L. McDowell, ed., *Journals of the Commissioners of the Indian Trade, September 10–August 29, 1718* (Columbia: South Carolina Archives Dept., 1955), 3–4.

41. McDowell, 11, 27.

42. David Crawley to William Byrd, July 30, 1715, and Journals of the Board of Trade, July 26, 1715, in *Records in the British Public Record Office Relating to South Carolina, 1663–1782*, 36 vols. (Columbia, S.C.: South Carolina Department of Archives and History, 1971), reel 2, vol. 6, pp. 140, 110–111 (hereafter SC Trans./microfilm.) For a characterization of Wright, see Gallay, *Indian Slave Trade*, 245–250.

43. Gallay, *Indian Slave Trade*, 328.

44. McDowell, *Journals of the Commissioners*, 65.

45. Huspaw King to Charles Craven King [governor of South Carolina], quoted in William L. Ramsey, *The Yamasee War: A Study of Culture, Economy, and Conflict in the Colonial South* (Lincoln: University of Nebraska Press, 2008), 228; "An Account of the Breaking Out of the Yamasee War [*Boston News*, June 13, 1715]," in B. R. Carroll, ed., *Historical Collections of South Carolina*, 2 vols. (New York: Harper & Brothers, 1836), 2:572.

46. "An Act to Confirm and Justify the Proceedings of the . . . Governor" [passed May 10, 1715], "An Act to Impower [Governor Craven] . . . to Carry on and Prosecute the War" [passed May 10, 1715], "An Act to Impower [Governor Craven] . . . to raise Forces [passed May 13, 1715], and Le Jau to the Secretary, May 14, 1715, in Klingberg, *Carolina Chronicle*, 155.

47. "Account of the . . . Yamassee War," in Carroll, *Historical Collections of South Carolina*, 2:572; Journals of the Board of Trade, July 16, 1715, in SC Trans./microfilm, reel 2, vol. 6, p. 138.

48. Board of Trade to Lord Stanhope, July 19, 1715, and [letter dated July 19, 1715, Charles Town], in SC Trans./microfilm, reel 2, vol. 6, pp. 101, 103–109.

49. Letter of Sam Eveleigh, October 7, 1715, and letter of John Tate, October 16, 1715, in SC Trans./microfilm, reel 2, vol. 6, pp. 119, 123; Francis Le Jau to the Secretary, November 16, 1716, in Klingberg, *Carolina Chronicle*, 188.

50. "Extract of a Memorial from the Agents of South Carolina," December 17, 1716, and "Humble Address of the Representatives & Inhabitants

of South Carolina," [February 24, 1717], CO 5/382, fol. 40 (oversize), fols. 55–56, British National Archives, Kew, UK.

51. John Alexander Moore, "Royalizing South Carolina: The Revolution of 1719 and the Evolution of Early South Carolina Government" (PhD diss., University of South Carolina, 1991), 199; Robert M. Weir, *Colonial South Carolina: A History* (Columbia: University of South Carolina Press, 1997), 100–102.

52. "A View of the Trade of South Carolina," [February 1723], in SC Trans./microfilm, reel 2, vol. 10 (unpaginated); Converse Clowse, *Economic Beginnings in Colonial South Carolina* (Columbia: University of South Carolina Press, 1971), 208–209; Crane, *Southern Frontier*, 328–329.

53. Voyage nos. 16101, 76487, 76685, in Voyages; Tattersfield, *Forgotten Trade*, 293; Donnan, *Documents Illustrative*, 4:259.

54. Voyages. Other investors included Noblet Ruddock, Robert Addison, Isaac Hobhouse, William Challoner, William Baker, Thomas Dolman, Henry Forrest, John Hawkins, Christopher Jones, William Brandale, Edmund Saunders, William Gibbons, and Andrew Allen. On the importance of the rice-growing peoples of West Africa, see Daniel C. Littlefield, *Rice and Slaves: Ethnicity and the Slave Trade in Colonial South Carolina* (Baton Rouge: Louisiana State University Press, 1981); and Judith Carney, *Black Rice: The African Origin of Rice Cultivation in the Americas* (Cambridge, Mass.: Harvard University Press, 2001).

55. [Report of Governor Robert Johnson, January 12, 1719], in Merrens, *Colonial South Carolina Scene*, 58; [James Glen], *A Description of South Carolina* (1749), repr. in *Colonia South Carolina: Two Contemporary Descriptions*, ed. Chapman Milling (Columbia: University of South Carolina Press, 1951), 30, 81; "Rice Exported"; Donnan, *Documents Illustrative*, 4:273; Voyages.

56. John J. TePaske, "The Fugitive Slave: Intercolonial Rivalry and Spanish Slave Policy, 1687–1764," in *Eighteenth-Century Florida and Its Borderlands*, ed. Samuel Proctor (Gainesville: University of Florida Press, 1975), 4. TePaske makes this argument and cites Crane, *Southern Frontier*, chap. 4, but neither scholar offers evidence that Carolina's Indian allies returned runaway Africans. Though speculative, the argument remains plausible.

57. "A List of the Negroe & Indian Slaves taken in the Year 1715 & carried to St. Augustine in the time of Our Indian War," CO 5/382, fol. 102, British National Archives, Kew, UK. For a rich account of postwar South Carolina, see Alejandra Dubcovsky, *Informed Power: Communication in the Early American South* (Cambridge, Mass.: Harvard University Press, 2016), 184–187.

58. Journals of the Board of Trade, and James Cochran and Jonathan Drake to Mr. Boone, March 8, 1718, in SC Trans./microfilm, reel 2, vol. 7, p. 100; [unsigned] to Mr. Boone, June 24, 1720, in SC Trans./microfilm, reel 2, vol. 8, pp. 24–25. In addition to this plot, nineteen enslaved Carolinians escaped to Saint Augustine in 1720 and 1721; see "A List of Negroes taken in the Year 1720 & 1721," CO 5/382, fol. 103, British National Archives, Kew, UK.

59. Information on these legislators was gleaned from Edgar, *Biographical Directory*, vol. 1, *Session Lists, 1692–1973*, ed. Joan Schreiner Reynolds Faunt and Robert E. Rector with David K. Bowden (Columbia: University of South

Carolina Press, 1974), 49–51; and Edgar, *Biographical Directory*, 2, 53–54, 74–75, 77–78, 139, 145, 152–154, 182–183, 234–235, 244–247, 313–314, 325–326, 339–340, 362–363, 365, 368–369, 405–406, 419, 443, 468–469, 472–473, 510, 513, 550, 601, 605, 614–615, 631–635, 639–640, 696–697, 703–705, 712–714, 724–725.

We have information on thirty-five members of this assembly: fourteen were born in the colony; twenty-seven were planters; seventeen were militia officers; and ten were involved in the Indian trade.

60. "An Act for the Better Ordering and Governing of Negroes and Other Slaves," [1722], in Cooper and McCord, *Statutes at Large of South Carolina*, 7:371–373, 376–377.

61. "Act for the Better Ordering and Governing of Negroes," [1722], 374, 378.

62. "Act for the Better Ordering and Governing of Negroes," [1722], 382.

63. "Act for the Better Ordering and Governing of Negroes," [1722], 382; *South Carolina Gazette*, March 23–30, 1734, and October 29–November 5, 1737; "An Act for the Better Ordering and Governing of Negroes," [1735], in Cooper and McCord, *Statutes at Large of South Carolina*, 7:385, 396. Slave marketers were probably women, but evidence from the 1730s is not clear on this point; see Robert Olwell, "'Loose, Idle and Disorderly: Slave Women in the Eighteenth Century Charleston Marketplace," in *More Than Chattel: Black Women and Slavery in the Americas*, ed. David B. Gaspar and Darlene C. Hine (Bloomington: Indiana University Press, 1996), 97–110.

64. "Act for the Better Ordering and Governing of Negroes," [1712], 352; "Act for the Better Ordering and Governing of Negroes," [1722], 371.

65. Governor Francis Nicholson to [Governor Antonio de Benavides], February 27, 1723, in SC Trans., reel 3, vol. 11, p. 34; Jane Landers, "Gracia Real de Santa Teresa de Mose: A Free Black Town in Spanish Colonial Florida," *AHR* 95 (February 1990): 15; Jane Landers, "Spanish Sanctuary: Fugitives in Florida, 1687–1790," *Florida Historical Quarterly* 62 (January 1984): 298–299; A. S. Salley, ed., *Journal of the Commons House of Assembly of South Carolina, February 23, 1724–June 1, 1725* (Columbia: Printed For the Historical Commission of South Carolina, 1945), 128.

66. Governor Middleton to President of the Board of Trade, June 13, 1728, in SC Trans./microfilm, reel 3, vol. 13, pp. 61–69.

67. Governor Middleton to President of the Board of Trade, June 13, 1728; Governor Middleton to Wargent Nicholson, Factor of the Royal Assiento Company in the Havana, March 27, 1728, in SC Trans./microfilm, reel 3, vol. 13, pp. 61–69, 187–189.

68. Deposition of James Howell, sworn in the Council Chamber April 21, 1738, in SC Trans./microfilm, reel 5, vol. 19, pp. 73–75; Landers, "Spanish Sanctuary," 301; Dubcovsky, *Informed Power*, 194–195.

69. J. H. Easterby, ed., *Journal of the Commons House of Assembly of South Carolina, November 10, 1736–June 7, 1739* (Columbia: Historical Commission of South Carolina, 1951), 578, 596, 631–632 (hereafter *JCHA, 1736–1739*); Oglethorpe to the Trustees of Georgia, July 4, 1739, CO 5/640, part 3, fol. 337, BNA.

70. *JCHA, 1736–1739*, 578, 590, 596, 631; *South Carolina Gazette*, January 25, 1739. The assembly passed an Act for the Further Security and Better Defence of This Province on September 18, 1738, but the text has been lost. Letters of Governor Montiano, January 3, 1739, and April 2, 1739, in *Collections of the Georgia Historical Society*, 19 vols. (Savannah: Georgia Historical Society, 1909), 7:29–30.

71. *JCHA, 1736–1739*, 673, 677, 698; Cooper and McCord, *Statutes at Large of South Carolina*, vol. 3, *Acts from 1716, Exclusive, to 1752, Inclusive*, ed. Thomas Cooper (Columbia, S.C.: printed by A. S. Johnston, 1838), 525. Cooper and McCord found only the title of the law that resulted from these deliberations, An Act for the Better Security of The Inhabitants of This Province against the Insurrections and Other Wicked Attempts of Negroes and Other Slaves. We do have part of the text, as reprinted in the *South Carolina Gazette*, August 11–18, 1739.

72. *South Carolina Gazette*, April 5–12, 1739.

73. Voyages.

74. This and the following paragraphs are based on the advertisements from 1732 to 1739 reprinted in Lathan A. Windley, ed. *Runaway Slave Advertisements: A Documentary History from the 1730s to 1790*, 4 vols. (Westport, Conn.: Greenwood Press, 1983), 3:1–39 (examples from pp. 13, 16, and 27); Morgan, *Slave Counterpoint*, 151–152.

75. See Chapter 2, notes 15, 16, 17.

76. David Northrup, "Igbo and Igbo Myth: Culture and Ethnicity in the Atlantic World, 1600–1850," *Slavery and Abolition* 21 (December 2000): 1–20; Gwendolyn Midlo Hall, *Africans in Colonial Louisiana: The Development of Afro-Creole Culture in the Eighteenth Century* (Baton Rouge: Louisiana State University Press, 1992), chap. 4; Philip Curtin, *Economic Change in Precolonial Africa: Senegambia in the Era of the Slave Trade* (Madison: University of Wisconsin Press, 1975), 178; Windley, *Runaway Slave Advertisements*, 3:8. Richard Anderson helped me understand the term "Pawpaw."

77. Windley, *Runaway Slave Advertisements*, 3:33.

78. John K. Thornton, "African Dimensions of the Stono Rebellion," *AHR* 96 (October 1991): 1101–1113.

79. "Account of the Negroe Insurrection in South Carolina," in *Stono: Documenting and Interpreting a Southern Slave Revolt*, ed. Mark M. Smith (Columbia: University of South Carolina Press, 2005), 14; "A Ranger's Report of Travels with General Oglethorpe, 1739–1742," in Smith, 7; J. H. Easterby, ed., *Journal of the Commons House of Assembly of South Carolina, Sept. 12, 1739–March 26, 1741* (Columbia: Printed for the Historical Commission of South Carolina, 1952), 64 (hereafter *JCHA, 1739–1741*).

80. "Account of the Negroe Insurrection," 15; Lt. Gov. William Bull to Board of Trade, October 5, 1739, in Smith, *Stono*, 17; *JCHA, 1739–1741*, 158, 230; Dubcovsky, *Informed Power*, 1–2.

81. "Account of the Negroe Insurrection," 15; Lt. Gov. William Bull to BT, October 5, 1739, 17; *Boston Gazette*, November 1–8, 1739, in Smith, *Stono*, 12; "Ranger's Report of Travels," 7.

82. Journal of William Stephens, [September 13, 1739], in Smith, *Stono*, 4; *JCHA, 1739–1741*, 16, 36, 50, 64–65, 86, 91, 100–101; "Thomas Elliott," in Edgar, *Biographical Directory*, 2:226.

83. *JCHA, 1739–1741*, 69. As in 1722, the Assembly of 1740 consisted almost entirely of planters—80 percent—and included men such as Henry Hyrne, whose father we have met, and Francis Le Jau, who became a planter despite his father's antislavery discontent with the colony; see Edgar, *Biographical Directory*, 1:80–83, 2:351–353, 2:399–400.

84. "An Act for the Better Strengthening of This Province," in Cooper and McCord, *Statutes at Large of South Carolina*, 3:556–557; Walter B. Edgar, ed., *The Letterbook of Robert Pringle*, 2 vols. (Columbia: University of South Carolina Press, 1972), 1:174–175, 186, 190.

85. Voyages; Willie Lee Rose, "The Domestication of Domestic Slavery," in *Slavery and Freedom*, ed. William W. Freehling (New York: Oxford University Press, 1982), 18–36.

86. "An Act for the Better Ordering and Governing of Negroes and Other Slaves," [1740], in Cooper and McCord, *Statutes at Large of South Carolina*, 7:397.

87. "Act for the Better Ordering and Governing of Negroes," [1740], 398.

88. "Act for the Better Ordering and Governing of Negroes," [1740], 397, 399, 413, 408, 412, 398, 413; *JCHA, 1739–1741*, 68.

89. "Act for the Better Ordering and Governing of Negroes," [1740], 411.

90. "Act for the Better Ordering and Governing of Negroes," [1740], 416–417.

91. Klaus G. Loewald, Beverly Starika, and Paul S. Taylor, eds., "Johann Martin Bolzius Answers a Questionnaire on Carolina and Georgia," *WMQ* 14 (April 1957): 221, 233–234, 255.

92. Loewald, Starika, and Taylor, 234, 259. I would like to thank my colleagues Emily Greenwood and Noel Lenski for help with the Latin.

93. Loewald, Starika, and Taylor, "Johann Martin Bolzius," 236; Richard S. Dunn, *A Tale of Two Plantations: Slave Life and Labor in Jamaica and Virginia* (Cambridge, Mass.: Harvard University Press, 2014), 32–35; Vincent Brown, *The Reaper's Garden: Death and Power in the World of Atlantic Slavery* (Cambridge, Mass.: Harvard University Press, 2008), 51–57; Barry Higman, *Slave Population and Economy in Jamaica, 1807–1834* (1976; repr., Kingston, Jamaica: University of the West Indies Press, 1995), 61–62.

94. Loewald, Starika, and Taylor, "Johann Martin Bolzius," 256, 260.

95. Governor William Bull [Jr.] to the Board of Trade, November 30, 1770, in Merrens, *Colonial South Carolina Scene*, 260; George C. Rogers Jr., *Charleston in the Age of the Pinckneys* (Norman: University of Oklahoma Press, 1969), 3.

CHAPTER 4   The Militarization of Slavery in Jamaica

1. Jamaica was also a key strategic asset of the British Empire, which maintained its largest naval squadron on the island. This fact contributed to the militarization of this slave society, but in my view the internal conflict between the masters and the slaves was primary; on the international dimen-

sions, see Richard Pares, *War and Trade in the West Indies, 1739–1763* (Oxford: Clarendon, 1936). For two very different but complementary portraits of eighteenth-century Jamaica, see Trevor Burnard, *Mastery, Tyranny, and Desire: Thomas Thistlewood and His Slaves in the Anglo-Jamaican World* (Chapel Hill: University of North Carolina Press, 2004); and Vincent Brown, *Reaper's Garden: Death and Power in the World of Atlantic Slavery* (Cambridge, Mass.: Harvard University Press, 2008).

2. Voyages (1700–1740).

3. John Kofi Fynn, *Asante and Its Neighbours, 1700–1807* (Evanston, Ill.: Northwestern University Press, 1971), 29.

4. Fynn, 31; Paul Lovejoy, *Transformations in Slavery: A History of Slavery in Africa* (New York: Cambridge University Press, 1983), 81.

5. Rebecca Shumway, *The Fante and the Transatlantic Slave Trade* (Rochester, N.Y.: University of Rochester Press, 2011), 90, 95; Robin Law, "Warfare on the West African Slave Coast, 1650–1850," in R. Brian Ferguson and Neil L. Whitehead, eds., *War in the Tribal Zone: Expanding States and Indigenous Warfare* (Santa Fe, N.M.: School of American Research Press, 2000), 114–118.

6. James Knight, "History of Jamaica," Add. MSS 12419, British Library, London, reproduced on microfilm in *Materials on the History of Jamaica in the Edward Long Papers* (Wakefield, UK: Microform Academic Publishers, 2006), reel 6.

7. Martha Beckwith, *Black Roadways: A Study of Jamaican Folk Life* (Chapel Hill: University of North Carolina Press, 1929), 185, 191; Joseph J. Williams, "The Maroons of Jamaica," *Anthropological Series of the Boston College Graduate School* 3, no. 4 (1938): 385–386; Mervyn C. Alleyne, *Roots of Jamaican Culture* (London: Pluto Press, 1988), 123; Jean Besson, "Caribbean Common Tenures and Capitalism: The Accompong Maroons of Jamaica," *Plantation Society in the Americas* 4 (Winter 1997): 216; Kenneth M. Bilby, *True-Born Maroons* (Gainesville: University of Florida Press, 2005), 4, 479.

8. Fynn, *Asante and Its Neighbors*, 57–60. For an insightful account of the formation of novel ethnicities in the Americas, see James Sidbury and Jorge Canizares-Esguerra, "Mapping Ethnogenesis in the Early Modern Atlantic," *WMQ* 68 (April 2011): 181–208; see also the citations in chap. 2 fn. 15.

9. Knight, "History of Jamaica," Add. MSS 12419, fols. 92–93, reel 6; "Anonymous History of the Revolted Negroes," Add. MSS 12431, fol. 70, British Library, reproduced on microfilm in *Materials on the History of Jamaica*, reel 8.

10. "Anonymous History," fol. 70.

11. "Anonymous History," fol. 71; Knight, "History of Jamaica," Add. MSS 12419, fol. 94.

12. "Anonymous History," fols. 74, 77; Knight, "History of Jamaica," Add. MSS 12419, fol. 96.

13. "An Act for Raising Parties," in *Acts of the Assembly Passed in the Island of Jamaica from the Year 1681 to the Year 1769*, 2 vols. (Kingston, Jamaica, 1787), 1:66.

14. Thomas Martyn to Lord Carlisle, July 25, 1702, Papers of the Earl of Carlisle Relating to Jamaica, Sloane MSS 2724, fol. 227, British Library; Lt.

Gov. Beckford to the BT, in *CSP*, vol. 20, *1702*, ed. Cecil Headlam (London: Her Majesty's Stationery Office, 1912), 600–602.

15. "Anonymous History," fols. 69–71; "A Plan of Port Antonio and parts adjacent, with the settlements of the REBELLIOUS NEGROES . . . 1730," Map Collection, Sterling Library, Yale University. For the belief in "nations" among the Windward Maroons today, see Bilby, *True-Born Maroons*, 79–87.

16. Voyages (1705–1720); "An Act for the more effectual punishing of Crimes committed by Slaves," in *Acts of the Assembly*, 1:113–116.

17. "An Act for the Encouragement of voluntary Parties to suppress rebellious and runaway Negroes," in *Acts of the Assembly*, 1:117–118.

18. "An Act to Encourage the Settling the North-east Part of this Island," in *Acts of the Assembly*, 1:121–125.

19. Duke of Portland to BT, August 2, 1725, in *CSP*, vol. 34, *1724–1725*, ed. Cecil Headlam and Arthur Percival Newton (London: His Majesty's Stationery Office, 1936), 408; "Account of what money has been paid for . . . Negroes taken in rebellion," Colonial Office: Jamaica, Original Correspondence (hereafter CO)140/29, fols. 71–73, British National Archives, Kew, UK.; Governor Hunter to the BT, August 3, 1728, in *CSP*, vol. 36, *1728–1729*, ed. Cecil Headlam and Arthur Percival Newton (London: His Majesty's Stationery Office, 1937), 167.

20. "Anonymous History," fol. 72.

21. Knight, "History of Jamaica," Add. MSS 12418, fol. 272; Thomas Beckford, Speaker of the House, Address to the Assembly, passed March 18, 1729, CO 137/18, fol. 82; "A Calculation of the Quantities & Value of ye Produce . . . of Jamaica [1729]," CO 137/18, fols. 102–103; Voyages (1725–1729). All figures are in pounds sterling.

22. Extracts of soldiers' letters from Jamaica, February 12, 1730–March 20, 1730, in CO 137/19, fols. 25–28.

23. Noel Deerr, *The History of Sugar*, 2 vols. (London, 1949), 1:198.

24. Hunter to the BT, January 16, 1731, CO 137/20, fol. 45; Col. Hayes to Maj. Sowle, Jamaica, March 11, 1730, CO 137/19, fol. 27; "Examination of Nicholas Physham," June 18, 1730, CO 137/18, fol. 84. Knight also wrote that while the troops were not useful against the Maroons, they "kept the Negroes in awe" and more easily managed on the plantations; see "History of Jamaica," Add. MSS 12418, fol. 273.

25. This narrative of the expedition is based on "Examination of Nicholas Physham"; "Examination of Samuel Soaper," June 25, 1730; and "Examination of Captain Ashcroft," June 18, 1730, CO 137/18, fols. 84–88.

26. Robert Hunter to BT, November 13, 1731, CO 137/19, fol. 112.

27. Capt. Thomas Peters to Gov. Robert Hunter, March 22, 1731, and Capt. Andrew Morrison to Gov. Robert Hunter, March 22, 1731, MS 438, NLJ.

28. Robert Hunter to the BT, September 20, 1732, CO 137/20, fols. 104–105.

29. This and the following paragraphs are based on "Extract of Capt. Lambe's Journal," [September 22–24, 1732], enclosed in Hunter to BT, November 18, 1732, CO 137/20, fols. 112–115.

30. "Capt. Lambe's Journal," fol. 114.

31. Jasper Ashworth to [Governor Hunter], June 7, 1733, and J. Draper to [Governor Hunter], June 7, 1733, both enclosed in Hunter to BT, July 7, 1733, CO 137/20, fols. 144–151. Also reported in *Gentleman's Magazine* (hereafter *GM*) 3 (June 1733): 329.

32. Hunter to BT, July 7, 1733; Council and Assembly of Jamaica to Sir Chaloner Ogle, July 6, 1733, in *CSP*, vol. 40, *1733*, ed. Cecil Headlam and Arthur Percival Newton (London: His Majesty's Stationery Office, 1939), 140–144.

33. "Extract of Lt. [Thomas] Swanton's Journal," [August 21, 1733], CO 137/20, fols. 192–193; Knight, "History of Jamaica," Add. MSS 12418, fols. 276, 278. Also reported in *GM* 3 (November 1733): 606.

34. "Confession made by Seyrus, A Negro belonging to Mr. Geo. Taylor," enclosed in Hunter to BT, August 25, 1733, CO 137/20, fol. 179; see also *CSP*, 40:172–173.

35. "Confession made by Seyrus, A Negro belonging to Mr. Geo. Taylor"; see also *CSP*, 40:172–173. The role of Jewish merchants was reported in the (London) *Grub-Street Journal*, October 3, 1734.

36. Hunter to BT, October 13 and November 11, 1733, and Hunter to the Duke of Newcastle, October 20, 1733, in *CSP*, 40:212–216, 222–223, 234–235.

37. "Further Examination of Sarra, alias Ned, taken by order of H.E.," [October 1, 1733], enclosed in Hunter to BT, October 13, 1733, in *CSP*, 40:212–216.

38. Hunter to BT, December 24, 1733, in *CSP*, 40:273–274.

39. Memorial transcribed in Knight, "History of Jamaica," Add. MSS 12418, fols. 279–280, also enclosed in Hunter to the BT, March 11, 1734, in *CSP*, vol. 41, *1734–1735* (London: Her Majesty's Stationery Office, 1953) 48–52; see also Hunter to the Duke of Newcastle, February 9, 1734, in *CSP*, 41:32.

40. *The Historical Register*, vol. 17, *For the Year 1732* (London: printed by S. Nevill, April 1732), 140; *GM* 3 (June 1733): 329; *GM* 4 (May 1734): 277; *Weekly Register* (London), June 15, 1734; *Grub-Street Journal* (London), October 3, 1734.

41. David Brion Davis, *The Problem of Slavery in Western Culture* (1966; repr., New York: Oxford University Press, 1988), 291–332; Steve Pincus, *The Heart of the Declaration: The Founders Case for an Activist Government* (New Haven, Conn.: Yale University Press, 2016), 35–36; "An Act for rendering the Colony of Georgia more defencible by prohibiting the imporation and use of black slaves or negroes," [January 9, 1734], in *Colonial Records of the State of Georgia*, 31 vols., ed. Allen D. Chandler (Atlanta, Ga., 1904), 1:50–52.

42. William Byrd II to the Earl of Egmont (John Perceval), July 12, 1736, in *The Correspondence of the Three William Byrds of Westover, Virginia, 1684–1776*, 2 vols., ed. Marion Trilling (Charlottesville: University of Virginia Press, 1977), 1:488. I thank Steven Pincus for this reference.

43. "This is a Black, *beware of him good Countryman*," *The Prompter* (London), January 10, 1735; Dickson D. Bruce Jr., *The Origins of African American Literature, 1680–1865* (Charlottesville: University of Virginia Press, 2001), 27–28.

44. "This is a Black, *beware of him good Countryman*," *The Prompter* (London), January 10, 1735.

45. "This is a Black, *beware of him good Countryman*," *GM* 5 (January 1735): 21–23.

46. Thomas W. Krise, *Caribbeana: An Anthology of English Literature of the West Indies* (Chicago: University of Chicago Press, 1999), 108; [Robert Robertson], *A Letter to the Right Reverend, the Lord Bishop of London: from an inhabitant of His Majesty's Leeward-Caribee Islands* (London: printed for J. Wilford, 1730), 10–11, 13 (quote). Valuable accounts of Robertson include Christopher Leslie Brown, *Moral Capital: Foundations of British Abolitionism* (Chapel Hill: University of North Carolina Press for the Omohundro Institute, 2006), 33–37; and Travis Glasson, *Mastering Christianity: Missionary Anglicanism and Slavery in the Atlantic World* (New York: Oxford University Press, 2011), 98–99.

47. "*The Speech of* Caribeus *in Answer to* Moses Bon Saam," *GM* 5 (February 1735): 91–93. Robertson acknowledges his authorship in "Case of Negroes and Planters Stated," *GM* 11 (March 1741): 145.

48. [Robert Robertson], *The Speech of Mr. John Talbot Campo-bell* (1736), reprinted in Krise, *Caribbeana*, 108–140 (quote, 109); see also Thomas W. Krise, "True Novel, False History: Robert Robertson's Ventriloquized Ex-Slave in 'The Speech of Mr. John Talbot Campo-Bell' (1736)," *Early American Literature* 30, no. 2 (1995): 152–164.

49. [Robertson], 109–111.

50. [Robertson], 122, 136–137.

51. "Some Considerations relating to the present State of Jamaica with respect to their Runaway Negroes. 16 October 1734," enclosed in Martin Bladen to Sir Robert Walpole, October 31, 1734, MS 1020, NLJ. "Polanky" refers to the Spanish name for a settlement of runaways, *palenque*, and indeed they were pervasive in Spanish America and Brazil; see Richard Price, *Maroon Societies: Rebel Slave Communities in the Americas*, 2nd ed. (Baltimore, Md.: Johns Hopkins University Press, 1979), esp. parts 1 and 4.

52. Knight, "History of Jamaica," Add. MSS 12418, fols. 284, 287; Hunter to the Duke of Newcastle, February 27, 1734, in *CSP*, 41:44–45; Ayscough to the Duke of Newcastle, October 21, 1734, in *CSP*, 41:257–259; Ayscough to the Duke of Newcastle, December 6, 1734, in *CSP*, 41:321–322. Most of these soldiers were drawn from regiments stationed in Gibraltar. See *Weekly Register* (London), June 15, 1734.

53. On the archeological evidence of this reoccupation, see Bilby, *True-Born Maroons*, 25.

54. Knight, "History of Jamaica," Add. MSS 12418, fol. 287; John Ayscough to the BT, February 27, 1735, in *CSP*, 41:383–385.

55. John Ayscough to the BT, February 27, 1735, 41:383–385.

56. Knight, "History of Jamaica," Add. MSS 12418, fols. 297–298, 300–301; John Gregory to the BT, July 7, 1736, CO 137/22, fol. 94; John Gregory to the BT, May 23, 1737, CO 137/22, fol. 141.

57. Knight, "History of Jamaica," Add. MSS 12418, fol. 301; "Database of Jamaican Inventories in the Jamaica National Archives, Spanish Town," created by Trevor Burnard, in possession of the author (hereafter Burnard database, 2010).

58. "Account of Negroes and Cattle in the Island of Jamaica [in 1734, 1740, and 1745]," in *JAJ*, vol. 1, *From January the 20th, 1663–4, . . . to April the 20th, 1709* . . . [Saint Jago de la Vega, Jamaica, 1811], 1: appendix, 49.

59. Frank Cundall, *The Governors of Jamaica in the First Half of the Eighteenth Century* (London: The West India Committee, 1937), 171–172.

60. Trelawney to the Duke of Newcastle, June 30, 1737, and "Humble Memorial of Edward Trelawney [1737]," CO 137/56, fols. 74–75, 76–80.

61. Trelawney to Newcastle, December 4, 1738, CO 137/56, fol. 158.

62. Trelawney to Newcastle, December 4, 1738, fol. 159.

63. Jamaica Council Minutes, July 5, 1738, CO 140/29.

64. Jamaica Council Minutes, July 5, 1738; "An Act for confirming the Articles executed by Colonel John Guthrie, Lieutenant Francis Sadler, and Cudjoe the Commander of the Rebels," in *Acts of Assembly*, 1:231; John Guthrie to Edward Trelawney, February 17, 1739, in Jamaica Council Minutes, February 24, 1739, CO 140/29; "Sugar Plantations in Jamaica . . . Christmas 1739," Edward Long Papers, Add. MSS 12431, fol. 153, in *Materials on the History of Jamaica*, reel 8; "Journal of the Expedition to Cudjoe Town by Lt Francis Sadler," in Jamaica Council Minutes, February 24, 1739; Guthrie to Trelawney, February 17, 1739, CO 137/56, fol. 193.

65. "Journal of the Expedition to Cudjoe Town by Lt Francis Sadler"; Knight, "History of Jamaica," Add. MSS 12419, fol. 99; Guthrie to Trelawney, February 18, 1739, CO 137/56, fol. 195.

66. Guthrie to Trelawney, February 18, 1739, fol. 199.

67. Trelawney to Guthrie, February 23, 1739; "[Trelawney's] Thoughts upon Cudjoe's proposal of submission," in Council Minutes, February 24, 1739.

68. Treaty with Captain Cudjoe and others, enclosed in Trelawney to the Board of Trade, March 30, 1739, CO 137/23, fols. 5–10.

69. Knight, "History of Jamaica," Add. MSS 12419, fols. 101–102.

70. Mavis Campbell, *The Maroons of Jamaica, 1655–1796: A History of Resistance, Collaboration and Betrayal* (Granby, Mass., 1988), 175–176, 283n33.

71. Bilby, *True-Born Maroons*, 263–273.

72. Trelawney to the Duke of Newcastle, June 30, 1739, CO 137/56, fol. 236; "An Act for confirming the Articles; An Act for confirming the Articles executed by Colonel Robert Bennett and Quao, the Commander of the Rebels," in *Acts of the Assembly*, 1:239–242; "An Act to encourage Colonel Cudjo and Captain Quaw, and the several Negroes under their Command . . . to pursue and take up runaway Slaves," in *Acts of the Assembly*, 1:251–252; Add. MSS 12435, in *Materials on the History of Jamaica*, reel 8; Edward Long, *History of Jamaica*, 3 vols. (London, 1774), 2:340.

73. Edward Trelawney to the Board of Trade, November 21, 1741, CO 137/23, fol. 149. For one example of these laws, see "An Act to enable the Inhabitants of the Parish of St. Anne to build a Barrack at or near the Head of Rio Bueno," in *Acts of Assembly*, 1:215–216.

74. Edward Trelawney to the Board of Trade, November 21, 1741, fol. 152.

75. Edward Trelawney to Henry Pelham, May 27 and June 1, 1741, Pelham Collection, MS 306, NLJ.

76. "Sugar Plantations in Jamaica . . . Christmas 1739," Add. MSS 12431; "Charges and Expenses in Jamaica," August 31, 1752, and "An Estimate of the Number of Negroes and Cattle in Jamaica . . . in 1768," Add. MSS 12435, in *Materials on the History of Jamaica*, reel 8.

77. Voyages; Deerr, *History of Sugar*, vol. 1.

78. [Edward Trelawney], *An Essay Concerning Slavery And the Danger Jamaica is Exposed to from the Too Great Number of Slaves, and the Too Little care that is taken to Manage them, And a Proposal to Prevent the Further Importation of Negroes* (London, 1746), 22; *JAJ*, vol. 4, *From March the 18th, 1745–46, . . . to December the 22d, 1756 . . .* (Spanish Town, Jamaica: printed by Alexander Aikman, 1797), 19–20. This pamphlet has long been attributed to Trelawney, and textual evidence suggests his authorship.

79. [Trelawney], *Essay Concerning Slavery*, 2, 5–6, 8; Davis, *Problem of Slavery in Western Culture*, 407. For a recent and insightful work on the laws of war, see John Fabian Witt, *Lincoln's Code: The Laws of War in American History* (New York: Free Press, 2012).

80. [Trelawney], *Essay Concerning Slavery*, 25–26. This story does not actually appear in the *Persian Letters*, and I do not know where Trelawney read it.

81. [Trelawney], 18–19, 22–23.

82. [Trelawney], 34–35.

83. [Trelawney], 24, 39, 46.

84. [Trelawney], 46, 48–50, 55–56.

85. Cundall, *Governors of Jamaica*, 200; Voyages.

86. David Northrup, *Trade without Rulers: Pre-colonial Economic Development in South Eastern Nigeria* (Oxford: Clarendon Press, 1978), 89–107; Fynn, *Asante and Its Neighbors*, 81–83; Robin Law, *The Oyo Empire: A West African Imperialism in the Era of the Transatlantic Slave Trade* (Oxford: Clarendon Press, 1977), 164–165.

87. Long, *History of Jamaica*, 2:447; Monica Schuler, "Akan Slave Rebellions in the British Caribbean" (1970), in *Caribbean Slave Society and Economy*, ed. Hilary Beckles and Verene Shepherd (Kingston, Jamaica: Ian Randle, 1991), 373–386; Michael Craton, *Testing the Chains: Resistance to Slavery in the British West Indies* (Ithaca, N.Y.: Cornell University Press, 1982), 99–104, 125–139; Burnard, *Mastery, Tyranny, and Desire*, 171; Vincent Brown, *Reaper's Garden*, 149.

88. The information about the name Tacky comes from my Ghanaian friend Wendell Adjetey.

89. Maria Alessandra Bollettino, "Slavery, War, and Britain's Atlantic Empire: Black Soldiers, Sailors and Rebels in the Seven Years War" (PhD diss., University of Texas, Austin, 2009), 200; Lt. Gov. Moore to the Board of Trade, April 19, 1760, CO 137/32, fol. 1; Long, *History of Jamaica*, 2:448; entry for December 5, 1760, in *JAJ*, vol. 5, *From September the 27th, 1757, . . . to September the 12th, 1766 . . .* (Spanish Town, Jamaica: printed by Alexander Aikman, 1798), 232; Richard Hart, *Slaves Who Abolished Slavery*, vol. 2, *Blacks in Rebellion* (Kingston: Institute of Social and Economic Research, University of the West Indies, Jamaica, 1985), 131. For an online interactive account of this rebellion and it suppression by colonial forces, see Vincent Brown, ed., Slave

Revolt in Jamaica, 1760–1761: A Cartographic Narrative, accessed August 12, 2016, http://revolt.axismaps.com/project.html.

90. *JAJ*, 5:232; Henry Moore to the Board of Trade, April 19, 1760, and Council Minutes, April 17, 1760, CO 137/32, fols. 1, 3–4; Burnard database; Trevor Burnard and John Garrigus, *The Plantation Machine: Atlantic Capitalism in French Saint-Domingue and British Jamaica* (Philadelphia, 2015), 129.

91. Henry Moore to the Board of Trade, June 9, 1760, CO 137/32, fol. 7; *JAJ*, 5:231–232.

92. Henry Moore to the Board of Trade, June 9, 1760, fol. 7; Douglas Hall, ed., *In Miserable Slavery: Thomas Thistlewood in Jamaica, 1750–1786* (Kingston, Jamaica: University of the West Indies Press, 1989), 105.

93. Law, "Warfare," 114–115.

94. "A List of White People killed since the Commencement of the Rebellion in Westmoreland 25 May 1760," ADM 1/236, fol. 60, British National Archives; Hall, *In Miserable Slavery*, 97; *JAJ*, 5:335.

95. Council Minutes, July 14, 1760, CO 137/32, fols. 23–24; letter of Charles Holmes, June 11, 1760, ADM 1/236, fol. 45, British National Archives.

96. Letter of Charles Holmes, June 11, 1760, fol. 45; Council Minutes, July 14, 1760, fol. 23; Hall, *In Miserable Slavery*, 98–100.

97. Letter of Charles Holmes, June 11, 1760, fol. 45; Council Minutes, July 14, 1760, fol. 23; Hall, *In Miserable Slavery*, 100–101.

98. *JAJ*, 5:231–232; Council Minutes, July 14, 1760, fol. 23.

99. Long, *History of Jamaica*, vol. 2, 457; Hall, *In Miserable Slavery*, 99, 109.

100. Hall, *In Miserable Slavery*, 104; Lawrence-Archer, J. H., ed., *Monumental Inscriptions of the British West Indies from the Earliest Date* (London: Chatto and Windus, 1875), 232; Long, *History of Jamaica*, 2:455–456; see also *JAJ*, 5:233, 240.

101. Hall, *In Miserable Slavery*, 107; letter of Charles Holmes, July 9, 1760, ADM 1/236, fol. 61, British National Archives.

102. "Testimony of John Venn," in Council Minutes, December 18, 1760, CO 140/43 [unpaginated]; *JAJ*, 5:229; Burnard database.

103. Hall, *In Miserable Slavery*, 112.

104. *JAJ*, 5:206, 234–236.

105. "An Act to oblige the Justices and Vestry Men of several Parishes in this Island, to build, repair, and keep in repair Barracks, Magazines, and Arsenals," in *Acts of Assembly*, 2:47–49.

106. "Act to oblige," 47.

107. "Act to oblige," 47–48.

108. "An Act to remedy the Evils arising from irregular Assemblies of Slaves," in *Acts of Assembly*, 2:52–57.

109. "Act to remedy the Evils," 52, 55. The cultural politics of this critical moment in Jamaican history have received considerable attention from Brown, *Reaper's Garden*, 144–152; Jerome S. Handler and Kenneth M. Bilby, *Enacting Power: The Criminalization of Obeah in the Anglophone Caribbean, 1760–2011* (Kingston, Jamaica: University of the West Indies Press, 2012), 46; Diana Paton, *The Cultural Politics of Obeah: Religion, Colonialism and Modernity in the Caribbean World* (New York: Cambridge University Press, 2015), chap. 1.

110. Hall, *In Miserable Slavery*, 113; "Copy of Governor Lyttleton's answers to the heads of inquiry relative to the state of the island of Jamaica . . . in 1764," in *JAJ*, vol. 1, appendix, 52.

111. Long, *History of Jamaica*, 2:462, 471.

112. Deerr, *History of Sugar*, 1:198; Voyages.

CHAPTER 5   The Transformation of Slavery's Politics

1. "Anglicanus," *London Chronicle*, September 29–October 2, 1764, 317. The *Gentleman's Magazine* estimated that there were twenty thousand black people in London in 1764; see *GM* 34 (October 1764), 493. Valuable accounts of black life in London include James Walvin, *The Black Presence: A Documentary History of the Negro in England, 1555–1860* (London: Orbach and Chambers, 1971); Peter Fryer, *Staying Power: The History of Black People in Britain* (London: Pluto Press, 1984); and Gretchen Holbrook Gerzina, *Black London: Life before Emancipation* (New Brunswick, N.J.: Rutgers University Press, 1995).

2. John Fielding, *Extracts from such of the Penal Codes, as Particularly Relate to the Peace and Good Order of this Metropolis* (London, 1769), 143–145 (quotes, 144).

3. Yorke-Talbot opinion reprinted in Travis Glasson, "'Baptism Doth Not Bestow Freedom': Missionary Anglicanism, Slavery, and the Yorke-Talbot Opinion, 1701–30," *WMQ* 67 (April 2010): 279; William Blackstone, *Commentaries on the Laws of England*, 2 vols. (London, 1765), 1:123, quoted in David Brion Davis, *The Problem of Slavery in the Age of Revolution, 1770–1823* (1975; repr., New York: Oxford University Press, 1999), 473; Robert J. Allison, ed., *The Interesting Narrative of the Life of Olaudah Equiano* (1789; Boston: Bedford/St. Martin's, 1997), 97.

4. Prince Hoare, *Memoirs of Granville Sharp, Esq. Composed from His Own Manuscripts*, 2 vols. (London, 1828), 1:48–49.

5. Hoare, 1:49–53.

6. Hoare, 1:54–55, 61; Granville Sharp, *A Representation of the Injustice and Dangerous Tendency of Tolerating Slavery in England* (London, 1769), 42, 82.

7. James Otis, *The Rights of the British Colonies Asserted and Proved* (Boston, 1764), 38. On the slavery metaphor in the works of radical Whigs, see Bernard Bailyn, *The Ideological Origins of the American Revolution* (Cambridge, Mass.: Harvard University Press, 1967), 232–246.

8. Otis, *Rights of the British Colonies*, 24, 29; John J. Waters, *The Otis Family in Provincial and Revolutionary Massachusetts* (Chapel Hill: University of North Carolina Press for the Omohundro Institute, 1968), 133; on the development of racial slavery in seventeenth century New England, see Wendy Warren, *New England Bound: Slavery and Colonization in Early America* (New York: Liveright, 2016)

9. Based on a reading of the pamphlets reprinted in Bernard Bailyn, ed., *Pamphlets of the American Revolution*, vol. 1, *1750–1765* (Cambridge, Mass.: Harvard University Press, 1965), 203–694, and all of the pamphlets listed in the chronology for Bailyn's projected volumes for 1765–1776 on pp. 749–750.

10. Stephen Hopkins, *Rights of the Colonies Examined* (Providence, R.I., 1765); John Dickinson, *Letters from a Farmer in Pennsylvania* (Philadelphia, 1768), 38.

11. Edmund S. Morgan and Helen M. Morgan, *The Stamp Act Crisis: Prologue to Revolution* (Chapel Hill: University of North Carolina Press for the Omohundro Institute, 1953), 103; Pauline Maier, *From Resistance to Revolution: Colonial Radicals and the Development of American Opposition to Britain, 1765–1776* (New York: Alfred A. Knopf, 1972), 54–55; E. Stanley Gobold Jr. and Robert H. Woody, *Christopher Gadsden and the American Revolution* (Knoxville: University of Tennessee Press, 1982), 58; Peter Wood, "'Liberty Is Sweet': African-American Freedom Struggles in the Years before White Independence," in *Beyond the American Revolution: Explorations in the History of American Radicalism*, ed. Alfred F. Young (DeKalb: Northern Illinois University Press, 1993), 157.

12. Lt. Gov. William Bull to the Lords of Trade, January 25, 1766, in SC Trans./microfilm, reel 10, vol. 31; Henry Laurens (hereafter HL) to John Lewis Gervais, January 29, 1766, in *The Papers of Henry Laurens* (hereafter *PHL*), vol. 5 of 16, *Sept. 1, 1765–July 31, 1768*, ed. George C. Rogers Jr. and David R. Chesnutt (Columbia: University of South Carolina Press, 1976), 53; Wood, "'Liberty Is Sweet,'" 158–159. See also *Newport Mercury*, February 10, 1766.

13. Christopher Gadsden to William Samuel Johnson, April 16, 1766, in *The Writings of Christopher Gadsden, 1746–1805*, ed. Richard Walsh (Columbia: University of South Carolina Press, 1966), 72; Andrew Jackson O'Shaughnessy, *An Empire Divided: The American Revolution and the British Caribbean* (Philadelphia: University of Pennsylvania Press, 2000), 84–104.

14. *South Carolina Gazette*, no. 1608 (October 31–June 2, 1766).

15. Philip D. Morgan and George D. Terry document a similar episode in "Slavery in Microcosm: A Conspiracy Scare in Colonial South Carolina," *Southern Studies* 21 (Summer 1982): 121–145.

16. "To the Planters, Mechanics, and Freeholders of the Province of South Carolina," *South Carolina Gazette*, June 22, 1769, in Walsh, *Writings of Christopher Gadsden*, 77–78.

17. Hoare, *Memoirs of Granville Sharp*, 1:72–73, 78–90, 103–105. See Adam Hochschild's graceful account of these stories in his *Bury the Chains: Prophets and Rebels in the Fight to Free an Empire's Slaves* (Boston: Houghton Mifflin, 2005), 43–50.

18. James Oldham, "New Light on Mansfield and Slavery," *Journal of British Studies* 27 (January 1988): 45–68; David Waldstreicher, *Slavery's Constitution: From Revolution to Ratification* (New York: Hill and Wang, 2009), 34.

19. *London General Evening Post*, May 28, 1772, quoted in Oldham, "New Light on Mansfield and Slavery," 53. The most detailed account of this case is Steven M. Wise, *Though the Heavens May Fall: The Landmark Trial That Led to the End of Human Slavery* (Cambridge, Mass.: Da Capo Press, 2005).

20. The best account of the arguments in the case can be found in *Somerset v. Stewart* (May 14, 1772), 1 Lofft 1–19, 98 Eng. Rep. 499, 499–510. For Dunning's argument, see pp. 504–506.

21. *Somerset v. Stewart*, 98 Eng. Rep. at 509–510.

22. *London Chronicle*, June 20–23, 1772, 598, *London Chronicle*, June 23–25, 1772, 608, *London Public Advertiser*, June 25, 1772, and Finnie and Jones, all quoted in Vincent Caretta, *Equiano the African: Biography of a Self-Made Man* (Athens: University of Georgia Press, 2005), 208, 212.

23. Ruth Paley, "After Somerset: Mansfield, Slavery and the Law in England, 1772–1830," in *Law Crime, and English Society, 1660–1830*, ed. Norma Landau (New York: Cambridge University Press, 2002), 165–184.

24. HL to John Lewis Gervais, May 29, 1772, in *PHL*, vol. 8, *Oct. 10, 1771–Apr. 19, 1773*, ed. George C. Rogers and David R. Chesnutt (Columbia: University of South Carolina Press, 1980), 353. American newspapers did cover the Somerset case, though generally without their own editorial comment; the *South Carolina Gazette* printed only one piece on the case; see *South Carolina Gazette*, August 10, 1772.

25. [Edward Long], *Candid Reflections Upon the Judgement lately awarded by the Court of King's Bench, in Westminster Hall, on what is commonly called The Negro Cause, by a Planter* (London, 1772). The only other planter response to the Somerset case was written by Samuel Estwick, agent of the Assembly of Barbados in London; see *Considerations on the Negroe Cause Commonly So Called, Addressed to the Right Hounourable Lord Mansfield, by a West Indian* (London, 1772).

26. Drew Gilpin Faust, *The Ideology of Slavery: Proslavery Thought in the Antbellum South, 1830-1860* (Baton Rouge: Louisiana State University Press, 1981); Michael O'Brien, *Conjectures of Order: Intellectual Life and the American South, 1810–1860*, 2 vols. (Chapel Hill: University of North Carolina Press, 2004).

27. [Long], *Candid Reflections*, 23–29, 37, 39, 42–43, 62.

28. Patricia Bradley, *Slavery, Propaganda, and the American Revolution* (Jackson: University Press of Mississippi, 1998), 72; *South Carolina Gazette*, August 10, 1772; *Some Fugitive Thoughts on a Letter Signed Freeman, Addressed to the Deputies Assembled at the High Court of Congress in Philadelphia, By a Back Settler* ([Charleston], S.C., 1774), 25.

29. Petition of December 31, 1773, Colonial Office: Jamaica, Original Correspondence (hereafter CO)140/52, British National Archives, Kew, UK.

30. John Dalling, "Observations on the present state of Jamaica, 14 May 1774," Osborn c524 unpaginated manuscript, Beinecke Library, Yale University; *Oxford Dictionary of National Biography Online*, s.v. "Dalling, Sir John, First Baronet," by Jonathan Spain, accessed November 2013, https://doi .org/10.1093/ref:odnb/53621.

31. Dalling, "Observations."

32. "From the Great Bible at Rosehill, Sussex," and Stephen Fuller to Zachary Bayly, April 5, 1764, in Stephen Fuller Letterbooks, 2 MS vols., vol. 1. John J. Burns Library, Boston College, Chestnut Hill, Mass. (hereafter Fuller Letterbooks); *Oxford Dictionary of National Biography Online*, s.v. "Fuller family" by J. S. Hodgkinson, accessed June 13, 2018 https://doi.org/10.1093/ref:odnb /47494; Walter Augustus Feurtado, *Official and Other Personages of Jamaica, from 1655 to 1790* (Kingston, Jamaica: W.A. Feurtado's, Sons, 1896), iv.

33. Stephen Fuller to Zachary Bayly, April 5, 1764, in Fuller Letterbooks, vol. 1. For more on the West Indian interest in London, see Douglas Hall, *A Brief History of the West India Committee* (Devon House, Barbados: Caribbean Universities Press, 1971); David Beck Ryden, *West Indian Slavery and British Abolition, 1783–1807* (New York: Cambridge University Press, 2009); Nicholas Draper, *The Price of Emancipation: Slave-Ownership, Compensation and British Society at the End of Slavery* (New York: Cambridge University Press, 2010), chap. 1.

34. Stephen Fuller to Committee of Correspondence, June 28, 1774, Fuller Letterbooks, 271; "An Account of the Ordinary and Extraordinary Expences of the Government of the Island of Jamaica out of the Annual Funds, 1774," Colonial Office: Jamaica, Original Correspondence (hereafter CO) 137/70, fol. 103, British National Archives, Kew, UK. Jamaican currency converted to pounds sterling at 1:40.

35. *To the King's Most Excellent Majesty in Council, the Humble Petition and Memorial of the Assembly of Jamaica* (Philadelphia, 1775), 3, 6. The First Continental Congress had resolved that the Intolerable Acts constituted "a system formed to enslave America"; see "Declaration and Resolves of the First Continental Congress, October 14, 1774," Avalon Project of the Yale Law School, Lillian Goldman Law Library, accessed December 2, 2013, http://avalon.law .yale.edu/18th_century/resolves.asp.

36. Josiah Smith to John Ray Jr., February 18, 1774, Letterbook of Josiah Smith, Southern Historical Collection, University of North Carolina, Chapel Hill; Basil Keith to the Earl of Dartmouth, January 4, 1775, CO 137/70, fol. 13. The Continental Congress had essentially cut off trade with Great Britain and its West Indian colonies by not importing, exporting, or consuming the products of the British Empire.

37. Basil Keith to the Earl of Dartmouth, January 4, 1775, fol. 14; "Extract of a Letter from a worthy Gentleman in Kingston, Jamaica, dated January 1, 1775," *Boston Evening Post*, February 2, 1775; also see n. 35.

38. Earl of Dartmouth to Basil Keith, March 3, 1775, CO 137/70, fol. 33; *Virginia Gazette*, March 30, 1775. The following papers reprinted the letter from the Kingston gentleman: *Boston Post-Boy*, February 13, 1775; *Essex Journal*, February 22, 1775; *Massachusetts Spy*, February 23, 1775; and *Virginia Gazette*, March 9, 1775. The following papers reprinted the entire petition: *Pennsylvania Evening Post*, February 23, 1775; *New York Journal*, February 23, 1775; and *New York Gazette*, February 27, 1775. See n. 32 for pamphlet citation.

39. J. William Harris, *The Hanging of Thomas Jeremiah: A Free Black Man's Encounter with Liberty* (New Haven, Conn.: Yale University Press, 2009), 73, 76–78; Wood, "'Liberty Is Sweet,'" 165–166; James Habersham to Robert Keen, May 11, 1775, in *Collections of the Georgia Historical Society*, vol. 6, *The Letters of Hon. James Habersham, 1756–1775* (Savannah: Georgia Historical Society, 1904), 244.

40. General Committee to Delegates for South Carolina at Philadelphia, May 8, 1775, and Resolutions of the General Committee of Charleston, quoted

in HL to John Laurens (hereafter JL), May 15, 1775, in *PHL*, vol. 10, *Dec. 12, 1774–Jan. 4, 1776*, ed. George C. Rogers and David R. Chesnutt (Columbia: University of South Carolina Press, 1985), 114n2, 119.

41. Josiah Smith to James Poyas, May 18, 1775, and Josiah Smith to George Appleby, June 16, 1775, Letterbook of Josiah Smith; William Campbell to Lord Dartmouth, August 31, 1775, in SC Trans./microfilm, reel 11, vol. 35, 192; William E. Hemphill, ed., *Extracts from the Journals of the Provincial Congress of South Carolina* (Columbia: South Carolina Archives Department, 1960), 39.

42. HL to JL, June 18, 1775, in *PHL*, 10:184; testimony of Jemmy and Sambo, enclosed in Campbell to Dartmouth, August 31, 1775, in SC Trans./microfilm, reel 11, vol. 35, 215. Campbell had also learned about the letter from Arthur Lee (p. 192). The trial of Jeremiah has been richly contextualized in two monographs: Harris, *Hanging*; and William R. Ryan, *The World of Thomas Jeremiah: Charles Town on the Eve of the American Revolution* (New York: Oxford University Press, 2010).

43. Thomas Hutchinson to Council of Safety, July 5, 1775, and Council of Safety to St. Bartholomew Committee, July 18, 1775, in *PHL*, 10:206–208, 231–232.

44. Harris, *Hanging*, 107–110; HL to JL, August 20, 1775, in *PHL*, 10:330.

45. Campbell to Dartmouth, August 31, 1775, in SC Trans., reel 11, vol. 35, 199–201. On the unusual nature of Smith's visit, see HL to JL, August 20, 1775, in *PHL*, 10:320.

46. Campbell to Dartmouth, August 31, 1775, 201; HL to William Campbell, August 20, 1775, in *PHL*, 10:329.

47. Campbell to Dartmouth, August 19 and 31, 1775, in SC Trans., reel 11, vol. 35, 186, 202; HL to JL, August 20, 1775, 10:321; HL to JL, July 14, 1775, in *PHL*, 10:220.

48. Harris, *Hanging*, 95.

49. Letter from Mr. T. L. Salmon, July 20, 1776, CO 137/71, fol. 248. These ethnic designations for the conspirators appear throughout the documents relating to this conspiracy. George Scott, a resident white, described the conspirators thus: "the most sensible of the Creoles both old and young, or rather middle-aged, and the old and most trusty of all others of other nations." See George Scott to John Allen, July 21, 1776, CO 137/71, fol. 254.

50. Lord Germain to Governor Basil Keith, January 24, 1776, CO 137/71, fol. 29; Basil Keith to Lord Germain, June 6, 1776, CO 137/71, fol. 153; letter from Lt. Col. Stiell of the 60th Regiment, May 21, 1776, CO 137/71, fol. 156; Hanover Magistrates to General John Palmer, July 19, 1776, CO 137/71, fol. 240.

51. Although Daphnis was the only woman named in this archive of rebellion, this does not mean that she was the only woman involved. For a brilliant exploration, see Marisa Fuentes, *Dispossessed Lives: Enslaved Women, Violence, and the Archive* (Philadelphia: University of Pennsylvania Press, 2016).

52. "Examination of Sam, taken 19 July 1776," CO 137/71, fols. 252–253.

53. "Examination of Peter, taken 23 July 1776," CO 137/71, fol. 262; "Examination of Adam, taken 17 July 1776," CO 137/71, fol. 234.

54. "Examination of Sam"; all numbers taken from "A List of Impeached Estates," CO 137/71, fol. 272.

55. Basil Keith to Lord Germaine, July 1 and September 5, 1776, CO 137/71, fols. 201–202, 231.

56. George Scott to John Allen, July 21, 1776, CO 137/71, fol. 254.

57. "Examination of Adam"; affidavit of James Tucker, July 19, 1776, CO 137/71, fol. 243. My analysis is informed by Winthrop Jordan, *Tumult and Silence at Second Creek: An Inquiry into a Civil War Slave Conspiracy* (Baton Rouge: Louisiana State University Press, 1993), 87–98.

58. "Examination of Sam"; Hanover Magistrates to General John Palmer, July 19, 1776, fol. 240; John Palmer to Basil Keith, July 20, 1776, CO 137/71, fols. 236–237.

59. Basil Keith to Lord Germaine, August 6, 1776, CO 137/71, fols. 227–229, 300; [a soldier in the Sixtieth Regiment] to Mrs. Manby, Kingston, August 6, 1776, Jamaican Slavery Letters, Special Collections, Duke University.

60. Thomas Thistlewood also wrote that Maroons might have been involved in the Lucea conspiracy; see Trevor Burnard, *Mastery, Tyranny, and Desire: Thomas Thistlewood and His Slaves in the Anglo-Jamaican World* (Chapel Hill: University of North Carolina Press, 2004), 145.

61. "Examination of Pontack, taken 28 July 1776"; "Examination of Charles, taken 29 July 1776"; Hanover Magistrates to Keith, August 7 and 9, 1776; Keith to Germaine, August 6, 1776, CO 137/71, fol. 228.

62. Edward Long, *History of Jamaica* (London, 1774), 2:410; Dalling, "Observations."

63. Quoted in Davis, *Problem of Slavery in the Age of Revolution*, 274.

64. Benjamin Rush, *An Address to the Inhabitants of the British Settlements in America, upon Slave Keeping* (Philadelphia, 1773), 5, 28, 30.

65. [John Allen], *The Watchman's Alarm to Lord N——h* (Salem, Mass., 1774), 25–30 (quote, 29). Allen drew from Isaiah 21:11. On the political print, see Lester C. Olson, "Pictorial Representations of British America Resisting Rape: Rhetorical Re-circulation of a Print Series Portraying the Boston Port Bill of 1774," *Rhetoric and Public Affairs* 12 (Spring 2009): 1–35.

66. Samuel Hopkins, *A Dialogue Concerning the Slavery of the Africans; Shewing it to be the Duty and Interest of the American Colonies to emancipate all their African Slaves* (Norwich, Conn., 1776); Thomas Paine, "African Slavery in America," *Pennsylvania Journal and Weekly Advertiser*, March 8, 1775; Samuel Johnson quoted in Davis, *Problem of Slavery in the Age of Revolution*, 275; Granville Sharp, *A Declaration of the People's Natural Right to a Share in the Legislature* (1774). Sharp's pamphlet was printed first in London, then twice in Philadelphia and again in Boston and New York.

67. "Declaration and Resolves of the First Continental Congress"; "A Declaration by the Representatives of the United Colonies of North America, Now Met in Congress at Philadelphia, Setting Forth the Causes and Necessities of Their Taking Up Arms," Avalon Project of the Yale Law School, Lillian Goldman Law Library, accessed December 2, 2013, http://avalon.law.yale.edu/18th_century/resolves.asp; http://avalon.law.yale.edu/18th_century/arms.asp.

68. Jefferson's draft quoted in Donald L. Robinson, *Slavery in the Structure of American Politics, 1765–1820* (New York: Harcourt Brace Jovanovich, 1971), 82.

69. Benjamin Quarles, *The Negro in the American Revolution* (1961; repr., New York: W.W. Norton, 1973), 42; Robinson, *Slavery in the Structure*, 83; Winthrop Jordan, *White over Black: American Attitudes toward the Negro, 1550–1812* (Chapel Hill: University of North Carolina Press for the Omohundro Institute, 1968), 301.

70. "Declaration of Independence, July 4, 1776," Avalon Project of the Yale Law School, Lillian Goldman Law Library, accessed December 2, 2013, http://avalon.law.yale.edu/18th_century/declare.asp; "Constitution of South Carolina—March 26, 1776," Avalon Project of the Yale Law School, Lillian Goldman Law Library, accessed December 2, 2013, http://avalon.law.yale.edu /18th_century/sc01.asp.

71. My account of this story has been enriched by the work of Gregory D. Massey; see his "The Limits of Antislavery Thought in the Revolutionary Lower South: John Laurens and Henry Laurens," *Journal of Southern History* 63 (August 1997): 495–530; and Gregory D. Massey, *John Laurens and the American Revolution* (Columbia: University of South Carolina Press, 2000).

72. HL to JL, August 14, 1776; JL to HL, October 26, 1776, in *PHL*, vol. 11.

73. JL to HL, January 14, 1778; JL to HL, February 2, 1778, in *PHL*, vol. 12, 305, 390–392.

74. HL to JL, January 22, January 28, and March 1, 1778; JL to HL, March 9, 1778, in *PHL*, vol. 12, 328, 367–8, 390–2. See also JL to HL, February 2, 9, and 15, 1778; HL to JL, February 6, 1778, in *PHL*, vol. 12, 390–2, 412–13, 430, 446–47.

75. JL to HL, February 17, 1779, in *PHL*, vol. 15, 60; Alexander Hamilton to John Jay, March 14, 1779, in *The Papers of Alexander Hamilton Digital Edition*, ed. Harold C. Syrett, accessed February 6, 2014, http://rotunda.upress .virginia.edu/founders/ARHN-01-02-02-0051; HL to George Washington, March 16, 1779, in *The Papers of George Washington Digital Edition*, ed. Theodore J. Crackel, accessed February 11, 2014, http://rotunda.upress.virginia .edu/founders/GEWN-03-19-02-0499.

76. *Journals of the Continental Congress, 1774–1789*, ed. Worthington C. Ford, vol. 13, *January 1–April 22, 1779* (Washington, D.C.: Government Printing Office, 1909), 386–388; David Ramsay to William Henry Drayton, September 1, 1779, in *Documentary History of the American Revolution*, ed. R. W. Gibbes, vol. 2 of 3, *1776–1782* (New York: D. Appleton, 1857), 121; Christopher Gadsden to Samuel Adams, July 6, 1779, in Walsh, *Writings of Christopher Gadsden*, 166.

77. Philipsburgh Proclamation quoted in Sylvia Frey, *Water from the Rock: Black Resistance in a Revolutionary Age* (Princeton, N.J., 1991), 113–114. See also Robert G. Parkinson, *The Common Cause: Creating Race and Nation in the American Revolution* (Chapel Hill, N.C., 2016), 463–465.

78. George Smith McCowen Jr., *The British Occupation of Charleston, 1780–1782* (Columbia: University of South Carolina Press, 1972); Rachel N.

Klein, *Unification of a Slave State: The Rise of the Planter Class in the South Carolina Backcountry, 1760–1808* (Chapel Hill: University of North Carolina Press for the Omohundro Institute, 1990), 78–108.

79. Stephen Fuller to the Committee of Correspondence, March 16, 1778, Fuller Letterbooks, vol. 1, fol. 83; *JAJ*, vol. 7, *From October the 21st, 1777, . . . to December 23d, 1783 . . .* (Spanish Town, Jamaica: printed by Alexander Aikman, 1802), 74.

80. *JAJ*, 7:85; affidavit of James Tucker, fol. 243; O'Shaughnessy, *Empire Divided*, 176–177.

81. "To Lord George Germain, the Humble Memorial of Stephen Fuller," December 24, 1778, Fuller Letterbooks, vol. 2, fol. 109; O'Shaughnessy, *Empire Divided*, 176–177. At a cost of £35 10d., Fuller printed dozens of copies of this memorial with the petition of 1773 appended, probably for distribution gratis among members of Parliament; see Fuller Letterbooks, vol. 2, fol. 204.

82. Fuller to the Committee of Correspondence, February 3, 1779, Fuller Letterbooks, vol. 2, fol. 117; Resolutions of a Meeting at Mr. Fuller's, September 29, 1779, Fuller Letterbooks, vol. 2, fol. 142; O'Shaughnessy, *Empire Divided*, 178.

83. Fuller to the Committee of Correspondence, October 14, October 30, and December 15, 1779, Fuller Letterbooks, vol. 2, fols. 164, 166, 174; Stephen Fuller to Governor Dalling, November 3, 1779, Fuller Letterbooks, vol. 2, fols. 218–219.

84. Nathanael Greene to John Rutledge, December 3 and 9, 1781, January 21, 1782, in *The Papers of Nathanael Greene*, ed. Denis M. Conrad et al., vol. 10 of 11, *3 December 1781–6 April 1782*, ed. Denis M. Conrad, Roger N. Parks, and Martha J. King (Chapel Hill: University of North Carolina Press, 1998), 20–22, 130, 228–229; Edward Rutledge to Arthur Middleton, February 8, 1782, in "Correspondence of Hon. Arthur Middleton (Cont.)," *SCHGM* 27 (January 1926): 4; George Washington to John Laurens, July 10, 1782, in *The Writings of George Washington from the Original Manuscript Sources, 1745–1799*, ed. John C. Fitzpatrick, vol. 24 of 39, *February 18, 1782–August 10, 1782* (Washington, D.C.: Government Printing Office, 1938), 421.

85. Excerpt from the House Journal, March 3, 1782, and *Minutes of a General Council of War . . . held on the 2nd and 3rd Days March 1782* (printed), both enclosed in Governor Archibald Campbell to Lord Germain, March 6, 1782, CO 137/82, fols. 155–156, 158; *JAJ*, 7:461. On the "unthinkable" nature of the slave rebellion in the slaveholding mind, see Michel-Rolph Trouillot, *Silencing the Past: Power and the Production of History* (Boston: Beacon Press, 1995), chap. 3.

86. Archibald Campbell, "A Memoir Relative to the Island of Jamaica," Kings MSS 214, British Library, London; "The Humble Memorial of William Henry Ricketts, Richard Bucknor James, Philip Vanhorne, and Thomas Barker," enclosed in Governor Archibald Campbell to Lord Germain, March 6, 1782, CO 137/82, fol. 204; entries for April 12 and 17, 1782, in *JAJ*, 7:467–468, 471; O'Shaughnessy, *Empire Divided*, 233, 237.

87. Campbell, "Memoir"; Laurent Dubois, *Avengers of the New World: The Story of the Haitian Revolution* (Cambridge, Mass.: Harvard University Press, 2004); Steven Hahn, *A Nation under Our Feet: Black Political Struggles in the Rural South from Slavery to the Great Migration* (Cambridge, Mass.: Harvard University Press, 2003), 66–115; Ada Ferrer, *Insurgent Cuba: Race, Nation, and Revolution, 1868–1898* (Chapel Hill: University of North Carolina Press, 1999), 15–89.

88. Massey, *John Laurens*, 225–227; Robinson, *Slavery in the Structure*, 223–224.

89. Maya Jasanoff, *Liberty's Exiles: American Loyalists in the Revolutionary World* (New York: Alfred A. Knopf, 2011), 73–77; Eldon Jones, "The British Withdrawal from the South, 1781–85," in *The Revolutionary War in the South: Power, Conflict, and Leadership*, ed. W. Robert Higgins (Durham, N.C.: Duke University Press, 1979), 270–272; Frey, *Water from the Rock*, 174–179; Cassandra Pybus, "Jefferson's Faulty Math: The Question of Slave Defections in the American Revolution," *WMQ* 62 (April 2005): 262–263; John W. Pulis, "Bridging Troubled Waters: Moses Baker, George Liele, and the African American Diaspora to Jamaica," in *Moving On: Black Loyalists in the Afro-Atlantic World*, ed. John W. Pulis (New York: Garland Publishers, 1999), 185.

90. Kamau Brathwaite, *The Development of Creole Society in Jamaica, 1770–1820* (1971; repr., Kingston, Jamaica: Ian Randle Publishers, 2005), 85–86; Richard B. Sheridan, "The Crisis of Slave Subsistence in the British West Indies during and after the American Revolution," *WMQ* 33 (October 1976): 615–641.

91. For two contrary views, see Waldstreicher, *Slavery's Constitution*, 40–41; and George Van Cleve, *A Slaveholder's Union: Slavery, Politics, and the Constitution in the Early American Republic* (Chicago: University of Chicago Press, 2010), 35–36.

92. Christopher Leslie Brown, *Moral Capital: Foundations of British Abolitionism* (Chapel Hill: University of North Carolina Press for the Omohundro Institute, 2006).

93. William Whipple to Josiah Bartlett, April 27, 1779, in *Letters of Delegates to Congress, 1774–1789*, ed. Paul H. Smith, vol. 12 of 26, *February 1–May 31, 1779*, ed. Paul H. Smith, Gerard W. Gawalt, and Ronald M. Gephart (Washington, D.C.: Library of Congress, 1985), 398; Aedanus Burke to Arthur Middleton, January 25, 1782, in Joseph W. Barnwell, "Correspondence of Hon. Arthur Middleton, Signer of the Declaration of Independence," *SCHM* 26, no. 4 (October 1925): 194.

CHAPTER 6   The Slaveholders Retrench

1. David Brion Davis, *The Problem of Slavery in the Age of Revolution, 1770–1823* (1975; repr., New York: Oxford University Press, 1999), 84–163; Adam Hochschild, *Bury the Chains: Prophets and Rebels in the Fight to Free an Empire's Slaves* (Boston: Houghton Mifflin, 2005), 1.

2. David P. Geggus, *Haitian Revolutionary Studies* (Bloomington: Indiana University Press, 2002); Julius S. Scott III, "The Common Wind: Currents of

Afro-American Communication during the Haitian Revolution (PhD diss., Duke University, 1986); David P. Geggus, ed. *The Impact of the Haitian Revolution in the Atlantic World* (Columbia: University of South Carolina Press, 2001).

3. For a reproduction of the map, and an insightful discussion of its relation to the historiography of abolition, see Christopher Leslie Brown, *Moral Capital: Foundations of British Abolitionism* (Chapel Hill: University of North Carolina Press for the Omohundro Institute, 2006), 3–8.

4. Biographical sketches of Sancho can be found in the introduction to *The Letters of Ignatius Sancho*, ed. Paul Edwards and Polly Rewt (Edinburgh: Edinburgh University Press, 1994), and in Gretchen Holbrook Gerzina, *Black London: Life before Emancipation* (New Brunswick, N.J: Rutgers University Press, 1995), 57–62.

5. *Edinburgh Magazine* 4 (December 1775): 4; "Historical Chronicle," in *GM* 46 (January 1776): 46; *Monthly Miscellany*, September 1776, 405–406.

6. Edwards and Rewt, *Letters of Ignatius Sancho*, 283; *Critical Review*, January 1784, 43. See also *European Magazine, and London Review*, September 1782, 199; *GM* 50 (December 1780): 591 (death notice); and *GM* 52 (September 1782): 437 (review).

7. Peter Peckard, *Piety, Benevolence, and Loyalty, recommended. A Sermon Preached Before the University of Cambridge, January the 30th, 1784* (Cambridge, 1784), 6.

8. Thomas Clarkson, *An Essay on the Slavery and Commerce of the Human Species* (London, 1787). On Clarkson's lasting influence, see James Henry Hammond, *Two Letters on Slavery in the United States, Addressed to Thomas Clarkson* (Columbia, S.C., 1845).

9. James Ramsay, *Essay on the Treatment and Conversion of African Slaves in the British Sugar Colonies* (London, 1784), 52–91 (quotes on 61 and 63).

10. Clarkson, *An Essay on the Slavery and Commerce of the Human Species*, 97, 100, 105.

11. "An Act for the better Order and Government of Slaves" (1696), in *Acts of Assembly, Passed in the Island of Jamaica, From 1681, to 1737, Inclusive*, comp. John Baskett (London, 1738), 226, 241, 242, 244, 249.

12. Gilbert Francklyn, *An Answer to the Rev. Mr. Clarkson's Essay on the Slavery and Commerce of the Human Species* (Kingston, Jamaica, 1788; London, 1789), 5; Lowell J. Ragatz, *The Fall of the Planter Class in the British Caribbean, 1763–1833: A Study in Social and Economic History* (New York: The Century Company, 1928), 259.

13. Stephen Fuller Account Book, 1786–1789, Perkins Rare Books Library, Duke University; Stephen Fuller to Lord Hawkesbury, January 29, 1788, Add. MS 38416, fol. 6, British Library, London. These hearings generated the highly influential "Report of the Lords of the Committee of Council Appointed to the Consideration . . . [of] the present state of the Trade to Africa, and particularly the Trade in Slaves; and concerning the present Effects and Consequences of this Trade, as well in Africa and the West Indies," *Parliamentary Papers*, 1789, vol. 69. https://parlipapers.proquest.com/parlipapers /docview/t70.d75.hcsp-001563?accountid=15172.

14. James Walvin, *England, Slaves and Freedom, 1776–1838* (Jackson: University of Mississippi Press, 1986), 110; Seymour Drescher, *Capitalism and Antislavery: British Mobilization in Comparative Perspective* (New York: Oxford University Press, 1987), 74–77; Ryden, *West Indian Slavery*, 194.

15. Francklyn, *Answer*, 4.

16. *The Act of Assembly of the Island of Jamaica, to repeal several acts, and clauses of acts, respecting slaves, and for the better order and government of slaves, and for other purposes, commonly called the Consolidated Act* (London: printed for B. White, and son, Fellet-Street; for J. Sewell, Cornhill; for R. Faulder, New-Bond Street; for J. Debrett and J. Stockdale, Piccadilly, 1788), 4–9.

17. *Consolidated Act*, title page; *Abstract of the Consolidated Act of Jamaica* (printed for the use of the House of Commons, 1791), sect. 5.

18. Francklyn, *Answer*, 236–240; Bryan Edwards, *A Speech Delivered at a Free Conference between the Honourable the Council and Assembly of Jamaica, 19th November, 1789, on the subject of Mr. Wilberforce's Propositions in the House of Commons, concerning the Slave Trade* (Kingston, Jamaica, 1789), 64. Sloane toured the island in the 1680s when there had been significant English settlement for only about twenty years; Hans Sloane, *Voyage to the Islands Madera, Barbados, Nieves, S. Christophers and Jamaica* (London, 1707).

19. *Two Reports from the Committee of the Honourable House of Assembly of Jamaica* (London, 1789), 2–4, 6.

20. *JAJ*, vol. 8, *From October the 19th, 1784, . . . to March the 5th, 1791 . . .* (Spanish Town, Jamaica: printed by Alexander Aikman, 1804), 4–5. This committee did revise several revenue laws.

21. Davis, *Problem of Slavery in the Age of Revolution*, 420–423; Drescher, *Capitalism and Antislavery*, 78–83.

22. Clarkson, *Essay*, vii; Eva Sheppard Wolf, *Race and Liberty in the New Nation: Emancipation in Virginia from the Revolution to Nat Turner's Rebellion* (Baton Rouge: Louisiana State University Press, 2006), 63; James Oliver Horton and Lois E. Horton, *In Hope of Liberty: Culture, Community and Protest among Northern Free Blacks, 1700–1860* (New York: Oxford University Press, 1997), chap. 3.

23. *Charleston Evening Gazette*, October 26, 1785.

24. Rachel N. Klein, *Unification of a Slave State: The Rise of the Planter Class in the South Carolina Backcountry, 1760–1808* (Chapel Hill: University of North Carolina Press for the Omohundro Institute, 1990), chap. 1; Jerome J. Nadelhaft, *The Disorders of War: The Revolution in South Carolina* (Orono: University of Maine at Orono Press, 1981), 62.

25. With the independence of the United States in 1783, "Charles Town" became "Charleston."

26. "Petition of the Inhabitants of Camden [1786]," South Carolina Department of Archives and History (hereafter SCDAH); Elizabeth Donnan, ed., *Documents Illustrative of the History of the Slave Trade to America*, vol. 4, *The Border Colonies and the Southern Colonies* (Washington, D.C.: Carnegie Institution, 1935), 483; Klein, *Unification of a Slave State*, 131–132. The principal debates were in September and October 1785, when the trade was at its peak;

proponents of the ban lost two votes: forty-seven to fifty-one in September, and forty-eight to sixty-three in October. Selections of these debates can be found in Donnan, *Documents Illustrative*, 4:472, 480–489, 492–494.

27. *South Carolina Gazette and General Advertiser* (Charleston), April 6, 1785; *South Carolina Weekly Gazette* (Charleston), April 9–13, 1785. It is intriguing to note that Henry Laurens may have planted these quotations. He had brought Price's pamphlet back from England in 1785 and presented it to the state legislature in January 1785. See Gregory D. Massey, "The Limits of Antislavery Thought in Revolutionary South Carolina: John Laurens and Henry Laurens" *Journal of Southern History* 63 (August 1997): 526–527.

28. *Charleston Morning Post*, January 21, 1786.

29. Richard Beeman, *Plain, Honest Men: The Making of the American Constitution* (New York: Random House, 2009), 59; *American National Biography Online*, s.v. "Butler, Pierce," by Robert Weir, accessed January 3, 2013, https://doi.org/10.1093/anb/9780198606697.article.0200350; *American National Biography Online*, s.v. "Rutledge, John," by Robert Weir, accessed January 3, 2013, https://doi.org/10.1093/anb/9780198606697.article.0100802; *American National Biography Online*, s.v. "Pinckney, Charles," by Robert Weir, accessed January 3, 2013, https://doi.org/10.1093/anb/9780198606697.article.0200258; *American National Biography Online*, s.v. "Pinckney, Charles Cotesworth," by Martin Zahniser, accessed January 3, 2013, https://doi.org/10.1093/anb/9780198606697.article.0200259. For a contemporary account of the delegates, see William Pierce, "Character Sketches of Delegates to the Federal Convention," in *The Records of the Federal Convention of 1787*, rev. ed., 3 vols., ed. Max Farrand (New Haven, Conn.: Yale University Press, 1966), 3:87–97. Pierce represented Georgia at the convention and served as a captain in the Continental army. Farrand's volumes are available at http://memory.loc.gov/ammem/amlaw/lwfr.html.

30. Davis, *Problem of Slavery in the Age of Revolution*, 122–131; David Waldstreicher, *Slavery's Constitution: From Revolution to Ratification* (New York: Hill and Wang, 2009); Beeman, *Plain, Honest Men*, chap. 17.

31. Edmund Morgan, *Inventing the People: The Rise of Popular Sovereignty in England and America* (New York: W. W. Norton, 1989); Farrand, *Records*, 1:196, 204, 562, 567, 581–582.

32. Farrand, *Records*, 1:201.

33. Waldstreicher, *Slavery's Constitution*, 51–55; Howard A. Ohline, "Republicanism and Slavery: Origins of the Three-Fifths Clause in the United States Constitution," *WMQ*, 3rd ser., 28 (October 1971): 570–571.

34. Farrand, *Records*, 1:580–581, 583, 587, 588.

35. Farrand, 1:597.

36. Farrand, 1:604–605. On Morris's reputation at the convention, see Pierce, "Character Sketches," 3:92.

37. Staughton Lynd, "The Compromise of 1787," *Political Science Quarterly* 81 (June 1966): 225–250; Waldstreicher, *Slavery's Constitution*, 87, 176n30; David C. Hendrickson, *Peace Pact: The Lost World of the American Founding* (Lawrence: University of Kansas Press, 2003), 228–229; Stanley

Harrold, *Border War: Fighting Over Slavery Before the Civil War* (Chapel Hill: University of North Carolina Press, 2010), 2–3.

38. Farrand, *Records,* 2:95.

39. Farrand, 2:220. On the Committee of Detail, see Donald L. Robinson, *Slavery in the Structure of American Politics, 1765–1820* (New York: Harcourt Brace, 1971), 217–219.

40. Farrand, *Records,* 2:221–223.

41. Farrand, 2:364–365.

42. Farrand, 2:370–371.

43. Farrand, 2:374, 415.

44. *Annals of Congress,* 1st Cong., 2nd Sess., Jan. 4, 1790–February 16, 1790, 1232, 1466, 1508; Richard S. Newman, "Prelude to the Gag Rule: Southern Reaction to Antislavery Petitions in the First Federal Congress," *Journal of the Early Republic* 16 (Winter 1996): 571–599. For a richly detailed history of the background of this petition (and those that followed), see Nicholas P. Wood, "A 'Class of Citizens': The Earliest Black Petitioners to Congress and Their Quaker Allies," *WMQ* 74 (January 2017): 109–144.

45. "Extract of the Register of Deliberation of the General Assembly of St. Domingo . . . from the session of the 24th August" (translation), enclosed in message of Governor Charles Pinckney, December 4, 1791, Governor's Messages #522, SCDAH; petition for aid from the Assembly at Saint-Domingue, enclosed in message of Governor Charles Pinckney, December 12, 1791, Governor's Messages #525, SCDAH; Michael E. Stevens and Christine M. Allen, eds., *The State Records of South Carolina: Journals of the House of Representatives, 1791* (Columbia: University of South Carolina Press, 1985), 319, 370, 392, 403, 417.

46. Governor Pinckney's answer to the Colonial Assembly of Saint Domingo, September 1791, enclosed in Governor's Messages #522, SCDAH; petition for aid, December 12, 1791, in Governor's Messages #525, SCDAH; letter from the President of the Colonial Assembly of St. Domingo, January 28, 1792, enclosed in message of Governor Charles Pinckney, December 2, 1792, Governor's Messages #554, SCDAH; Donald R. Hickey, "America's Response to the Slave Revolt in Haiti, 1791–1806," *Journal of the Early Republic* 2 (Winter 1982): 364; David Geggus, "Jamaica and the Saint-Domingue Slave Revolt, 1791–1793," *The Americas* 38 (October 1981): 227–229; Laurent Dubois, *Avengers of the New World: The Story of the Haitian Revolution* (Cambridge, Mass.: Harvard University Press, 2004), 117.

47. Geggus, "Jamaica," 221–222; Frederick Douglass, "Lecture on Haiti [January 2, 1893]," in *The Life and Writings of Frederick Douglass,* ed. Philip S. Foner, vol. 4 of 5, *Reconstruction and After* (New York: International Publishers, 1955), 484–486; see also the essays in David Barry Gaspar and David Geggus, eds., *A Turbulent Time: The French Revolution and the Greater Caribbean* (Bloomington: Indiana University Press, 1997); David Geggus, ed., *Impact of the Haitian Revolution in the Atlantic World* (Columbia: University of South Carolina Press, 2001); David Geggus and Norman Fiering, eds. *World of the Haitian Revolution* (Bloomington: Indiana University Press, 2009).

48. Lt. Gov. Adam Williamson to Henry Dundas, November 27, 1791, and minutes of the Council of War called on November 30, 1791, Colonial Office: Jamaica, Original Correspondence (hereafter CO) 137/90, fols. 17, 44.

49. B. W. Higman, "Jamaican Port Towns in the Early Nineteenth Century," in Franklin Knight and Peggy Liss, eds., *Atlantic Port Cities: Economy, Culture and Society in the Atlantic World*, 1650–1850 (Knoxville: University of Tennessee Press, 1991), 117–137.

50. Williamson to Dundas, November 27, 1791, CO 137/90, fol. 110; "St. James. Minutes of the Proceedings of the Committee of Security & Safety, 10 January 1792," CO 137/90, fols. 116–121; "Examinations of Sundry Slaves in the parish of St. Ann, Jamaica, respecting an intention to revolt, 12 February 1792," CO 137/90, fol. 123; "Examinations of Sundry Slaves in the parish of Trelawney, Jamaica, respecting an intention to revolt, [January 1792]" CO 137/90, fol. 130.

51. Williamson to Dundas, January 15, 1792, CO 137/90, fol. 73. On the size of the Jamaican garrison in 1792, see Williamson to Dundas, November 4, 1791, CO 137/90, fol. 2.

52. Charles Douglas to Patrick Douglas, undated letter [1792], Letters of Charles Douglas, Boswell Collection, General MSS 150, Series 1 Correspondence, Douglas of Garallan Family Subseries, Beinecke Library, Yale University. On martial law, see Kamau Brathwaite, *The Development of Creole Society in Jamaica, 1770–1820* (1971; repr., Kingston, Jamaica: Ian Randle Publishers, 2005), 26–31.

53. "The Petition of Stephen Fuller, Esq., Agent for Jamaica," March 30, 1792. An excerpt of the petition was printed; the full text appears in CO 137/90, fols. 358–360.

54. Williamson to Dundas, September 14, 1792, CO 137/90, fol. 332; extract of a letter from Simon Taylor, dated May 20, 1798, Kingston, enclosed in R. Taylor to Henry Dundas, July 6, 1798, MS 624, NLJ; David Geggus, "The Enigma of Jamaica in the 1790s: New Light on the Causes of Slave Rebellions," *WMQ*, 3rd ser., 44 (April 1987): 279–280; Mavis Campbell, *The Maroons of Jamaica, 1655–1796: A History of Resistance, Collaboration and Betrayal* (Granby, Mass.: Bergin & Garvey, 1988), chap. 7; Kenneth M. Bilby, "A Treacherous Feast: A Jamaican Maroon Historical Myth" *Bijdragen tot de Taal-, Land- en Volkenkunde* 140; *Anthropoligica* 26 (1984), 1–31.

55. Message of Gov. Pinckney, December 4, 1791, Governor's Messages #522, SCDAH; *Charleston City Gazette*, May 25 and 27, 1791; *Charleston City Gazette*, June 17, 1791 (quote); the *Gazette* concluded Paine's essay on July 19, 1791. George D. Terry, "A Study of the Impact of the French Revolution and the Insurrections in Saint-Domingue upon South Carolina: 1790–1805" (MA thesis, University of South Carolina, 1975), 34–37. Important studies of this critical moment in U.S. history include: Stanley Elkins and Eric McKitrick, *The Age of Federalism* (New York: Oxford University Press, 1993), chap. 8; Ashli White, *Encountering Revolution: Haiti and the Making of the Early Republic* (Baltimore: Johns Hopkins University Press, 2010); James Alexander Dun,

Dangerous Neighbors: Making the Haitian Revolution in Early America (Philadelphia: University of Pennsylvania Press, 2016).

56. Jeremy D. Popkin, *You Are All Free: The Haitian Revolution and the Abolition of Slavery* (New York: Cambridge University Press, 2010), chap. 6.

57. Lt. Gov. James Wood to Gov. Alexander Moultrie, Richmond, August 14, 1793, with the following enclosures: Thomas Newton to James Wood [undated], and William Nelson to Thomas Newton, York, August 8, 1793, with "Secret Keeper" letter enclosed; all enclosed in message of Governor William Moultrie, November 30, 1793, in Governor's Messages # 577, SCDAH. Governor Moultrie's orders quoted from Terry, "Study of the Impact," 59.

58. *Charleston City Gazette*, September 7, 1793; unsigned letter enclosed in Governor's Messages #577, SCDAH; Pierce Butler to John Holmes, November 6, 1793, Pierce Butler Letterbook, South Caroliniana Library, University of South Carolina, Columbia.

59. *Charleston City Gazette*, October 9, 1793, cited in Terry, "Study of the Impact," 61–63.

60. "A Black" to His Excellency the Governor, recd. October 10, 1793, enclosed in Governor's Messages #577, SCDAH, reprinted in *A Documentary History of the Negro People in the United States*, ed. Herbert Aptheker (New York, 1951), 29.

61. Terry, "Study of the Impact," 62–63; *Charleston City Gazette*, October 17 and November 13, 1793. On the political significance of funerals, see Vincent Brown, *The Reaper's Garden: Death and Power in the World of Atlantic Slavery* (Cambridge, Mass.: Harvard University Press, 2008), chap. 2.

62. Letters of Rusticus, South Carolina Historical Society, Charleston. For a similar expression of concern regarding the French National Convention's abolition, see Ralph Izard to John Parker, June 21, 1794, Ralph Izard Family Papers, Library of Congress, Washington, D.C.; Ralph Izard to Mathias Hutchinson, November 20, 1794, South Caroliniana Library.

63. *Worcester Gazette*, December 20, 1797; "The Petition of John Desbeaux to the Honorable House of Representatives," December 4, 1798, General Assembly Petitions 1798 #116, SCDAH; "Memorial of Sundry Citizens of Charleston Respecting the Importation of Negroes," December 11, 1797, General Assembly Petitions 1797 #87, SCDAH.

64. William Read to Jacob Read, Charleston, September 20, 1799, February 15 and March 12, 1800, Read Family Papers, South Carolina Historical Society, Charleston; *South Carolina State Gazette*, February 14 and 15, 1800. For more on the Sasportas plot in Jamaica, see Philippe Girard, "Isaac Sasportas, Toussaint Louverture, and Jamaica's Failed Slave Uprising of 1799" (paper presented at the Annual Meeting of the Association of Caribbean Historians, Curaçao, May 2012).

65. "An Act to Prevent Negro Slaves and other Persons of Colour, From Being Brought into or Entering this States" and "An Act Respecting Slaves, Free Negroes, Mulattoes, and Mestizoes; For Enforcing the More Punctual Performance of Patroll Duty; And to Impose Certain Restrictions on the Emancipation of Slaves," in *The Statutes at Large of South Carolina*, ed. Thomas

Cooper and David J. McCord, vol. 7, *Acts Relating to Charleston, Courts, Slaves, and Rivers*, ed. David J. McCord (Columbia, S.C.: printed by A. S. Johnston, 1840), 436–443; Terry, "Study of the Impact," 146, 155; Howard A. Ohline, "Georgetown, South Carolina: Racial Anxieties and Militant Behavior, 1802," *SCHM* 73 (1972): 130–140.

66. Voyages; Ryden, *West Indian Slavery*, 222; B. W. Higman, "Jamaican Coffee Plantations, 1780–1860: A Cartographic Analysis," *Caribbean Geography* 2 (1986): 73–74; S. D. Smith, "Sugar's Poor Relation: Coffee Planting in the British West Indies, 1720–1833," *Slavery and Abolition* 19 (December 1998): 72–73.

67. Jed Handelsman Shugerman, "The Louisiana Purchase and South Carolina's Reopening of the Slave Trade in 1803," *Journal of the Early Republic* 22 (Summer 2002): 271; Lacy Ford, *Deliver Us from Evil: The Slavery Question in the Old South* (New York: Oxford University Press, 2009), 94.

68. Shugerman, "Louisiana Purchase," 279; Ford, *Deliver Us from Evil*, 102; "An Act to Alter And Amend the Severall Acts Respecting the Importation Or Bringing into this State, from beyond Seas Or Elsewhere, Negroes and Other Persons of Colour," in McCord, *Statutes at Large of South Carolina*, 7:449–451.

69. Shugerman, "Louisiana Purchase," 282; Voyages; James A. McMillin, *Final Victims: Foreign Slave Trade to North America, 1783–1810* (Columbia: University of South Carolina Press, 2004).

70. Bryan Edwards, *The History, Civil and Commercial, of the British Colonies in the West Indies*, 4 vols. (Philadelphia, 1806), 4: xv.

71. Seymour Drescher, "Whose Abolition? Popular Pressure and the Ending of the British Slave Trade," *Past and Present* 143 (May 1994): 136–166; Matthew E. Mason, "Slavery Overshadowed: Congress Debates Prohibiting the Atlantic Slave Trade to the United States, 1806–1807," *Journal of the Early Republic* 20 (Spring 2000): 59–81.

72. Reinhart Koselleck, "Representation, Event, and Structure," in Koselleck, *Futures Past: On the Semantics of Historical Time*, trans. Keith Tribe (Cambridge, Mass.: MIT Press, 1985), 105–115. Rafael Marquese suggested this source.

73. Significant accounts of the transition to the second slavery include Rafael Marquese et al., *Slavery and Politics: Brazil and Cuba, 1790–1850*, trans. Leonardo Marques (Albuquerque: University of New Mexico Press, 2016), 59–60; Ada Ferrer, *Freedom's Mirror: Cuba and Haiti in the Age of Revolution* (New York: Cambridge University Press, 2014), 81–82, 283–284. On slavery's expansion in the US South, see Adam Rothman, *Slave Country: American Expansion and the Origins of the Deep South* (Cambridge, Mass.: Harvard University Press, 2005); Steve Deyle, *Carry Me Back: The Domestic Slave Trade in American Life* (New York: Oxford University Press, 2005); Walter Johnson, *River of Dark Dreams: Slavery and Empire in the Cotton Kingdom* (Cambridge, Mass.: Harvard University Press, 2013); and Edward Baptist, *The Half Has Never Been Told: Slavery and the Making of American Capitalism* (New York: Basic Books, 2014).

CHAPTER 7   The Political Significance of Slave Resistance

1. John Moultrie to Isaac Ball, February 18, 1823, Ball Family Papers, South Caroliniana Library, University of South Carolina, Columbia; Edward Ball, *Slaves in the Family* (New York: Farrar, Staus and Giroux, 1998).

2. John Moultrie to Isaac Ball, March 17, 1823, Ball Family Papers.

3. William Wilberforce, *An Appeal to the Religion, Justice, and Humanity of the Inhabitants of the British Empire, in Behalf of the Negro Slaves in the West Indies* (London: printed for J. Hatchard and Son, 1823); Thomas Clarkson, *Thoughts on the Necessity of Improving the Condition of the Slaves in the British Colonies, with a View to Their Ultimate Emancipation* (London, printed for the Society for the Mitigation and Gradual Abolition of Slavery, 1823).

4. James Walvin, *England, Slaves and Freedom, 1776–1838* (Jackson: University of Mississippi Press, 1986), 127–128.

5. *Report from the Select Committee of the House of Assembly . . . [on] the Origins, Causes, and Progress of the Late Insurrection* (Barbados, 1816), 29. For a rich analysis of this revolt and how whites understood it, see David Lambert, *White Creole Culture, Politics and Identity during the Age of Abolition* (New York: Cambridge University Press, 2005), esp. chap. 4.

6. Michael Craton, *Testing the Chains: Resistance to Slavery in the British West Indies* (Ithaca, N.Y.: Cornell University Press, 1982), 264; *Report from the Select Committee*, 13.

7. Robert Pierce Forbes, *The Missouri Compromise and Its Aftermath* (Chapel Hill: University of North Carolina Press, 2007), 35–36; Leonard L. Richards, *The Slave Power: The Free North and Southern Domination, 1790–1860* (Baton Rouge: Louisiana State University Press, 2000), 52–54.

8. Matthew Mason, *Slavery and Politics in the Early American Republic* (Chapel Hill: University of North Carolina Press, 2006).

9. Rufus King, *Substance of Two Speeches . . . on the Subject of the Missouri Bill* (New York, 1819); Robert Ernst, *Rufus King, American Federalist* (Chapel Hill: University of North Carolina Press for the Omohundro Institute, 1968), 370–371.

10. *Annals of Congress*, 16th Cong., 1st Sess. (1820), 259–75.

11. William W. Freehling, *Prelude to Civil War: The Nullification Controversy in South Carolina, 1816–1836* (New York: Harper & Row, 1965), 97–98.

12. *Annals of Congress*, 16th Cong., 1st Sess., 264–267, 269.

13. *Annals*, 267.

14. *Annals*, 268–269.

15. John C. Calhoun to H[enry] W. DeSaussure, April 28, 1820, DeSaussure Family Papers, South Carolina Historical Society, Charleston.

16. Richard John, *Spreading the News: The American Postal System from Franklin to Morse* (Cambridge, Mass.: Harvard University Press, 1995), 36–37.

17. W. Jeffrey Bolster, *Black Jacks: African American Seamen in the Age of Sail* (Cambridge, Mass.: Harvard University Press, 1997).

18. Julian J. Petty, *The Growth and Distribution of Population in South Carolina* (Columbia, S.C.: State Council for Defense, 1943), 214, 231; Emma Hart,

Building Charleston: Town and Society in the Eighteenth-Century British Atlantic World (Charlottesville: University of Virginia Press, 2010).

19. Bernard E. Powers Jr., *Black Charlestonians: A Social History, 1822–1885* (Fayetteville: University of Arkansas Press, 1994), 267; Richard S. Newman, "'A Chosen Generation': Black Founders and Early America," in *Prophets of Protest: Reconsidering the History of American Abolitionism*, ed. Timothy Patrick McCarthy and John Stauffer (New York: New Press, 2006), 62. See also Marina Wikramanayake, *A World in Shadow: The Free Black in Antebellum South Carolina* (Columbia: University of South Carolina Press, 1973).

20. James Oliver Horton and Lois E. Horton, *In Hope of Liberty: Culture, Community, and Protest among Northern Free Blacks, 1700–1860* (New York: Oxford University Press, 1997), 101–154; Erica Armstrong Dunbar, *A Fragile Freedom: African American Women and Emancipation in the Antebellum City* (New Haven, Conn.: Yale University Press, 2008), 5; Edward B. Rugemer, "Emancipation Day Traditions in the Anglo-Atlantic World," in *The Routledge History of Slavery*, ed. Gad Heuman and Trevor Burnard (London: Routledge, 2011), 316–318.

21. Albert J. Raboteau, *Slave Religion: The Invisible Institution in the Antebellum South* (New York: Oxford University Press, 1978), 135–137; Mary Turner, *Slaves and Missionaries: The Disintegration of Jamaican Slave Society, 1787–1834* (1982; repr., Kingston, Jamaica: Press University of the West Indies, 1998), 89–92; Sylvia R. Frey and Betty Wood, *Come Shouting to Zion: African American Protestantism in the American South and the British Caribbean to 1830* (Chapel Hill: University of North Carolina Press, 1998), 84–85

22. Vincent Harding, *There Is a River: The Black Struggle for Freedom in America* (San Diego: Harcourt Brace, 1981), 67; Horton and Horton, *In Hope of Liberty*, 141; Powers, *Black Charlestonians*, 20–22.

23. *Camden (S.C.) Gazette*, November 9, 1820.

24. "An Act to Restrain the Emancipation of Slaves," in *The Statutes at Large of South Carolina*, ed. Thomas Cooper and David J. McCord, vol. 7, *Acts Relating to Charleston, Courts, Slaves, and Rivers*, ed. David J. McCord (Columbia, S.C.: printed by A. S. Johnston, 1840), 459–460.

25. While I disagree with Michel Johnson's account of this conspiracy in his "Denmark Vesey and His Co-Conspirators," *The Making of a Slave Conspiracy*, pt. 1, *WMQ*, 3rd ser., 58 (October 2001): 915–976, his provocative, award-winning article generated a fruitful debate, continued in *The Making of a Slave Conspiracy*, pt. 2, *WMQ*, 3rd ser., 58 (January 2002): 135–202. My narrative of this slave conspiracy has drawn principally from the excellent document collection edited by Douglas R. Egerton and Robert L. Paquette, *The Denmark Vesey Affair: A Documentary History* (Gainesville: University of Florida Press, 2017). See also Douglas R. Egerton, *He Shall Go Out Free: The Lives of Denmark Vesey* (Madison, Wis.: Madison House, 1999); James O'Neil Spady, "Power and Confession: On the Credibility of the Earliest Reports of the Denmark Vesey Slave Conspiracy," *WMQ*, 3rd ser., 68 (April 2011): 287–304.

26. Egerton, *He Shall Go Out Free*, 83–90.

27. [James Hamilton], *Account of the Late Intended Insurrection among a Portion of the Blacks of this City* (Charleston, 1822), 3–4.

28. "Examination of [William Paul]," in Egerton and Paquette, *Vesey Affair*, 285.

29. Egerton, *He Shall Go Out Free*, 156–157. See the useful chronology, sometimes with a day-to-day progression of events, in Egerton and Paquette, *Vesey Affair*, xxix–xlii.

30. "Testimony of Joe La Roche (Enslaved)," in Egerton and Paquette, *Vesey Affair*, 287; see also p. 211.

31. Egerton and Paquette, *Vesey Affair*, 158.

32. James Hamilton to Charles Harris, [July 3, 1822], quoted in Martha Proctor Richardson to Dr. James Screven, July 6, 1822, in Egerton and Paquette, *Vesey Affair*, 383.

33. "Examination of Rolla Belonging to Thomas Bennett," [June 25, 1822], in Egerton and Paquette, *Vesey Affair*, 294; "Trial of Jack, a Mulato Man, Belonging to Mrs. Purcell," in Egerton and Paquette, 213–214. Purcell's trial took place on July 12; see Egerton and Paquette, 214n1.

34. "Examination of Joe a Negro Man Belong to Mr. La Roche," [June 20, 1822], in Egerton and Paquette, *Vesey Affair*, 287.

35. "Examination of Benjamin Ford," [June 26, 1822], in Egerton and Paquette, *Vesey Affair*, 296.

36. James Hamilton to Charles Harris, [July 3, 1822], quoted in Martha Proctor Richardson to Dr. James Screven, July 6, 1822, in Egerton and Paquette, *Vesey Affair*, 383 a sampling of northern newspaper coverage is in Egerton and Paquette, *Vesey Affair*, Part 5.

37. George Hibbert to the Committee of Correspondence, Assembly of Jamaica (hereafter GH to the Comm.), April 9, 1823, Jamaica National Archives, Spanish Town (hereafter JNA); Trevor Burnard and John Garrigus, *The Plantation Machine: Atlantic Capitalism in French Saint-Domingue and British Jamaica* (Philadelphia: University of Pennsylvania Press, 2016), 57; Lowell J. Ragatz, *The Fall of the Planter Class in the British Caribbean, 1763–1833: A Study in Social and Economic History* (New York: The Century Company, 1928), 98–99; *Oxford Dictionary of National Biography Online*, s.v. "Hibbert, George (1757–1837), Merchant," by David Hancock, accessed December 22, 2017, https://doi.org/10 .1093/ref:odnb/13194.

38. GH to the Comm., April 9, 1823.

39. GH to the Comm., April 9, 1823.

40. Resolutions of the Standing Committee of West Indian Planters and Merchants, [April 25, 1823], CO 854/1, fols. 119–120, British National Archives, Kew, UK.

41. Resolutions of the Standing Committee of West Indian Planters and Merchants, fols. 119–120. For a list of those present at the meeting, see fol. 119.

42. Extract from the proceedings of the subcommittee, Colonial Office: Jamaica, Original Correspondence (hereafter CO) 854/1, fols. 122–123. While some evidence suggests that the ameliorative efforts of West Indian planters did result in improved living conditions, the nineteenth century rebellions dem-

onstrate that slavery remained so offensive to human dignity as to inspire sustained resistance. On amelioration, see especially J.R. Ward, *British West Indian Slavery, 1750–1834: The Process of Amelioration* (Oxford, U.K.: Clarendon Press, 1988); and Ward, "The Amelioration of British West Indian Slavery: Anthropometric Evidence," *The Economic History Review* (2018), forthcoming.

43. Petition of George Hibbert, CO 137 / 155, fols. 174–175 ;GH to the Comm., May 9, 1823, JNA.

44. GH to the Comm., May 8 and 9, 1823, JNA.

45. *Hansard's Parliamentary Debates*, 3rd ser. (London: Printed by T.C. Hansard, 1823) vol. 9, 265.

46. "At a Meeting of the Standing Committee of West India Planters and Merchants . . . 5 June 1823," CO 137 / 155, fol. 128.

47. "Report to Be Transmitted to the Colonial Assemblies," [written after June 5, 1823], CO 137 / 155, fols. 115–117.

48. "Report to Be Transmitted," fols. 115–117.

49. "Report to Be Transmitted," fols. 115–117.

50. Emilia Viotti da Costa, *Crowns of Glory, Tears of Blood: The Demerara Slave Rebellion of 1823* (New York: Oxford University Press, 1994), 19–21.

51. Reprinted in *The Annual Register, or a View of the History, Politics, and Literature of the year 1823* (London: printed for Baldwin, Cradock, and Joy, 1824), 130–131.

52. Ragatz, *Fall of the Planter Class*, 412; "Proclamation," and accompanying letter of intent, dated Colonial Office, May 1823," CO 854 / 1, fols. 153–154.

53. Da Costa, *Crowns of Glory*, 178; William Law Mathieson, *British Slavery and Its Abolition, 1823–1838* (London: Longman's, Green, and Co., 1926), 127–128.

54. Da Costa, *Crowns of Glory*, 179, 196.

55. Da Costa, 181.

56. Da Costa, 197.

57. Edwin Angel Wallbridge, *The Demerara Martyr: Memoirs of the Reverend John Smith* (London: Charles Gilpin, 1848).

58. George Hibbert to Lord Bathurst, October 18, 1823, CO 137 / 155, fols. 188–189.

59. "Complaints of the Free People of Color," enclosed in Michael Hanly to Bathurst, September 22, 1823; Hanly also noted that the "Complaints" was also sent to Jamaica's governor, the Duke of Manchester, in October 1823, CO 137 / 155, fols. 67–68.

60. Gad Heuman, *Between Black and White: Race, Politics, and the Free Coloreds in Jamaica, 1792–1865* (Westport, Conn.: Greenwood Press, 1981), 10, 33–34. See also Daniel Livesay, *Children of Uncertain Fortune: Mixed-Race Jamaicans in Britain and the Atlantic Family, 1733–1833* (Chapel Hill: University of North Carolina Press, 2018).

61. Thomas Cooper to Rev. L. L. Tarns, May 12, 1818, Thomas Clarkson Papers, Add. MS 41266, British Library, London; Heuman, *Between Black and White*, 10.

62. Michael Hanly to Bathurst, September 22, 1823, CO 137/155, fol. 67. According to the petitioners, racial degrees worked like so in Jamaica: White is the legal equivalent of musteefine. Musteefines descend from a white and a mustee. Mustees descend from a white and a quadroon. Quadroons descend from a white and a mulatto. Mulattoes are the children of blacks and whites.

63. Michael Hanly to Bathurst, September 22, 1823, CO 137/155, fol. 68.

64. Heuman, *Between Black and White*, 27.

65. Heuman, 35. On free colored mobilization in the eastern Caribbean, see Edward L. Cox, *Free Coloreds in the Slave Societies of St. Kitts and Grenada, 1763–1833* (Knoxville: University of Tennessee Press, 1984).

66. Manchester to Bathurst, July 12, 1824, CO 137/156, fol. 294. This and the following paragraph draw on Heuman, *Between Black and White*, chap. 3.

67. Manchester to Bathurst, May 18, 1824, CO 137/156, fol. 223.

68. "Resolutions Passed at a General Meeting of the Magistrates and Freeholders . . . St. Ann's Jamaica, 15 September 1823," Add. MSS 75000KK, British Library. See also Crister Petley, *Slaveholders in Jamaica: Colonial Society and Culture during the Era of Abolition* (London: Pickering & Chatto, 2009).

69. G. T. Gilbert to the Duke of Manchester, October 28, 1823, CO 137/155, fol. 62.

70. Manchester to Bathurst, January 12, 1824, CO 137/156, fol. 6. On this revolt see Richard Hart, *Slaves Who Abolished Slavery*, 2 vols., (Kingston, Jamaica: Institute of Social and Economic Research, 1985), vol. 2 *Blacks in Rebellion*, 227–243.

71. Manchester to Bathurst, February 9, 1824, CO 137/156, fols. 137, 151.

72. Campbell to Wm. Bullock, June 14, 1824, enclosed in Manchester to the Earl of Bathurst, June 16, 1824, CO 137/156, fol. 275.

73. Examination of Richard Hemmings, June 14, 1824, CO 137/156, fol. 276.

74. Examination of Richard Hemmings, fol. 276.

75. Manchester to the Earl of Bathurst, June 16, 1824, CO 137/156, fols. 282–283.

76. Manchester to the Earl of Bathurst, June 16 and July 31, 1824, CO 137/156, fols. 283–284, 304–305.

77. *Charleston Courier,* July 14, 1823, quoted in Alan January, "The South Carolina Association: An Agency for Race Control in Antebellum Charleston," *SCHM* 78 (July 1977): 192–193; Undated broadside in South Carolina Department of Archives and History (hereafter SCDAH). The broadside's text is reproduced in Egerton and Paquette, *Vesey Affair*, 605–620.

78. Egerton and Paquette, *Vesey Affair,* 611–620. On hegemony, see Eugene Genovese, *Roll Jordan Roll: The World the Slaves Made* (New York: Vintage Books, 1972), 25–49.

79. "An Act for the Better Regulation and Government of Free Negroes and Persons of Color," in Cooper and McCord, *Statutes at Large of South Carolina*, 7:461–462.

80. Egerton and Paquette, *Vesey Affair,* 606–608.

81. Egerton and Paquette, 609.

82. [Edwin C. Holland], *A Refutation of the Calumnies Circulated against the Southern and Western States respecting the Institution and Existence of Slavery* (Charleston, 1822), 61; *Furman's Exposition of the Views of the Baptists Relative to the Coloured Population* (Charleston, 1823); [Frederick Dalcho], *Practical Considerations Founded on the Scriptures, Relative to the Slave Population of South Carolina* (Charleston, 1823); [Robert J. Turnbull], *The Crisis, or, Essays on the Usurpations of the Federal Government, by Brutus* (Charleston, 1827); Freehling, *Prelude to Civil War,* 79–82.

83. [Turnbull], *Crisis,* 17.

84. [Turnbull], 26–27, 122. On the far different relationship between slaveholders and federal power, see Don E. Fehrenbacher, *The Slaveholding Republic: An Account of the United States Government's Relations to Slavery,* completed and edited by Ward M. McAfee (New York: Oxford University Press, 2001); Matthew Karp, *This Vast Southern Empire: Slaveholders at the Helm of American Foreign Policy* (Cambridge, Mass.: Harvard University Press, 2016).

85. [Turnbull], 128–129, 132.

86. James Brewer Stewart, *Holy Warriors: The Abolitionists and American Slavery,* rev. ed. (New York: Hill and Wang, 1997), 30–31; David Brion Davis, *The Problem of Slavery in the Age of Emancipation* (New York: Alfred A. Knopf, 2014), 144–192; Manisha Sinha, *The Slave's Cause: A History of Abolition* (New Haven, Conn.: Yale University Press, 2016), 163–165. 144–192.

87. "Speech Used in Forming the Committees in 1823 & 1824," CN 73, Thomas Clarkson Papers, Huntington Library, San Marino, Calif.; Adam Hochschild, *Bury the Chains: Prophets and Rebels in the Fight to Free an Empire's Slaves* (Boston: Houghton Mifflin, 2005), 324.

88. Ragatz, *Fall of the Planter Class,* 426–430; G. W. Bridges, *A Voice from Jamaica; in Reply to William Wilberforce, Esq. M. P.* (London, 1823). Augustus Beaumont edited the *Jamaica Courant,* which was full of such vitriol.

89. Ragatz, *Fall of the Planter Class,* 419; Elizabeth Heyrick, *Immediate, Not Gradual Abolition* (London, 1824), 4.

90. Heyrick, *Immediate, Not Gradual Abolition,* 13, 22; Clare Midgley, *Women against Slavery: The British Campaigns, 1780–1870* (London, 1992), 43–44, 50; David B. Davis, "The Emergence of Immediatism in British and American Antislavery Thought" (1962), in *From Homicide to Slavery: Studies in American Culture* (New York: Oxford University Press, 1986), 249; Sinha, *Slave's Cause,* 197.

91. *West India Colonies: Slave Insurrection* (London, 1832), 3; Belmore to Goderich, September 6, 1831, Belmore to Goderich, May 2, 1832 CO 137/179, fols. 201–207, 268; Augustus H. Beaumont, *The Jamaica Petition for Representation in the British House of Commons, or for Independence* (Cornhill, UK, 1831), 16.

92. Heuman, *Between Black and White,* 60; CO 137/179, fol. 204.

93. "Examination of Thomas McNeel," and "Confession of Linton," in *Report of a Committee of the House of Assembly of Jamaica, Appointed to Inquire into . . . the Recent Rebellion* (London, 1832), 13, 29.

94. Turner, *Slaves and Missionaries,* 156; *West India Colonies,* 14.

95. "Trial of Elizabeth Ball, free woman," CO 137/185, fols. 116–117; Turner, *Slaves and Missionaries*, 152–153.

96. Turner, *Slaves and Missionaries*, 153–154.

97. "Confession of Nicholas Simpson, a Slave under sentence of death on Friday morning the 13th January 1832," "Trial of Solomon Athenson, a slave to Fairy Hill Estate, January 18, 1832," CO 137/185, fols. 729–731.

98. *West India Colonies*, 19–20, 22.

99. *West India Colonies*, 29–30, 37; Audra Diptee, *From Africa to Jamaica: The Making of an Atlantic Slave Society* (Gainesville: University of Florida Press, 2010).

100. "Trial of Elizabeth Ball," "Trial of George Shaw, Court Martial, January 9, 1832," "Trial of Phoebe of Mocho Plantation [undated]," "Trial of Joseph Curry, Lambert Taylor, Frederick Fisher, and George Murray, slaves to Fairy Hill Estate, and Richard Buckley of Fairfield Estate, January 19, 1832," in CO 137/185, fols. 116, 465, 702, 734; Turner, *Slaves and Missionaries*, 162.

101. Turner, *Slaves and Missionaries*, 165–167; Belmore to Goderich, May 2, 1832; Lord Mulgrave to Goderich, December 31, 1832, CO 137/182, fols. 268, 567.

102. John Cannon, *Parliamentary Reform, 1640–1832* (New York: Cambridge University Press, 1973).

103. *Hansard's Parliamentary Debates*, 3rd series, vol. 13 (London: Printed by T.C. Hansard, 1832), 34–36, 38, 41, 49.

104. *Hansard's Parliamentary Debates*, 13:55, 66, 80, 86–87, 97; Ragatz, *Fall of the Planter Class*, 453

105. Mathieson, *British Slavery*, 224–225; Ragatz, *Fall of the Planter Class*, 448.

106. Nick Draper, *The Price of Emancipation: Slave Ownership, Compensation, and British Society at the End of Slavery* (New York: Cambridge University Press, 2009).

107. Harding, *There Is a River*, 75–100; Sinha, *Slave's Cause*, 211; General Assembly Petition, 1831, #170, #59, SCDAH. See also Patrick Breen, *The Land Shall Be Deluged in Blood: A New History of the Nat Turner Revolt* (New York: Oxford University Press, 2015).

108. Message of Governor James Hamilton Jr., December 6, 1831, in Governor's Messages #2 SCDAH.

109. Message of Governor James Hamilton Jr., December 6, 1831, SCDAH.

110. Freehling, *Prelude to Civil War*, 155–159, 228–229; John Calhoun to Virgil Maxcy, September 11, 1830, in *The Papers of John C. Calhoun*, vol. 11 of 28, *1829–1832*, ed. Clyde N. Wilson (Columbia: University of South Carolina Press, 1978), 229.

111. "Report of a Committee of the Convention, to Whom Was Referred an Act to Provide for Calling a Convention of the People of South Carolina," in *State Papers on Nullification* (Boston, 1834), 17, 21; Freehling, *Prelude to Civil War*, 219–297; Richard Ellis, *The Union at Risk: Jacksonian Democracy, States' Rights, and the Nullification Crisis* (New York: Oxford University Press, 1987).

112. Leonard Richards, *"Gentlemen of Property and Standing": Anti-abolition Mobs in Jacksonian America* (New York: Oxford University Press, 1970); Stewart, *Holy Warriors*, 51; Sinha, *Slave's Cause*, 225, 233–234, 242, 252.

113. "Remarks on Receiving Abolition Petitions," in *The Papers of John C. Calhoun*, vol. 13, *1835–1837*, ed. Clyde N. Wilson (Columbia: University of South Carolina Press, 1980), 392–394.

114. "Remarks on Receiving Abolition Petitions," 13:394–395.

115. Eric Foner, *The Fiery Trial: Abraham Lincoln and American Slavery* (New York: W.W. Norton, 2010); James Oakes, *Freedom National: The Destruction of Slavery in the United States, 1861–1865* (New York: W. W. Norton, 2013); William Freehling, *The Road to Disunion*, 2 vols. (New York: Oxford University Press, 1990–2007).

116. Frederick Douglass, "West India Emancipation, a Speech Delivered at Canandaigua, New York, August 3, 1857," in *Frederick Douglass: Selected Speeches and Writings*, ed. Philip S. Foner and Yuval Taylor (Chicago: Lawrence Hill Books, 1999), 359; Seymour Drescher, *Abolition: A History of Slavery and Anti-slavery* (New York: Cambridge University Press, 2009); Christopher Schmidt-Nowara, *Slavery, Freedom, and Abolition in Latin America and the Atlantic World* (Albuquerque: University of New Mexico Press, 2011); Marcela Echeverri, "Slavery in Mainland Spanish America in the Age of the Second Slavery," in *Atlantic Transformations in the Age of the Second Slavery*, ed. Dale Tomich (Binghamton, N.Y., forthcoming).

Acknowledgments

The research and writing of this book has inspired me for more than a decade. The basic idea for the book occurred to me late in graduate school as I completed my dissertation at Boston College, but the execution of this project has been my work at Yale University since I began to teach there in the fall of 2007. I have been richly supported by many brilliant people along the way, and by the institutions that enable them.

Archival research is the foundation of this book. My time in the archives has been precious, insightful, and creatively supported by librarians and archivists. While I cannot name them all, I would like to begin by acknowledging the people who work at the National Library of Jamaica, Kingston; the Jamaica National Archives, Spanish Town; the South Caroliniana Library at the University of South Carolina, Columbia; the South Carolina Department of Archives and History, Columbia; the South Carolina Historical Society, Charleston; the Charleston Public Library; the Charleston Library Society; the British National Archives, Kew, England; the British Library, London; the Southern Historical Collection in the Louis Round Wilson Library at the University of North Carolina, Chapel Hill; the David M. Rubenstein Rare Book and Manuscript Library of Duke University, Durham, North Carolina; the Huntington Library of San Marino, California; the Law School Library, the Houghton Library, and the Widener Library of Harvard University, Cambridge, Massachusetts; the John J. Burns Rare Books Library at Boston College, Chestnut Hill, Massachusetts; the DiMenna-Nyselius Library of Fairfield University, Connecticut; and the libraries of Yale University:

the Sterling Department of Manuscripts and Archives; the Sterling Map Collection; the Lillian Goldman Law Library; and the Beinecke Library. Whether I was carrying my camera, a laptop, or simply a notebook and a cup of coffee, visits to these libraries have sustained the research and the writing of this book.

My efforts to think through the history of racial slavery have been encouraged and deepened by the intellectual communities I have been a part of at Yale and beyond. I began to clarify the project while applying for the Morse Junior Faculty Fellowship at Yale and had valuable feedback from Glenda Gilmore and David Blight. I began the research and writing as a fellow at the Charles Warren Center for the Study of American Civilization at Harvard University. We lived in Jamaica Plain, Boston, at the time, and this fellowship made life simpler; it allowed me to begin. I also had the great fortune to convene regularly with Kristen Block, Vincent Brown, Joyce Chaplin, Marisa Fuentes, Josh Guild, Walter Johnson, Paul Kramer, Gunther Peck, Suzanna Reiss, Cynthia Young, and the late Patrick Wolfe, may he rest in peace. It was a memorable year that taught me very much.

As the writing progressed, Chandra Manning and Adam Rothman invited me to share what became Chapter 6 with the 19th Century U.S. History Workshop at Georgetown University. I presented a later version of that chapter to the Rocky Mountain Early America Seminar in Salt Lake City, Utah, at the generous invitation of Matt Mason and Eric Hinderaker. In 2014, the *William and Mary Quarterly* and the Early Modern Studies Institute of the University of Southern California included a draft of Chapter 5 in their annual workshop at the Huntington Library in San Marino, California. We worked through eight chapter-length essays on the Age of Revolutions, including my essay, in two days. It was exhausting but, as an intellectual experience, unmatched; comments from Kate Engel, Julia Gaffield, Sarah Knott, Peter Mancall, Brett Rushforth, Eric Slauter, and Karin Wulf were particularly valuable. More recently, Rafael Marques organized a colloquium of his graduate students at the University of São Paolo to read my work, and Jim Oakes organized a manuscript workshop with colleagues and graduate students at the City University of New York Graduate Center; both groups offered excellent feedback that proved to be invaluable.

The book has further benefited from several of the working groups that make Yale such a vibrant place. Steve Pincus invited me to present the seventeenth-century material to the British History Colloquium; John Witt included me in the Legal History Forum at Yale Law School; Joanne Freeman invited me to present work to the Yale Early American History Workshop (twice!); and the Working Group on Race and Slavery in the Atlantic World at Yale, which I began with Anne Ruderman in 2014, read my chapter on eighteenth-century South Carolina.

Invitations from fellow scholars to give lectures from the project have also been valuable exercises. I would like to thank the organizers and audiences at the "Economies of Empire in the Eighteenth Century" conference at the Huntington Library; "Charting New Courses in the History of Slavery and Emancipation" at the University of Southern Mississippi, Long Beach; "Atlantic Migrations" at Virginia Commonwealth University, Richmond, Virginia; the History Department Seminar at Boston College; "Fear in the Revolutionary Americas" at Tufts University, Somerville, Massachusetts; the "Politics of the Second Slavery" conference at Binghamton University in New York; "A Escravidão e os Novos Mundos" at the Universidade Estadual Paulista, Franca, São Paolo, Brazil; and Brooklyn College in New York City. I have also presented papers from this project at my two regular conferences: the annual meeting of the Association of Caribbean Historians and that of the Society of Historians of the Early American Republic. To share work in progress is to try to tell a new story, or to advance a new idea, for a live, thinking audience, and I've always left the room a little wiser than before.

That goes for teaching, too. Whether it's my first-year seminar course in the Beinecke, my lectures on the rise and fall of Atlantic slavery, or a graduate course, I have found the act of teaching to be the best instructor in the clear explanation of ideas. Working closely with graduate students on their own research projects has also helped me think through my own, especially when I realize that I ought to follow the advice I try to impart. I have learned much in working with Joseph Yannielli, Katherine Mooney, Jayne Ptolemy, Alison Gorsuch, Anne Ruderman, Richard Anderson, James Shinn, Danya Pilgrim, Brandi Waters, Kyra Daniel, Alycia Hall, Patrick Barker,

Ben Parten, Teanu Reid, and Connor Williams, who have all been a part of this endeavor.

The best writing gets done when the teaching subsides, and writing can be quite solitary. Yet I have benefited tremendously from the time taken by friends, colleagues, and mentors to read and critique countless proposals and drafts. David Davis, Stanley Engerman, Gad Heuman, Peter Kolchin, and Lynn Lyerly read versions of the proposal that conceptualized this book. As I began to write the chapters, David Blight, Lissa Bolletino, Vince Brown, Trevor Burnard, David Davis, Alejandra Dubcovsky, Marcela Echeverri, Anne Eller, Joanne Freeman, Jerry Handler, Naomi Lamoreaux, Jane Landers, Rafael Marques, Matt Mason, and Steven Pincus read chapters and made suggestions. Vince, Trevor, Alejandra, Steve, and Jane also shared research materials and unpublished work. In July 2013, I published "The Development of Mastery and Race in the Comprehensive Slave Codes of the Greater Caribbean during the Seventeenth Century," *William and Mary Quarterly* 70 (July 2013): 429–458; some of the ideas originally explored in this article are revisited in Chapters 1 and 2, and I appreciate the journal providing an initial venue in developing my arguments. My former colleagues Alejandra Dubcovsky and Steve Pincus deserve special mention, for they both took time away from their own projects to read numerous chapters, sometimes more than once, on top of countless conversations about the eighteenth-century Atlantic. Joyce Seltzer enthusiastically signed on as the editor of this project in 2011, and like many scholars before me, I have benefited tremendously from her wisdom and expertise. Over numerous lunches, Joyce helped me to shape the research into a book with chapters and a narrative arc. She marked up the chapters—in pencil—as I wrote them, and then read the whole thing once again at the end. Stacey Maples, a fellow father of three boys, drew all the maps. Copyeditor Ashley Moore refined my prose and caught my many mistakes.

Financial support to conduct the research, and to write, has come from the Charles Warren Center for the Study of American History, Harvard University; the Huntington Library in San Marino, California; and, at Yale University, from the Whitney and Betty Mac-Millan Center for International and Area Studies; the Whitney

Humanities Center; and the Gilder Lehrman Center for the Study of Slavery, Resistance, and Abolition. Some of these funds paid for essential research assistance from Dawn Whitehead, who first helped me chart the historiography; Jayne Ptolemy, who spent hours scrolling through South Carolina newspapers; Adrian Abel-Bey and Christian White, who helped me organize the runaway slave ads of South Carolina; and Alice Baumgartner, Anna Duensing, and Emily Yankowitz, who transcribed hundreds of manuscript pages from images taken in the archives.

I wrote this book with both the pressure and the generous support of Yale's previous tenure system, which a series of department chairs—Paul Freedman, Laura Engelstein, George Chauncey, and Naomi Lamoreaux in the History Department; and Robert Stepto, Elizabeth Alexander, Jonathan Holloway, and Jackie Goldsby in the African American Studies Department—helped me to navigate. And colleagues such as Ned Blackhawk, David Blight, Hazel Carby, Marcela Echeverri, Anne Eller, John Mack Faragher, Crystal Feimster, Joanne Freeman, Glenda Gilmore, Matt Jacobsen, Gil Joseph, Gerry Jaynes, Stuart Schwartz, and Anthony Reed, have offered important mentorship and camaraderie throughout this whole process.

I close this note of thanks with friends and family, whose love and support have sustained me. My parents, Ted and Virginia Rugemer, have been there for me since the beginning, and I am forever grateful. Our friends in Jamaica Plain, and in New Haven, offer an anchor apart from academe. Joanne and Terence Cooney of Great Barrington, Massachusetts, brought Kate into the world, and she is my rock. Our first son, Henry, arrived before I had begun this project, but Philip arrived as I wrote the first proposals, and James is three. The great effort necessary to complete this book compelled many late nights in the office and numerous solitary sojourns to distant libraries. Yet those days and nights were intertwined with the pitter-patter of little feet, early in the morning, countless afternoons on baseball fields, one hundred thousand loads of laundry, and road trips to Boston. I would never have it any other way.

Edward Rugemer
New Haven, Connecticut

Notes on the Maps

Map 1. The Early Atlantic World, based on Ira Berlin, *Many Thousands Gone: The First Two Centuries of Slavery in North America* (Cambridge, Mass.: Harvard University Press, 1998), vi-vii; John Iliffe, *Africans: The History of a Continent* (New York: Cambridge University Press, 1995), 128; David Eltis and David Richardson, *Atlas of the Transatlantic Slave Trade* (New Haven, Conn.: Yale University Press, 2010), 112.

Map 2. South Carolina in 1707, based on Alejandra Dubcovsky, *Informed Power: Communication in the Early American South* (Cambridge, Mass.: Harvard University Press, 2016), x; "An Act to Limit the Bounds of the Yamasee Settlement, to Prevent Persons from Disturbing Them with Their Stocks, and to Remove Such as Are Settled," in *The Statutes at Large of South Carolina*, ed. Thomas Cooper and David J. McCord, vol. 2, *Acts from 1682 to 1716*, ed. Thomas Cooper (Columbia, S.C.: printed by A. S. Johnston, 1837), 2:317–318; Jane Landers, *Black Society in Spanish Florida* (Urbana: University of Illinois Press, 1999), 31.

Map 3. South Carolina in 1740, based on S. Max Edelson, *Plantation Enterprise in Colonial South Carolina* (Cambridge, Mass.: Harvard University Press, 2006), 128; Verner W. Crane, *The Southern Frontier, 1670–1732* (1929; repr., Tuscaloosa: University of Alabama Press, 2004), 326. Denise Bossy advised me on situating the Yamasee in 1740.

Map 4. Jamaica in 1750, based on Alvin O. Thompson, *Flight to Freedom: African Runaways and Maroons in the Americas* (Kingston, Jamaica: University of the West Indies Press, 2006), 117; Christer Petley, *Slaveholders in Jamaica: Colonial Society and Culture during the Era of Abolition* (London: Pickering and Chatto, 2009), 3.

Map 5. Lucea Bay and Surrounding Plantations, 1775, based on Thomas Jefferys, *Jamaica from the Latest Surveys* (London: Laurie and Whittle, 1794), in the Sterling Map Collection, Beinecke Library, Yale University, New Haven, Conn.

All maps drawn by Stacey Maples.

Index